AMERICA'S AMERICANS

PHILIP DAVIES AND IWAN MORGAN

AMERICA'S AMERICANS:
Population Issues in U.S. Society and Politics

PHILIP DAVIES AND IWAN MORGAN

INSTITUTE FOR THE STUDY OF THE

AMERICAS

UNIVERSITY OF LONDON · SCHOOL OF ADVANCED STUDY

The Institute for the Study of the Americas (ISA) promotes, coordinates and provides a focus for research and postgraduate teaching on the Americas – Canada, the USA, Latin America and the Caribbean – in the University of London.

The Institute was officially established in August 2004 as a result of a merger between the Institute of Latin American Studies and the Institute of United States Studies, both of which were formed in 1965.

The Institute publishes in the disciplines of history, politics, economics, sociology, anthropology, geography and environment, development, culture and literature, and on the countries and regions of Latin America, the United States, Canada and the Caribbean.

ISA runs an active programme of events – conferences, seminars, lectures and workshops – in order to facilitate national research on the Americas in the humanities and social sciences. It also offers a range of taught master's and research degrees, allowing wide-ranging multi-disciplinary, multi-country study or a focus on disciplines such as politics or globalisation and development for specific countries or regions.

Full details about the Institute's publications, events, postgraduate courses and other activities are available on the web at *www.americas.sas.ac.uk*.

© Institute for the Study of the Americas, 2007

British Library Cataloguing-in-Publication Data
A catalogue record for this book is available
from the British Library

ISBN   978 1 900039 79 6

INSTITUTE FOR THE STUDY OF THE
A M E R I C A S
UNIVERSITY OF LONDON · SCHOOL OF ADVANCED STUDY

Institute for the Study of the Americas
31 Tavistock Square
London
WC1H 9HA
Telephone: 020 7862 8870
Fax: 020 7862 8886
Email: americas@sas.ac.uk
Web: www.americas.sas.ac.uk

Contents

		Page
A Note on Contributors		vii
Introduction: America's Americans: Population Issues in U.S. Society and Politics		
Iwan Morgan		xi

Part 1: Overviews of Population Change

1	The Three Americas: Reflections on America's Americans in Regional Context *William Frey*	3
2	Through the Prism of Demographics: America's Political Scene *Rhodes Cook*	15

Part 2: The Socioeconomic and Cultural Contexts of Population Issues

3	Population Matters in Native America *Joy Porter*	31
4	Inventing the Matron: American Women Redefine Middle Age *Jay S Kleinberg*	50
5	From Exile Community to 'Hy'-Society: Cuban American Literature and Cultural Identity *Annabel Cox*	74
6	The Continuing Significance of Race and Ethnicity in the Melting Pot *Natasha Kumar Warikoo*	94
7	Living Together – Living Apart: Racial and Ethnic Integration in Metropolitan Neighborhoods, 1970–2000 *David Fasenfest and Jason Booza*	120

8 Integrating New Americans   145
   Bill Ong Hing

9 Demographic Change and Concentrated Poverty in Rural America   168
   Kenneth M. Johnson and Daniel T. Lichter

Part 3: The Politics and Public Policy of Population Change

10 Social Change, Families, and Values: Morality Politics   199
   in Contemporary America
   Christopher J. Bailey

11 Native American Self-Determination: From Nixon to Reagan   222
   Dean J. Kotlowski

12 Race, Class, Age and Punitive Segregation: Prisons and   246
   Prison Populations in the Contemporary United States
   Vivien Miller

13 The Shifting Politics of Immigration Reform   263
   Andrew Wroe

14 The Cuban Adjustment Act and Immigration from Cuba   288
   Jessica Gibbs

15 Urban Electoral Coalitions in an Age of Immigration: 312
   Time and Place in the 2001 and 2005 Los Angeles Mayoral
   Primaries
   Raphael J. Sonenshein and Mark H. Drayse

16 California and the Third Great Demographic Transition: 346
   Immigrant Incorporation, Ethnic Change, and
   Population Aging, 1970–2030
   Dowell Myers

A Note on Contributors

Christopher J. Bailey is Professor of U.S. Politics at Keele University. Among his publications are *Congress and Air Pollution, The U.S. Congress,* and *The Republican Party in the U.S. Senate, 1974–84.*

Jason Booza is a doctoral student in Political Science at Wayne State University. He has authored numerous journal articles and reports on racial and ethnic integration in metropolitan areas and is interim director of the Michigan Metropolitan Information Center in the Center for Urban Studies at Wayne State.

Rhodes Cook has written widely on U.S. electoral politics, including most recently *The Presidential Nomination Process: A Place for Us* and *Race for the White House: Winning the 2004 Nomination.* Formerly a reporter and commentator for *Congressional Quarterly,* he now authors on a freelance basis *The Rhodes Cook Letter,* the highly regarded tracking analysis of national and state elections and voting behavior.

Annabel Cox is a doctoral student in the Department of Hispanic Studies and Italian, Queen Mary University, London.

Philip Davies is Director of the Eccles Centre for American Studies at the British Library and Professor of U.S. Studies at de Montfort University, Leicester. He was formerly chair of the British Association of American Studies and is presently chair of the (UK) American Politics Group. Among his publications are *Elections USA* and (co-edited with George Edwards) *New Challenges for the American Presidency.* He is co-editor of *Right On? Political Change and Continuity in George W. Bush's America,* also published by the Institute for the Study of the Americas.

Mark H. Drayse is Associate Professor of Geography at California State University, Fullerton. He has written extensively on political and demographic geography, and is the co-recipient (with Raphael Sonenshein) of a Russell Sage Foundation grant to research immigrant political incorporation and political coalitions.

David Fasenfest is Associate Professor in the Douglas Fraser Center for Workplace Issues at Wayne State University. He has written widely in scholarly journals and produced numerous reports on racial and ethnic integration in metropolitan areas. He is editor of the journal *Critical Sociology* and has also co-edited *Critical Evaluations of Economic Development Policies*.

William Frey is Research Professor in the Population Studies Center at the Institute for Social Research, University of Michigan, and Senior Fellow in Demographic Studies at the Milken Institute. One of America's leading demographers, he is contributing editor to *American Demographics* and has authored many scholarly articles and reports for public and private organizations on the subject of population change. Among his most recent publications is (with Bill Abresch and Jonathan Yeasting), *America by the Numbers: A Field Guide to the U.S. Population.*

Jessica Gibbs has a doctorate in history from the University of Cambridge and lectures in History at Reading University. She is presently writing a book on U.S.-Cuban Relations since the end of the Cold War to be published by Routledge.

Bill Ong Hing is Professor of Law and Asian American Studies at the University of California, Davis. He has written extensively on immigration and integration, including *Defining America Through Immigration Policy, To Be an American: Cultural Pluralism and the Rhetoric of Assimilation,* and *Making and Remaking Asian America Through Immigration.*

Kenneth M. Johnson is Professor of Sociology at Loyola University Chicago and is the author of numerous reports and articles on demographic issues.

Jay Kleinberg is Professor of American Studies at Brunel University. A former editor of the *British Journal of American Studies,* she has written widely on social history, including *Widows and Orphans First: The Family Economy and Social Welfare Policy, 1880–1939; Women in the United States, 1830–1945;* and *The Shadow of the Mills: Working Class Families in Pittsburgh, 1870–1907.*

Dean J. Kotlowski is Associate Professor of History at Salisbury University, Maryland. Among his numerous publications in the field of civil rights is *Nixon's Civil Rights: Politics, Principles and Policy.* He is presently working on a biography of Paul McNutt for publication by Indiana University Press.

Daniel T. Lichter is Professor of Policy Management and Analysis, Ferris Family Professor of Life Course Studies, and Director of the Bronfenbrenner Life Course Center at Cornell University. He has authored over a hundred articles and chapters on the distribution of poverty and other sociological and demographic issues.

Vivien Miller was formerly Reader in American History at Middlesex University and is currently a freelance researcher. Among her publications are *Crime, Sexual Violence and Clemency: Florida's Pardon Board and Penal System in the Progressive Era* and *The Prison Farm and the Chain Gang: Race, Gender and Punishment in Twentieth Century Florida*.

Iwan Morgan is Professor of U.S. Studies at the Institute for the Study of the Americas, University of London. He has written widely on U.S. political history and political economy. He is co-editor of *Right On? Political Change and Continuity in George W. Bush's America*, also published by the Institute for the Study of the Americas, and is presently writing a book on presidents and the budget deficit to be published by the University Press of Kansas.

Dowell Myers is Professor of Urban Planning and Demography at the University of Southern California and is a fellow of the Lincoln Institute for Land Policy. He has authored many reports and studies of immigrant adaptation and assimilation, including the most widely referenced work on census analysis, *Analysis with Local Census Data: Portraits of Change*. His book, *Immigrants and Boomers: Forging a New Social Contract for the Future of America* was published by the Russell Sage Foundation in 2007.

Joy Porter is Lecturer in American Studies and Associate Dean of Humanities at the University of Swansea. Among her publications are *To Be an Indian: The Life of Seneca-Iroquois Arthur Caswell Parker* and (co-edited with Kenneth Roemer) *The Cambridge Companion to Native American Literature*. She is presently working on two monographs, *The American Indian Pet of World War I: Modernism and the Indian identity of Frank 'Toronto' Prewett 1893–1962* and *Native American Freemasonry*, research for which was supported by a Leverhulme Research Fellowship.

Raphael J. Sonenshein is Professor of Political Science at California State University, Fullerton. Among his publications are *Politics in Black and White: Race and Power in Los Angeles* and *The City at Stake: Secession, Reform and the Battle for Los Angeles*. He was executive director of the Los Angeles Charter Reform Commission, which helped to produce the 'unified charter' proposal for the ballot that in 1999 approved the first comprehensive update of the Los Angeles charter of 1925.

Natasha Kumar Warikoo is Lecturer in U.S. Studies at the Institute for the Study of the Americas, University of London. She recently gained her doctorate in Sociology from Harvard University and has published numerous articles on ethnic youth.

Andrew Wroe is Lecturer in Politics at the University of Kent. He has published numerous papers on immigration issues and his book, *The Republican Party and Immigrant Politics*, was published by Palgrave in 2007.

Introduction: America's Americans: Population Issues in U.S. Society and Politics

Iwan Morgan

The United States is the third most populous country in the world after China and India and accounted for about 4.6 percent of the world's population in 2006. Its population size underwent dramatic expansion from 200 million in 1966 to 300 million forty years later. This growth rate was remarkable in comparison to other industrialized nations. In the second half of the twentieth century the population of the United States increased by 85 percent, around four times the growth rate of the United Kingdom (20 percent), Germany (20 percent) and Italy (22 percent). America's population growth will almost certainly slow in the first half of the twenty-first century but it is equally likely to remain significant. The Census Bureau projects that the United States will have a population of 420 million in 2050, whereas more pessimistic estimates by the United Nations and the Social Security Administration put the figure at 395 million and 390 million respectively.

With the population of the United States on the cusp of passing the 300 million mark, the British Library's Eccles Centre for American Studies and the University of London's Institute for the Study of the Americas commemorated this symbolically significant development by co-organizing the first ever academic conference to be held in Europe on the topic of American population issues. This took place at the British Library on May 8 and 9, 2006 and drew presenters from both Britain and the United States. The present volume is the outgrowth of that conference, titled *America's Americans: The Populations of the United States.*

Population growth is a critical issue in the study of America's changing population, but it is by no means the only one. As William Frey notes in this volume, the United States population is not only getting bigger, it is also getting older and becoming more racially and ethnically diverse. America's population had been relatively 'young' in the first half of the twentieth century due to high fertility, declining infant and childhood mortality and high rates of net immigration by young workers and families. However, the baby-boom generation that produced a bulge at the lower end of the nation's age structure in the two decades after World War II is having the same effect at the opposite end of the age structure in the early twenty-first century. Moreover, the removal of immigration restrictions on some nationalities by the Immigration and Nationality Act of 1965 generated a new flow of immigrants to the United States, particularly from Latin America and East and South Asia. Net immigration to the United States (immigrants minus emigrants) rose from 2 million in 1951–60 to 6.75 millions in 1991–2000. In 2004, the leading source countries (of birth) for legal immigrants were Mexico (175,000 persons or 18.5 percent of total), followed by India (7.4 percent), the Philippines (6.1 percent), China (5.4 percent), Vietnam (3.3 percent), and the Dominican Republic (3.2 percent).

In addition to these aggregate changes, many developments on a smaller, but still significant scale, have important implications for America's population. Just a few examples can serve to convey this. The mean age for first-time mothers in the United States reached an all-time high of 25.2 years in 2003. This attests to women's changing socioeconomic circumstances whereby enhanced labor market participation and career prospects have resulted in postponement of childbearing. The proportion of Americans who are poor has effectively fallen by nearly half since the 'discovery' of poverty in the 1960s, but poverty rates are now highest among children instead of among the aged, the most impoverished demographic group some fifty years ago. Finally, population growth has been strongest in the South and Southwest and weakest in the old industrial areas of the Northeast and Midwest that used to be magnets in their manufacturing heyday for newcomers from home and abroad. Many of America's fastest growing states are those with large Hispanic and Asian ethnic populations. In 2004, as in every year since 1971, the primary destination states for legal immigrants were California, New York, Texas, Florida, New Jersey, and Illinois. Nearly two out of every three people immigrating to the United States that year lived in these six states. Significantly, the two most populous states – California and Texas – attained majority-minority status (whereby members of minorities make up more than 50 percent of the population) in 1998 and 2004 respectively.

This volume offers a multi-disciplinary perspective on U.S. population issues. The contributors are drawn from the fields of demography, planning, sociology, political science, history, geography and literary studies. The sixteen essays in the book explore a wide range of topics encompassing not only the socioeconomic and cultural significance of population change but also the implications for politics and public policy in early twenty-first century America.

The first two essays offer overviews of population change. In *The Three Americas: Reflections on America's Americans in Regional Context*, William Frey emphasizes the importance of considering demographic change in regional terms rather than in national aggregates. He analyzes the emergence of three demographic regions – the new Sunbelt that attracts domestic in-migration to its suburban areas, the increasingly diverse Melting Pot region that attracts immigration, and the slow-growing Heartland that attracts neither in-migration nor immigration. In his assessment, the conventional labels of rural, urban and suburban with their intra-regional connotations are increasingly less appropriate than regional classifications as indicators of lifestyles, race profiles, and age structures.

In *Through the Prism of Demographics: America's Political Scene*, Rhodes Cook suggests that the familiar political loyalties of 'Red' and 'Blue' America are already showing signs of erosion under the impact of population change. In his view the political parties will have to compete for voters driven by demographic concerns, but neither the Democrats nor Republicans can be certain of winning their loyalties. He contends that in the short term the demographics of age, notably relating to the aging of 'baby boomers,' will have key importance in shaping electoral outcomes, but will eventually be overtaken by the demographics of race and ethnicity as the Hispanic vote grows in size and significance.

The next section of the book deals with the socioeconomic and cultural contexts of population change. In *Population Matters in Native America*, Joy Porter explores the politics of demography pertaining to the original Americans. As she shows, the measurement and interpretation of population data on Native Americans has always been hotly contested because of its impact on the welfare, status and identity of native peoples. Her chapter focuses on three key issues: the highly controversial question of how many North American Indians perished in the first century of European contact; the political, cultural and social complexity of Indian population measurement; and the implications of the ongoing renaissance in Indian numbers from the low of the 1890 census to the high of the 2000 count.

Jay Kleinberg's essay *Inventing the Matron: American Women Redefine Middle Age* offers a valuable historical perspective on the socioeconomic transformation of gender roles. Women experienced significant life transitions at different ages and in different ways from previous generations as the twentieth century progressed. In particular, their lives altered as middle age developed into a lengthy, distinct stage of the life cycle for women. Profiting from education and employment opportunities denied their forebears, women aged 40 to 64 moved in growing numbers into the labor force over the course of the twentieth century. This development, in combination with the radical changes in their domestic and maternal functions, imbued middle-aged women with a new and distinctive identity.

In *From Exile Community to 'Hy'-Society: Cuban American Literature and Cultural Identity*, Annabel Cox uses literary texts to explore the identity issues of one immigrant group, Cuban Americans. She focuses on works by members of the so-called 1.5 generation who reflected the experience of refugee youth making a dual transition from adolescence to adulthood and from one socio-cultural environment to another. Her analysis reveals the importance of not using simplistic ethnic labels for immigrant literature in general. She shows that there are as many creative responses to the dilemma of identity following migration for Cuban American authors as there are Cuban American texts. This underlines the diversity not only within Cuban American literature but also within Latino and ethnic American literature itself, of which Cuban American writing is a part.

In *The Continuing Significance of Race and Ethnicity in the Melting Pot* Natasha Warikoo also focuses on immigrant youth identity, but from a sociological perspective. She demonstrates the strong salience of ethnicity and race in the self-identity and social life of teenagers in a New York City multiethnic public high school, in contrast to a similar school in London. She argues that diversity in school alone goes only so far in breaking down racial and ethnic barriers – schools need the right structures in place to promote integration. The contrasting organizational structures of the New York and London schools along with outside structural influences – U.S. residential segregation, historical processes of racial formation, and patterns of migration – led to the continuing significance of race among the New York student population, in spite of the 'super-diversity' in their school.

In *Living Together – Living Apart: Racial and Ethnic Integration in Metropolitan Neighborhoods, 1970–2000*, David Fasenfest and Jason Booza explore an issue that forms a backdrop to Warikoo's essay. They find that incidence of black and white residential proximity declined in the late twentieth century, but that each race experienced greater residential diversity because of Hispanic influx into their neighborhoods. The interaction of blacks and whites with this new group rather with each other may become the key issue of integration in the future. Nevertheless, as Frey cautions in his essay, the authors find that regional patterns reveal things which national aggregates do not. In some regions a new form of ethnic segregation is taking root as Hispanics have mainly moved into communities with residents like themselves. However, the authors conclude that there have been significant changes in the dynamics of racial and ethnic residential patterns and they expect the urban demographic landscape to change even more dramatically in the first thirty years of this century.

In his essay *Integrating New Americans* Bill Ong Hing addresses some of the issues raised by Warikoo and Fasenfest and Booza. In his view, the time is ripe for renewed civic engagement efforts directed at newcomers to the United States, in the manner of the Americanization movement in the early twentieth century era of immigration. He sees this as a matter of mutual interest since immigration meets America's economic needs. In his view state and local governments should lead the way but he also deems it imperative that other institutions are involved – notably schools, daycare centers, local businesses, chambers of commerce, churches, recreation clubs, neighborhood groups, senior groups and youth groups. His essay provides interesting and inspiring examples of successful civil engagement.

Newcomers primarily head for America's urban areas where economic opportunities are greater than in rural areas, which traditionally suffered higher rates of poverty in the twentieth century. In *Demographic Change and Concentrated Poverty in Rural America*, Kenneth Johnson and Daniel Lichter examine the extent and etiology of changing patterns of concentrated rural poverty. Their empirical research indicates a significant departure from historical trends in rural poverty in the 1990s and highlights the role of population change in this development. In particular, it shows that reductions in poverty in persistently poor counties resulted both from reductions in the number of poor people and from overall population growth. Less optimistically, their results indicate that poverty rates remained higher in rural than in urban areas in the 1990s, that general rural poverty rates had turned up again after 2000, and that the number of non-metropolitan counties with high levels of child poverty is much higher than the number of persistent poverty counties.

The final section of the book deals with the politics and public policy of population issues. In *Social Change, Families, and Values: Morality Politics in Contemporary America*, Christopher Bailey explores how social changes and an assertion of group identities have stimulated a political debate about America's core values between 'progressives' seeking to defend and extend the cultural legacy of the 1960s and 'traditionalists' seeking to roll it back. In his view, however, the so-called 'morality war' has been waged largely by issue activists and political elites. While a bitter struggle over issues such as abortion, homosexuality, stem cell research and a raft of moral issues is undoubtedly taking place in the United States, he finds little indication that the public is fully engaged in these battles. Through careful examination of poll data and other evidence, he concludes that the majority of Americans have met the social changes of the last four decades with an equanimity and tolerance that belies the vitriolic debate among issue activists.

In *Native American Self-Determination: From Nixon to Reagan*, Dean Kotlowski deals with public policy concerning the group identity of American Indians. His analysis explains the transformation in federal Native American policy in the 1970s and 1980s. It examines how successive administrations in this era departed from the longstanding goal of assimilating Indians into Euro-American society and the policy of terminating Indian treaty privileges and tribal land rights to promote the new policy of 'self-determination without termination' that promised to respect and to enhance, rather than to destroy, tribal authority and Indian distinctiveness. This change was in large part a response to the activism of Native Americans, who used a variety of tactics – lobbying, civil disobedience, and litigation – in a successful campaign to reclaim tribal land, fishing and water rights.

Like America's population in general, the U.S. prison population is getting bigger, more non-white, and older, but this is primarily attributable to public policy rather than to demographic trends. In *Race, Class, Age and Punitive Segregation: Prisons and Prison Populations in the Contemporary United States*, Vivien Miller explores the reasons for the 'blackening' and 'browning' of the inmates of the state and federal penal systems, whose numbers quadrupled between 1980 and 2005. Her analysis examines the link between racialized rates of incarceration and the 'war on drugs,' which has been waged disproportionately in poor, urban and non-white areas. She contends that media and political attention on the U.S. drugs problem has helped shape the racialized and gendered images of drugs abuse and abusers. Her essay also considers the impact of major sentencing changes on the shift to mass incarceration and its consequences for the 'graying' of the U.S. prison population, among whom elderly prisoners (age 55 and over) constitute the fastest growing age group in the twenty-first century.

The population growth at the center of political and public attention in the late twentieth and early twenty-first centuries has been the expansion of Latino immigration. In *The Shifting Politics of Immigration Reform*, Andrew Wroe charts the changing politics of this issue. He explores the rise of anti-immigrant politics in California, where voters approved a number of popular referenda targeted against Latinos and Latino immigrants in the 1990s. He focuses in particular on the political calculation of key Republican politicians, initially at state level and later at federal level, who chose to use the immigration issue for electoral gain. His essay also examines how that calculus changed as the Latino population mobilized against the anti-immigration agenda and its growing numbers made it a significant electoral force. Immigration was consequently a major issue in George W. Bush's second term, when the president found himself at odds with many in his own party over his preference for liberalization of immigration policy.

In *The Cuban Adjustment Act and Immigration from Cuba*, Jessica Gibbs offers a case study of the problems of making immigration policy. Her analysis examines the significance of the Cuban Adjustment Act of 1966 with regard both to the formation of the Cuban American community and – equally significantly – to its unintended consequences. As she shows, policymakers failed to anticipate or even consider the long-term impact of the legislation. In the forty years since its enactment the lax terms of the measure have served to encourage illegal immigration from Cuba. More significantly, it has been a complicating factor in the

U.S. response to any prospective mass migration episode since the Mariel boatlift emergency of 1980. Finally, the essay examines efforts in the 1990s to repeal the legislation and explains why the Cuban American community has been instrumental to date in preserving it.

While politicians debate immigration at national level, it is evident that urban politics has been fundamentally reshaped by the arrival of so many newcomers from abroad. In *Urban Electoral Coalitions in an Age of Immigration: Time and Place in the 2001 and 2005 Los Angeles Mayoral Primaries*, Raphael Sonenshein and Mark Drayse consider coalition patterns in the new urban environment. Examining the 2001 and 2005 Los Angeles mayoral primaries, their dependent variable is voting for Antonio Villaraigosa, a liberal Latino who ran against James Hahn, a white candidate with African American support. They found that Villaraigosa benefited from a stable coalition that combined Latinos and some white liberals, but Hahn's black support eroded. However, if Los Angeles had operated partisan primaries like New York, a third group of white moderates could have won a Republican primary. The authors note that racial and ethnic bloc voting was reinforced by the residential concentration of ethnic groups. They conclude that space and time are related to the stability and maintenance of coalitions surrounding immigration.

Finally, Dowell Myers shows in his essay, *California and the Third Great Demographic Transition: Immigrant Incorporation, Ethnic Change, and Population Aging, 1970–2030*, that the Golden State is leading the U.S., and indeed the world, through a third great transition, one centering on immigrant incorporation in the context of an aging society. California's foreign-born population is growing fast and already constituted 27 percent of the state's total population in 2006. Meanwhile, the ethnic mix is passing from majority-white to majority-minority and then majority-Latino. Near the middle of the transition from 1990 through 2010, there was substantial political friction over immigration. Long-established residents view immigrants as a burden and resist the decline of their own ethnic group. Not yet seeing their own interests as tied to the rising generation, they often voted against the interests of the incoming majority who are the future. This study integrates political opinion data with demographics of age, ethnicity, and nativity. It contends, firstly, that a longer run perspective and understanding of the great transition helps place current decisions in better context and, secondly, that how California resolves the tensions over these may hold lessons for other states and nations.

Since this work is a collaborative venture, the editors would like to express their thanks to the individuals and organizations involved in bringing the project to fruition. First and foremost, they thank the contributors for their engagement with and commitment to the initial conference and then the publication of their research in the present volume. Their always cheerful and helpful support, not least in submitting their papers on time, made our task as editors an enjoyable one. Secondly, we would like to thank our respective institutions, the British Library's Eccles Centre for American Studies and the University of London's Institute for the Study of the Americas (ISA) not only for their financial support for the venture but also the input of our colleagues into making the conference a success and bringing this book towards publication. In the latter regard, we particularly thank Kate Bateman and Jean Petrovic of the Eccles Centre, Olga Martinez, and Karen Perkins of ISA, and Emily Morrell and Jane Winters of the Institute of Historical Research who oversaw publication matters. Thirdly, we gratefully acknowledge the financial support of the United States Embassy in London that enabled us to bring two keynote speakers, William Frey and Rhodes Cook, to the conference. Finally, we have great pleasure in thanking our colleague, Dr Natasha Warikoo, for her multi-faceted contributions to the project not only as one of the academic contributors but also for her assistance in helping us to reach out to U.S. colleagues working in this field. However, Natasha's most important contribution to *America's Americans* was to give birth to one of the three hundred million. We hope that her daughter Zoya, born shortly after our conference, brings her much happiness.

PART ONE
Overviews of Population Change

1

The Three Americas: Reflections on America's Americans in Regional Context

William Frey

The population of the United States expanded from 200 million to 300 million in the forty-year period from 1966 to 2006. The principal drivers of this growth were immigration, racial-ethnic change and the baby-boom generation born in the quarter-century after World War II. These three elements will continue to shape the national demographic patterns of the United States for the first half of the twenty-first century. They will generate different trends at the opposite ends of the generational scale in the form of the graying of the white population as the baby-boomers age into retirement and a younger cohort of multi-cultural, globalized new Americans. Adjustment to the consequences of these demographic developments will be one of the major challenges facing the United States in the early decades of the twenty-first century. However, demographic change cannot be understood simply through the prism of national aggregates. It also has to be analyzed through a regional dimension. This essay suggests that in terms of demographic character there are three different regions in the United States, whose changing population profiles set the context for the broader changes at national level.

America's Americans: Some National Trends

To make sense of regional trends, we first have to consider the broad pattern of national population change in the late twentieth and early twenty-first centuries. At its most basic level, population change can be summed up in one simple sentence: 'The U.S. is getting bigger, older, and more diverse.' (Scommegna, 2004)

A bigger America: The U.S. population nearly doubled from its 1950 level of 152 million to 283 million in 2000. In addition to declining mortality rates and fertility levels that are hovering around the generational 'replacement' level, the net gain from immigration has been the key factor driving population growth. The 1965 reform of immigration law brought to an end the so-called 'immigrant pause' that began around World War I, but its effects were not fully felt until the 1980s (Martin and Midgley, 2003). Net immigration to the United States rose from 2.09 million in 1951–60 to 2.4 million in 1961–70 and then grew in succeeding decades to 3.3 million (1971–80), 5.7 million (1981–90) and 6.8 million (1991–2000). The net gain of 2.6 million immigrants in 2001–4 suggests that numbers in the first decade of the twenty-first century will break the previous decennial record. (Shrestha, 2006)

An older America: The population of the United States had been relatively young in the first half of the twentieth century, a consequence of high fertility rates, declining infant/child mortality and high rates of net immigration. Since 1950, however, the U.S. has been in the process of aging, a development that will intensify in the first decade of the new century. In 1950 the population resembled a Christmas tree – the most populous group was the youngest one at the base of the age structure (10.8 percent of the population was aged 5 or under) and the 65 and over group was, at 8.1 percent, a relatively small share of all Americans. In 2000, however, those aged 5 or under constituted only 6.8 percent of the population compared to the 12.4 percent represented by those aged 65 and over. The significant presence of the baby-boomers in the 2000 population (those aged 35–54) created a population bulge in the middle of the national age profile. As this group ages, the 65 and over share of the population will grow steadily and is projected to be more than 20 percent of all Americans by 2050. To put this change in perspective, the 'oldest' state in the 2000 census was Florida with just 17.6 percent of its population aged 65 and over.

A more diverse America: The 2000 census returns recorded 81 percent of the population as white, 12.7 percent as black, 3.8 percent as Asian, 1 percent as 'other' and 1.4 percent as being of more than one race. The white share is projected to fall to 72 percent and the Asian share to rise to 8 percent by 2050. In the 2000 census, 48 percent of Hispanics classified themselves as 'white' and a staggering 42 percent as 'some other race' (i.e. they did not identify with any of the 14 categories offered). The Census Bureau's modified estimates suggested that those of Hispanic origin numbered 35.3 million or 12.6 percent of the population in 2000. Their share of the population is projected to grow steadily to 24.4 percent by 2050 (Crieco and Cassidy, 2001).

The Three Americas in Regional Perspective

The development of distinctive regional demographic trends marks a significant change from the conventional boundaries of local culture that characterized twentieth-century America's intra-regional demarcation as urban, suburban and rural. Analysis of the 2000 Census data shows that local cultural boundaries are being superseded by increasingly sharp regional ones based on distinctive culture and demography. This development flies in the face of the conventional view that the United States is a single 'melting pot' nation. The new regional variations are being driven by very different patterns of immigration and domestic migration. As such, the twenty-first century United States can be viewed as a nation of three distinctive demographic regions. These are: the suburb-like 'New Sunbelt' that attracts domestic in-migration; an increasingly diverse 'Melting Pot' region that attracts immigration; and a slow-growing 'Heartland' region that attracts neither in-migration nor immigration.

Of course, there are internal nuances and micro-level features in the demography of these three regions that do not conform to their macro-level character in my proposed categorization. Dallas, for example, is a 'Melting Pot' city in my schema because it is a magnet for immigration, but it could equally be designated a 'New Sunbelt' city because it attracts considerable domestic in-migration. Moreover, some cities in my 'Melting Pot' regional category manifest New Sunbelt features because white families, who are attracted by the affordability of their suburban housing, drive their population growth. Obvious examples of this are the interior California cities of Riverside and Sacramento, where homes are a good deal less expensive than in the coastal areas of San Diego, greater Los Angeles and San Francisco.

Even allowing for such nuances, it is still possible to make a strong case for the existence of three regions with distinctive population profiles. In demographic character, the New Sunbelt shows features of being, in comparison to other regions, more suburban and middle-class, whiter – at least in its younger and middle-aged population – and with a more dispersed population wanting to live in a safe neighborhood. The most distinctive element of the Melting Pot's population, by contrast, is that it is younger, culturally vibrant, and probably more tied to the global economy and America's future. Finally, the Heartland's population is getting older and whiter and showing signs of stagnation in terms of growth. The state make-up of these three broad regions is tabulated below.

Table I: The Three Americas: A State Profile

The New Sunbelt	The Melting Pot	The Heartland
Arizona	Alaska	Alabama
Colorado	California	Arkansas
Delaware	Florida	Connecticut
Georgia	Hawaii	Indiana
Idaho	Illinois	Iowa
North Carolina	New Jersey	Kansas
Nevada	New York	Kentucky
Oregon	New Mexico	Louisiana
South Carolina	Texas	Maine
Tennessee		Maryland
Utah		Massachusetts
Virginia		Michigan
Washington		Minnesota
		Mississippi
		Montana
		Nebraska
		New Hampshire
		North Dakota
		Ohio
		Oklahoma
		Pennsylvania
		Rhode Island
		South Dakota
		Vermont
		West Virginia
		Wisconsin
		Wyoming

The New Sunbelt

The Sunbelt concept, as originally designated, focused on states south of 37 degrees latitude which had experienced rapid population growth and economic expansion since World War II – notably the big three of California, Texas and Florida (Abbott, 1990). In my regional reconfiguration based on the 2000 census data, the 'old' Sunbelt superstates have been re-classified as 'Melting Pot' states based on their highly urbanized and ethnically diverse character. My category of 'New Sunbelt' states are also fast-growing in terms of their population, which increased by 24 percent in the 1990s compared with 13 percent for the nation as a whole. However, the bulk of national population growth in the last decade of the twentieth century was driven by new immigrant minorities, particularly Latinos and Asians. In contrast, the New Sunbelt states grew as a result of domestic in-migration on the part of white Americans and African Americans, which outpaced the growth of their immigrant population by a ratio of five to one. Indeed, these 13 states absorbed 79 percent of the nation's white population gain in the 1990s.

The New Sunbelt attracts newcomers from different ends of the generational scale because of the relative affordability of suburban housing in these states compared to the very high prices in suburbs in the established Sunbelt superstates and the northern metropolises. Young Generation-Xers, especially those forming families, find that a decent home in a low-density neighborhood is still within their economic reach. Significantly, white married couples with children declined as a share of the national population in the 1990s, but nine of the ten states that recorded gains in such families were located in the New Sunbelt, led by Nevada where their numbers grew by 25 percent. At the other end of the age scale, retirees – a group whose numbers will explode in the early twenty-first century – showed a marked trend of in-migration to the New Sunbelt in the 1990s. They could trade in pricey homes in congested commuting suburbs elsewhere for the more spread-out residential communities and slower pace of life in the New Sunbelt (Frey, 2002).

The fastest population growth in the New Sunbelt occurred in outer suburban areas, ex-urban rural counties and smaller metropolitan areas. Significantly, the fastest growing counties in the United States in the 1990s were predominantly white and white-gaining counties on the peripheries of New Sunbelt metropolitan areas. The creation of this new demographic region is being shaped by migrants from other parts of the country quitting the largely cosmopolitan, liberal-leaning urban areas in a new form of white suburban flight from the inner cities of the industrial metropolises in the 1950s and 1960s. This earlier population movement produced local political cleavages between central cities and outlying areas. The more recent migration is more likely to generate political and cultural differences on a regional level between the New Sunbelt and the Melting Pot. In this regard, it should be noted that the growth trajectory of the 'Old' Sunbelt superstates has peaked but growth trajectories in the New Sunbelt continue to rise. The implications of this for a redistribution of regional political power in the twenty-first century were signaled by congressional reapportionment of seats based on the 2000 census. This produced seven additional seats for New Sunbelt states compared to only five for California, Texas and Florida combined. In contrast, the reapportionment following the 1990 census gave 14 new seats to the latter and only five to the former.

The Melting Pot

While it is true that the United States is becoming more racially and ethnically heterogeneous, this diversity is hardly spread evenly across the country. Most counties in the United States gained Hispanic and Asian residents in the 1990s, but these population groups were heavily clustered in the Melting Pot region. In 2000 the nine states that I classify as being part of the 'Melting Pot' contained 70 percent of the U.S. foreign-born population and 76 percent of all Americans who speak Spanish at home. Conversely, they were home to only 37 percent of the nation's native-born population and only 34 percent of those who speak only English at home. In a further mark of regional diversity, 55 percent of the nation's mixed-race couples reside in these states.

California makes a particularly interesting case of a 'Melting Pot' state that has evolved from being the archetype of the 'old' Sunbelt region which enjoyed substantial population growth during the long post-World War II economic boom. However, the waves of newcomers who went to seek jobs in California in the 1940s through the 1970s were Americans from other states, particularly those who were natives of the Midwest and the South. In this sense, California was America's America – a magnet for in-migration by Americans themselves rather than the golden door for immigration from abroad that the Northeastern and Great Lakes states had once been for Europeans. Around the middle of the twentieth century, more than half of the Golden State's population had been born in another state. However, the 2000 Census showed for the very first time that there were more people born in another country living in California than were born in another state. California is still the Golden State, but it has become the land of opportunity more for people from abroad rather than for native-born Americans.

The states of the Melting Pot region have been the main destinations for the newcomers who have entered the United States since the immigration reform of 1965 swept away many of the discriminatory restraints on immigrant national origins imposed in the 1920s. In 2000 they were home to 74 percent of the nation's combined Hispanic and Asian populations but only to 41 percent of its total population. Six of these states – California, New York, Texas, Florida, Illinois and New Jersey – led the nation in terms of the growth of their immigrant populations in the 1990s. In total the nine Melting Pot states grew in population by 13 percent in the last decade of the twentieth century. This growth was dominated by immigrants and immigrant minorities, with Asians and Hispanics accounting for 76 percent of the gains and other non-white, non-black races (including American Indians, other races and mixed races) contributing an additional 17 percent. In contrast, these states as a group lost white population in the 1990s. Even the 'Melting Pot' states that registered gains in white population – Florida, Texas, New Mexico and Alaska – experienced far greater increases in their immigrant and immigrant minority populations. The significance of immigration for population growth in the Melting Pot region is further underlined by the fact that these states collectively experienced a net domestic out-migration in the 1990s.

The attraction and retention of immigrant minorities in this region is influenced by a national immigration policy that emphasizes family reunification and encourages immigration to occur in chains that connect co-nationals at both origin and destination. It is also shaped by the establishment in these areas of real ethnic communities replete with their own institutions – small businesses, clubs, churches and social networks – that are not easily replicated in other regions of the country. For new ethnic minorities from Latin America, Asia or elsewhere, a move to the suburbs or another community within the Melting Pot region is likely to be more comfortable than being an 'outrider' in another part of the country. As a result, the suburbs in the nine Melting Pot states are in the process of becoming almost as multi-ethnic as their cities. In this region, over half of younger residents (under 35 years of age) are non-white or Hispanic, as these age, the proportion of older residents (35 years and over) in these groups – currently only a third – will increase (Frey, 2001 and 2003). Accordingly, the cities and suburbs of the Melting Pot are unlikely to reflect the old local tensions between these zones because they have more in common with each other than with cities and suburbs in the New Sunbelt.

The out-migration of whites reinforces the demographic distinctiveness of the Melting Pot. In the 1990s, the greater Los Angeles area lost 800,000 whites, the greater New York City area lost over 600,000 whites, and other immigrant gateway cities such as Miami, Chicago, San Diego and Houston experienced smaller losses. This population shift, which affects both central cities and suburban communities, reflects a flight from urbanism rather than from diversity. However, the white migrants belong to those groups that are moving to the New Sunbelt: young people, married couples, parents and retirees. This out-movement represents the ongoing displacement of the white middle-class core populations of suburbs surrounding the nation's largest urban areas, which for the most part, are located in the Melting Pot states.

On the other hand, there are grounds to be optimistic that Melting Pot cities and suburbs are not going to become civically dysfunctional communities because of the loss of old-stock Americans. They are being infused with new immigrant minorities who, by virtue of their age and proclivity for more traditional families, can help in developing a new sense of community in these areas based on their own experience and aspirations. The 2000 census showed that the large city with the highest percentage of families with children was Santa Ana, California, where they comprised 42 percent of all households (Frey, 2002). Close behind were Anaheim, California, and El Paso, Texas, where at least three out of ten households were traditional families.

The Heartland

The Heartland region consists of the remaining 28 states and the District of Columbia. It includes all the Northeastern and Midwestern states that are not classed as Melting Pot and Southern and Western states that have lagged in population growth. The dominant demographic characteristics of the region are relatively modest population growth and a largely white population. The Heartland, which contained 39 percent of the nation's population in 2000, was the least racially diverse of America's three demographic regions. Whites made up 81 percent of its population and African Americans, who were primarily concentrated in its industrial cities, constituted 12 percent. In the 1990s, the Heartland only accounted for about 14 percent of the nation's Asian and Hispanic population growth, but this small infusion helped stem the overall population loss that several of its declining cities would otherwise have experienced.

Many of the Heartland states have not attracted migrants in sizeable numbers for decades. Consequently, the region has an older age structure than the New Sunbelt and the Melting Pot. It also has a higher percentage of population born in-state – for example, 78 percent in the case of Pennsylvania compared with only 24 percent for Nevada in 2000. Its suburbs contain more middle-aged residents and are poised towards rapid 'graying' in contrast to those of the other two regions, which have attracted Generation-Xers and immigrants. Put another way, Heartland states have larger shares of Baby Boomers born in the quarter-century after World War II and coming to or approaching retirement in the early twenty-first century. This population group has considerable influence on the Heartland's politics, but in a way, that often blurs what we understand as the difference between 'Red State' and 'Blue State America.' Since pensions, healthcare provision and the wellbeing of elderly parents weigh large as issues for many in this cohort, the Heartland boomers seemingly constitute a fertile constituency for the Democrats. On the other hand, many are socially conservative on issues like abortion, gay rights and affirmative action, which can incline them towards the Republicans. As a result, many of these states are swing states whose partisan loyalties are unpredictable but can affect the outcome of national elections, as Ohio demonstrated in the 2004 presidential contest.

The Implications of Regional Population Developments

The increased saliency of regional demographic distinctions raises the issue of how well they can be bridged and whether they portend the growth of socio-cultural divisions in twenty-first century America. In this regard it may be tempting to transcribe regional differences into the emerging political stand-off between 'Blue America,' where voters are broadly identified as being liberal, individualistic and secular, and 'Red America,' where the majority is deemed to be conservative, community-oriented and strongly tied to religious beliefs (Barone, 2001; Brooks, 2001). Nevertheless, closer examination suggests that the parallels between regional demography and political geography are by no means so clear-cut.

The Melting Pot region admittedly shows some approximation with 'Blue America.' With the exception of Alaska, Florida and Texas, all its states favored the Democratic presidential candidate in 2000 and 2004. As a group, the residents of these states are culturally diverse, economically heterogeneous and broadly supportive of a larger role for government, especially regarding education, employment and social welfare programs. Moreover, this region's middle- and upper-income groups tend to be more cosmopolitan in outlook, educated to a higher level and less devout in their religious beliefs (at least measured by regularity of church attendance) than their counterparts in other regions.

However, it would be difficult to define 'Red America' as comprising the other two regions. The New Sunbelt in particular does not fit this mold. Many of its new residents are out-migrants from the more urban Melting Pot. While they may, by and large, be in quest of family-friendly neighborhoods and hold economically conservative views, their roots tend to make them more moderate on social issues like abortion, gun control and affirmative action. One possible exception to this trend, as discussed below, is their attitude to immigration control. Overall, however, their effect is likely to strengthen the political center in the region rather than to sharpen polarization. In fact, it is the Heartland, with its older, whiter and more socially conservative population profile, that most closely fits the 'Red America' stereotype. Nevertheless, many of its states, particularly those of the upper Midwest, New England and the mid Atlantic, were solidly in the Democratic column in both 2000 and 2004. In addition, many pundits were surprised that the suburban voters in many of these states were a competitive constituency rather than an automatic Republican one in these elections.

Rather than reflecting the two political Americas, I would prefer to cast the three regions as reflecting the older local distinctions of urban, suburban and rural. The new regional 'white flight' from the Melting Pot to the New Sunbelt is analogous to the older local 'white flight' from central cities to their suburban rings. The key differences in the first decade of the twenty-first century from the post-World War II era are that, firstly, both residents *and* jobs are now much more mobile, and, secondly, for middle-class Americans lifestyle rather than just economics is important in selecting a destination. Hence, while the Melting Pot region provides the intensity, ethnic diversity, and close contact that used to be associated only with cities, the New Sunbelt offers the quieter setting, large lot sizes and local control that have always attracted people to the suburbs. Finally, large swathes of the Heartland region now replicate the older, slower growing and more conservative rural areas of the second half of the twentieth century.

What is absent from this new scenario is the opportunity that used to exist for daily, face-to-face interactions among people from these different worlds. In the context of the old local cultural divisions, commuters, shoppers and theatergoers from the suburbs still had to interact with urbanites on a regular basis. Children in young suburban families still had relatively close contact to grandparents who lived in the city or countryside. In *Bowling Alone*, sociologist Robert Putnam (2000, p. 215) refers to a 'sprawl civic penalty' that has contributed to American society's overall civic disengagement. The fact that young couples, empty-nest boomers and retirees will increasingly populate the New Sunbelt region where sprawl is expanding rapidly suggests that greater social isolation will result from this trend.

Additionally, there is the potential for social dislocation between native-born Americans, particularly whites, and immigrant non-white newcomers outside the Melting Pot. Significantly, the states with the highest rate of increase (though this rarely translated into significant aggregate growth) in their foreign-born population between 1990 and 2005, led by North Carolina, Tennessee, Georgia and Nevada, were almost entirely located in the New Sunbelt. They also included Heartland states like Alabama, Iowa and Kentucky. Immigrants moving into the New Sunbelt states usually take jobs – notably in construction, retail and service industries – created by the growth of white, middle-class in-migration. Many of the immigrants into these new destination states arrived in the United States after 2000, are likely to be low income or poor in terms of economic status, and relatively lacking in skills and education compared to the more long-established foreign born in the Melting Pot. They also manifest a higher proportion of undocumented or illegal immigrants than the foreign born in the 'old' destination states. In essence, the white residents of the new destination states are not seeing the full panoply of immigration but a small and unrepresentative portion that is bestowed with a negative imagery in their eyes. For this reason, these are the states where demand for immigration control tends to be strongest, thereby creating the potential for disharmony with Melting Pot states that broadly favor liberal immigration policy.

On the other hand, there are positive features of social cohesion growing as a result of demographic change. Within the Melting Pot states, the evidence from the 1990s and the first years of the new century points to greater inter-racial and inter-cultural dating and marriage, residential coexistence, and the propensity for second-generation immigrant children to become proficient in English as well as the language of their parents. 'Melting' is indeed happening within the Melting Pot regions, if not across the broader national landscape.

These trends imply that an important national challenge for the twenty-first century will be to find ways of bridging these new regional divisions among communities with different demographics, lifestyles and values – but similar aspirations. The increased relevance of regional diversity will have significant implications for the national political parties, business corporations, state and local government, and civic and religious organizations. The saliency of immigration control as an issue of national debate in the early twenty-first century has already pointed to the capacity of issues relating to population change to create regional political differences. Well-worn local labels such as urban, suburban and rural, with their conventionally intra-regional connotations, are becoming less descriptive of lifestyles, racial profiles and age structures than is the regional classification of states into the 'Three Americas.' The differences between the racially diverse 'Melting Pot,' the suburb-like 'New Sunbelt' and the slow-growing, aging 'Heartland' are rooted in distinct redistribution patterns of immigrant minorities, who have concentrated mostly in coastal areas, and streams of largely white domestic migrants, who have gravitated to newer, economically prosperous areas in the Southeast and West. These regional variations will shape the diversity of America's Americans well into the twenty-first century.

Bibliography

Abbott, C. (1990) 'New West, New South, New Region,' in Raymond Mohl (ed.), *Searching for the Sunbelt: Historical Perspectives on a Region* (Knoxville: University of Tennessee Press), pp. 7–24.

Barone, M. (2001) '49 Percent Nation,' *National Journal* (June 8), pp. 1710–16.

Brooks, D. (2001) 'Are We Really One Country? A Report from Red and Blue America,' *Atlantic Monthly* (December), pp. 53–65.

Crieco, E.M. and Cassidy, R.C. (2001) 'Overview of Race and Hispanic origin,' *U.S. Census Bureau: Census 2000 Brief*, C2KBR/01–1

Frey, W. (2001) 'Meltingpot Suburbs: A Census 2000 Study of Suburban Diversity,' Census Survey (Washington, DC: Brookings Institution Center on Urban and Metropolitan Policy)

Frey, W. (2002) 'Ozzie & Harriet meet Will and Grace,' *Milken Institute Review*, no. 2, pp. 5–7.

Frey, W. (2003) 'Boomers and Seniors in the Suburbs: Changing Patterns in Census 2000' *Cities and Suburbs*, The Brookings Institution (January).

Martin, P. and Midgley, E. (2003) 'Immigration: Shaping and Reshaping America,' *Population Bulletin*, vol. 58, pp. 1–39.

Putnam, R.D. (2000) *Bowling Alone* (New York: Touchstone).

Scommegna, P. (2004) 'U.S. Growing Bigger, Older, and More Diverse,' *Population Reference Bureau* (April), www.prb.org

Shrestha, L. (2006) *The Changing Demographic Profile of the United States*, Congressional Research Service Report for Congress.

2
Through the Prism of Demographics: America's Political Scene

Rhodes Cook

From its inception in 1789 as a new nation of less than 4 million people, the United States has never stopped growing. By 1850, the population approached 25 million; by 1900, it had surpassed 75 million; by 2000, it exceeded 280 million; and in 2006 it passed the 300 million mark (Guide to U.S. Elections, 2005, pp. 1614–15). America has never really stopped to catch its breath. Assimilation of new groups has come on the fly, and inclusiveness in the political process has often come grudgingly. In the early years of the Republic, voting was largely limited to the landed gentry. Suffrage was not widely extended to non-property-owning adult white males until the early 1800s. Women were not given the right to vote until 1920. As for blacks, their road to full political participation came in fits and starts, beginning after the Civil War but not fully realized until the 1960s. And it was not until 1971, in the midst of the Vietnam War, that the national voting age was lowered from 21 to 18, giving many young soldiers who were fighting and dying in Southeast Asia a vote in the democracy that they were defending. In short, the American electorate was constantly evolving and expanding but it included some groups at a slower pace than others.

In the period since George W. Bush's father was elected president in 1988, the electorate – at least the portion that votes in presidential elections – has grown older, better educated, more racially diverse and much larger. Voter turnout jumped from barely 90 million in 1988 to more than 120 million in 2004, with a majority of the vote shifting from the states of the Frost Belt (the Northeast and Midwest) to those of the Sun Belt (the South and West). (Scammon et al., 2005, p. 11) In the early twenty-first century, Republican strength is concentrated in geographic terms in the American heartland, a large swath of the country that includes the fast-growing South and Mountain West, as well as the slower-growing Great Plains. Democrats dominate in the populous Northeast and the Pacific West, generally not as fast-growing but the locale of many of the nation's largest states. As for voting groups, Republicans have scored perceptible gains since 1988 among Hispanics, the less educated, and the elderly. Democrats have gained ground among the well educated, the young, and self-described independents (Stanley and Niemi, 2006, pp. 124–5).

Population changes on the political horizon will probably have an even more profound impact on the American electorate than those of the recent past – certainly altering the demographic composition and possibly even the partisan advantage. In the short run, politics will be affected by the demographics of aging, with the maturing mass of 'baby boomers' poised for their last hurrah. The advance guard of this hefty post-World War II generation turned 60 in 2006, with the tail end turning 42. Roughly 75 million strong, the boomers will have the numbers to push the nation toward one party or the other. Or just maybe, they will exhibit an independence of thought and action and steer the nation's politics on a new course that places neither the Democrats nor the Republicans in the lead role (Fineman, 2006).

In the long run, however, nothing will shape the American political scene more than the demographics of race. The nation's minority population has been growing so quickly of late, especially its Hispanic element, that it is not hard to imagine an American electorate a generation or so from now where whites comprise a tenuous majority, at most. If the changing demographics of age represent quiet evolution, the changing demographics of race could produce nothing less than a political revolution. It has already unleashed plenty of passion, on full display over the issue of immigration. Neither the Democratic nor Republican parties know quite how to handle this issue, in large part because the stakes are so high – both for them and for the nation as a whole.

The Demographics of Age: 'Baby Boomers' and the Politics of the Present

While the demographics of race are apt to drive the politics of the future, the demographics of age are molding the politics of the present, as the American electorate grows steadily grayer. When Bill Clinton was elected president in 1992, more than 55 percent of voters were under the age of 45. When George W. Bush was re-elected in 2004, nearly 55 percent were aged 45 or older, with roughly one-third of all voters aging 'baby boomers' (Stanley and Niemi, 2006, p. 124).

Voters at either end of the age spectrum – the young and the old – tend to get the most attention. The young are always a curiosity; they are new to the political process, with partisan preferences that are largely unknown. So, too, is even their interest in the political process, as it is always in question how many in the highly mobile 18-to-29 year old age group will even register to vote. The elderly (those 60 and older) are another matter. They tend to vote at a higher rate than any other age group in the electorate, at least up to age 75. Living longer each generation, those aged 60 and over cast nearly one-quarter of all the votes in the 2004 presidential election (Stanley and Niemi, 2006, p. 124).

It is assumed that a commonality of interests at least loosely binds the youngest and the oldest with their chronological peers. But that has not been the case as yet with the boomers, the largest generation of voters in American history. Born between 1946 and 1964, they came of age at vastly different times. Older boomers can recall the dawn of television and the threat of nuclear war in the 1950s; the Kennedy assassinations, the civil rights struggle and the Vietnam War in the 1960s; all capped by the tumultuous 1968 Democratic convention in Chicago, where the forces unleashed in the previous decade seemed to come to a head. Younger boomers do not remember any of this. They have a different frame of reference, with early memories that start with Richard Nixon and Watergate, and a coming of age that coincided with the Ronald Reagan years.

But as the boomers age, there is the chance that for the next decade or so they will not only be a hugely influential group in numbers but an increasingly homogenous one, as they focus more and more on common issues such as economic security, health care and the legacy they wish to leave their children, the country, and the planet. Up to now, the boomers have been political free agents, not firmly committed to one party or the other. If anything, they have been a national barometer in their voting behavior. As young voters in 1976, they leaned slightly to Democrat Jimmy Carter in an election that Carter narrowly won. As the vanguard of boomers reached early middle age in the 1980s, they voted decisively like the rest of the country for Republicans Ronald Reagan and George Bush Snr., before switching in the 1990s – as the nation did – to Democrat Bill Clinton.

As the leading edge of the boomers approached late middle age with the new millennium, they reflected almost exactly the national result of the last two presidential elections – splitting nearly evenly between George W. Bush and Al Gore in 2000 and favoring Bush by the same 51-to-48 percent margin by which he won nationally in 2004 (Stanley and Niemi, 2006, p. 124).

What is next for this largest, if not greatest, of American generations? To be sure, boomers are part of a generation blessed like no other. Generally better educated and more affluent than their parents, they often project themselves as independent thinkers with a healthy dose of skepticism about politicians and the major parties. This is a group that is not likely to exit the national stage quickly or quietly. The last two presidents, Clinton and George W. Bush – both born in 1946 – are in the advance guard of boomers; and the country is likely to be led for years to come by others in this generation. All the while, rank-and-file baby boomers stand ready to flex their political muscle. They can be found almost everywhere in large numbers, comprising (according to the 2000 census) at least 25 percent of the total population in every state except Utah, where they constituted 23 percent (U.S. Census Bureau, 2001, p. 10).

As the large boomer population ages, voter turnout for presidential elections has inched upward – from barely 50 percent of the citizen voting-age population in 1996, to 54 percent in 2000, to more than 60 percent of eligible citizens in 2004. And election turnouts are apt to stay high for years to come (Gans, 2005). To be sure, the nature of the individual contests and the perceived stakes involved have affected voter turnout in recent elections. The Clinton–Dole race in 1996 was considered dull and the outcome was predictable. On the other hand, the Bush–Kerry face-off was considered more consequential than any election in a generation and was nip and tuck virtually from start to finish. But regardless of the political fireworks (or lack thereof) that surrounds each election, it is a simple fact that the nation's population is aging. And a basic truth of American politics is that the turnout rate tends to increase with age.

If nothing else, boomers are apt to be a tough sell in the years ahead – as they were for President Bush's plan to privatize Social Security in 2005, and President Clinton's complex program to overhaul the nation's health care system more than a decade earlier. Try to take away a portion of their Social Security or their Medicare, as politicians may want to try in the future, and things could get ugly. As for their partisanship, the boomers have given few hints as to how they might vote in the future. A Gallup Poll survey on party identification in April 2006 showed that Republicans have a two-point edge among 30–49 year-olds (who include younger boomers), while Democrats have a five-point edge among 50–64 year-olds (who include older boomers). Yet one-third of the respondents in both age groups labeled themselves as independents (Gallup Poll, 2006).

If the boomers finally come down firmly in favor of one party or do something really unusual and mount a challenge to the two-party system itself, they could transform their political legacy from a national barometer that reflects public opinion to a national trend-setter that leads it.

The Demographics of Race: Hispanics and the Politics of the Future

While the demographics of aging reflect a quiet and natural evolution, the changing demographics of race are different. It is a visceral matter that engages passions, and may produce nothing less than a political revolution as the twenty-first century unfolds. As the nation's minority population steadily grows, not only will the racial composition of the electorate gradually change but who sits at the head of the political table could shift as well. In 2004, there were already four states with a majority-minority population (that is, whites form less than 50 percent of the population) – Hawaii, New Mexico, California and Texas – and five others where minorities made up around 40 percent of the population – Maryland, Mississippi, Georgia, New York and Arizona (Caldwell, 2005; Pear, 2005).

Which party is likely to benefit from the changing hue of the electorate? At first glance, it would seem to be a clear bonanza for the Democrats. On second glance, it may not be that simple. For the last half century or so, Democrats have dominated the minority vote – up from 15 percent of the total vote cast in 1988 to more than 20 percent in 2004. But the Democrats have done better with some racial groups than others. With black Americans they are golden, consistently drawing upwards of 90 percent of this group's vote in presidential elections since the Republican Party took a sharp turn south in the mid-1960s. Hispanics and Asians have been more competitive, on the other hand, with Democratic candidate John Kerry only winning between 55 percent and 60 percent of their ballots in 2004 (Connelly, 2004, p. 4).

Smaller in numbers, Native Americans are not tracked to the same degree in national Election Day exit polls as the larger minority groups. However, looking at election results from heavily Indian counties, they appear to be decidedly Democratic. Shannon County, South Dakota, for instance, a county that is 94 percent Native American – the highest percentage in the United States – went 85 percent for John Kerry in the 2004 presidential election. Menominee County, Wisconsin, which is 87 percent Native American, went 83 percent for Kerry. Apache County, Arizona, which is 77 percent Native American, went 65 percent for Kerry (Cook, 2005, p. 149). With results like these, Native Americans may not vote as Democratic as blacks, but they are consistently more so than Asians or Hispanics.

In the 2004 presidential election, blacks cast an estimated 11 percent of the nationwide vote, Hispanics 6 to 8 percent (depending on the source), and Asians 2 percent. But the focus of late has been on the role of Hispanics, who have emerged in the early twenty-first century as the nation's largest and fastest-growing minority group. They are not only found in swelling numbers in vote-rich states along America's southern border, but they are also the leading minority in disparate far-flung states to the north, such as Idaho, Kansas and New Hampshire (U.S. Census Bureau, 2005). In short, Hispanics are a group that both Democrats and Republicans covet as they plot their long-range strategies.

However, the battle for the Hispanic vote is a fight for the future since it represents potential rather than current political power. More than half of Hispanic ballots in 2004 were cast in just three states – California, Florida and Texas – only one of which (Florida) was an actual battleground state (Suro et al., 2005, p. 170). Nationally, there were more than 41 million Hispanics living in the United States in 2004. Nevertheless, according to a Census Bureau survey, just 16 million were eligible to vote, less than 10 million reported being registered to vote, and barely 7.5 million Hispanics actually reported voting. (U.S. Census Bureau, 2006, p. 4) This was in sharp contrast to the voting participation of blacks. Of America's estimated 39 million African Americans in 2004, 23 million were eligible to vote, 16 million reported being registered, and 14 million reported voting. In short, the number of ballots cast by blacks in 2004 was nearly twice as large as the number cast by Hispanics. (U.S. Census Bureau, 2006., p. 4).

The 25 million Hispanics not eligible to vote in 2004 were split between those who were citizens but too young to vote and adults of voting age who were not citizens. The latter comprise a majority of the 11 million or so illegal immigrants presently living in the United States, a group that may never become eligible to vote unless an amnesty affects their status. In contrast, young Hispanic citizens will become voters, and are certain to be a growing force in American politics.

However, answers to questions regarding the likely consequences of Hispanic electoral assimilation necessarily involve a degree of speculation. Firstly, will Hispanics register to vote in larger numbers than they have in the past? Judging from their increased activism in the form of demonstrations in 2005–6, they appear more energized and organized than they have ever been before. They are also beginning to bridge their internal racial differences to unite Puerto Ricans in New York, Cubans in Florida, and Mexicans in the Southwest in the pursuit of a common cause. It therefore seems reasonable to expect with regard to the 2008 elections and beyond an increased rate of voter registration among Hispanics, which after citizenship is the biggest hurdle to voting.

Secondly, could increased Hispanic involvement in American politics spur a shift in the partisan voting behavior of whites, blacks and Asians? This could well happen. As demonstrated by the defection of white Southerners to the Republicans in the wake of the enfranchisement of African Americans in the 1960s, the entry of a large racial or ethnic group in the electorate can have a ripple effect that brings changes in the partisan voting behavior of other groups, who seek to maintain their own place in the political sun.

Finally, does either party have an immediate advantage in wooing Hispanics? Democrats start with the inside track because they have won a clear majority of the Hispanic vote in every presidential election in the past generation. If 2004 voting patterns were to hold, the Hispanic vote for the Democrats would be

500,000 higher in 2008 simply as a result of the growth in numbers of this population group. The impact is even stronger further into the future. According to the Hispanic Voter Project conducted by Johns Hopkins University, had the 2004 election been held in an electorate based on the one forecast for 2020, with all other factors held constant, the higher Hispanic vote would have given John Kerry a slight victory in both the electoral college and popular vote over Bush (Edsall and Goldfarb, 2006).

Moreover, the Democrats appear less divided than the Republicans in their sympathies toward immigrants. The latter are split between a Hispanic-friendly White House and business community desirous of cheap labor, and a conservative rank-and-file upset with the legal and cultural implications of a massive Hispanic influx. In addition, Republicans have their fingerprints all over House-passed legislation in December 2005 which emphasized border security and criminal punishments to reduce illegal immigration. To many Hispanics, it was a reminder of California Proposition 187, approved in 1994 with considerable Republican help, which denied public services to the children of illegal immigrants.

It remains to be seen whether George W. Bush, who speaks Spanish and has featured outreach to Hispanics throughout his political career, can help mute any widespread Hispanic antipathy to his party during his last years as president. As a public official, Bush has personally worn well among Hispanics. When he ran for re-election as governor of Texas in 1998, he won roughly 50 percent of the Hispanic vote. In 2004, as president, Bush drew roughly 40 percent, the best showing by any Republican presidential candidate among Hispanics in more than a quarter century. However, defending his party from a possible Hispanic backlash is a greater challenge than promoting his candidacy among Hispanic voters (Riley, 2004, p. A15). Bush and GOP leaders face the problem that conservative white Republicans are the most adamantly opposed of all political and demographic groups to what the president dubbed his 'rational middle ground' policy towards allowing more undocumented workers to become legal and eventually acquire citizenship (Edsall and Goldfarb, 2006).

In 2004, Democrats largely took the Hispanic vote for granted, expecting to replicate Al Gore's 2000 lead of nearly two to one over Bush with this group. Meanwhile, Republicans ran carefully targeted appeals to Cuban Americans in Florida and Mexican Americans in the Southwest, delivered in Spanish to first-generation Hispanics and in English to those in the second and third generations. Republican ads emphasized patriotism, family values, and basically portrayed the Republicans as the party of strength and opportunity and the Democrats as the party of grievance. (Campo-Flores and Fineman, 2005, p. 27) Bush's most pronounced gains were among the increased share of Hispanics who are evangelical Christians and among Hispanics who immigrated to the United States rather

than among those born there. (Edsall and Goldfarb, 2006) However, this promising trend towards the Republicans was abruptly halted in the midterms of 2006.
Exit polls suggested that 69 percent of Hispanic ballots went to the Democrats
in these elections (Pena, 2006).

One thing is certain, immigration – and by extension, the place of Hispanics
in America's future – is now a hot button political issue. Like the contents of
Pandora's box, once out in the open it is likely to remain there. At the core of
the debate for many voters are two quite elemental and as yet unanswered
questions: first, what will the country look like demographically and culturally a
generation from now; and second, who will be running it?

Clues from the Map

Arguably the last partisan realignment in American politics occurred in 1968,
when Republicans brought down the curtain on the long-running Democratic
New Deal era and launched a Republican era of their own. It has seen them win
seven of the last 10 presidential elections, gain control of the Senate from 1981
through 1987, and finally establish control over both branches of the legislature
from 1995 to 2007. The outline of the current GOP dominance was presciently
outlined by political analyst Kevin Phillips in his book, *The Emerging Republican
Majority* (published shortly after the 1968 election of his boss, Richard Nixon).
Phillips correctly foresaw a GOP majority anchored in America's heartland and
burgeoning Sun Belt. But the Republican majority that Phillips envisioned also
included California and suburbia, and did not take into account a growing
minority population that Democrats have a head start in wooing (Phillips, 1969).

As a result, Republicans do not have a muscular majority, but a tenuous one.
They have consolidated the South, pulling states across the Deep South that
voted that year for former Alabama Governor George C. Wallace into the
Republican column to join other states that were already there. But Republicans
have been consistently beaten of late in the Northeast and the Pacific West, as
well as major Midwestern battleground states such as Illinois and Michigan. In
short, whether one is discussing control of the White House or of Congress,
America's electoral geography consists of the L-shaped Republican heartland in
one corner versus the Democratic coasts in the other, with the states of the
industrial Midwest these days holding the balance of power for control of both
ends of Pennsylvania Avenue.

The national political map has rarely been as geographically synchronized as in
2004. In the 26 states of the Republican 'L' – comprised of the South, the Plains
states and the Rocky Mountain West (including Alaska) – the GOP came out of

the 2004 election holding two-thirds of the House seats, more than three-fourths of the Senate seats, and all 232 electoral votes. In the 16 states on the Democratic coasts – the Pacific West and the Northeast (including the District of Columbia) – the Democrats won nearly two-thirds of the House seats, fully three-fourths of the Senate seats, and all but five of its 199 electoral votes (losing only West Virginia) (Cook, 2006, p. 12). Meanwhile, in the eight Midwestern battleground states, the tallies on nearly all counts were roughly equal between the two parties. Some have dubbed this geographical phenomenon of Republicans living in one place and Democrats in another as the 'big sort'. It is most apparent in the crisply delineated Republican 'red states' and Democratic 'blue states' on recent presidential election maps. But this growing link between geography and partisanship is not limited to states and regions. Increasingly, it now extends all the way down to the county level (Bishop, 2004).

Although the 2004 presidential race was very close nationally, that was not the case in county-by-county voting. A vast majority of the nation's 3,100 or so counties were won by one party or the other decisively with at least 60 percent of the vote. There were more of these 'landslide' counties in 2004 – over 1,800 of them in all – than in any close presidential election in modern history (Cook, 2005, p. 121). There are three clear reasons for this development: Republicans have tightened their hegemony in rural America; Democrats dominate more than ever in the cities; and the suburbs, while a battleground when viewed as a whole, have their sharp partisan distinctions. Democrats have a clear edge in older, inner suburbs adjoining central cities, while Republicans tend to prevail in fast-growing outlying areas, commonly known as exurbs.

This political archaeology is vividly on display in the Northern Virginia suburbs of the nation's capital. The inner suburbs just across the Potomac River from Washington, D.C., have a high minority population and vote loyally Democratic. The middle suburbs that straddle the proverbial beltway about 10 miles out from Washington have a lower minority population and tend to be politically marginal. The outer suburbs, originally areas of 'white flight,' have low minority populations and are usually found in the Republican column.

A byproduct of this 'sortedness,' not just in the Washington, D.C. area, but the nation as a whole, has been a striking decline in electoral competition. It has been seen at the congressional level in both high re-election rates and a falloff in recent years in the number of closely contested races. Both trends have been particularly evident in races for the U.S. House of Representatives, where not only have the incumbent reelection rates approached unanimity but few winners have even had to break a sweat to win their seats. The 2006 midterms broke this particular mold, but it remains to be seen whether this results in a new cycle of incumbency advantage or enhanced competitiveness. A winning percentage below 55 is often used to define a competitive race. In 1992, contests in 111 of the 435 House districts met this standard. In 2004, races in only 32 districts did – an almost total absence of competition that more closely resembles a banana republic than a nation that fashions itself as a 'world-class' democracy (Cook, 2005, p. 121).

Hand in hand with declining competition has come an increasing congruency in the nation's electoral map, particularly as one compares the vote for president and the U.S. House by congressional district. The closing decades of the twentieth century were the heyday of split-ticket voting in the United States – regularly producing divided government, with a president from one party and a congress from the other. But for now, that is a thing of the past. No longer does the South vote Republican for president and Democratic for members of Congress, nor does the Northeast vote Democratic for president while electing a large complement of moderate Republicans to seats on Capitol Hill. Few congressional districts split their vote for president and the House anymore. In 1984, there were nearly 200 ticket-splitting districts around the country. In 1988, there were still close to 150. In 2004, there were just 59 such districts, the lowest number in any presidential election since World War II (Stanley and Niemi, 2006, p. 46).

Looking Ahead

For good measure, the national electoral map has stayed virtually the same the last two presidential elections, giving the sense that the famous red and blue shadings are in semi-permanent balance. But below the state level, in the 3,100 or so counties across the country, there is an ongoing movement of voters between the two parties that hints at the emerging shape of the future of American politics. More than 200 counties switched party hands in 2004. Most of these moved from the Democrats in 2000 to George W. Bush and the Republicans in 2004. But more than 60 counties moved the other way – to John Kerry and the Democrats. To be sure, many of the counties that changed parties were small, rural ones. And in many cases, only a few votes were needed to tip a county from one party to the other. But nearly three dozen of the counties that switched party hands in 2004 were populous ones, each with more than 100,000 residents. And their movement from one party to the other represented the seeds of change in American politics that when reaching full flower can bring historic shifts (Cook, 2006, pp. 11–14).

In 2004, both Democrats and Republicans made inroads in a far-flung array of states and an eclectic assortment of counties. Many of the counties that Bush gained in 2004 had not voted for a Republican presidential candidate since his father in 1988. On the other hand, many of the counties that Kerry picked up from the GOP had voted Democratic as recently as 1996, taking a one-election sabbatical from the party in 2000 when defections to Ralph Nader's independent candidacy temporarily reduced the Democratic vote. Republicans pulled into their column a number of retirement-oriented counties on the Florida Gulf Coast, a heavily Hispanic county on Texas's southern border with Mexico, and the Indiana county that contains America's most famous Catholic university, Notre Dame. Democrats also made cross-country gains at the county level in 2004, from one in central Maine that includes the state university to a pair of mountain counties in California that had not voted for a Democratic presidential candidate since Franklin D. Roosevelt.

Probably most intriguing for the future, however, were the inroads that Republicans scored in 'blue' America and that Democrats managed in 'red' America. Republicans registered breakthroughs in a number of blue-collar counties across the industrial Frost Belt in 2004. In Michigan, they picked up Macomb County, the fabled home of ethnic, working-class 'Reagan Democrats' just outside Detroit. In Pennsylvania, they gained Lawrence County, in the old iron and steel country outside Pittsburgh. And in New York, Bush brought into the Republican column the borough of Staten Island, home to many of New York City's police and firemen and located just across the harbor from the site of the World Trade Center. But if there was one county that exemplified the Republican trend in 'blue' America, it was Cambria in mountainous, southwest Pennsylvania. The county is the gateway to industrial western Pennsylvania, a region known for its ethnic diversity, intense patriotism, and longtime loyalty to organized labor and the Democratic Party. The Cambria County seat of Johnstown is home to John Murtha, the pro-military Democratic congressman who has become a vocal critic of the Bush administration's Iraq War policy. Yet in 2004, Cambria County voted for Bush, the first time in 32 years that it supported the Republican presidential candidate (Scammon et al., 2005).

Democratic inroads in 'red' America in the last election were of a different sort. They made gains in generally affluent counties, including a number of ski resorts in Colorado's 'granola belt' (which stretches from the southwest corner of the state to Boulder, by way of places like Aspen and Vail). And the Democrats won Teton County, the Wyoming home of Vice President Richard Cheney, which includes the resort town of Jackson Hole.

Their most notable gains were in populous cosmopolitan areas in the South – such as the counties that contain Savannah, Ga., Charlotte, N.C., and Austin, Texas – as well as Indiana's capital city of Indianapolis, which had not voted for a Democratic presidential candidate since 1964 (Judis and Teixeira, 2002). Yet, if there is one county that personified the Democratic trend in 'red' America, it is Fairfax in suburban Northern Virginia. Situated a few miles west of the nation's capital, it is the most populous jurisdiction in the Washington, D.C. area, with more than 1 million residents. It is fast-growing, having more than doubled its population since 1970, and is one of the most affluent counties in the country. Fairfax County also has a substantial number of minority residents, comprising an estimated one-third of the population and growing. And until recently, it was reliably Republican in presidential voting. But in 2004, Fairfax County voted for Kerry, the first time in 40 years that it supported the Democratic presidential candidate. And in 2005, it overwhelmingly backed the party's candidate for governor, enabling the Democrats to retain the state's executive mansion. (Scammon et al., 2005)

In summary, there is not only an ongoing movement of populations within America, there is ongoing change among its voters. There is a blue-collar trend to the Republicans; a white-collar trend to the Democrats; an electorate that in the short run will be dominated by older voters, and in the long run dramatically impacted by a growing minority population. All of these factors portend change, maybe big change, for America's electoral map. Let us enjoy the familiar red and blue shadings while we can. They may not last much longer.

Bibliography

Bishop, Bill (2004) 'The Great Divide: An Utterly Polarizing U.S. Election,' *Austin American-Statesman* (4 December).

Caldwell, Alicia A. (2005) 'Non-Whites Now a Majority in Texas,' *Boston Globe* (11 August).

Campo-Flores, Arian and Fineman, Howard (2005) 'A Latin Power Surge,' *Newsweek* (30 May).

Connelly, Marjorie (2004) 'How Americans Voted: A Political Portrait,' *The New York Times* (7 November).

Cook, Rhodes (2005) 'The Electoral Map: Where You Live is How You Vote,' *Mapping the Political Landscape 2005* (Washington, D.C.: Pew Research Center).

Cook, Rhodes (2006) 'Through the Prism of Demographics: America's Political Scene,' *The Rhodes Cook Letter* (April).

Edsall, Thomas and Goldfarb, Zachary (2006) 'Bush is Losing Hispanics' Support, Polls Show,' *Washington Post* (21 May).

Fineman, Howard (2006) 'The Last Hurrah,' *Newsweek* (23 January).

Gallup Poll (2006) *Gallup Poll Social Series*, 10–13 April (Princeton, N.J.: The Gallup Organization), unpublished data.

Gans, Curtis (2005) 'Turnout Exceeds Optimistic Predictions' (Washington, D.C.: The Committee for the Study of the American Electorate).

Guide to U.S. Elections, 5th ed (2005) (Washington, D.C.: CQ Press)

Judis, John B. and Teixeira, Ruy (2002) *The Emerging Democratic Majority* (New York: Scribner).

Pear, Robert (2005) 'U.S. Minorities are Becoming the Majority,' *International Herald Tribune* (13–14 August).

Pena, Maria (2006) 'Hispanic Voters Punish Republicans in Mid-term Elections,' *La Oferta* (November 13), www.laoferta.com/index.php?option=com

Phillips, Kevin (1969) *The Emerging Republican Majority* (New York: Arlington House).

Riley, Jason L. (2004) 'Ignore the Anti-Immigrant Right. Bush Did.' *The Wall Street Journal* (22 November).

Scammon, Richard M., McGillivray, Alice V. and Cook, Rhodes (2005) *America at the Polls 1960–2004* (Washington, D.C.: CQ Press).

Scammon, Richard M., McGillivray, Alice V. and Cook, Rhodes (2005) *America Votes 26* (Washington, D.C.: CQ Press).

Stanley, Harold W. and Niemi, Richard G. (2006) *Vital Statistics on American Politics 2005–2006* (Washington, D.C.: CQ Press).

Suro, Roberto, Fry, Richard and Passel, Jeffrey S. (2005) 'The Hispanic Vote: Electoral Strength Lags Population Growth,' *Mapping the Political Landscape 2005* (Washington, D.C.: Pew Research Center).

U.S. Census Bureau (2001) 'Age: 2000,' *Census 2000 Brief* (Washington, D.C.: U.S. Census Bureau).

U.S. Census Bureau (2005) 'Texas Becomes Nation's Newest "Majority-Minority" State, Census Bureau Announces' (11 August) (Washington, D.C.: U.S. Census Bureau).

U.S. Census Bureau (2006) 'Voting and Registration in the Election of November 2004' (Washington, D.C.: U.S. Census Bureau).

PART TWO
The Socioeconomic and Cultural Contexts of Population Issues

3
Population Matters in Native America

Joy Porter

Bestselling books such as Charles C. Mann's *1491* have made accessible to the reading public recent scholarship that radically challenges conventional notions of what the western hemisphere was like before Columbus (Mann, 2005). What is particularly interesting about such work is the growing awareness it reflects not only of new conclusions being reached but also their implications. Increasingly, there is a general understanding that the measurement and interpretation of data about Native American populations is hotly contested because it has always impacted upon, and to a degree reflected, the welfare, representation and status of native peoples in North America. This chapter examines the politics of population within Native America to explore three areas where debate reverberates within and across disciplinary boundaries:

- the hotly contested question of whether one, eighteen or tens of millions of North American Indians perished in the first century of contact, and the contrasting ways in which this issue has been addressed by both native and non-native scholars over time;
- the political, cultural and social complexities of Indian population measurement, and the long-term impact of the U.S. policy inflection to perceive Indians as 'vanishing' that lasted up until the 1960s;
- the implications of the on-going renaissance in Native American Indian numbers from an all-time low of 228,000 in 1890 to 4.1 million (American Indian & Alaskan Native alone or in combination with other races) in the 2000 Census and 4.4 million (1.5 percent of the U.S.) population as of 1 July 2004.

Perhaps the most polarized topic of all within Native American Studies is the debate over pre-contact Native population numbers. It is a story of scholarly estimates that have significantly inflated over time. In sum, changes in how the academy estimated Indian numbers before the onset of colonialism have mirrored changes in how Indians have been perceived within American society generally. This is not to suggest that scholars of population up until now have failed to make objective use of the data available to them. It is to say, however, that defining objectivity in relation to Indian population numbers is, as Peter Novick put it when defining historical objectivity more generally, like 'nailing jelly to the wall' (Novick, 1988, p. 6).

During the 1920s, in an era when the least assimilated Indian communities were beginning to be seen by American intellectuals as holistic and capable of producing 'good personality' (in comparison to non-Indian communities which at the time seemed beset by anomie and all the fracturing stresses of modern, industrial life), scholars began a process of reassessment. Remarkable as it may seem today, for a long time prior to the 1920s, the 1560 estimate by Spanish priest Bartolomé de Las Casas that 40 million Indians died in Latin America between 1492 and 1560 had been generally thought of as a gross exaggeration (Denevan, 1976). However as William M. Denevan has pointed out, the 1920s saw a fresh debate begin between the geographer Karl Sapper (1924) and the anthropologists Paul Rivet (1924) and Herbert Spinden (1928) suggesting that Columbian contact numbers stood at between 37 and 50 million. This stimulated a wave of region- and culture-specific research, begun by James Mooney (1928) that produced another swing of the pendulum on Native numbers. From the late 1920s until the watershed of the 1960s, scholarly orthodoxy hewed in favor of conservative estimates, such as 8.4 million advanced by anthropologist Alfred Kroeber's calculations in 1934 and 1939, 13.4 million proposed by philologist Ángel Rosenblat in 1935, and 15.6 million put forward by Julian Steward in 1949 (Sapper, 1924; Rivet, 1924; Spinden, 1928; Mooney, 1928; Kroeber, 1934 and 1939; Rosenblat, 1935; Steward, 1949).

James Mooney's early twentieth century estimate (1928, also 1910) at the time of 'first extensive contact' for individual tribal populations in regions north of the Rio Grande was of only 1.15 million Native Americans (that is, American Indians, Eskimos and Aleuts). The only challenge of note to this estimate was voiced by the then less influential Berkeley geographer Carl Sauer – supported by fellow geographer Peveril Meigs and physiologist Sherburne F. Cook (the first, in 1937, to systematically study Indian population decline due to epidemic disease) – who produced larger estimates. Their dissenting position was later endorsed by Lesley Simpson, Woodrow Borah and Homer Aschmann. Conservative estimates still dominated, but Sauer and his School began the approach of respecting early counts, estimates and documentary data, and they stressed the importance of epidemics in prompting catastrophic decline in Indian numbers. Uniquely, they emphasized the significance of the context and larger processes that accompanied the maintenance of empire (Denevan, 1996; Meigs, 1935; Cook, 1937; Borah, 1964; Aschmann, 1959).

An immediate question that arises from the above is why did it take so long for scholars to begin to focus on what might seem the obvious first place to start when estimating pre-contact population numbers – that is, with early counts and documentary evidence. No doubt some would argue in a blanket fashion that non-Indian intellectuals were simply beset by racist preconceptions, but in one sense at least early twentieth century scholars should be forgiven for choosing to discount historical testimony when they came to formulate their estimates. After all, early records are replete with the preposterous and the overtly propagandistic, especially when it comes to descriptions of native peoples. Europeans traveled to the New World with preconceptions, fully expecting to find the monstrous and the forbidden. Early descriptions did not fail to deliver them. Consider, as one example, the tract *Mundus Novus* (ca. 1504–1505) produced by the Florentine merchant Amerigo Vespucci, after whom the Americas are named. He wrote about Brazilian natives:

> First then, to the people. We found in those parts such a multitude
> of people as nobody could enumerate (as we read in the
> Apocalypse), a race I say gentle and amenable. All of both sexes go
> about naked, covering no part of their bodies; and just as they spring
> from their mother's wombs so they go until death.[6]

Vespucci went on to discuss native bodies and native sexual practices in depth, deviating momentarily to dwell on native cannibalism, stating 'I knew one man whom I also spoke to who was reputed to have eaten more than three hundred human bodies.' He continues, spending much time on the nakedness, cleanliness, beauty and libidinousness of native women, noting that, 'When they had the opportunity of copulating with Christians, urged by excessive lust, they defiled and prostituted themselves.' Furthermore, he noted 'their women, being very lustful, cause the private parts of their husbands to swell up to such a huge size that they appear deformed and disgusting. And in consequence of this many lose their organs which break through lack of attention, and they remain eunuchs.' Vespucci concludes with the remark, 'They live one hundred and fifty years and rarely fall ill...' (*Mundus Novus*). Although Vespucci is not usually relied upon as a platform from which to base population estimates (more usually it is Bartolomé de Las Casas and conquistador Hernán Cortés), he illustrates the point that the propagandistic and exaggerated elements within early records and testimonies served to obscure their worth as clues to population numbers in the eyes of scholars until the cultural and conceptual changes inaugurated by the twentieth century (for a discussion on invented chronicles, see Zamora, 1988).

The next groundswell of change within Native American studies and within Indian population estimates came at another watershed era in the United States's history, the 1960s. The key voice making population estimates was the anthropologist Henry Dobyns. He picked up on (some have suggested, became obsessed with) Sauer's emphasis on disease, arguing that European pathogens could have cut a swathe through Indian population numbers long before actual face-to-face encounters between European settlers and Indians actually occurred (Henige, 1989). Using mortality rates from epidemics and regional estimates of environmental carrying capacity, Dobyns estimated that there were up to 18 million Indians north of Mesoamerica when Europeans began to make contact (Dobyns, 1966 and 1983). This was a huge jump in estimates and one that cannot be divorced from the intellectual climate of the time. The 1960s, like the 1920s, were a decade of investigation into Indian conditions and, as in the 1920s, reform pressure stimulated policy change that led to ongoing improvement in Indian conditions, Indian economics, and population levels. Dobyns' work can usefully be thought of in juxtaposition with the variety of studies carried out at the time that brought the grim and unwholesome conditions Indians were experiencing into sharp relief. These made a plea for 'self-determination' to replace 'termination,' a call echoed in the 1961 'Declaration of Indian Purpose' produced by the American Indian Chicago Conference. This was repeated by the National Indian Youth Council, founded in 1961, by the Alaskan Federation of Natives (AFN), formed in 1966, and by the controversial American Indian Movement (AIM), formed in 1968. Further Indian activism was spurred by strong Indian involvement in the war in South-East Asia. What came to be known as the 'Red Power' insurgency was to last from 1969 to 1973 and range from non-violent political demonstrations to occasional armed resistance.

This political mobilization of American Indians, and the consequent reduction in the perceived stigma associated with Indian identity, may also have contributed to the growth in Indians enumerated by the U.S. census since 1960, alongside the changes that were made in how the census defined 'Native American.' A large part of the leap in Indian figures since 1960 (from 523,591 in 1960 to 1.9 million including Eskimos and Aleuts in 1990), has been explained not just by higher rates of fertility relative to the dominant population but by people identifying themselves as Indian who had not done so before. Clearly, in the 1960s a new ethos surrounded all things Indian, heralding a change not only in how Indians thought of themselves, but also in how non-Indians thought about Indians in general. This is not an insignificant cultural phenomenon, especially when looked at from a 'long' perspective. As Karl Kroeber has pointed out, 'The implications of this cultural phenomenon dwarf those of the Indians' not inconsiderable demographic expansion, dramatizing a radical transformation in the attitude of Old World immigrants to native New Worlders.' For well over a quarter-century now, the growth in Indian numbers within the United States has decisively surpassed the realms of biological possibility, forcing us to recognize a new phenomenon in North America, a phenomenon Kroeber describes as 'an eagerness of immigrants to align themselves genetically with American Indians' (Kroeber, 1994).[1] As a codicil, however, it is worth noting that whilst changes in self-identification are recognized as accounting for much of the huge increase in Indian numbers since 1950, a debate persists about its exact extent (Passel, 1976; Passel and Berman, 1986).

Although one could say that Indian identity was reconceived by the dominant American culture during the 1960s and 1970s and that a version of things Indian again captured popular attention during the 1990s, it is also the case that since 1966, few scholars have approached Dobyns' heights in their estimates. Douglas Ubelaker estimated an aboriginal population north of Mexico of 1.85 million; William Denevan (1992) estimated 3.79 million and A.J. Jaffe in the same year, one million for the same area. Cherokee demographer Russell Thornton (1987) has estimated over 5 million in the U.S. mainland in 1492 with another 2 million in present-day Alaska, Canada and Greenland combined, while Kirkpatrick Sale (1990) has suggested that the correct figure is actually 15 million for all of the U.S. and Canada. In 1987, Thornton suggested that a 75 million aboriginal figure was a reasonable estimate for the hemisphere (Thornton, 1987; Sale, 1990; Denevan, 1992; Jaffe, 1992). The debate continues, with further work put forward, in 1983 and 1989, by Dobyns, whose scholarship and premises have been much critiqued; by Milner, Joralemon, Ramenofsky, Snow and Lanphear, Ubelaker, Henige, Johansson, Upham, Thornton and Marsh-Thornton, and Peter H. Wood (Dobyns, 1989a and 1989b; Milner, 1980; Joralemon, 1982; Ramenofsky, 1987; Snow and Lanphear, 1988; Ubelaker, 1976 and 1988; Henige, 1989; Johansson, 1982; Upham, 1986; Wood, 1989).

The vehemence contained within some of the arguments about pre-contact population numbers listed above, notably concerning the level of scholarly professionalism and the politics said to underlie scholarly conclusions, has been mirrored in the often equally vehement debate over just how long Native peoples have existed within the American landscape. When Europeans first encountered Native Americans they speculated that they had been there only a few hundred years. Estimates grew to 5000 years in 1900 and have recently leapt again with

---

[1] Arguably, one of the most intriguing instances of this phenomenon was on July 9, 1998 when President Clinton told Sherman Alexie and others on the PBS show *A Dialogue on Race With President Clinton*, hosted by Jim Lehrer, that his grandmother in Arkansaw had one-quarter Cherokee blood. Further specifics on the Clinton family Indian connection have not been provided thereafter.

the discovery of archaeological remains off the California coast, dated to 28,000 BCE. Contemporary scholars like Michael Crawford think the first people in the Americas might have come from Siberia. The theory is that the earliest inhabitants crossed a land, or perhaps ice, 'bridge,' exposed during the last glacial period between Siberia and Alaska in an area called the Bering Strait (Crawford, 1998).

As with the pre-contact demography debate, this idea and its implications have been fundamentally contested. Perhaps the key voice has been the late Lakota scholar Vine Deloria, Jr., who took particular exception to it, dwelling at length upon the political implications of an Indian 'discovery' of the Americas and suggesting that instead traditional accounts of indigenous origins would be a much more fruitful and appropriate focus for study (Deloria, 1973, 1995). Deloria's concerns about the social and political implications of this 'origins' scholarship seemed to be borne out in 1999 when anthropologists suggested that the earliest North Americans were neither Indian nor Asian but were in fact Western Europeans who arrived around 18,000 years ago.[2] Interestingly, while it is true to say that the dominant thinking about Paleo-Indian migration is that ancient peoples came from northeast Asia at points when land bridges were exposed during cold periods and that they arrived in Alaska at around 13000–12000 yr BP, there is currently a great deal of dissent. Anthropologists are increasingly recognizing inconsistencies in the archaeological and geological record with reference to the 'bridge' theory and instead finding the idea of early coastal migration (along the archipelagos of Australasia and the Pacific coast by boat) more plausible. Whether we choose Deloria or the anthropologists as our best guide, as Joseph F. Powell reminds us, it remains the case that, 'Regardless of how the first Americans came to the Americas, their camps, burial sites, and skeletal remains are scattered from Alaska to Patagonia' (Powell, 2005).[3]

Currently, both sets of arguments, over contact Indian populations estimates and over indigenous origins, are carried out under the larger shadow of the ongoing debate over who should be permitted to articulate things Indian and, indeed, who the appropriate audience should be for scholarship by or about

[2]   Dennis Stanford and Bruce Bradley received a great deal of popular attention for their suggestion of a possible colonization of the Americas by Upper Paleolithic Solutrean peoples of Western Europe. Stanford, D.J. and Bradley, B. (2002) 'Ocean Trails and Prairie Paths? Thoughts About Clovis Origins,' in N.G. Jablonski (ed.), *The First Americans: The Pleistocene Colonization of the New World* (San Francisco: Memoirs of the California Academy of Sciences no. 27), pp. 255–72. For a comprehensive rebuttal of the Solutrean theory, see Straus, L.G. (2000) 'Solutrean Settlement of North America? A Review of Reality,' *American Antiquity* vol. 65, no. 2, pp. 209–26.

[3]   For a critique of the Bering Strait theory, see Dixon, E.J. (1999) *Bones, Boats and Bison* (Albuquerque: University of New Mexico Press).

Indians of any sort. Questions about 'ownership' of information about Indians have been voiced increasingly strongly since the 1960s – when larger numbers of Indian intellectuals began to enter the academy. The concern expressed is that all Indian history to date has tended to reflect only what non-Indians think is significant. An illustrative example here might be the Plains histories of 1833, which tend to emphasize cholera, the fur trade and intertribal warfare. By comparison, Indian winter counts or pictographs emphasize the spectacular shower of meteors that fell to earth during 'the winter the stars fell' (Edmunds, 1995, p. 737). It is suggested that this sort of ethnocentrism is much exacerbated by the fact that very few scholars of the Native American past are conversant with a Native language. That said, perhaps the largest challenge is that most academic historians approach their subjects within the framework of traditional European or American methodology – that is, as Donald Grinde puts it, with 'the rhetoric and scholarly inventions of empire' (Grinde, 1994).

The problem in this regard is that an Indian epistemological perspective on history can often be incompatible with that of the modern non-Indian historian or demographer. Consider, for example, the Brulé Sioux historian Clyde Dollar's remarks that:

> The idea of an historical fact... from the Indian side – is something one has been told by his elders and therefore is not to be questioned. Indeed, among the High Plains people, there is little interest in the subject matter of history *per se* beyond the repeating of its stories, and a deeply searching pursuit of data and facts on which to build veracity in history is frequently considered rather pointless, perhaps ludicrous, decidedly nosy, an occupation closely associated with eccentric white men. (Dollar, 1998)

As Arnold Krupat has explained, this difference is not simply a matter of perspective. Most scholars writing North American history look for facts about the past, not stories and symbolism about it, and have a commitment to what they deem to be plausible according to what they know about the world. There is a tendency, therefore, to view traditional Indian-authored histories as myth, or at least, as messages that are irrationally bereft of any concern for verifiable fact (Krupat, 1998). Indian intellectuals, on the other hand, also have a very specific relationship to history and to the idea of intellectualism, with significant numbers adopting bio-regional, community-specific and spiritually orientated approaches to the life of the mind. If the Black intellectual could be said to be, as James Baldwin put it, 'a kind of bastard of the West,' then the Indian intellectual is in an even more complex position.

Many Indian traditional communities prioritise the sacred over the secular and many Indian traditions conflict directly with Western notions of how history, meaning and time are constituted. Often, within Indian groups, the idea of voice and agency operating outside of community (as they may be seen to do in individual book authorship) is problematic.[4] In sum, Indian intellectuals run up against some of the same conflicts with conventional academic enquiry as do indigenous African peoples. 'We have,' as Kwame Appiah explains, 'to decide whether we think the evidence obliges us to give up the invisible ontology [that is, beliefs in spiritual agencies]' (Appiah, 1993). Added to this, work done without the sanction of and unrequested by a specific Indian community can be construed as utterly redundant. As the Maori scholar Linda Tuhiwai Smith has remarked when recalling her own community upbringing, 'Research was talked about both in terms of its absolute worthlessness to us, the indigenous world, and its absolute usefulness to those who wielded it as an instrument. It told us things already known, suggested things that would not work, and careers for people who already had jobs' (Tuhiwai Smith, 1999). The conceptual disparities separating non–Indian and Indian intellectuals can therefore be deep and numerous, and it remains to be seen just how diverse arguments about the Indian presence across time, including those concerning Indian pre-contact numbers, can be reconciled within an increasingly heterogeneous academic community.

How then should those who are not demographers, whether Indian or non–Indian, proceed? Would we be well advised to throw our hands in the air and, like Nietzsche, declare that scholars (and especially demographers) simply 'knit socks for the spirit' (Nietzsche, 1954)? That is, should we avoid making a decision about which of these divergent pieces of scholarship is most valid and take recourse in phrases that discuss 'the spectrum of debate about pre-contact population numbers?' Or, should we take firm evaluative decisions about the work available on Indian numbers pre-contact and, in so doing, risk further re-inscribing the scholarly and ethnic divisions that increasingly haunt the discipline?

The implications intellectually of fully assimilating the ideas put forward by 'high counters' such as Dobyns are enormous. It means accepting that Indian losses occurred of a magnitude unmatched at any other time in history, caused not only by the ugly realities of the colonial process but by a conjunction of factors including the introduction of European diseases to which American populations were uniquely susceptible. It means accepting this as the preferred starting

---

[4]   For a discussion of such issues including the Crow Creek Sioux writer Elizabeth Cook-Lynn's assertion that certain successful female Native writers exude 'excesses of individualism' see Mihesuah, Devon A. (2000) 'A Few Citations at the Millennium on the Merging of Feminist Studies with American Indian Women's Studies,' *Signs* vol. 25, no. 4 (Summer), pp. 1247–51.

point for the story of European life on the American continent and dealing with its moral and cultural implications. These involve dispensing with long-held heroic American narratives, such as that of the 1890s historian Frederick Jackson Turner, where Indian absence and dispossession are posited as a minor footnote to the story of American progress. Some would argue that it would also obliterate the immature and malevolent sort of innocence that Graham Greene once suggested was particularly American: 'innocence... like a dumb leper who has lost his bell, wandering the world, meaning no harm' (Greene, 1980).

Be that as it may, any choice made between the existing contrasting scholarship must reconcile the fact that all of the available estimates by necessity extrapolate and their margin of error is substantial. As Dean R. Snow is quoted as saying in *1491,* 'you can make the meager evidence from the ethnohistorical record tell you anything you want. It's really easy to kid yourself' (Mann, 2005, p. 4). Others, such as James Merrell, are equally explicit. His conclusion about Dobyns' work is that 'the most important lesson may be how little confidence one can place in estimates of native population.' Most explicit of all in this regard has been David Henige, who has accused Dobyns and other 'high counters' of conjuring 'numbers from nowhere' in an attempt to answer 'a thoroughly unanswerable question.' In his sarcastic, funny and strongly felt book, Henige finds it impossible to concur with the assumptions which he feels underlie their work, namely that early European observers could count accurately, did so and communicated this accurately within written sources. He makes the point that whilst estimates have changed very significantly across time, the amount of direct evidence available to answer the question has not. Furthermore, he suggests that the impact of disease has been vastly overestimated (Merrell, 1984; Henige, 1998).

Even bearing all of this in mind, certain key, new themes still remain inescapable. Mooney and Kroeber's estimates have now firmly been superseded and an awareness has grown that, prior to 1492, Indian populations may have been much larger than had been thought and, as a corollary, may well have been much more complex than commentators had imagined. Although fundamental debate persists about exactly how many Native peoples died following contact (with, at one end of the spectrum, David Stannard citing 100 million deaths and claiming American Indian death to have been 'the most massive act of genocide in the history of the world'), there is now a great deal of scholarship to suggest that the depletion in Indian numbers was substantial and that Old World diseases played a key role (Stannard, 1993, p. 151).

Recent work has argued persuasively that the resultant population decline was unlikely to have been uniform and that in fact, and here again one hears echoes of Sauer, the indirect effects of epidemics may well have played a more central role in long-term Indian population decline. Repeated pummeling from cyclical bouts of disease would have had a devastating effect when compounded with, as Thornton, Miller and Warren put it, 'the indirect effects of wars (and genocide), enslavements, removals and relocations, and the destruction of the "ways of life" and subsistence patterns of American Indian societies accompanying contact with Europeans' (Thornton et al., 1991, p. 39). Thornton has added his voice to Larsen who in 1994 was at pains to warn against an overemphasis upon disease as a factor in decline at the expense of other factors such as relocation, forced labor, and changes in diet. Instead, he has stressed the many factors attendant upon colonialism, arguing 'Native American societies were removed and relo- cated, warred upon and massacred, and undermined ecologically and economi- cally. All of these effects of colonialism caused population decline through reduced fertility as well as increased mortality' (Larsen, 1994; Thornton, 1997, p. 311).

Similarly, when Nancy Shoemaker carried out her studies concerning the processes that underlie the phenomenon of twentieth century Indian population recovery and, specifically, what explains Indian natural increase since 1900, she placed an analogous stress upon how heterogeneous Indian responses to colo- nialism and disease were. She analyzed the demographic histories of five differ- ent sets of peoples – the Seneca Nation in New York State, the Oklahoma Cherokees, the Red Lake Ojibways in Minnesota, the Yakamas in Washington State, and the Navajos in the Southwest – and showed clearly that depopulation was something that happened at different times and at different rates among dif- ferent groups. Disease susceptibility, family economy and household structure all affected her sample groups with, she suggests, a nuclear-family residence pattern at the time of European contact having a positive effect upon group survival.

Moving on from pre-contact Indian population figures does not necessarily make Indian demography more straightforward. The first U.S. decennial census held was in 1790. It collected data on race but American Indians were not enu- merated as a separate group until the census of 1860 and, even then, those in American Indian territories and on American Indian reservations were not included. It was not until 1890 that Indians were finally counted throughout the country. As stated at the outset, Indian population within the United States is deemed to have reached an all-time low of just 228,000. It then turned a corner and began a recovery that culminated in 4.1 million in the 2000 census (2.5 mil- lion American Indian and Alaskan Native, 1.6 million American Indian and Alaskan Native as well as one or more other races). Whilst there has been rapid Indian population growth in the last several decades and improvements made in healthcare provision on reservations, these figures point clearly towards repeated under-enumeration within the federal population censuses. As already noted, the biggest change has stemmed from the shift to self-identification starting in 1960 and, to a lesser degree, from shifts in how Indians have been defined by the Bureau of the Census (Snipp, 1989; Shumway and Jackson, 1995, p. 186).

As the reader is no doubt aware by now, few things about Indian numbers are not complex. Indeed, just in terms of federal definitions, 'Indianness' is an identity defined in thirty-three different ways in assorted pieces of legislation (Brownell, 2000). In contemporary America, whilst burgeoning numbers are choosing to claim Indian identity, there has been increasing resistance to granting such claims to legitimacy both amongst scholars and within Indian communities themselves. These conflicts are linked to the inconsistent and often illogical legacy of the Indian relationship to the federal government. Generally, as Eva Marie Garroutte has detailed in the first half of her book, *Real Indians: Identity and the Survival of Native America,* the government body with responsibility for Indian concerns, the Bureau of Indian Affairs, demands a one-quarter Indian blood quantum and/or tribal membership before an individual can be counted as Indian. Various tribes have different requirements, but around two-thirds of all federally recognized tribes specify a minimum blood quantum, and most often it is one-quarter. This being the case, significant numbers of individuals who live as Indians, think of themselves as Indians and who are accepted by other Indians as Indians, can nonetheless find themselves excluded from legal status as Indian. For example, since 2000, Americans have been able to choose more than one race with which to identify themselves. Those who register Indian ancestry from more than one tribe risk exclusion if their tribe specifies that the one-quarter Indian blood quantum registered comes from their tribe only.

There has also been concern expressed that the rise in the number of Americans self-identifying as Indian reflects 'ethnic switching' towards an Indian identity for a variety of reasons. These include a perception that Indian identity carries a certain cultural cachet and the fact that a legal Indian identity carries with it various rights, protections and privileges. These can include various economic rights guaranteed by treaty, such as subsistence rights on designated lands, exemption from state property tax and the right as an Indian parent for your children, should it be deemed necessary that they be removed from their home, to be placed with another family member in keeping with the dictates of the 1978 Indian Child Welfare Act. This Act was intended as a means of redressing what had been an up to 35 percent loss in some states of Indian children to foster and adoption care within non-Indian families, a phenomenon perceived by many as a symptom of cultural incomprehension on the part of largely white, middle-class social workers. Legally defined Indian individuals are also protected from prosecution for using certain prohibited items, such as eagle feathers and the hallucinogen peyote; enjoy further rights under the 1990 Native American Graves Protection and Repatriation Act; are allowed to market their work as 'Indian produced' under the 1990 Indian Arts and Crafts Act; and can benefit from 'Indian preference' in federal employment, particularly within the Bureau of Indian Affairs and the Indian Health Service.

Another great anomaly stems from the fact that evaluation of Indian status at the tribal level most often revolves upon written tribal rolls even though traditional methods for retaining and passing on knowledge within many tribes were oral. Such rolls were often compiled in the nineteenth century by non-Indians in a most biased, over-complicated and unsystematic fashion at a time when a fundamental and deep-seated program of Indian discrimination and cultural obliteration was taking place. The Dawes Rolls, for example, were compiled between 1898 [the Curtis Act] and 1906 by the Dawes Commission as an attempt to persuade tribes who had resisted the Dawes Act of 1887 to go along with its dictates. The Dawes Act was one of the most invidious pieces of Indian legislation ever passed by Congress, since its purpose was to pulverize Indian cultures and force assimilation to the lifeways of the dominant culture within a single generation. It required Indians to accept allotment of tribal land according to status in return for which they would be extended citizenship and the proceeds from the sale of unallotted tribal lands would be used for Indian education. Rather than fostering Indian assimilation into the mainstream, what actually got assimilated into non-Indian hands as a result of the Dawes Act were Indian lands. Close to two-thirds of Indian lands nationally went into white ownership, an estimated 86 million acres by 1934 when policy changed. Even though the Dawes Commissioners enrolled only a small percentage of those who applied and, according to Garroutte, acknowledged that they had denied many people of indubitable tribal ancestry, the Dawes Rolls remain the basis for the award of Certificates of Degree of Indian Blood (CDIBs, which are known in Canada as Indian status cards) for people of Cherokee, Choctaw, Creek, Chickasaw and Seminole blood.[5] Unsurprisingly, Indians actively resisted the enrollment process and their descendants therefore are disenfranchised from Indian status. Non-Indian people also made it on to the rolls, including non-Indian spouses of Indians and on occasion, upon remarriage, their non-Indian children and their subsequent non-Indian partners. As well as the notorious 'five dollar Indians' (non-Indians said to have paid this amount to bribe unscrupulous census enumerators), there were also African American slaves with no Indian

---

[5] Garroutte quotes Thomas Bolshoi's evidence of Sicangu Lakota peoples who, when queuing for a census that would determine rations, ensured that they were counted more than once. Census enumerators duly recorded names that translate as 'Dirty Prick' and 'Shit Head'. Garroutte, Eva Marie (2003) *Real Indians: Identity and the Survival of Native America* (Berkeley: University of California Press), p. 24; Bolshoi, Thomas (1995) 'The Birth of the Reservation: Making the Modern Individual Among the Lakota' *American Ethnologist*, vol. 22, no. 1 (February), pp. 28–49.

ancestry formerly owned by Oklahoma tribes who were made into tribal members. Garroutte concludes, 'It is impossible to estimate the number of modern-day descendants of those non-Indian "Indians", but it could be quite large.'

Garroutte makes the valid point that acquiring and maintaining Indian identity is something that requires effort and indeed certification, whereas to be socially attributed as black or African American is much easier, since it has focused since the Civil War upon the 'one-drop rule,' or rule of hypodescent, which she claims held sway within American state courts up until 1970. She concurs with the Powhatan/Lenape/Saponi scholar Jack Forbes' ironic comment that modern Americans 'are always finding "blacks" (even if they look rather un-African), and ... are always losing "Indians".' Forbes' remark invokes a centuries old settler desire to find in the 'New World' Indian continent 'virgin territory,' bereft of inhabitants and to construe Indians surviving colonialism nostalgically as 'vanishing' or as departing vestiges or remnants (Garroutte, 2003, pp. 47–48). It is also worth noting that the legal characteristics of tribal enrollment today are inconsistent with what are usually thought of as 'traditional' concepts of tribal membership (Deloria, 1974). This leads some Indian people to boycott the whole tribal enrollment process for reasons once powerfully summed up by the Ojibwa-Sioux activist and long-term federal prisoner Leonard Peltier. He said, 'This is not our way. We never determined who our people were through numbers and lists. These are the rules of our colonizers... I will not comply with them' (Peltier, 2001, p. 65).

Indian enumeration using blood quantum was thought up by the U.S. government rather than by Indian peoples themselves at a time when the stated aim of the U.S. government was to annihilate Indian peoples as discrete, viable cultures. As the noted assimilationist Captain Richard H. Pratt recommended in 1892, 'all the Indian there is in the race should be dead.' It therefore seems odd that so many tribes should themselves adhere to the blood quantum system of defining Indian identity (*Official Report*). Obviously, it is wholly unsuited to tribes which are small and therefore need to marry outside the tribe. More importantly, if tribes and the government continue to adhere to it long term, potentially there will cease to be any Indians left to count. Indians have the highest rate of intermarriage of any ethnic group, which is perhaps unsurprising given their history of engulfment since 1492. Therefore, continuing to adhere to or to tighten existing blood quantum requirements in the long term could bring about Indian self-destruction, at least in terms of how Indians are enumerated and formally defined. Given that the numbers of 'mixed-blood' Indians are continually increasing, voices within Indian communities have gone so far as to argue that 'by choosing to forsake traditional modes of community membership in exchange for blood quantum, Native nations are committing the ultimate act of self-colonization in that not only are they excluding a growing number of their "mixed-blood" brethren, American Indian people are, in a self-colonizing act, breeding themselves out of an "authentic" Indian identity' (Waters, 2005, p. 31).

How Indian communities choose to respond to this challenge in the future remains to be seen but it is certainly the case that blood and direct descent have a unique significance within Indian thinking that cannot easily be displaced. Reference to 'memory in the blood' in one form or other is a characteristic of each of the Kiowa Pulitzer Prize winner N. Scott Momaday's major works and the idea is so central that a critical text, *Blood Narrative*, has been devoted exclusively to the nexus of blood-land-memory that held to inform much Indian writing (Allen, 2002). This is not to say that Indian and non-Indian ideas about blood and genealogy are the same or that an Indian emphasis upon blood can routinely be dismissed as racist. Eva Garroutte (2003, pp. 125–27) points out, for example, that Indian thinking does not imply that Indian identity is diluted as the degree of Indian blood decreases. Instead, she stresses that Indian ideas about kinship differ greatly from those of non-Indians and she demands recognition of the fact that 'there are indigenous essentialisms quite different from the biologistic, social scientific varieties' dependent upon the idea of race.

Intermarriage has a long history within Native America and its contemporary significance in terms of demographics is linked to the biggest shift of recent decades, the shift from Indian rural to urban living. Although in modern times Indians have never been a predominantly urban population, it is worth bearing in mind that this phenomenon is not without extremely long-term precedent in Native America. Prior to 1492, especially in the Southwest and in the Mississippi river valley, there is good evidence to suggest that Indians lived in large, complex settlements. Cahokia, for example, near present-day St Louis, Missouri, could have had a population as large as 40,000 (Peregrine, 1991; Thornton et al., 1982). By the turn of the twentieth century, only 0.4 percent of Indians lived in urban areas, whereas in 1990 it was 56.2 percent, a transformation aided by government relocation programs begun in the 1950s. Even though growth rates are higher for Indians living away from Indian-owned land, the shift towards urban living combined with increases in Indian intermarriage is likely to continue reducing the strength of tribal identity and further decreasing the degree to which Indian languages are spoken.

Remarkably, Russell Thornton suggests, these are changes which may make it appropriate in the future to begin speaking primarily of Native American ancestry or ethnicity, rather than of specific tribal members or of 'full-blood Indians.' In his view, 'a Native American population comprised primarily of "old" Native Americans strongly attached to their tribes will change to a population with a predominance of "new" Native Americans who may or may not have tribal attachments or even tribal identities' (Thornton, 2000, p. 41). In contrast, however, Nancy Shoemaker has argued that the tribe will remain the primary Indian entity of the future. She is candid about the fact that with Indian population numbers at 1.5 percent of the overall United States population in 2004, Indians are never likely to have a strong voice as a cohort within American politics as a whole. Echoing Stephen Cornell, she feels that real Indian political power in the foreseeable future is always likely to remain within the tribe, however it is defined (Shoemaker, 1999, pp. 101, 103; Cornell, 1988). Although Indians are the ethnic group whose population is currently growing fastest through natural increase, even if projected growth rates occur, the proportion of Indians within the United States will still only be 2 percent in 2050 (Day, 1993). Indian voters tend to vote for the Democratic Party and came out strongly for Kerry in the 2004 election.[6] Yet, as the preceding chapter has hopefully made clear, the power and impact of Indian identity have never simply or directly correlated with the number of Indian individuals enumerated. As Indian sovereignty, treaty, and humanitarian rights are promoted within international frameworks such as the Organization of American States, the World Council of Indigenous Peoples, and the United Nations's Working Group on Indigenous Populations, United States Indian voices are no longer alone. They are part of a chorus of growing transnational claims for indigenous rights, often linked to various environmental movements, whose significance in the twenty-first century has yet to be fully appreciated.

Bibliography

Allen, Chadwick (2002) *Blood Narrative: Indigenous Identity in American Indian and Maori Literary and Activist Texts* (Durham: Duke University Press).

Appiah, Kwame Anthony (1993) *In My Father's House: Africa in the Philosophy of Culture* (New York: Oxford University Press), p. 103.

Aschmann, H. (1959) *The Central Desert of Baja California: Demography and Ecology* (Berkeley: University of California Press).

Borah, W. (1964) 'America as Model: The Demographic Impact of European Expansion upon the Non-European World,' *Actas y Memorias, XXXV Congreso International de Americanistas* vol. 3, pp. 379–87.

Brownell, Margo (2000) 'Who is an Indian? Searching for an Answer to the Question at the Core of Federal Indian Law,' *University of Michigan Journal of Law Reform* vol. 34, pp. 273–320.

---

[6] I am indebted to Dr Rhodes Cook for information on Indian voting patterns. See Cook, Rhodes (2005) *Mapping the Political Landscape* (Washington D.C.: Pew Research Center), p. 149.

Cook, S.F. (1937) *The Extent and Significance of Disease Among the Indians of Baja California, 1697–1773* (Berkeley: University of California Press).

Cornell, Stephen (1988) *The Return of the Native: American Indian Political Resurgence* (New York: Oxford University Press).

Crawford, Michael (1998) *The Origins of Native Americans: Evidence From Anthropological Genetics* (Cambridge: Cambridge University Press).

Day, J.C. (1993) 'Population Projections of the United States by Age, Sex, Race and Hispanic Origin: 1993–2050,' *Current Population Report*, pp. 25–110 (Washington D.C.: U.S. Bureau of the Census).

Deloria Jr., Vine (1974) *Behind the Trail of Broken Treaties: An Indian Declaration of Independence* (Austin: University of Texas Press).

Denevan, William M. (1976) 'The Caribbean, Central America, and Yucatán: Introduction,' in W.M. Denevan (ed.), *The Native Population of the Americas in 1492* (Madison: University of Wisconsin Press), pp. 35–41.

Denevan, William M. (ed.) (1992) *The Native Population of the Americas in 1492* (Madison: University of Wisconsin Press).

Denevan, William M. (1996) 'Carl Sauer and Native American Population Size,' *The Geographical Review*, vol. 86 no. 3, pp. 385–97.

Dobyns, Henry F. (1966) 'Estimating Aboriginal American Population: An Appraisal of Techniques with a New Hemispheric Estimate,' *Current Anthropology*, vol. 7, pp. 395–416.

Dobyns, Henry F. (1983) *Their Number Became Thinned: Native American Population Dynamics in Eastern North America* (Knoxville: University of Tennessee Press).

Dobyns, Henry F. (1989a) 'More Methodological Perspectives on Native American Demography,' *Ethnohistory* vol. 36, pp. 285–299.

Dobyns, Henry F. (1989b) *Their Number Became Thinned* (Knoxville: University of Tennessee Press).

Dollar, Clyde (1998) quoted in Arnold Krupat 'America's Histories,' *American Literary History* vol. 10, no. 1, p. 125.

Edmunds, R. David (1995) 'Native Americans, New Voices: American Indian History, 1895–1995,' *The American Historical Review* vol. 100, no. 3 (June), pp. 717–40.

Garroutte, Eva Marie (2003) *Real Indians: Identity and the Survival of Native America* (Berkeley: University of California Press).

Greene, Graham (1980) quoted in Richard Drinnon *Facing West: The Metaphysics of Indian Hating and Empire Building* (New York: Meridian).

Grinde, Donald A., Jr. (1994) 'Teaching American Indian History: A Native American Voice,' *Perspectives* vol. 32, pp. 11–16.

Henige, David (1989) 'On the Current Devaluation of the Notion of Evidence: A Rejoinder to Dobyns,' *Ethnohistory* vol. 36, no. 3 (Summer), pp. 304–07.

Henige, David (1998) *Numbers from Nowhere: the American Indian Contact Population Debate* (Norman: University of Oklahoma Press), pp. 6, 8, 9, 79.

Jaffe, A. J. (1992) *The First Immigrants from Asia: A Population History of the North American Indians* (New York: Plenum Press).

Johansson, Ryan S. (1982) 'The Demographic History of the Native Peoples of North America: A Selective Bibliography,' *Yearbook of Physical Anthropology* vol. 25, pp. 133–52.

Joralemon, Donald (1982) 'New World Depopulation and the Case of Disease,' *Journal of Anthropological Research* vol. 38, pp. 108–127.

Kroeber, A.L. (1934) 'Native American Population,' *American Anthropologist* vol. 36, no. 1, pp. 1–25.

Kroeber, A.L. (1939) *Cultural and Natural Areas of Native North America* (Berkeley: University of California Press).

Kroeber, Karl (ed.) (1994) *American Indian Persistence and Resurgence* (Durham: Duke University Press), p. 2.

Krupat, Arnold (1998) 'America's Histories,' in *American Literary History* vol. 10, no. 1, p. 125.

Larsen, Clark Spencer (1994) 'In the Wake of Columbus: Native Population Biology in the Postcontact Americas,' *Yearbook of Physical Anthropology* vol. 37, pp. 109–154.

Mann, Charles C. (2005) *1491: New Revelations of the Americas Before Columbus* (New York: Alfred A. Knopf).

Meigs, P. (1935) *The Dominican Mission Frontier of Lower California* (Berkeley: University of California).

Merrell, James H. (1984) 'Playing the Indian Numbers Game,' *Reviews in American History* vol. 12, no. 3 (September), p. 357.

Milner, George R. (1980) 'Epidemic Disease in the Postcontact Southeast: A Reappraisal,' *Midcontinental Journal of Archaeology* vol. 5, pp. 39–56.

Mooney, James (1928) *The Aboriginal Population of America North of Mexico*, Smithsonian Miscellaneous Collections, vol. 80, no. 7 (Washington, D.C.: Smithsonian Institution).

Mundus Novus Albericus Vespucius Laurention Petri de medicis salutem plurimam dicit as *Vespucci Reprints, Texts and Studies*, vol. 5, trans. by George T. Northrup (1916) (Princeton University Press) quoted in Robert F. Berkhofer, Jr. (1978) *The White Man's Indian: Images of the American Indians From Columbus to the Present* (New York: Vintage Books), pp. 7–9.

Nietzsche, Friedrich (1954) *Thus Spoke Zarathustra*, translated by Walter Kaufmann, New York: Random House; reprinted in *The Portable Nietzsche*, New York: The Viking Press, 1954, p. 237.

Novick, Peter (1988) *That Noble Dream: The 'Objectivity Question' and the American Historical Profession* (Cambridge: Cambridge University Press).

Official Report of the Nineteenth Annual Conference of Charities and Correction (1892) reprinted in Richard H. Pratt (1973) 'The Advantages of Mingling Indians with Whites,' *Americanizing the American Indians: Writings by the 'Friends of the Indian' 1880–1900* (Cambridge: Harvard University Press), pp. 260–71.

Passel, J.S. (1976) 'Provisional Evaluation of the 1970 Census Count of American Indians,' *Demography* vol. 12, pp. 397–409

Passel, J.S. and Berman, P.A. (1986) 'Quality of 1980 Census Data for American Indians,' *Social Biology* vol. 33, pp. 163–82.

Peltier, Leonard (2001) quoted in Jack Utter *American Indians: Answers to Today's Questions*, 2nd ed. (Norman: University of Oklahoma Press).

Peregrine, P (1991) 'Prehistoric Chiefdoms on the American Midcontinent: A World System Based on Prestige Goods,' in C. Chase-Dunn and T.D. Hall (eds.) *Core/Periphery Relations in Precapitalist Worlds* (Boulder: Westview Press).

Powell, Joseph F. (2005) *The First Americans: Race, Evolution, and the Origin of Native Americans* (Cambridge: Cambridge University Press), pp. 126–127.

Ramenofsky, Ann F. (1987) *Vectors of Death: The Archaeology of European Contact* (Albuquerque: University of New Mexico Press).

Rivet, Paul, Stresser-Péan, G. and Loukotka, C. (1924) 'Langue Américaines,' in A. Meillet and M. Cohen (eds.), *Les Languages du Monde* vol. 16 (Paris: Société de Linquistique de Paris), pp. 597–712.

Rosenblat, A. (1935) 'El desarrollo de la población indígena de América,' *Tierra Firme*, vol. 1, no. 1, pp. 115–33; vol. 1, no. 2, pp. 117–48; vol. 1 no. 3, pp. 109–41.

Sale, Kirkpatrick (1990) *The Conquest of Paradise: Christopher Columbus and the Columbian Legacy* (New York: Plume).

Sapper, K. (1924) 'Die Zahl und die Volkdichte der indianischen Bevölkerung in Amerika vor der Conquista und in der Gegenwart,' *Proceedings of the 21st International Congress of Americanists* vol. 1, pp. 95–104.

Shoemaker, Nancy (1999) *American Indian Population Recovery in the Twentieth Century* (Albuquerque: University of New Mexico Press).

Shumway, J. Matthew and Jackson, Richard H. (1995) 'Native American Population Patterns,' *Geographical Review* vol. 85, no. 2 (April), pp. 185–201.

Snipp, C.M. (1989) *American Indians: The First of this Land* (New York: Russell Sage Foundation).

Snow, Dean R. and Lanphear, Kim M. (1988) 'European Contact and Indian Depopulation in the Northeast: The Timing of First Epidemics,' *Ethnohistory* vol. 35, pp. 15–33.

Spinden, Herbert J. (1928) 'The Population of Ancient America,' *Geographical Review* (18 October), pp. 641–60.

Stannard, David E. (1993) *American Holocaust: The Conquest of the New World* (Oxford: Oxford University Press).

Steward, J.H. (1949) 'The Native Population of South America,' in J.H. Steward (ed.), *Handbook of South American Indians* vol. 5, pp. 655–68, Bureau of American Ethnology Bulletin no. 143 (Washington D.C.: Smithsonian Institution).

Thornton, Russell (1987) *American Indian Holocaust and Survival: A Population History Since 1492* (Norman: University of Oklahoma Press).

Thornton, Russell (1997) 'Aboriginal North American Population and Rates of Decline, ca. AD 1500–1900,' *Current Anthropology* vol. 38, no. 2 (April).

Thornton, Russell (2000) 'Population History of Native North Americans' in Michael R. Haines and Richard H. Steckel (eds.), *A Population History of North America* (Cambridge: Cambridge University Press).

Thornton, Russell, Miller, Tim and Warren, Jonathan (1991) 'American Indian Population Recovery Following Smallpox Epidemics,' *American Anthropologist,* New Series vol. 93, no. 1 (March).

Thornton, Russell, Sandefur, G.D. and Grasmick, H.G. (1982) *The Urbanization of the American Indian* (Bloomington: University of Indiana Press).

Tuhiwai Smith, Linda (1999) *Decolonizing Methodologies: Research and Indigenous Peoples* (London: Zed Books), p. 3.

Ubelaker, Douglas H. (1976) 'Prehistoric New World Population Size: Historical Review and Current Appraisal of North American Estimates,' *American Journal of Physical Anthropology* vol. 45, pp. 661–66.

Ubelaker, Douglas H. (1988) 'North American Indian Population Size, A.D. 1500 to 1985,' *American Journal of Physical Anthropology* vol. 77, pp. 289–94.

Upham, S. (1986) 'Smallpox and Climate in the American Southwest,' *American Anthropologist* vol. 88, pp. 115–28.

Waters, Tiffany (2005) 'Biometrics in Indian Country: The Bloody Fight for Authenticity,' *Fourth World Journal: A Publication of the Center for World Indigenous Studies* vol. 6, no. 1.

Wood, P.H. (1989) 'The Changing Population of the Colonial South: An Overview by Race and Region, 1685–1790,' in P.H. Wood, Gregory A. Waselkov and M. Thomas Hatley, *Powhatan's Mantle* (Lincoln: University of Nebraska Press), pp. 35–108.

Zamora, Margarita (1988) *Language, Authority and Indigenous History in the Comentarios reales de los Incas* (Cambridge: Cambridge University Press).

4
Inventing the Matron: American Women Redefine Middle Age

S. Jay Kleinberg

As the twentieth century progressed, women experienced significant life transitions at different ages and in different ways from previous generations. Their lives altered radically as middle age developed into a lengthy, distinct stage of the life cycle for women. Various demographic and technological transformations had a profound impact on women's lives and the way that women moved through the stages of the life course. The new markers by which society categorized women and by which they measured themselves, such as sustained levels of economic activity and social/organizational participation throughout their lives, developed in response to industrialization, urbanization, and their associated phenomena of increased education, health, and longevity. The rapid movement of women aged 40 to 64 into the labor force during the twentieth century resulted from fundamental shifts in education and economic opportunities, leading women to restructure their lives to fight for and take advantage of opportunities denied their foremothers. A combination of new employment structures and radical alterations in domestic and maternal functions imbued middle-aged women with a new and distinctive identity. Over time there has been convergence in the employment patterns of the various racial and ethnic groups that make up the American population and in the levels of economic activity between women of different age groups and marital statuses. Thus examining middle-aged women's demographic and economic behavior in the twentieth century informs us about major changes in gender roles and American society (Tienda and Glass, 1985).

This essay first examines the major demographic shifts in women's lives before it turns to the employment revolution that occurred in middle-aged women's lives (Giele and Elder, 1998). It traces the rapid movement of these women into the labor force during the twentieth century and hypothesizes that a combination of different types of employment and new domestic and maternal patterns altered middle-aged women's roles and place in society. Middle-aged women also constituted a larger portion of America's female population, rising from 17 percent of females in the United States in 1880 to 27 percent 100 years later. Increasingly, they perceived themselves and came to be regarded as a separate and distinctive group, with terms such as 'empty nest syndrome' and 'displaced homemaker' indicating public and academic awareness of changes in women's relationship to the family and the economy (Raup and Myers, 1989).

Defining Middle Age

Although age demarcators can have an element of arbitrariness, sociologists in the 1960s and 1970s and activist groups, notably the Older Women's League founded in 1980, selected 40 as the beginning of middle age and the empty nest phenomenon. The United States Congress also recognized 40 as an important dividing line when it passed the Age Discrimination in Employment Act in 1967, prohibiting employment discrimination against people over this age (United States Employment, 2006). Altered patterns of female economic activity in the twentieth century manifested themselves when women reached their late 30s and early 40s, which means that the U. S. Census division, '45 to 64,' obscures some of the shifting patterns in middle-aged women's lives. Thus, this paper terms 'middle age' as the period from 40 to 64 years of age. The annual data from which these conclusions are drawn comes from the Integrated Public Use Microdata Sample, which holds between 76,000 and 909,000 cases depending upon the year.[1]

As Bernice Neugarten and Joan Moore explained in their pioneering sociological study of middle age in 1968, all societies have age-status systems which distribute 'duties, rights, and rewards' according to socially defined age groups (Neugarten and Moore, 1968, p. 5). Through the end of the nineteenth century most American women devoted their lives to rearing large families, giving birth to their last child in their late 30s or early 40s. Motherhood and household care dominated their lives well into their 50s and sometimes even through their 60s (Spence and Lonner, 1971). The age-status system altered in the twentieth century when the interval between childbearing, children leaving home, and mother's age at death all lengthened. Staying in school through graduation from

---

[1] The sample sizes were as follows: 1880, 176,275; 1900, 136,102; 1910, 133,359; 1920, 388,672; 1930, 75,861; 1940, 540,243; 1950, 700,657, 1960, 541588; 1970, 620,031; 1980, 742,262; 1990, 807,68; 2000, 908,788. For each census year we ran the SPSS data file provided by IPUMS to be representative of the U.S. population as a whole. Then using the SPSS 'select cases' option, we selected the ages either for female or total population and then derived the necessary subsample for each year.

high school or college contributed to children's longer dependency upon their parents. At the same time, women began to substitute for children in helping to support the family, using their monetized labor to purchase consumer durables and college educations. American women invented new economic and domestic roles for themselves and moved through the life course at a very different pace from their mothers and grandmothers.[2] However, these changes have not all been in one direction, nor did they necessarily occur at the same time for different groups of women. As a generalization, between 1890 and 1960 the women's median age at first marriage fell from 22 to about 19 years, although it varied between groups, with Southern rural African Americans having much lower ages at marriage than white women.[3] Since that time, the average age at marriage has risen, reaching 25 by 2000. Instead of marrying just after high school (characteristic of many baby boom marriages), women in the late twentieth century have tended to wait until after college or beyond before tying the knot, if they get married at all (Simmons and Lawler Dye, 2004). These changes in marital behavior had repercussions, not least for the role of the family in women's lives.

There were concomitant alterations in fertility patterns, with family sizes shrinking in the first decades of the century, returning to near 1900 levels during the baby boom which followed World War II, then falling sharply in the last decades of the century. At the turn of the twentieth century, the average woman had around four children, with rural families being larger. African American farmwomen, for example, had an average of seven children in 1900, with their birth rate falling to around five children in 1940.[4] Overall birth rates decreased between 1900 and 1930, fell during the Great Depression and World War II, but skyrocketed in post-war America. In 1960, more than half (52.5 percent) of all women aged 20 to 24 had given birth to at least one child, as had four-fifths of all 25 to 29 year olds. By the age of 40, only 12 percent of women in 1960 had no children. But toward the end of the century, women increasingly either delayed maternity or eschewed it altogether, so that only one-third of young women had given birth to their first child by the time they were 24, while

---

[2] Thistle, Susan (2006) *From Marriage to the Market: The Transformation of Women's Lives and Work* (Berkeley: University of California Press) discusses women's changing relation to marriage, motherhood, and the market place.

[3] Tolnay, Stewart E. (1999) *The Bottom Rung: African American Family Life on Southern Farms* (Urbana: University of Illinois Press), pp. 49–72, discusses the timing of marriage in different groups within society.

[4] Tolnay, Stewart E. (1999) *The Bottom Rung: African American Family Life on Southern Farms* (Urbana: University of Illinois Press), pp. 49–72, p. 17, observes that such large families were an economic benefit in a non-mechanized agricultural environment.

three-fifths were childless throughout their twenties. In 1960 about 13 percent of women in their thirties were childless, while by the 1980s and 1990s that proportion had risen to about 22 percent as more women chose education and employment rather than early marriage or childbearing (National Center for Health Statistics, 2005, p. 137). Divorce rates rose as the proportion of women who married declined, so that many more women either lived on their own or with their children, and depended upon their own labor rather than husbands for support (Thistle, 2006, pp. 114–115).

In addition, the average age at death for women rose from 57 to 79 between 1890 and 2000, meaning that many more women survived through middle age and into old age with few or no children at home. Once again, there were racial and regional variations, with the average life expectancy for rural black women being 40 in 1900, but climbing to 58 by 1940 (Tolnay, 1999, p. 17). The post-World War II compression of the family cycle with a period of concentrated childrearing in the first decade of marriage left many women with a sense of malaise by their late 30s and early 40s as they passed out of the stage of intensive mothering. Betty Friedan famously labeled this feeling 'the problem that has no name' and helped construct a woman's movement which fostered the employment of middle-aged, middle-class women (Friedan, 1963). Late twentieth-century women delayed having children in order to establish themselves on their career ladders and increasingly depended upon paid childcare substitutes in order to stay in the labor force (Neugarten and Moore, 1968, p. 6; National Center for Health Statistics, 2005, p. 64).[5]

Despite middle-aged women's growing public presence, there have been few historical analyses of their experiences or the complex factors that led to the description of middle age as a discrete phase in the life cycle.[6] Sociologists, in contrast, began discussing middle age in the post-war era. Many post-war sociological and medical studies of women in this age group indicate a perception of

[5] On political activism see Murray, Sylvie (2003) *The Progressive Housewife: Community Activism in Suburban Queens, 1945–1965* (Philadelphia: University of Pennsylvania Press) and Swerdlow, Amy (1993) *Women Strike for Peace: Traditional Motherhood and Radical Politics in the 1960s* (Chicago: University of Chicago Press), among others.

[6] Spence Bocock, Sarane (1978) 'Historical and Sociological Research on the Family and the Life Cycle,' *American Journal of Sociology* vol. 84 (supplement), pp. 366–94 and Elder, Glen Jr. (1985) *Life Course Dynamics: Trajectories and Transitions* (Ithaca, NY: Cornell University Press) explore the phases of the life cycle from an historical/sociological perspective. There has been no sustained historical analysis of middle age, although much attention has been devoted to childhood, adolescence, young parenthood, and old age. Also see Thistle, Susan (2006) *From Marriage to the Market: The Transformation of Women's Lives and Work* (Berkeley: University of California Press), who examines women's shift from marriage to marketplace between 1970 and 2006, but with relatively little analysis by age.

middle age as a time of trouble for women. In this view, the empty-nest syndrome marred middle age because women supposedly lost their primary role as mothers.[7] Moreover, doctors regarded middle age as complicated (or blighted) by menopause, as women's bodies underwent chemical changes that resulted in them no longer being able to procreate. Typical of this approach, Le Mon Clark, M.D., from Oklahoma City, when addressing the Groves Conference on the Conservation of Marriage and the Family in 1948, warned of the emotional, physiological, and psychological changes that affected sexual relations in middle life. This doctor described the 'burden of growing old' as seemingly falling more heavily upon the wife:

> She develops a sense of insecurity. Will her husband love her? As the children grow up and leave home she has a great sense of loss. She may even feel that she is no longer needed and what is worse, that she is no longer really wanted. To the extent that she has 'lived for her children,' and 'devoted her life to them,' this sense of loss is that much greater. (Clark, 1947–48, p. 59)

He thus portrays middle age as a time of loss and physical degeneration and warns middle-aged women to keep their figures in order to keep their husband's love. 'The modern American man has not been brought up to like the Rubens type of figure.' (Clark, 1947–48, p. 58).

This post-war medical perception of middle age as a particular problem for women followed on from the derogatory remarks made by social commentator Philip Wylie in his attack on American mothers during World War II. He offered a (dys)functional description of these women's life experiences earlier in the century and indicated a growing awareness that middle-aged women's roles were changing. In 1942 Wylie claimed that 'until very recently, mom folded up and died of hard work somewhere in the middle of her life,' rendering her invisible and unproblematic. By the middle of the century, 'mom' did not die in middle age; she continued to be a presence in her family and, increasingly, in the labor force (Wylie, 1942, p. 185).

As lives lengthened and families shrank, mid-life women refocused their energies, undertook new challenges in the market place, shifted the balance of power within and outside the home, and asserted their right to full participation in society. They were able to do so in part because the material conditions of their lives

---

[7] Houck, Judith A. (2006) *Hot and Bothered: Women, Medicine, and Menopause in Modern America* (Cambridge, MA: Harvard University Press) discusses the medicalization of menopause. Here, I explicitly reject the notion that menopause and middle age are synonymous.

had changed. Middle and upper class women, in particular, took advantage of the burgeoning consumer market in the early years of the century to decrease their own domestic labor and reduce their reliance on unpaid or paid household help from their own daughters or servants, respectively (Sutherland, 1988, pp. 188–9). The massive substitution of mechanical for human energy in the home proved to be a real generator of economic activity for much of the century. The total amount expended on canned fruit and vegetables in the first three decades of the twentieth century rose from $162 million (in 1909) to $930 million (1929). Electrical appliances became commonplace, with families purchasing $152 million dollars worth of refrigerators, sewing machines, washing machines, and stoves in 1909, a figure that increased to $804 million in 1929 (McGovern, 1969, p. 321).[8] Thus women's choice of bought rather than homemade food and their use of household appliances both helped drive the economy and freed them and their daughters for participation in activities outside the home, whether education, employment, or political and social activism.

Working class women's access to domestic technology and substitutes for their own domestic labor burgeoned after World War II, closing the gap between women of different social classes. In post-war America almost all homes had central heating, indoor plumbing, electricity and gas, which would have characterized only the most affluent dwellings earlier in the century. New homes, whether in working or middle class suburbs, came equipped with stoves and refrigerators, while small appliances such as steam irons, vacuum cleaners, toasters, and electric mixers were commonplace. In the last quarter of the century, clothes washers and driers, dishwashers, and freezers joined the list of widely purchased labor-saving devices (Matthews, 1987; Schwartz Cowan, 1983).

Such domestic technology had several effects: it freed unmarried daughters to remain in school or enter the labor force; it also relieved married women of onerous household duties, enabling them to deploy their free time either in social and political affairs or to undertake paid employment. Scholars disagree over the causality contained in the link between the diffusion of domestic technology and married or middle-aged women's employment. While it may well be the case, as Valerie Kincade Oppenheimer has argued, that the expansion of women's employment initially occurred among poorer women who acquired domestic technology more slowly, nevertheless such technology facilitated their employment and ability to combine two roles, those of homemaker and wage earner (Kincade Oppenheimer, 1972, pp. 29–30; Hetzler, 1969, p. 16; Klein

---

[8]   On working-class use of domestic technology see Kleinberg, S.J. (1976) 'Technology and Women's Work: The Lives of Working Class Women, Pittsburgh, 1870-1900,' *Labor History* vol. 17, no. 1, pp. 58–72.

and Myrdal, 1968). It is difficult to determine the precise combination of factors that motivated or impelled middle-aged women into employment, but
shifting family roles played a clear part. Mothers substituted for children as
ancillary wage earners once state laws required children to go to school and stay
out of the labor force, and parents wanted additional income to pay for consumer durables and children's college education. Moreover, the structure of
education and employment altered, providing greater opportunities to obtain an
education and opening up jobs that were acceptable to a broader range of
women.[9]

At the end of the nineteenth century, the typical white family, whether
native- or foreign-born, either had a single, adult male wage earner or relied
upon the combined employment of father and children. Married white women
rarely took jobs outside the home. Few had direct or sustained participation in
the formal economy, although a sizeable proportion earned some income during their married years by taking in boarders or perhaps washing clothes.
Immigrant families were apt to have lodgers when the children were small and
could not contribute to the family coffers. They typically used their children's
employment to enable women to stay out of the labor force through middle and
older age. If these married women worked, they frequently did so in tenement
industries where they could combine family care and income generation (Bodnar
et al., 1982, p. 108). Large families and minimal household technology meant
that most middle-aged women remained enmeshed in domestic and household
duties. A number moved in and out of wage earning, although census takers frequently overlooked their economic contributions to their families because of the
sporadic nature of their remunerative labors.[10]

But even at the turn of the twentieth century not all women experienced their
middle years in a domestic fashion. In some parts of the United States, especially
in textile mill and tenement industry areas, many middle-aged women held jobs
(Kleinberg, 2006b; Hareven, 1982; Yans McLaughlin, 1977). A high proportion
of mid-life African American women remained in the labor force long after their
white counterparts left it to concentrate upon domesticity, working either as

[9]   On the substitution of maternal for child labor see Kleinberg, S.J. (2005) 'Children's
and Mothers' Employment in Three Eastern Cities' Social Science History vol. 29, no. 1,
pp. 45–76.
[10]   Prewitt, Kenneth (2005) 'Politics and Science in Census Taking,' in Reynolds Farley and John
Haaga (eds.), The American People: Census 2000 (New York: Russell Sage Foundation), pp. 3–48.
Census definitions of employment also varied from year to year. See footnote 24, below. Also see
Amott, Teresa L. and Matthaei, Julie A. (1991) Race, Gender, and Work: A Multicultural Economic
History of Women in the United States (Boston: South End Press), pp. 399–406 for definitions of major
occupational categories and the difficulties of comparisons between census years.

servants or agricultural laborers. As historian Shirley Carlson observed, African American women remained in the public domain, frequently combining maternity and wage labor (Kleinberg, 2003; Carlson, 1992, p. 62).

African American families relied on working women to augment household incomes. When their children had jobs outside the home (as distinct from agricultural labor with their families) they typically retained their wages rather than contributing them to the family as African American parents tried to foster independence in their children (Bodnar et al., 1982, p. 108; Landry, 2000). Urban middle-aged black women frequently rented out rooms as a means of leaving the labor market or combined day work and other occupations with caring for lodgers at home.[11] Amongst subsistence agriculturalists, such as Native Americans and many of the Spanish-speaking peoples of the Southwest, all family members worked, with varying degrees of waged labor among women in their middle years. As Vicki Ruiz observed in her history of Mexican women workers, 'the family remained the unit of production in agricultural labor well into the twentieth century' (Ruiz, 1998, p. 17). Whether or not the census counted their labor as 'work,' however, depended upon both the vagaries of the individual census enumerator and shifting official Census Bureau policy towards women's agricultural labor.[12]

Economic Changes in Middle-Aged Women's Roles

The growth in women's labor force participation was quite steady through the middle of the twentieth century, with the exception of the unusual labor demands caused by World War II. Women's employment levels rose from 27.6 to 37.0 percent between 1940 (when the United States was still emerging from the Great Depression) and 1945, when wartime demands on the civilian labor force peaked. However, even during the sharp decline in women's economic activity in 1947 at the beginning of the baby boom, women's employment levels were still considerably higher than they had been the previous decade (Schweitzer, 1980, pp. 89–95). Moreover, female labor force participation ramped up steeply in the latter half of the twentieth century, so that three out of

[11] It is nevertheless the case that the majority of married black women, as Thistle observes, did not have jobs outside the home. Thistle, Susan (2006) *From Marriage to the Market: The Transformation of Women's Lives and Work* (Berkeley: University of California Press), pp. 29–33.

[12] Anderson, Margo J. (1988) *The American Census: A Social History* (New Haven: Yale University), pp. 221–5 discusses the politics behind the separate enumeration of Hispanics and the undercounts of African Americans. Also see Goldin, Claudia (1990) *Understanding the Gender Gap* (Oxford: Oxford University Press), p. 22.

Table 1: Percentage of Women in the Labor Force, 1890–2000

Year

1890	1900	1910	1920	1930	1940	1950	1960	1970	1980	1990	2000
18.2	20.0	22.7	23.6	25.4	27.6	33	41	49	63	74	74

Percentage of Women in the Labor Force

Sources: U.S. Department of Labor, Women's Bureau (1965) *Handbook on Women Workers* (Washington, DC: Government Printing Office), p. 6.
Cotter, David A., Hermsen, Joan M. and Vanneman, Reeve (2005) 'Gender Inequality at Work,' in Reynolds Farley and John Haaga (eds.), *The American People: Census 2000* (New York: Russell Sage Foundation), p. 109.

every four women were economically active in 2000 compared with one out of every six in 1890.

To some extent, World War II can be seen as a turning point in women's employment generally (Chafe, 1972; Campbell, 1984; Enders, 2002). An examination of age-specific employment profiles, however, reveals that certain groups of women participated in the female employment boom to a greater extent than others. The sharp increase in older women's employment rates in the second half of the century reflected a desire on the part of families to increase their income, the declining use of children as ancillary wage earners, and women's desire to protect themselves from the consequences of rising divorce rates (Hernandez, 1994, p. 4). What is most noticeable in Figure 1, which examines the proportion of women in the labor force by age categories, is that middle-aged women's employment levels rose at a faster rate than that of other groups of women and overtook younger women's employment levels in 1960 and 1970. This graph also confirms the significant demographic shift in 25–39-year-olds' employment pattern, namely that by the 1980s their proportion in the labor force rose sharply, exceeding that of younger women for the first time. Their pattern of delayed motherhood and/or working even if they had young children became firmly established in the last quarter of the twentieth century.[13] Younger women, those aged 16 to 24, who had dominated the female labor force at the end of the nineteenth and beginning of the twentieth centuries, exhibited quite a different pattern. Their employment levels peaked in 1910, stagnated or decreased until

[13] Umansky, Lauri (1996) *Motherhood Reconceived: Feminism and the Legacies of the Sixties* (New York: New York University Press) discusses changing patterns of motherhood while Michel, Sonya (1999) *Children's Interests/Mothers' Rights* (New Haven: Yale University Press) explores the tensions between home and work responsibilities and public policy.

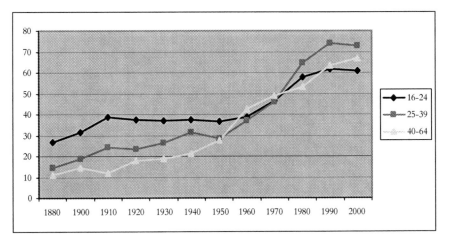

Figure 1: Proportion of Women in Labor Force by Age Category (%)

1950, and only began to rise again as the baby boom tapered off in the 1960s. Not even World War II altered this trend line, and, indeed, a slightly lower proportion of this age group was economically active in 1950, a reflection of their greater immersion in marriage and family life.[14]

The counter-currents and complexities of the female labor force in the United States in the twentieth century mean that even examining women in their discrete age groups masks the changing racial and ethnic dynamics of their labor force participation. The timing of middle-aged women's movement into and out of the labor force varied by race as well as by age. Middle-aged women in various racial/ethnic groups moved in and out of the labor force at different ages. For example, African American women constituted a disproportionate share of the economically active middle-aged women at the beginning of the twentieth century. However, their labor force participation rates decreased between 1920 and 1940, while European immigrants and native-born white women's levels of economic activity rose. Consequently, any analysis of female labor force participation must disaggregate the category of 'women workers' into its component parts so that the trends of the numerical majority do not hide those of particular minorities.

As Figure 2 illustrates, the employment levels of native- and foreign-born white middle-aged women were quite similar between 1880 and 1920. European-born women had slightly greater representation in the labor force in

---

[14]   I am excluding elderly women entirely from this analysis, largely because they had, and continue to have, very low levels of participation in the formal economy.

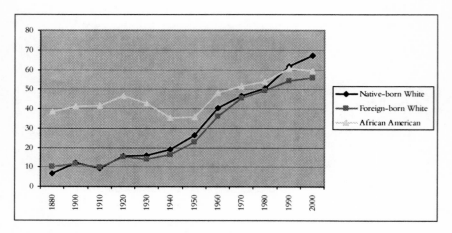

Figure 2: Proportion of Middle-Aged Women in the Labor Force by Race and Nativity

1880, but their employment levels closely resembled those of native-born white women from 1900 to 1920. By 1930, the labor force participation rates of middle-aged white women born in the United States began to overtake those born abroad and remained higher throughout the rest of the century. The gap between their employment levels was most marked at the end of the twentieth century, when foreign-born white women constituted a much smaller proportion of the white population than a century earlier and were somewhat less apt to work outside the home.[15]

However, the differences in employment levels of native- and foreign-born middle-aged white women were insignificant when compared to those of African American women, especially in the early years of this study. In 1880, 7.5 percent of middle-aged white women had jobs compared with 38 percent of African American women in that age bracket.[16] By 1920, the employment levels of white women doubled, to 15.5 percent, while that of black women increased to 46.5 percent. The tendency of black women to work outside the home moved in the opposite direction from that of white women between 1920 and 1950, as they actually began to depart from the labor force (See Figure 2). Their departure stemmed from a number of factors: the mechanization of

---

[15]   In 1880, foreign-born white women accounted for 31 percent of the sample population; this proportion fell to 24 percent in 1920 and by the late twentieth century accounted for only 7 percent.

[16]   These figures are derived by combining foreign- and native-born white women's employment levels in accordance with their relative sample sizes and comparing this combined proportion with that of black women.

agriculture, urbanization, and the declining market for household help. African American men's ability to get higher paying jobs in industrial establishments in the North and West also decreased pressure on their wives to undertake employment, even though they were, as Bart Landry expressed it, 'pioneers of the American family through their sustained presence in the labor force and more egalitarian family patterns' (Landry, 2000, p. 6; Collins, 2000). Subsequent structural shifts in the American economy, the growth of the service sector – especially in the cities where post-World War II African Americans lived in increasing numbers – and improved educational opportunities all facilitated black women's employment in a much broader range of occupations. They left domestic service as opportunities in public service, teaching, and manufacturing opened to them (Woody, 1992, p. 6).[17]

The data presented here for middle-aged women shows that these long term trends affected white women in a somewhat different fashion, although as economists Francine Blau and Marianne Ferber concluded it is difficult to see why, given similar economic circumstances, white women had lower employment levels than black women (Blau and Ferber, 1992). Taking an expanded time frame puts the developments in black and white women's employment into context and shows the extent to which white women adopted black women's immersion in the labor force. However, it also indicates that levels of middle-aged African American women's economic activity tapered off toward the end of the century. While middle-aged white women's employment outside the home doubled between 1920 and 1960, African American women's barely increased. By 1970, middle-aged white women's labor force participation levels came close to matching black women's employment levels.[18] This convergence continued until the millennium when middle-aged white women's employment rates actually exceeded those of African American women for the first time in American history.[19]

[17] There is no space here to discuss the impact of the Civil Rights Movement on African American women's employment, but see Wallace, Phyllis (1982) *Women in the Workplace* (Boston: Auburn House).

[18] Landry, Bart (2000) *Black Working Wives: Pioneers of the American Family Revolution* (Berkeley: University of California Press), p. 88, paints a different picture of the relative engagement of black and white women in the post-war labor force. However, he is examining the labor force participation of all married women regardless of age which gives a rather different picture. According to Landry, married white women's employment increased by about 10 percent per decade with a slight tapering off by 1990. Married black women's employment increased at a slower rate and actually fell between 1990 and 1995.

[19] The reasons for this need investigation. Sokolof, Natalie J. (1992) *Black Women and White Women in the Profession: Occupational Segregation by Race and Gender, 1960–1980* (London: Routledge) finds that black women still suffered segregation within professional jobs even as their access to them increased.

Table 2: Middle-Aged African American and White Women's
Employment Levels

	1880 No.	%	1920 N	%	1960 N	%	2000 N	%
White (a)	37,667	7.5	99,779	15.5	222,158	40.0	352,751	66.0
African American	4,657	38.3	8,672	46.5	22,462	48.1	45,832	59.6

(a) The numbers in the 'White' column are derived by combining foreign- and native-born white women's employment levels in accordance with their relative sample sizes.
Source: All tables and figures are based on the Integrated Public Use Microdata Survey Sample, unless otherwise attributed.

In the first half of the twentieth century, marital status was an important predictor of middle-aged women's employment for white women. Both among native and foreign-born whites, married middle-aged women had negligible levels of economic activity as measured by the census employment surveys in 1880 and 1900. They started entering the labor force in somewhat larger numbers by 1910 and 1920. As Figure 3 shows, the proclivity of married women residing with their husbands to take jobs outside the home increased during the Great Depression, World War II, and thereafter. Non-married women exhibited a different profile, both in their levels of employment and in the distinctions between native- and foreign-born. The labor force activities of those born in the United States were more tightly grouped than those born abroad, indicating a greater similarity in their tendency to work, especially in the Progressive Era when widows and those with absent spouses had lower, and very similar, levels of economic activity when compared with divorced or never-married women (Kleinberg, 2006a, ch. 4). Moreover, native-born white divorcees (a small but growing proportion of American women) had higher rates of employment than did their single sisters. The employment levels of all native-born white middle-aged women increased by 1950. It was only then, however, that single women exceeded the rate of divorced women in this group. Yet foreign-born white women who never married had a greater presence in the labor force than those who were or had once been married. Their employment levels were much higher than their native-born counterparts, growing from about three-fifths to four-fifths of the group between 1880 and 1950.

The graphic depiction of middle-aged African American women's employment in the first half of the twentieth century presents a distinctive trajectory. There was little divergence in the employment patterns of different categories of non-married black women in the first half of the century. The only exception

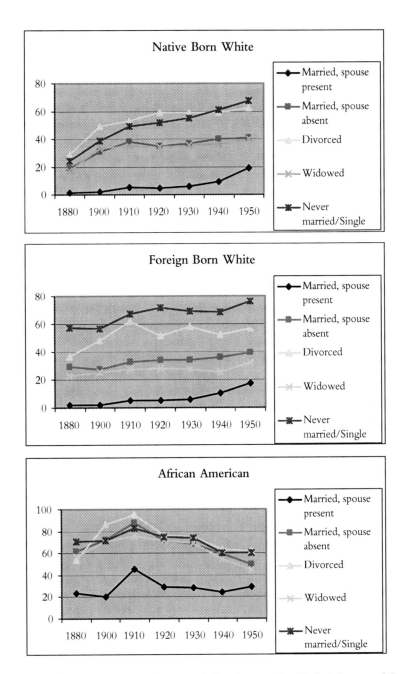

Figure 3a, b and c: Middle-Aged Women's Employment by Marital Status and Race/Nativity

to this came from divorced women who had lower levels of employment in 1880 and then higher ones in 1900 and 1910. All black middle-aged women's rates of economic activity rose in 1910, declined through 1940, and then rose somewhat in 1950. The increase in 1910 may be related to the way the census decided what constituted work or gainful employment, with women who worked on their own (or sharecropped) farms being included as employed in 1910, but not in either 1900 or 1920.[20] As the U. S. Census Bureau noted, special efforts were made to secure a more careful return of occupations at the Thirteenth Census [1910]. The 1920 Census, taken at a slack period in the farming year, returned fewer women in agriculture. It also discounted much of married women's agricultural labor, which helps explain some of the seeming decline of married black women in the labor force. At this time, farming was the single largest occupational classification for African American women, so these shifts in timing and definitions may explain the apparent decrease in middle-aged African American women's employment in 1920, especially among widows. Another factor could be the move north during the Great Migration, which disrupted employment patterns and possibly prompted some decrease in employment levels. Nevertheless, it is likely that the higher enumeration in 1910, combined with the stricter definition of employment in 1920, explains some of the apparent rise and subsequent decrease in married African American women's employment between 1900 and 1920.[21]

The employment levels of middle-aged widows in the first half of the twentieth century show the limited effectiveness of widows' pension and the Social Security Act (SSA) in resolving their plight. To be sure, neither pensions nor the SSA had middle-aged women in mind as beneficiaries (Kessler-Harris, 1995). Middle-aged widows' rising employment levels indicate a shift from economic reliance upon children to self-support in this era, on the part of native-born white women and to a lesser extent among foreign-born or African American widows. Between 1880 and 1900 the proportion of economically active native-born white middle-aged widows doubled from 16.8 to 33.6 percent and then remained stable until it rose to 40 percent in 1950. The employment levels of

[20] Tolnay, Stewart E. (1999) *The Bottom Rung: African American Family Life on Southern Farms* (Urbana: University of Illinois Press) describes the dreadful conditions under which most black farm families lived, and their need to incorporate both women and children directly in agricultural labor.
[21] United States Department of Commerce, Bureau of the Census (1923) *Fourteenth Census of the United States Population, 1920, Occupations* vol. iv (Washington, DC: Government Printing Office), pp. 10, 13. The Census decided that 'a woman who works *only occasionally, or only a short time each day* at outdoor farm or garden work, or in the dairy, or in caring for live stock or poultry' should not be counted as working. 'A woman who worked *regularly* and *most of the time* at such work' should be returned as a farm laborer (p. 30 – italics in original).

foreign-born white women were somewhat higher in 1880, at 22.7 percent, but increased at a lower rate than their native-born counterparts, rising to 32.1 percent in 1950 (Kleinberg, 2006b, ch. 5).

The economic activity rates of African American widows in their middle years differed both from native- and foreign-born white women. In 1880, their employment rates were two and one-half to three times greater than white women's. Their employment levels increased more than white women's between 1900 and 1930, but by 1940 had fallen below the employment level of their grandmothers' generation. As discussed above for married black women, a number of factors may account for this. As middle-aged African American widows moved into cities in larger numbers, they might have turned to taking in boarders as a means of sustaining their households, which was not included by the census in its calculations of women's employment. The levels of augmented and extended families remained higher in the African American community as more blacks moved into cities and sought accommodation with family, former neighbors, or simply within the black community as widespread discrimination prevented them from obtaining housing elsewhere.[22] In 1940, unemployment levels were still very high among domestic servants, so they might either have no occupation recorded for them or subsisted on public relief, especially in northern cities.

Some clue to the underlying reasons for African American widows' lower levels of economic activity by 1950 might be found in analyzing the overall patterns of black women's employment throughout the century. Rates of labor force participation among middle-aged African American women peaked in 1910 in all marital statuses but fell sharply in 1920 and continued to fall through 1950. Nationally, there was a decrease in the proportion of employed African American women of all ages in these years and a very sharp decline in agriculture. In 1910, 52 percent of all African American women worked in agriculture, compared with only 39 percent in 1920 (United States Department of Commerce, 1923, p. 340). Thus, it is possible that some of the decline is related to the increased urbanization and decreased importance of agricultural employment among African Americans (Newman, 1986).

Another way to analyze the changing levels of economic activity among race/ethnicity groups is to look at women's position within the household, whether as heads, wives, children, or other relatives, servants, and boarders.

---

[22]   See the essays in Trotter, Joe William Jr. (1991) *The Great Migrations in Historical Perspective: New Dimensions of Race, Class, and Gender* (Bloomington: Indiana University Press) especially that of Darlene Clark Hine, 'Black Migration to the Urban Midwest: The Gender Dimension, 1915–1945,' pp. 127–146.

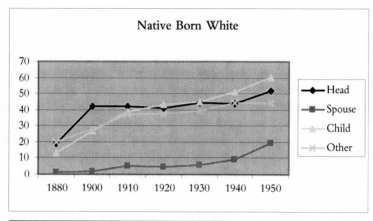

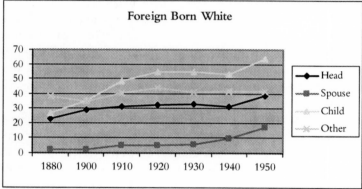

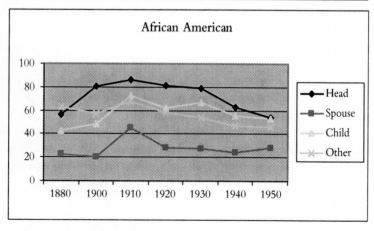

Figure 4a, b and c: Middle-Aged Women's Employment by Relation to Head of Household and Race /Nativity

Figure 4 shows that women who headed households tended to have higher rates of economic participation than other widows. What is most interesting here is the way in which women of different racial/nativity groups related to the labor force and to supporting their household. For an African American woman to head a household she almost had to be economically active, although the level of labor force participation changed over time. In 1880 nearly three-fifths of all black female household heads had jobs. This figure rose to over 80 percent in 1900 and stayed at that level until the Great Depression, when black women's inability to get jobs and their growing likelihood of getting either relief or other forms of federal assistance helped them leave the labor force. By 1950, the proportion who worked was actually lower than it had been in 1880.

A number of factors contributed to the different employment trajectories of the races in the 1940s and 1950s. It is possible that a combination of urbanization, the prosperity of the immediate post-war era, and deliberate choices made by African Americans to deploy women's labor within their own homes rather than on white men's farms or in white women's kitchens coalesced in post-war America to enable black women to focus on their own families. This hypothesis is suggested by the reaction of African American families to emancipation after the Civil War, when black women's economic activity decreased sharply.[23]

The role of adult children in supporting their parents is important in understanding how the elderly survived in the early twentieth century.[24] Co-resident adult children over the age of 40 constituted another important group sustaining African American families throughout this era. In 1880, 40 percent of all middle-aged black women residing with their parents worked to support them. By 1910, this figure had risen to over 70 percent, and tapered off to just over half by 1950. White families had a somewhat different trajectory. In 1880, around 12 percent of native-born white women in their middle years worked to support their parents, as did about 28 percent of foreign-born white women. But whereas African American women's direct support for their parents tapered off after 1910, that of white women, whether born in the United States or abroad, continued to increase on a steady basis until 1950, when it reached over 60 percent.

Foreign- and native-born white women who headed households had lower levels of employment than African American women. However, the employment of native-born white female household heads rose faster and higher than that of foreign-born white female household heads. The latter continued to rely

---

[23] Ransom, Roger and Sutch, Richard (2000) *One Kind of Freedom*, 2nd ed. (Cambridge: Cambridge University Press), discuss the impact of emancipation upon the black family.

[24] Znaniecki Lopata, Helena (1973) *Widowhood in an American City* (Cambridge, MA: Schenkman Publishing Company) discusses the way in which Social Security liberated the elderly from dependence upon their families.

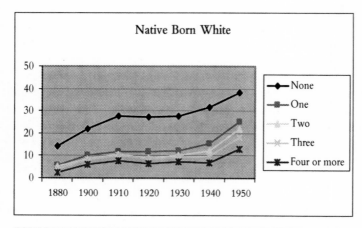

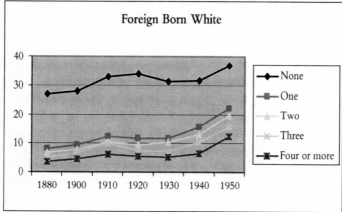

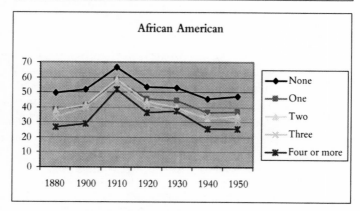

Figure 5a, b and c: Middle-Aged Women's Employment by Number of Children and Race/Nativity

upon the labor of their children for support, but their employment levels rose by about 10 percent for both groups between 1940 and 1950.

Another important dimension of middle-aged women's role in the family can be found in their growing propensity to enter the labor market when they had children of their own still living at home. Once again, race is crucial in understanding mothers' relation to the economy. For African American mothers, motherhood had a different influence on their decision to undertake employment than for white women, since they viewed their labor force participation as compatible with being good mothers (Landry, 2000, p. 98). Urban reformers attributed high levels of maternal employment among African Americans to a desire to foster independence among the children of the race. Analysts of black rural dwellers explain their high levels of employment on the great poverty of black agricultural families (White Ovington, 1969; Pleck, 1978; Tolnay, 1999, pp. 35–9). In 1880, two-fifths of all black women with one to three co-resident children had jobs. Even in larger families more than one-fourth of mothers worked, compared with one-half of those without children at home.[25] By 1910, between one-half to three-fifths of black middle-aged mothers were economically active, and again, having a large family still at home made only a slight difference to employment rates. Even when middle-aged black women's levels of economic activity dropped during the 1930s and 1940s, there was little change in the influence of co-resident children upon maternal employment, with the same level of maternal employment among middle-aged black women as there was in 1880.[26]

Middle-aged white mothers had a very different relation to the labor market. A mere 5 percent of native-born white mothers were in the labor force in 1880, with the number of children still at home making little difference in their proclivity to undertake employment. The proportion of foreign-born white mothers with jobs was slightly higher, with a few more mothers of one child working than those with four or more. The somewhat higher employment levels of middle-aged women without co-resident children, even in 1880, show how important ancillary wage earners were to the family economy. In 1880, about 15 percent of native-born and 28 percent of foreign-born middle-aged white women with no children (or no children living at home) had jobs. As with African American women, employment levels rose for white mothers through 1910, but at a very slow rate. These rates stabilized through the 1930s, in contrast

[25] The way in which Census data are organized make it difficult to differentiate between women who never had children and those whose children were living away from home.

[26] Tolnay, Stewart E. (1999) *The Bottom Rung: African American Family Life on Southern Farms* (Urbana: University of Illinois Press), pp. 110–14, discusses the extent to which children lived away from their family of origin, but only discusses children under the age of 14.

to African American mothers whose employment decreased in this decade. The major difference between the races comes in 1940 and 1950. The employment of middle-aged black mothers in these decades remained virtually static, while white mothers' employment levels rose sharply. Black middle-aged mothers with children at home were still more likely to hold jobs than white women with the same number of children, but it is clear that the economic patterns were converging between the races, at least in terms of presence in the labor force.

What stands out in this examination of middle-aged women's participation in the labor force is the growing similarity between these groups of middle-aged women over the course of the twentieth century in their levels of employment and approaches to the labor market. The finding that their employment patterns had in some respects converged before either the Civil Rights or Women's Liberation Movements occurred emphasizes both women's agency and fundamental social and economic changes taking place in American society in the twentieth century. The debates over the status of mid-life women and the place of people of color in American society were, at least in part, a reflection of the shifts that had already taken place in their lives. By the 1960s and 1970s the role of the state in preventing discrimination expanded as employment and age discrimination legislation, pension splitting, and protection for displaced homemakers became political issues.[27] Middle-aged women became the core of many civil rights organizations, the National Organization for Women, the longest-lived feminist organization in the United States, and the Older Women's League.[28] Thus, the changing experiences of middle-aged women can be said to have helped give birth to some of the most important social movements of the twentieth century and to have changed the way in which Americans regarded women's roles inside and outside the home.

---

[27] Huckle, Patricia (1991) *Tish Sommers, Activist, and the Founding of the Older Women's League* (Knoxville: University of Tennessee Press) explores many of these issues.

[28] Mary McLeod Bethune, Rosa Parks, Fannie Lou Hamer, and Septima Clark played crucial roles in the Civil Rights Movement, even if they were not credited with the leadership they provided. See Curtin, Mary Ellen (2007) 'Strong People and Strong Leaders: African American Women and the Modern Black Freedom Struggle,' in S. J. Kleinberg, Eileen Boris, and Vicki Ruiz (eds.), *Crafting U.S. Women's History: Narratives, Intersections, Dialogues* (New Brunswick, NJ: Rutgers University Press).

Bibliography

Blau, Francine and Ferber, Marianne (1992) *The Economics of Women, Men, and Work* (Englewood Cliffs, NJ: Prentice Hall), pp. 80–99.

Bodnar, John, Simon, Roger and Weber, Michael P. (1982) *Lives of Their Own: Blacks, Italians, and Poles in Pittsburgh 1900–1960* (Urbana: University of Illinois Press).

Campbell, D'Ann (1984) *Women at War with America: Private Lives in a Patriotic Era* (Cambridge, Mass., Harvard University Press).

Carlson, Shirley J. (1992) 'Black Ideals of Womanhood in the Late Victorian Era,' *Journal of Negro History* vol. 77, no. 2 (Spring).

Chafe, William (1972) *The American Woman: Her Changing Social, Economic, and Political Roles, 1920–1970* (New York: Oxford University Press).

Clark, Le Mon (1947–1948) 'Sex Life of the Middle-Aged,' *Marriage and Family Living* vol. 11, no. 2 (Spring).

Collins, William J. (2000) 'African-American Economic Mobility in the 1940s: A Portrait from the Palmer Survey,' *The Journal of Economic History* vol. 60, no. 3 (September), pp. 756–781.

Endres, Kathleen L. (2002) *Rosie the Rubber Worker: Women Workers in Akron's Rubber Factories During World War II* (Kent, Ohio: Kent State University Press).

Friedan, Betty (1963) *The Feminine Mystique* (New York: Norton).

Giele, Janet Z. and Elder, Glen H. (1998) *Methods of Life Course Research: Qualitative and Quantitative Approaches* (Thousand Oaks, CA: Sage).

Hareven, Tamara (1982) *Family Time and Industrial Time: The Relationship between the Family and Work in A New England Industrial Community* (Cambridge: Cambridge University Press).

Hernandez, Donald J. (1994) 'Children's Changing Access to Resources: An Historical Perspective,' *Social Policy Report* vol. 8, no. 1 (Spring).

Hetzler, Stanley (1969) *Technological Growth and Social Change: Achieving Modernization* (London: Routledge).

Kessler-Harris, Alice (1995) 'Designing Women and Old Fools: The Construction of the Social Security Amendments of 1939,' in Linda Kerber, Alice Kessler-Harris, and Kathryn Kish Sklar (eds.), *U.S. History as Women's History: New Feminist Essays* (Chapel Hill: University of North Carolina Press), pp. 87–106.

Klein, Viola and Myrdal, Alva (1968) *Women's Two Roles at Home and at Work* (London, Routledge).

Kleinberg, S. J . (2003) 'Black and White Women's Employment Contrasted,' unpublished paper presented to the 'In Our Time Conference' (University of East Anglia).

Kleinberg, S. J. (2006a) *The Family Economy and Social Welfare Policy, 1880 – 1939* (Urbana: University of Illinois Press).

Kleinberg, S. J. (2006b) *Widows and Orphans First: The Family Economy and Social Welfare Policy, 1880–1939* (Urbana: University of Illinois Press).

Landry, Bart (2000) *Black Working Wives: Pioneers of the American Family Revolution* (Berkeley: University of California Press).

Matthews, Glenna (1987) *Just a Housewife: The Rise and Fall of Domesticity in America* (New York: Oxford University Press).

McGovern, James R. (1969) 'The American Woman's Pre-World War I Freedom in Manners and Morals,' *Journal of American History* vol. 55, no. 1 (July).

National Center for Health Statistics (2005) *Health, United States, 2005* (Hyattsville, MD: Government Printing Office).

Neugarten, Bernice L. and Moore, Joan W. (1968) 'The Changing Age-Status System,' in Bernice L. Neugarten, *Middle Age and Aging* (Chicago: University of Chicago Press).

Newman, Debra Lynn (1986) 'Black Women Workers in the Twentieth Century,' *Sage* vol. 3, no. 1 (Spring), pp. 10–15.

Pleck, Elizabeth H. (1978) 'A Mother's Wage: Income Earning Among Married Italian and Black Women, 1896–1911' in Michael Gordon (ed.), *The American Family in Social Historical Perspective*, 2nd ed. (New York: St. Martin's Press), pp. 490–510.

Raup, Jana L. and Myers, Jane E. (1989) 'Empty Nest Syndrome: Myth or Reality?' *Journal of Counselling and Development* vol. 68, no. 2 (November-December), pp. 180–183.

Ruiz, Vicki (1998) *From Out of the Shadows: Mexican Women in the Twentieth Century* (Oxford: Oxford University Press).

Schwartz Cowan, Ruth (1983) *More Work for Mother: The Ironies of Household Technology from the Open Hearth to the Microwave* (New York: Basic Books).

Schweitzer, Mary M. (1980) 'World War II and Female Labour Force Participation Rates,' *The Journal of Economic History* vol. 40, no. 1 (March), pp. 89–95.

Simmons, Tavia. and Dye, Jane (2004) 'What Has Happened to Median Age at First Marriage Data?' Paper presented at the annual meeting of the American Sociological Association, Hilton San Francisco & Renaissance Parc 55 Hotel, San Francisco, CA,, Aug 14, 2004 Online. www.allacademic.com/meta/p109114_index.html, accessed 5 October 2006

Spence, Donald and Lonner, Thomas (1971) 'The "Empty Nest": A Transition Within Motherhood,' *The Family Coordinator* vol. 20, no. 4 (Oct.), pp. 369–75.

Sutherland, Daniel (1988) *Americans and Their Servants: Domestic Service in the United States from 1800 to 1920* (Baton Rouge: Louisiana State University Press).

Thistle, Susan (2006) *From Marriage to the Market: The Transformation of Women's Lives and Work* (Berkeley: University of California Press).

Tienda, Marta and Glass, Jennifer (1985) 'Household Structure and Labor Force Participation of Black, Hispanic, and White Mothers,' *Demography* vol. 22, no. 3, pp. 381–94.

Tolnay, Stewart E. (1999) *The Bottom Rung: African American Family Life on Southern Farms* (Urbana: University of Illinois Press).

United States Department of Commerce, Bureau of the Census (1923) *Fourteenth Census of the United States Population, 1920, Occupations* vol. iv (Washington, DC: Government Printing Office).

United States Employment Opportunities Commission 'Facts about Age Discrimination,' www.eeoc.gov/employers/overview.html accessed 8 May 2006.

White Ovington, Mary (1969 – orig. 1911) *Half a Man* (New York: Schocken Books).

Woody, Bette (1992) *Black Women in the Workplace* (Westwood, CN: Greenwood Press).

Wylie, Philip (1942) *Generation of Vipers* (New York: Farrar, Rinehard).

Yans McLaughlin, Virginia (1977) *Family and Community: Italian Immigrants in Buffalo, 1880–1930* (Ithaca, NY: Cornell University Press).

5

From Exile Community to 'Hy'-Society: Cuban American Literature and Cultural Identity

Annabel Cox

Introduction

Cuban migration to the United States has a long history. However, since the Revolution on the island in 1959, the size and nature of this migration has altered dramatically. Numbers of migrants have been large, and Cuban migration has been subject to varying policy changes by both the Cuban and United States governments over time. Furthermore, not only have the waves of migration and governmental policy in relation to them been subject to change, so too have the cultural responses to the experience of migration by these Cuban migrants themselves, especially following extended time spent in the U.S. This essay examines some of the range of perspectives witnessed in certain literature produced by some Cuban American writers, namely Gustavo Pérez Firmat's poem 'Bilingual Blues,' Cristina García's novel *Dreaming in Cuban*, and Achy Obejas's poem 'Sugarcane,' regarding their new American environment. For these particular individuals the situation is especially interesting, as the migration itself took place during youth – that is, before the development of a solid, established, sense of wholly Cuban identity.

The term 'Cuban American' is used here very specifically to signify those people now resident in the United States who were born in Cuba but came to the U.S. as adolescents, children, or infants. Yet this is not the way in which the term is always employed by others. For example, it can be used to mean anyone of Cuban origin now living in the U.S. – people who arrived at 70 as much as people who arrived at 7. It is also applied by some to the U.S.-born children of those who came earlier – that is, to people who are in fact second-generation Cuban, being both born and raised in the United States. Rather than just country of origin (or parents' origin) and present country of residence, the way in which the term is utilized here places far greater emphasis upon the bicultural (by which is suggested double, although this may in fact be multiple) nature of identity for these people. It is important to note, however, that due to the continuous waves of Cuban migration to the United States it is not possible to place Cuban American generations within any particular time frame. They are not tied to any one era, although this essay focuses upon writers who first came to the U.S. as children in the early 1960s.

The term 'Cuban American' is also linked to the idea of the '1.5 generation' in this discussion, a concept formulated by the Cuban sociologist Rubén Rumbaut in reference to Indo-Chinese teenage exile and migration. Rumbaut depicts the particular circumstances of '1.5ers' in terms of the fact that:

> These refugee youth must cope with two crisis-producing and identity-defining transitions: (1) adolescence and the task of managing the transition from childhood to adulthood, and (2) acculturation and the task of managing the transition from one sociocultural environment to another. (1991, p. 61)

Pérez Firmat has theorized that Cuban American cultural development has for the most part been the result of the efforts of this generation within his own community, as 'their intercultural placement makes them much more likely to undertake the negotiations and compromises that produce ethnic culture' (1999, p. 4). Yet Pérez Firmat does not consider, as this essay does, that different waves of migration have created and will continue to create different waves of Cuban American 1.5ers.

Rather, Pérez Firmat argues 'precisely because of its link to a specific generation, the varieties of Cuban American culture ... have a limited life expectancy' (1999, p. 17). Similar to an exile perspective, there is the assertion of an element of exceptionality witnessed in such a position, even at the same time as the writer is arguing himself to be part of a bridging generation found in many migrant Latino/a and non-Latino/a cultures. Still, as the critic himself has argued: 'Once an exile, always an exile; but it doesn't follow that once an exile, always *only* an exile' (Pérez Firmat, 1999, p. 11). Pérez Firmat considers himself to be not only an exile but also a Cuban American, but other writers assert different identifications than this. For example, García identifies herself not only as a Cuban American but also a Latina. The Latino/a label itself is rejected by Pérez Firmat, however.

Many critics do consider Cuban-origin people to be part of a larger grouping termed Latinos/as, but this is not to say that all differences between the communities linked under this umbrella term must be sublimated. Indeed, of all the Latino groups writing in the U.S., according to Efraín Barradas, the

'Cuban-American case is perhaps the most problematic' (1992, p. 93). Just as some Cuban Americans do not know whether to consider themselves exiles or migrants, 'Cuban-American writers do not know if their work will be seen, in the long run, as part of the body of island literature or as a historical curiosity within North American literature' (Barradas, 1992, p. 93). This essay examines the responses encountered in the selected works of fiction to this dilemma and the identity question in general, as expressed through language, theme, imagery, and intertextual reference. Furthermore, some of the material discussed here is also theoretical, and in the case of Pérez Firmat and García a brief comparison between the authors' theoretical positions and those witnessed in some of their fictional literature is given. In addition, how Cuban American identity is conceptualized and expressed in relation to both the exile and Latino/a label is also considered. Finally, the ways that Obejas in particular moves beyond the brackets of exile, Cuban American, and Latino/a identity towards what can be termed a bycultural position is discussed.

Cuban American Biculturation and 'Bilingual Blues'

Pérez Firmat coins and defines the term 'biculturation' to describe the Cuban American situation:

> Biculturation designates not only contact of cultures; in addition, it describes a situation where the two cultures achieve a balance that makes it difficult to determine which is the dominant and which is the subordinate culture. Unlike acculturation or transculturation, biculturation implies an equilibrium, however tense or precarious, between the two contributing cultures. Cuban-American culture is a balancing act. (1999, p. 6)

Whilst his theory of biculturation may not be amenable to 'a fashionable view of relations between "majority" and "minority" cultures,' Pérez Firmat argues that 'the oppositional model, accurate as it may be in other situations, does not do justice to the balance of power in Cuban America' (1999, p. 6). Still, despite Pérez Firmat's insistence upon equilibrium in his theories, a much less balanced and equitable picture emerges when we turn to his own poem, 'Bilingual Blues.' In this, Pérez Firmat declares that he has 'mixed feelings about everything' (1995, p. 28) and emotional as well as linguistic reverses and revisions are reflected in the poem, which swings from humorous and celebratory to aggressive and isolated. William Luis notes 'defiance, frustration, and anger against the established norms' in the piece, exemplified by the retort of 'tu madre' (1997, p. 169). However, the poem also rejoices in the range of cultural references available to the bicultural Cuban American subject, with Pérez Firmat adapting not only the ideas of the Cuban anthropologist Fernando Ortiz but also the Anglo-U.S. songs 'Let's Call the Whole Thing Off' and 'Consider Yourself at Home.'

The first song is concerned with both the pains and pleasures of difference and how opposites simultaneously attract and repel, whereas the second concerns the idea of belonging (or not, as the case may be). Originating from the musical *Oliver*, it has strong associations with the idea of being orphaned – that is, of being without roots and a sense of identity and history. It is important to note that the themes of division and rootlessness are both configured within the Anglo cultural realm in the poem through these songs, whilst perhaps more positive images of displacement and difference are accessed through the poet's Cuban cultural inheritance, particularly in reference to Ortiz.

Ortiz's work has been of immense value and interest in recent years to Cuban Americans and Cuban exiles. In the exile context in particular, he has been of supreme importance because he 'defines a Cuban simply as someone who wants to be Cuban: Cuban is he who is aware and desirous of his *cubanidad*' (Pérez Firmat 1999, p. 30). Furthermore, Ortiz proposes that beyond even *cubanidad* exists the state of *cubanía*. This is defined as 'cubanidad plena, sentida, consciente y deseada,' that is full Cubanness, deeply felt, aware, and desired (Ortiz 1991, p. 14). As Pérez Firmat notes, 'unlike *cubanidad*, which is essentially a civil status, *cubanía* is a spiritual condition, but a spiritual condition identified by an act of the will, one that is fundamentally a desire, a wanting .... To want *cubanía* is already to possess it' (1989, p. 30). Given the pain of Cuban exile and migration to the United States, Ortiz's ideas concerning national identity can provide comfort and affirmation. They allow a continuation, if not in fact a heightening, of the sense of Cubanness for exiles and migrants.

Referring to Ortiz's 1939 essay 'Los factores humanos de la cubanidad,' Pérez Firmat declares in the opening line of 'Bilingual Blues' (and twice afterwards): 'Soy un ajiaco de contradicciones,' that is, 'I am a stew of contradictions' (1995, pp. 28, ll 1, 7, 20). An *ajiaco* is a traditional Taíno dish, cooked in a pit in the ground and topped up frequently by the addition of extra foodstuffs. In this *ajiaco* description Pérez Firmat is asserting the enduring nature of change and growth for himself personally, just as he argues Ortiz had also asserted it in reference to Cuban culture as a whole. Pérez Firmat summarizes the metaphor of Ortiz's *ajiaco* thus:

> First, since the *ajiaco* is made by combining a variety of meats and vegetables ... it conveys the ethnic diversity of Cuba. Second, the

> *ajiaco* is agglutinative but not synthetic; even if the diverse
> ingredients form part of a new culinary entity, they do not lose their
> original flavor and identity ... Third, an *ajiaco* is indefinitely
> replenishable, since new ingredients can be added to the stew as old
> ones are used up. In this respect, the dish symbolizes the continuing
> infusion of new elements into the Cuban cultural mix. (1989, p. 30)

With Ortiz's emphasis upon flux, cultural interchange and migration in the metaphor of the *ajiaco*, it is apparent that this can hold a deep relevance in the Cuban exile and Cuban American context, providing an alternative to the model of the melting pot.

The continuing relevance of the *ajiaco* exists for a number of differing, if inter-related, reasons. Firstly, Ortiz's *ajiaco*, as understood by Pérez Firmat, furnishes the poet with a metaphor for cultural interaction between Cuban Americans and Cubans in exile and mainstream U.S. culture that suggests the former do not have to relinquish their *cubanidad*. It assures their cultural agency to influence as well as to be influenced. Secondly, this island stew also suggests impermanence to Cuban culture, which can provide hope for those wanting political change upon the island, especially when it is a prerequisite for return. Thirdly, the image of replen-ishment indicates that Cubans who have resided outside the island will have some-thing of value to contribute if return does become possible – that is, that any foreign acculturation will merely provide yet more flavour to what remains a Cuban mix. According to Pérez Firmat, Cuban culture is depicted by Ortiz as in a process of coming into being that is considered open to new or returning influ-ences, helping to allay fears concerning the cultural relevance of exiles and Cuban Americans in both their present time and location and also in the future.

Furthermore, this reference to Ortiz's *ajiaco* is paradoxically both an affirma-tion of Cubanness as well as a declaration of the poet's own mixed cultural loca-tion as a biculturated Cuban American. Unlike certain more staunchly exile-writers, Cuban American writers such as Pérez Firmat insist that 'they have a niche in their own national literature – whether this is written inside or out-side the homeland' not because 'their work is primarily defined by their native, *Cuban* experience' (Rivero, 1986, p. 165) but because Cuban experience itself is being redefined by such writers to include that of Cuban exiles and Cuban Americans. As hybridity is propounded to be essentially Cuban by Ortiz, his work is employed as a tool by Cuban Americans with which to broaden the understanding of Cuban identity to include hybridities encountered by those residing outside of the island itself.

In addition to references to Ortiz, there are also echoes of Nicolás Guillén's poem 'Digo que yo no soy un hombre puro' ('I declare myself an impure man')

in Pérez Firmat's description of himself as 'un puré de impurezas,' that is, a purée
of impurities (1995, pp. 28,). Whilst the image of the *puré* is much less comfortable than the *ajiaco*, carrying the idea of violent (possibly) mechanical pulveriza-
tion and an immediate loss of individual texture and flavour, the positive
elements of the concept of impurity are foregrounded by association with
Guillén's work. To Guillén, purity was an overrated virtue, involving hypocrisy
and a refusal to engage with the world in a vital, creative and sexual fashion.
Similarly, Pérez Firmat configures sexuality as a form of true and creative identity, and one that provides him with a sense of membership.

As Luis notes: 'home, in the poem, is defined in sexual terms by the *hueco* (the
hole) and the *cosa* (the thing) and by communion with the other: "and if the cosa
goes into the hueco, | consider yourself at home"' (1997, p. 170). Indeed rather
than calling the whole thing off, in this poem Pérez Firmat calls the hole/thing
home. Furthermore, the poet feels most 'like a cubano' when he is 'straddling'
(1995, p. 28), a term that calls to mind not only sexual intercourse but also the
creative bridging of all opposites, including the linguistic and cultural. Herein is
found the poet's sense of union, liberation, and belonging, communicated via
what the poet considers to be the Cuban aspects of his sexuality.

Indeed, the Cuban aspects of identity are clearly central to Pérez Firmat in
'Bilingual Blues,' and there is an identification with an exile position witnessed.
In his 2000 memoir, the author identifies himself in such terms, declaring: 'As
an exile, my experience is different from that of immigrants in that I came to this
country fully intending to return to my homeland as soon as possible' (2000,
p. 10). When discussing the possibility of return to Cuba if the Revolution fell,
however, Pérez Firmat also declares: 'For me, homecoming would feel like
departure' (2000, p. 12). He asks 'What happens to the exile who can go back
but who decides not to? What does he become then, a post-exile? An ex-exile?'
(2000, p. 10). This suggests that his own assertions of identity are problematic
even to himself. Whilst Pérez Firmat states that he will never feel truly at home
in the U.S., he is also aware that as the years have gone by the possibility that
Cuba could ever be home again has also diminished.

The poet also asserts that 'nadie nunca acoplará' (nobody will ever fit together)
his divided self (1995, p. 28). That there will never be this coming together or
coupling for him undermines all the previous sexual imagery wherein is depicted
the chance of joyful union, and even a brief respite from the overriding loneli-
ness and feelings of separation from both Cuba and the U.S. In addition,
'Bilingual Blues' ends with the line '(Cha-cha-chá)' (1995, p. 28), which makes
a mockery of all the poet's earlier witticisms regarding the United States. This
Latin American musical reference, positioned as it is within parentheses, makes
a lonely after-thought to the main body of the poem. The dwindling of bravado

encountered in the poem's final lines draws attention to the fact that, despite all
the gleeful puns and sexual imagery, the poem nevertheless is ultimately about
the Blues. Like the displaced and disenfranchised African slaves from whom this
musical genre originated in the United States, one cannot presume that Pérez
Firmat's singing is an indication of his happiness.

However, that the Spanish language and Cuban cultural references still have a
central place in the poem alongside English and Anglo-U.S. allusions suggests
that all is not lost. This poem, like all bilingual work, reflects merely partial
assimilation. Rather than either full acculturation or, conversely, a refusal to
acculturate, what many Cuban-origin people in the U.S. have practiced is 'a
strategy of paced, selective assimilation' which Alejandro Portes and Min Zhou
have described as possibly 'the best course for immigrant minorities' (1994,
p. 33). They argue that:

> ... adopting the outlook and cultural ways of the native born does
> not necessarily represent the first step towards social and economic
> mobility. It may, in fact, lead to exactly the opposite. [...] This
> situation stands the common understanding of immigrant assimilation
> on its head. As presented in innumerable academic and journalistic
> writings, the expectation is that the foreign born and their offspring
> will acculturate and seek acceptance among the native born as a
> prerequisite for social advancement. If they did not, they would
> remain confined to the ranks of the 'ethnic' lower and lower-middle
> classes. This portrayal of the path to mobility, so deeply embedded in
> the national consciousness, stands contradicted today by a growing
> number of empirical studies. (1994, p. 21)

Whilst they acknowledge that 'the expected consequences of assimilation have
not changed entirely,' Portes and Zhou emphasize that this process has become
'segmented' (1994, p. 21), wherein 'rapid economic advancement' is combined
with 'deliberate preservation of the immigrant community's values and solidarity' (1994, p. 22). According to 'Bilingual Blues,' these values and solidarity are
found in language and cultural history, and such matters are as essential to survival for migrants as economic success.

Beyond Bifocal Perspectives: From Exile via Cuban American to Latina/o Identification

Furthermore, it can be argued that Pérez Firmat's affiliations extend beyond the
Cuban and Anglo-U.S. realms in 'Bilingual Blues.' When the poet describes

himself as 'a little square from Rubik's Cuba' (1995, p. 28) this brings to mind the idea of the self as a small piece in a much larger and shifting puzzle not only in terms of culture (and perhaps race through the association with colour) but also politically as well. The Rubik's cube was invented in Hungary, a country that was under Communist rule in the Cold War. Many Hungarians fled to the United States after the Russian invasion put down the attempted revolutionary overthrow of Communism in 1956 and, according to Felix Masud-Piloto, the 'Hungarian refugee operation's overwhelming success convinced the administration that it could solve another refugee crisis from a Communist country the same way' (1996, p. 37). However, it soon became apparent that 'Cuban migration ... did not fit the Hungarian blueprint' (Masud-Piloto, 1996, p. 37). Not only was it spread over a much greater period of time and involved much larger numbers of people, it also, until the policy and status changes implemented by the Clinton administration in May 1995 at least, was privy to an open-door policy that Hungarian migration was not (Masud-Piloto, 1996, p. 128).

When Pérez Firmat came to the U.S. at the age of 11 in 1960 this open-door policy was in full effect, yet the poet still describes himself as 'illegally alienated' (1995, p. 28). In relation to the word 'complexed' in the previous line of the poem (1995, p. 28) the term 'alienated' appears to refer to a psychological rather than political state of being, wherein regardless of immigration status in the U.S. all non-natives face similar experiences of isolation and displacement. However, in the Cuban American context it is possible that Pérez Firmat is actually depicting his alienation from Cuba rather than the United States. Unlike, for example, a Puerto Rican American, this poet does not feel able to return to the land of his birth. Therefore a phrase which at first appears to draw parallels between Cuban exiles and Cuban Americans and other, arguably more voluntary Latino and non-Latino migrant groups ultimately constitutes a statement of difference. Pérez Firmat's affiliations in 'Bilingual Blues' appear based more upon shared political relations of exile to the homeland than cultural and political identifications in the U.S.

The fact that the poet voices his declaration of not fitting in Spanish, 'nadie nunca acoplará' (1995, p. 28), suggests a deep sadness on his part for the losses that have occurred through displacement, a nostalgia for the past, and a profound sense of isolation, all of which are recurring themes of exile literature. Nevertheless, whilst placing himself within the exile rather than immigrant and/or Latino/a bracket, Pérez Firmat still considers himself very much part of the 1.5 generation and shares this group's ability to move between cultural realms. However, some other Cuban American authors more readily identify themselves as 1.5ers with more of a migrant and/or Latino/a perspective than an exile one. Like Rumbaut's 1.5 theory, Cristina García's *Dreaming in Cuban* focuses upon adolescence and biculturality, but Pérez Firmat regards it as exemplifying the movement away from Cuban and Cuban-exile literature towards ethnic-American identification in Cuban American literature (1999, pp. 143–44).

Garcia's background is half way between the 1.5 and second generations in that she was born in Cuba but almost entirely raised in the United States. However, Pérez Firmat places her in literary terms as an ethnic-American writer of Cuban origin alongside second-generation Cuban American authors such as Oscar Hijuelos. In his view, such authors write '"from" Cuba but "toward" the United States,' as for them 'Cuban culture is [the] narrative point of departure.' 'The voice that speaks ...,' he avows, 'is that of someone who retains ties to Cuba but is no longer Cuban' (1999, p. 136). As well as being written from Cuba and towards the U.S., Pérez Firmat argues that ethnic-American writing of Cuban origin is written '"from" Spanish but "toward" English,' something that he sees as 'common among American "ethnic" writers ... but rather atypical of Cuban-American writers' as 'by and large Cuban-Americans have so far written for other Cuban-Americans' (1999, pp. 143–44). Pérez Firmat argues this to be the case 'even when they write in English,' and asserts that only 'in the last couple of years, with the appearance of novels by Hijuelos, Virgil Suárez, and Cristina García, have Cuban-American authors sought to reach a broader audience' (1999, p. 144).

Yet García appears to consider herself as much a part of the 1.5 generation as Pérez Firmat, and has asserted that, like his *cubano* (Pérez Firmat, 1995, p. 28), she too is one of the subjects that is able to 'straddle both cultures' (López, 1995, p. 109). In doing so García argues that she and other children of exile:

> are in a unique position to tell our stories, to tell our family stories. We're still [EBS1] very close to the immigration, we're in the wake of that immigration, and yet we weren't as directly affected by it as our parents and grandparents were. So we are truly bilingual, truly bicultural, in a way that the previous generation were not. (López, 1995, p. 109)

However, whilst García herself may feel a part of this bicultural, bilingual generation, it is clear that *Dreaming in Cuban* itself is not a bilingual text. In comparison to 'Bilingual Blues,' *Dreaming in Cuban*'s linguistic and, perhaps by extension, cultural identity clearly is much more Anglo-identified.

Rocío C. Davis concurs with Pérez Firmat, identifying *Dreaming in Cuban* as an ethnic-American text. García's first novel centers on familial relationships, especially those between mothers and daughters. Davis argues that often 'Ethnic texts ... highlight questions of identification with and differentiation from the mother, emphasizing a need for understanding between mothers and daughters as a fundamental step towards self-awareness and mastery of the culture' (2000, p. 60). Here, the tensions of the mother-daughter relationship represent not only the realm of the personal but also the cultural, and are the arena in which attitudes and feelings towards both the home and the host nation and culture are played out.

Yet, whilst the mother-daughter dynamic is often problematic in *Dreaming in Cuban*, other female relationships are also present in the text. These help to counterbalance the difficulties in the relationship of Pilar Puente, the protagonist, with her mother, Lourdes. The novel is woman-centered, and, as Eliana Ortega and Nancy Saporta Sternbach note:

> In Latina writing, the entire extended family of women – mothers, daughters, sisters, aunts, cousins, godmothers, lovers, neighbors, fortune-tellers, *curanderas* (healers), midwives, teachers, and friends, especially girlhood friends – makes up a cast of characters. (1989, p. 12)

So whilst Davis argues that the focus upon the mother-daughter relationship is characteristic of ethnic-American literature, Ortega and Saporta Sternbach see this relationship as just one of many between women that predominate in Latina literature. Still, whilst evidencing such possible links to Latina-identified literature, García does not allow distinctions between different Latino/a groups to go unexamined in her text.

Indeed, *Dreaming in Cuban* on several occasions asserts the differences rather than similarities between Cuban Americans and other Latino/a groups in the United States, which suggests that García herself is not totally comfortable with the homogenizing tendencies of concepts such as Latino/a identity. For example, Pilar acknowledges the class differences between herself and her Mexican American boyfriend, Max, whose mother is a single parent and a cleaner (García, 1992, p. 137). In addition, regarding her next boyfriend, Rubén, who is Peruvian, she sees the similarity between their families in that his is also 'divided over politics' (García, 1992, p. 179). Yet she cannot ignore the fact that Rubén can at least return to his country of origin: 'This makes me ache for the same possibility' (García, 1992, p. 179).

Still, García's position is not divisive, and common causes amongst Latinos/as are also highlighted. In Pilar's painting, *SL-76*, the image of the Statue of Liberty, and by extension the national mythologies that this represents, are transformed through their encounter with punk imagery and lyrics. Luis describes

'García's rendition of Liberty as a political commentary on how immigrants are treated in the United States' (1997, p. 218), an issue that he connects to Latino migration: 'Whereas in the past many European immigrants were welcomed to the United States ..., today's (Hispanic) immigrants have not been received with the same enthusiasm' (1997, p. 219). Furthermore, Luis also argues that we can see in Pilar's picture that the young woman 'is disillusioned by the contradiction between what the United States is and what the country is supposed to represent' (1997, p. 219).

The term 'Latina' suggests a place at the margins, and this is what García herself focuses upon in an interview when discussing her own work and that of other writers such as Oscar Hijuelos, the Dominican-born Julia Álvarez, and Sandra Cisneros, the daughter of a Mexican father and Chicana mother. The author, at ease with her interviewer's placement of her alongside these other writers of Latin-American origin, declares:

> I think it is a matter of time before Latino writers are recognized.
> Even though our literature is now called 'minority' writing,
> population studies show that we're really becoming the mainstream,
> and the literature of the future will be what has traditionally been
> called 'the margins'. (López, 1995, pp. 109–10)

Furthermore, García argues that a place in the mainstream does not necessitate the assumption of mainstream U.S. attitudes and identity:

> What I mean is not that we'll become part of the melting pot nor
> that our identity and culture will become diluted, but that the
> mainstream itself will be redefined to include us. We'll be part of the
> mainstream not by becoming more like 'them' and less like 'us', but
> by what it means to be an American in the twenty-first century.
> This is changing and its definition will be necessarily broader and
> more inclusive. I don't think this means leaving our culture in the
> dust. (López, 1995, p. 110)

Yet García's novel sometimes indicates otherwise. Although it is not entirely abandoned, García does indeed both display and depict the loss of a certain amount of Cubanness in her text.

This is most obviously seen in the author choosing to write in English, and Ortega and Saporta Sternbach emphasize that above all 'Latina writing is bilingual' (1989, p. 14). Yet, as we have seen with the bilingual poetry of Pérez Firmat, bilingual writing does not always equate to Latino/a identification.

Furthermore, Ortega and Saporta Sternbach go on to argue of Latina writers that even 'when, as speakers, they are not bilingual, the majority of their discourses are informed by a Spanish mothertongue [sic]' (1989, pp. 14–15), and García's novel does contain elements of this. Issues relating to the Spanish language are explicit in *Dreaming in Cuban*, and García's novel discusses both the loss and recovery, to a certain extent, of Spanish. Nevertheless, the representation and discussion of this author's Spanish-language heritage does not alter the fact that García provides not only linguistic translations for events depicted in Spanish but also cultural ones to help Anglo readers understand unfamiliar practices and experiences.

This suggests that whilst this novel may be written from the margins as Latina or ethnic-American literature, it ultimately seeks an audience within the Anglo mainstream and caters to this rather than encourages the mainstream to alter to a significant degree.

For example, when Pilar refers to 'outdated stores with merchandise that's been there since the Bay of Pigs' (García, 1992, p. 25), some knowledge of U.S.-Cuban history is needed to understand her remark. However, had García referred to Playa Girón, the level of this would have increased, perhaps too far beyond García's expectations of her intended (Anglo) readership. Unlike bilingual literature such as 'Bilingual Blues,' which is written from the margins and to the margins and may be considered singular in its untranslatability, García's text holds the art of translation, in a cultural if not necessarily linguistic sense, at its core.

However, this is not to suggest that the reader is presented with a picture of complete assimilation in García's work either. Originally believing that she would experience a sense of homecoming in Cuba, having revisited the island Pilar finds herself able to accept that she cannot stay: 'sooner or later I'd have to return to New York. I know now it's where I belong – not *instead* of here, but *more* than here' (García, 1992, p. 236, italics as in the original). Yet the retention of a certain degree of Cubanness is still witnessed in the protagonist's and the text's relationship to Pilar's home language. Although Spanish is one of 'the languages lost' in the text (the title of the third and final section of the novel), this is not entirely the case for Pilar. After returning to Cuba, Pilar notes, 'I've started dreaming in Spanish' (García, 1992, p. 235), but even prior to this she observes: 'English seems an impossible language for intimacy' (García, 1992, p. 180). Considering the importance of both sexual maturation and the inner psychological world in this text concerning adolescence and familial and cultural identity, the centrality of the language of dreaming and intimacy – that is, Spanish – cannot be underestimated. Through Pilar's capacity to dream in Spanish García is asserting that there are certain areas of the self that remain resistant and resilient, and are unable to be assimilated. In terms of Pilar's every-day interactions, Spanish takes second place to English. However, the areas in which Spanish does predominate are so important that one of them, dreaming, in fact informs the title of the novel itself.

Furthermore, this is not a text only concerned with language as identity, as would have been suggested had the title been *Dreaming in Spanish*, but one firmly grounded in the story of Cuban exile and displacement. However, as well as being a marker of Cuban specificity, the novel's title suggests a criticism of U.S. founding ideologies. This is not an immigrant's tale of the American Dream, something of which Pilar is herself deeply critical, but Cuban dreaming that is, an alternative version to the myths, aspirations and desires of the U.S. main-stream. As such, the title *Dreaming in Cuban* ties together the two main branches of identity formation that the novel discusses: on the one hand, the psychologi-cal world of Cuban family as evidenced in the novel's emphasis upon mothers and daughters, and on the other, identity in terms of cultural politics in the United States.

'Sugarcane' and Hycultural Identity

The final piece of writing considered here is the poem 'Sugarcane' by Achy Obejas. Like Pérez Firmat's work, Obejas's piece is interlingual, issuing the same challenges to Anglo-hegemony despite the differing positions witnessed in each poem. 'Sugarcane,' furthermore, makes reference to poetry by Nicolás Guillén, as well as to the song lyrics of Celia Cruz and Benny Moré. There is also an emphasis on the Caribbean in general, rather than just Cuba, through the image of the plantation found in 'Sugarcane,' but by transposing this upon the inner city environment of Chicago the poem concerns not only the slaves of the past in these locations but also the contemporary situation for blacks and those who are referred to as 'browns' (Obejas, 1996a, p. 93): 'Chicanos and Latinos as well as African Americans' (Rivero, 1986, p. 178). In addition, Obejas also does not overlook the existence of the indigenous population of either the Caribbean or the United States prior to colonization, drawing a much wider historical per-spective than encountered in the other two works considered.

According to Eliana S. Rivero, the image of sugarcane, often employed in earlier Cuban exile writing to nostalgically symbolize pre-Revolutionary Cuba, is subverted by Obejas to direct the reader to consider 'the slavery and oppres-sion suffered in the Hispanic Caribbean by peoples of African origin' (1986, p. 178). Furthermore, Obejas, like García, critiques not only the Cuban society in which she was born, both in its present-day and historical manifestations, but also her current socio-cultural environment, the United States. As Rivero argues, the poem 'subtly shifts the Caribbean colonial system to American society, where large numbers of ethnic minorities with darker skin are still on the lowest rungs of the socioeconomic ladder' (1986, p. 178). That the United States shares with the colonial Caribbean a history of slavery that informs its present-day inequalities is a matter that the poem appears to wish to highlight.

The image of sugarcane, alongside performing the function of critiquing nostalgic Cuban exile discourse and U.S. national mythology through an examination of both past and present inequality, also serves as a metaphor for the strength and vitality of the blacks and browns in modern Chicago. Districts that formerly were the territory of gangsters are depicted as 'overgrown taken | over by the dark | and poor' (Obejas, 1996a, p. 92), and this verdant growth and life stands in stark contrast to the 'hard cold | stone of the great gritty city' (Obejas, 1996a, p. 92). According to the poem, without the blacks and browns there would be no 'azuca' in Chicago (Obejas, 1996a, p. 92), and this idea, combined with the poem's repeated refusal to allow division amongst the marginalized, gives 'Sugarcane' a resistant and resilient tone. Whereas sugarcane can be read as a metaphor for the first step in the process of whitening, here it becomes an image of sweetness and fluidity already complete in itself. Obejas's cane is a powerful raw material that needs no refinement.

Obejas draws non-white identifications in 'Sugarcane,' and these are at points also non-Anglo in character. Such cultural and racial affiliations are constructed not only through the image of the plantation and direct references to black and brown skin color but also through the poem's use of both English and Spanish. Not only does the poet directly mention the Hispanic Caribbean islands of 'quisqueya | cuba y borinquen [sic]' (utilizing the Taíno language in this naming), she also joins them with the Spanish conjunction 'y' and utilizes the English language as well (1996a, pp. 93–94). Whilst the employment of Spanish as well as English could also be seen to invite a generally Latino or even just a broadly Spanish/English bilingual audience in the U.S., the poem's bilingualism in combination with the image of the plantation and Taíno naming of Cuba, Puerto Rico and the Dominican Republic suggests its focus is much more specifically towards a migrated Hispanic Caribbean identification. So, rather than just a broadly Caribbean identity, Obejas in 'Sugarcane' appears to separate the Hispanic islands from the others and the employment of the Spanish language, with its highlighting of colonial divides in the region, plays a central role in this separation.

Nevertheless, Spanish, although tied to ideas of separation, is not a site of loss in 'Sugarcane.' In fact, in common with the work of Pérez Firmat and García, the importance of the Spanish language as a site of both identity and resistance is displayed. However, it is important to note that it is only by Spanish being employed within Obejas's own current cultural context of the Anglo-speaking United States that it signifies resilience and defiance. In the earlier context of slavery and the plantation in the Hispanic Caribbean that 'Sugarcane' keenly evokes, Spanish was in fact the language of domination and not the dominated. Therefore, it could be argued that the poet inconsistently transforms and manipulates certain aspects of Cuban cultural history and identity in order to suit her own purposes and present location. Nevertheless, it is also possible to view Obejas's reconfiguration of Spanish as the language of the oppressed rather than the oppressor in the context of the plantation as an ironic comment upon the idea of subordinate and dominant cultures, as also critiqued in Pérez Firmat's theory of biculturation. Languages, and by extension cultures, are shown not to be stable in terms of power relations. In depicting the former language of the allegedly orderly and civilized European masters in the Caribbean now as part of the vivacious and jubilant language of the underdog in the U.S., 'Sugarcane' critiques essentializing theories of linguistic (and often, by extension, racial and/or social) inferiority and superiority. Such matters have nothing to do with the intrinsic value of one language over another, but are based upon cultural context alone.

This critique is furthered in the fact that Obejas's use of Spanish in the poem is distinctly of an island or Caribbean variety, in that in certain words particular consonants are absent, replaced by an apostrophe to indicate this. For example, sugar is '*azuca*' (Obejas, 1996a, p. 92) rather than *azúcar*, and the cane is something that '*no se pue'e cortar*' as opposed to *no se puede cortar* (Obejas, 1996a, p. 93). The distinction made by these spellings is not only between a more oral than written language but also between Caribbean and mainstream (specifically non-Anadalusian) peninsular usage. Furthermore, it is not only island Spanish that is used in 'Sugarcane' but also African American Vernacular English is employed. It is, therefore, arguable that beyond even being just bilingual, 'Sugarcane' is an at least trilingual piece, interspersing as it does Cuban Spanish, Standard American English and AAVE. Through the employment of AAVE alongside island Spanish in her portrait of Chicago, the poet makes a connection between Hispanic Caribbean (including Cuban) and Cuban American linguistic identity, and that of inner city black populations in the United States.

Just as Spanish is employed in order to demonstrate a refusal to submit to a completely English-speaking version of both the self and reality in Cuban American literature, AAVE is utilized by Obejas in order to express a refusal to accept solely white-identified versions of these either. This is a critique aimed at not only Anglo-American culture, but also conservative Cuban exile perspectives that attempt to sublimate the extent of the African influence upon the present-day nature of their own identity. With the use of both AAVE and island Spanish, Obejas appears to identify Cuban American identity as being strongly tied to

Afro-Cuban and black culture in general including the African American. Her vision is transformative, reconfiguring the shackles of slavery as shared blood and history, and a common bond(age) amongst those who have experienced diaspora. When the poet instructs the reader to 'dig it down to the | roots' (1996a, p. 92), we are presented with an image that suggests not only the search for common ancestry (literally the common ground) but also a celebration of African American linguistic input through this word 'dig.' The poem's ethos 'digs' both roots and linguistic versatility itself. Similarly, its repeated utilization of the term 'bro' (1996a, pp. 92, 93) again suggests familial connectivity, expressed not only in language but also through it.

Ultimately, therefore, like García, Obejas refuses to submit to divisions. The poet instead reconfigures the conflicts of migration and exile in terms of creative possibilities. These include (as they do in Pérez Firmat's work also) the artistic opportunities found in linguistic contact and exchange. However, in 'Sugarcane' these are examined and taken beyond the tensions of just Spanish versus English. Obejas, by introducing a third element, AAVE, bypasses a dualized conception of bicultural identity entirely. In addition, Obejas's inclusion of a variety of languages also highlights an undermining of the idea and value of not only national boundaries as defined by race, language, and ethnicity, but also more generally the concept of purity itself. This is also seen in Pérez Firmat's description of himself as a '*puré de impurezas.*' Like both Pérez Firmat and Nicolás Guillén, Obejas too is proud to declare herself impure in a linguistic sense.

Furthermore, Obejas's poem's impurity concerns not only its mixing of languages but also the presence of varying literary and cultural references. Most immediately notable of these is its intertextual reference, like 'Bilingual Blues,' to the poetry of Guillén. The title of Obejas's poem is the English translation of the leading Afro-Cuban poet's 1930 piece 'Caña.' Through this referencing Obejas seems not only to be drawing parallels between certain thematic similarities such as anti-racism and anti-U.S. imperialism in her writing and that of Guillén, but also more generally to be highlighting her own familiarity with and grounding in her Cuban cultural heritage. This is something that the poet desires to show extends beyond political, racial, temporal and/or geographical divides. It is not only Guillén's work that Obejas makes reference to, however. As Rivero notes, 'the lyrics' of a fifties' Afro-Cuban song by Celia Cruz ... constitute a takeoff point for the refrain "*no se pue'e cortar*"' (1986, p. 177). Indeed Cruz's cry of '¡*azuca!*' is even granted the final, triumphant, word in 'Sugarcane' (Obejas, 1996a, pp. 94, 160).

In yet another intertextual reference relating to popular song, this time to the work of Benny Moré (in a song also recorded by Celia Cruz), Obejas too mentions '*siguaraya*' (1996a, pp. 92, 93) as these singers had done before her.

According to Rivero, this is 'a tree especially revered for its magic properties in the belief system of the Yoruba religion' (1986, 177), so once again Africannness is highlighted. In addition, the central and repeated refrain of Obejas's poem, that of not being able to cut, features in Moré's recording of 'Mata Siguaraya' as well. These words being echoed by the Cuban American author add an element of spirituality to her text. As in the song when the siguaraya tree may only be felled with the blessing of the orishas, the implication is that the (African-origin) 'blood | lines from this island | train' depicted in the poem (Obejas, 1996a, pp. 92, 93) are also subject to divine protection.

Latino/a Identification and Beyond

Through the subversion of the image of sugarcane, an insistence on links related to Africa, a knowledge of non-white Cuban traditions, and an identification with the experience of the suffering of racial prejudice in the U.S. Obejas is clearly displaying a different approach to the subject of cultural identity than is found in conservative Cuban exile literature. This is in no doubt partly owing to the fact that Obejas was raised from the age of six in the environment of the U.S. However, other factors relating to Cuban migration may also have influenced her position. As María de los Ángeles Torres notes, prior to 1980 'common mythology characterized the Cuban exile community as mainly "white", conservative and middle-class, as many of its members indeed were' (1998, p. 50), and parts of the Cuban exile community appeared proud of these factors that differentiated them from some other ethnic migrant groups. However, the position of the conservative Cuban exile group as well as the Anglo majority and other Latino communities had to be forcibly reevaluated following the Mariel exodus of 1980.

What differentiated the Mariel exodus from previous migratory waves was not only the sheer scale of it but also the fact that the 'Mariel immigration was visibly more racially and economically diverse' (Torres, 1998, p. 50). As de la Campa argues:

> The 'Marielitos' ... comprised a different sort of Cuban from the
> white, successful, professional image Miami had carved out for itself.
> Indeed, Marielitos were largely representative of a racial and class
> composition that disturbed Cuban Miami's collective memory:
> Was Cuba really that poor and black – in short, similar to other
> Caribbean countries? (2002, p. 95)

As Obejas's 'Sugarcane' suggests, some Cuban-origin people adjusted to and accepted, even celebrated, this more diverse perspective on not only Cuban but also U.S.-Cuban culture and identity. Others, however, found it more difficult to accept and integrate with some of the newcomers, and such feelings were echoed in the Anglo-American community as well.

Portes and Stepick argue that there were several important cultural impacts of Mariel on Cuban exiles and Cuban Americans: 'up to that point, the self-image of Cuban exiles had been a happy mix: they were not only America's allies in the global anticommunist struggle but also a "model" minority' (1993, p. 30). However, with Mariel 'this positive image faded quickly; Cuban-Americans now found themselves classed with the most downtrodden and discriminated against minorities' (Portes and Stepick, 1993, p. 30), and some reacted to this situation by in turn rejecting and distancing themselves from the *Marielitos* (Portes and Stepick, 1993, p. 32). Nevertheless, others were 'forced to turn their attention inward and confront their condition as a domestic ethnic minority' (Portes and Stepick, 1993, p. 33) in a way that had in the main been previously avoidable, due to both their economic success and special immigration status.

As Rivero accurately states, in 'Sugarcane' Obejas is asserting 'a Cuban American ethnic consciousness, identified politically and racially with other historically marginalized groups' (1986, p. 177), and this is a stance that has often been actively rejected and resisted previously within the conservative Cuban exile community.

Furthermore, her poem also displays a very different position toward history than that often found in Cuban exile discourse. Through its mixing of the Cuban with the American, many times as well as places are drawn together in the poem: the Taíno culture prior to conquest, the plantation and the history of slavery both in Cuba and the U.S., the 1920s and 30s in Chicago, 1930s and 40s in Cuba through allusions to 'Caña,' as well as the modern day through descriptions of spray-paint and graffiti. 'Sugarcane,' by widening the historical panorama, moves away from the more often heard immediate concerns of Cuban exile writing which tends to often focus upon Cuba just prior to the Revolution. Starting from the initial point of her own contemporary identifications in the United States and reaching back beyond nostalgia, thus historically contextualing her migrated position, Obejas reconfigures the issues of memory and history and broadens their meaning.

In doing so, rather than asserting just a 'bicultural world vision,' as has been argued by Rivero (1986, p. 176), it is more accurate to say that Obejas more than the other authors examined here draws attention to the at least bicultural nature of Cuban identity prior to exile and migration. Furthest from an exilic perspective, 'Sugarcane' is firmly grounded in and celebrates the polyglot and multicultural existence of its author. Owing to its racially and culturally inclusive perspective, twinned with a broad historical framework highlighting the centrality of cultural contact within this, 'Sugarcane's' position can be defined as hycultural. In hycultural identity, notions of origin, purity and linearity are disrupted and undermined. This leads us to ask about the point at which we consider the quest for our sense of ourselves to have reached its definitive source – that is, how far back does one legitimately search for and indeed claim one's identity in one's roots? However, it is important to note that these questions are posed alongside an acute awareness of, rather than disregard for, history, recognizing the power of this to shape individual lives as well as communities and nations. Nonetheless, simultaneously such constructs as the idea of nation and indeed even legitimacy are also interrogated in the hycultural, the term signifying skepticism towards the more traditional perspectives of memory and history that support these.

Yet such a hycultural perspective is not shared by all the literature examined here. Pérez Firmat's 'Bilingual Blues' has more in common with an exile perspective, despite its author's solid grounding in the 1.5 generation. García's *Dreaming in Cuban* focuses more upon exploring how Cuban American identity both intersects with and differs from Latino/a identity in general. Therefore, from the writings considered here, it is possible to argue that there are as many creative responses to the dilemma of identity following migration for Cuban American authors as there are Cuban American texts. This serves to promote not only diversity within Cuban American literature but also within Latino/a and ethnic-American literature itself, of which the Cuban American can be considered a part.

Bibliography

Primary texts

García, Cristina (1992). *Dreaming in Cuban* (London: HarperCollins).

Obejas, Achy (1996) 'Sugarcane,' in Virgil Suárez and Delia Poey (eds.), *Little Havana Blues: A Cuban-American Literature Anthology* (Houston: Arte Público), pp. 92–94.

Pérez Firmat, Gustavo (1995) 'Bilingual Blues' in *Bilingual Blues* (Tempe: Bilingual Press), p. 28.

Secondary texts

Barradas, Efraín (1992) 'North of the Caribbean: A History of Spanish-Caribbean Literature in the United States,' in Arnold A. James (ed.), *History of Literature in the Caribbean, Vol. 1: Hispanic and Francophone Regions* (Amsterdam: John Benjamins Publishing), pp. 85–94.

Campa, Román de la (2002) *Cuba on My Mind: Journeys to a Severed Nation* (London: Verso).

Davis, Rocío C. (2000) 'Back to the Future: Mothers, Languages, and Homes in Cristina García's *Dreaming in Cuban*,' *World Literature Today*, vol. 74, no. 1, pp. 60–67.

López, Iraida H. (1995) "' ... And There is Only My Imagination Where Our History Should Be"': An Interview with Cristina Garcia,' in Ruth Behar (ed.), *Bridges to Cuba/ Puentes a Cuba* (Ann Arbor: University of Michigan Press), pp. 102–114.

Luis, William (1997) *Dance Between Two Cultures: Latino Caribbean Literature Written in the United States* (Nashville: Vanderbilt University Press).

Masud-Piloto, Felix (1996) *From Welcomed Exiles to Illegal Immigrants: Cuban Migration to the US, 1959–1995* (Lanham, MD: Rowman and Littlefield).

Ortega, Eliana, and Saporta Sternbach, Nancy (1989) 'At the Threshold of the Unnamed: Latina Literary Discourse in the Eighties,' in Asunción Horno-Delgado et al. (eds.), *Breaking Boundaries: Latina Writings and Critical Readings* (Amherst: University of Massachusetts Press), pp. 2–25.

Ortiz, Fernando (1991) 'Los factores humanos de la cubanidad,' in Isaac Barreal Fernández (ed.), *Estudios Etnosociológicos* (Havana: Editorial de Ciencias Sociales), pp. 10–30.

Pérez Firmat, Gustavo (1999 – first published 1994) *Life on the Hyphen: The Cuban-American Way* (Austin: University of Texas Press).

Pérez Firmat, Gustavo (2000) *Next Year in Cuba: A Cubano's Coming-of-Age in America* (Houston: Scrivenery Press).

Portes, Alejandro and Stepick, Alex (1993) *City on the Edge: The Transformation of Miami* (Berkeley: University of California Press).

Portes, Alejandro and Zhou, Min (1994) 'Should Immigrants Assimilate?,' *The Public Interest*, vol. 18, pp. 18–33.

Rivero, Eliana S. (1986) '(Re)writing Sugarcane Memories: Cuban Americans and Literature,' in Fernando Alegría and Jorge Ruffinelli (eds.), *Paradise Lost or Gained? The Literature of Hispanic Exile* (Texas: Arte Público), pp. 164–82.

Rumbaut, Rubén (1991) 'The Agony of Exile: A Study of Migration and Adaptation of Indochinese Refugee Adults and Children,' in F.L. Ahearn and J. L. Athey (eds.), *Refugee Children: Theory, Research and Services* (Baltimore: Johns Hopkins University Press), pp. 59–91.

Torres, María de los Angeles (1998) 'Encuentros y Encontronazos: Homeland in the Politics and Identity of the Cuban Diaspora,' in Antonia Darder and Rodolfo D. Torres (eds.), *The Latino Studies Reader: Culture, Economy and Society* (Malden, MA: Blackwell), pp. 43–62.

6

The Continuing Significance of Race and Ethnicity in the Melting Pot

Natasha Kumar Warikoo

The author is grateful for guidance and assistance on this research from Mary C. Waters, Michéle Lamont, and Prudence Carter. This research has also benefited from the support of the Multidisciplinary Program in Inequality and Social Policy at Harvard University, funded by the National Science Foundation; the National Science Foundation's Dissertation Improvement Award; and Harvard University's Minda de Gunzburg Center for European Studies Graduate Dissertation Research Fellowship, funded by the Krupp Foundation.

In this volume William Frey has documented three major demographic areas of the United States. Of the three, the *Melting Pot* includes traditional immigrant destinations like New York. These places have the highest rates of intermarriage in the country. David Fasenfest and Jason Booza in this volume come to similar conclusions about New York while analyzing U.S. demographics using smaller units of analysis. They look at Census tracts, which are typically around 4,000 people. They find that the northeast has had a decline in black-white neighborhoods and an increase in other kinds of mixed neighborhoods, such as black–Hispanic and white-Asian. (see also Alba et al., 1995; Fong and Shibuya, 2005; Frey and Farley, 1996). What does this increasing diversity of the populations of places like New York City mean for youngsters, in terms of ethnic identities and race relations? That is, how do multiethnic environments influence ethnic identities? And will living among and attending school with diverse peers lead to weaker boundaries between racial and ethnic groups? What are the mitigating factors that lead to stronger or weaker boundaries between groups, given racially diverse environments? This chapter addresses these questions, by presenting research with U.S.-born children of immigrants attending a diverse New York City school, and comparing them with similar children in a London school. I draw upon ethnographic data, 120 in-depth interviews with students in both cities, and a survey of 191 students in the two schools. The international comparison allows me to distill what is unique to the urban *American* multiethnic school environment.

The research shows that ethnic identities in New York are significant parts of daily life, both in terms of self-identities and social life; it also shows that diversity in school alone goes only so far in breaking down racial and ethnic barriers – schools need the right structures in place to promote integration. This chapter will demonstrate the strong salience of ethnicity and race for teenagers in a New York City multiethnic public high school, in contrast to a similar school in London, where race and ethnicity matter much less. The contrasting organizational structures of the schools along with structural influences outside the school – U.S. residential segregation, historical processes of racial formation, and patterns of migration – led to the continuing significance of race among the New York student population, in spite of the 'super-diversity' (Vertovec 2006) in their school. Race and ethnicity of course mattered in London as well, but not nearly as much as they did in New York.

Methodology

This research was part of a larger study on peer culture among second generation teens in New York City and London. A multi-method approach triangulates the research: ethnographic observations, a random survey with 191 teenagers, and 120 in-depth interviews with second-generation Indians and Afro-Caribbeans in both cities, white English students in London, and second generation Indo-Caribbeans in London. I spent one semester in each of two schools, one in New York and one in London. In the schools I shadowed teachers and students and wrote detailed field notes. Surveys were conducted with random groups of students in school during four heterogeneous classes (by ethnicity/race, gender, skills) in each site; they gave a sense of overall interests, attitudes, identities and backgrounds in the schools.[1] 65 per cent of survey respondents in London were second generation (U.K.-born or arrived by age 5 with foreign-born mother), as were 48 per cent in New York. Another 33 per cent in New York were first or 1.5 generation[2], as were an additional 7 per cent in London (see Table 1). Survey responses provided an overview of student backgrounds in each school as well as answers to questions on social interactions across ethnic and racial groups, facilitating the New York-London comparison.

Finally, in-depth interviews elicited explanations for identities and social groups. Interviews were conducted with two ethnic groups in both cities:

---

[1]   The survey was administered in Personal, Social, and Health Education (PSHE) classes in London, and in mixed humanities classes in New York. Although students could opt out of the survey, none in either city chose to do so. Students who were absent on the day of the survey were not included in the data.

[2]   First or 1.5 generation defined as foreign-born children arriving after age 5.

Table 1: Survey Respondents

Mean age	New York 15.8 years		London 15.1 years	
Gender	Number	Percentage	Number	Percentage
Boys	33	42	64	58
Girls	46	58	46	42
Mother's birthplace				
West Indies	30	38	12	11
India	4	5	27	24
East Africa (Kenya, Uganda)	0		7	6
Dominican Republic, Puerto Rico	10	13	0	
Morocco	0		7	6
Pakistan	0		7	6
U.S./Britain	14	18	31	28
Other	17	21	19	17
No answer	5	6	1	1
Second Generation*		48		65
First or 1.5 Generation**		33		7
Total	80		111	

*　Second generation defined as U.S./U.K.-born children with foreign-born mothers, or foreign-born children who arrived at or before age 5.

**　First or 1.5 generation defined as foreign-born children arriving after age 5.

second-generation Afro-Caribbeans and second generation Indians. In addition, in London I interviewed native white students, and in New York second-generation Indo-Caribbeans. There were twenty students of each ethnic group in each city (half girls and half boys), for a total of 120 in-depth interviews (see Table 2). Interview respondents in both cities ranged in age from 14 to 18, with the exception of one 20-year-old student in New York. In both cities, interviews lasted from 40 minutes to 90 minutes, and were subsequently transcribed.

The New York school, York High School,[3] lies on the border of Brooklyn and Queens. Median household income of its surrounding neighbourhood is $40,900[4] which is 3 percent below the U.S. median (U.S. Census 2000, Summary File 3).

[3]　Throughout this article I have changed the names of the schools, students, and teachers in the interest of confidentiality.

[4]　I have used the zip-code area for this figure.

Table 2: In-Depth Interview Subjects

		New York	London
2nd Generation			
Indians	Boys	10	10
	Girls	10	10
2nd Generation			
Afro-Caribbeans	Boys	10	10
	Girls	10	10
UK-born whites with UK-born parents	Boys		10
	Girls		10
2nd Generation Indo-Caribbeans	Boys	10	
	Girls	10	
Total: 120 Interviews		60	60

As with many urban areas (and the London school's neighborhood), the better off population of the neighborhood sends its children to parochial, private, and specialized public schools, and students from neighboring more disadvantaged neighborhoods commonly come by bus or subway to attend the school.[5] York High is quite diverse. Hispanics (42 per cent) and Asians (about 37 per cent)[6] are the largest groups at the school, but the statistics mask the internal diversity of the groups. Hispanics include significant numbers of Puerto Ricans and Dominicans as well as other Latino origin groups in smaller numbers. Asians include significant numbers of Indians, Indo-Caribbeans, and Pakistanis. Black students make up 14 per cent of the school population, and this includes African Americans and Afro-Caribbeans. Lastly, whites are 7 per cent of the school population. Hence, there is no majority ethnic group at York High School. The school is home to over 3,000 students. One-third of students are eligible for free student lunches. Finally, in the 2003–2004 school year at York, 55 per cent of students who took the Regents English exam passed it, in comparison to 66 per cent of students citywide, and in Math A (first of two math exams), 64 per cent of students passed, in comparison with 68 per cent of students citywide (NYC Department of Education School

[5]   In the 3-digit zip code area of York High School, 14.2% of K-12 students attended private or parochial schools (U.S. Census 2000, Summary File 3). Others attend alternative public high schools that have admissions criteria, such as passing an entrance exam or high grades in a particular subject.

[6]   Because school statistics count Asians together with those in the 'other' category, this figure may be slightly high.

[7]   Students in New York State are required to attain a minimum score on the Regents math and English exams in order to graduate high school, in addition to passing the required classes.

Table 3: The Schools in Comparison

		New York: York High School		London: Long Meadow Community School
Free Lunch Eligibility		34%		33%
Racial Makeup	Black (includes Afro-Caribbean, African American)	14%	Afro-Caribbean	15%
	Asian and Others (includes Indian, Indo-Caribbean, other Asians, Mixed, Native American)	37%	Indian	16%
	White	7%	White	17%
	Hispanic	42%	Mixed, Other, or Unspecified	25%
Number of Students		3,100		1,180
Exam/Graduation Results	graduation rate	44%	At least 5 A-C GCSEs	43%

Sources: U.K. Office of Standards in Education School Reports, 1998, 2004; NYC Department of Education School Report Card, 2003–2004 School Year

Report Cards 2004). [7] The school's official graduation rate is 44 per cent, although a group of 1,100 ninth grade students in 2002 dwindled to 430 twelfth grade students by 2005[8] (see Table 3). I focused my research on grades 9–11, ages 14–17.

Because I found that the majority of black students at York High were African American with U.S.-born parents, I approached a neighboring school in the same Board of Education Region, a school I call Harrison High School, to complete interviews with Afro-Caribbeans. Although not ideal, because the schools are demographically similar, this did not affect my findings. Harrison High School is less than 2 miles from York High School, and no other high schools lie between the two. Harrison High School's student body was quite similar to York High

---

[8]   The number of ninth grade students is much higher than the number of students entering the school each year, since those who don't pass enough classes remain as ninth graders, sometimes for three or even more years. Still, reported graduation rates are often inflated (Orfield, 2004).

School's in terms of ethnicity and race: 9 per cent non-Hispanic white, 26 per cent non-Hispanic black, 37 per cent Hispanic, and 33 per cent Asian and others (NYC Department of Education School Report Cards 2004). 49 per cent of Harrison's over 3,500 students were eligible for free school lunches.[9] A school administrator at York High called Harrison their 'sister school'. Many students at Harrison reported having friends at York, and vice versa.

The London school, Long Meadow Community School, sits in the northwest borough of Brent. Over 60 percent of Brent's population is of non-British origin, which is the highest percentage of minorities in all of Britain's boroughs (2001 UK Census KS06, Office of National Statistics). Brent is not the poorest London borough, but it includes a range of classes, from quite poor to quite wealthy. Its unemployment rate is almost 50 per cent greater than all of England's (2001 UK Census). Long Meadow's 1,100 students reflect the ethnic and racial diversity of the borough. No ethnic group predominates, and there is also a significant 'mixed race' population. The largest ethno-racial groups are white British students (17 per cent), Indians (16 per cent), and Afro-Caribbeans (15 per cent); still, these groups together comprise less than half the student population. One-third of Long Meadow's students are eligible for free student lunches. In terms of educational outcomes, in 2003 some 43 per cent of Long Meadow eleventh grade students attained five grades of C or above on the General Certificate of Secondary Education (GCSE) exams (the national average is 52%) (2004 OFSTED Report) (see Table 3).[10] Although Long Meadow hosts students from ages 11–18 (including a Sixth Form for ages 16–18), I focused my research on Years 10–11 and the Lower Sixth Form, which included ages 14–17, in order to coincide with the ages of my New York research.

---

[9]   A school administrator at York High School explained to me that because many students do not have a lunch period at her school, many do not bring in their free/reduced lunch form. She estimated that closer to 50% or more of York students would be eligible for free lunches, if they brought their forms in to school. She cited Harrison High School as a school with similar students but one where administrators pushed students to bring in lunch forms in order to get enough low-income forms to qualify for Title I federal school funding, which goes to the most disadvantaged schools. As a result in that year the eligibility shot up to 49%, from 28% the previous year (NYC Department of Education 2004).

[10]   The GCSE exams are the exit exams for schooling in the U.K., taken at age 16. Five C or above GCSE grades (one grade is awarded for each subject) is the minimum requirement for entering most British universities, and five A–G grades is the minimum standard for saying one has finished school 'with qualifications'.

Findings

In what follows I analyze the ethnic identities and symbolic boundaries[11] of teens at both schools. Ethnic identities are discussed through students' self-descriptions of ethnic and racial identities, British/American identities, and the meanings of those identities. Symbolic boundaries are discussed through the nature of social groups and social interactions in both schools. Finally I turn to the causes of the differences between the U.S. and Britain.

Ethnic and National Identities

In order to understand the impact of multiethnicity on ethnic and racial identities, I asked interview respondents to describe their ethnic and racial identities. Although I had categorized respondents into three categories in each city (Indian, Afro-Caribbean, and Indo-Caribbean in New York and Indian, Afro-Caribbean, and white English in London), they themselves gave myriad responses, only some of which matched the ones I used. In New York they called themselves American Indian, Punjabi, half Indian-half American, African American, black, African Jamaican, Guyanese, Muslim, West Indian, and more. Black meant African American and Afro-Caribbean; Guyanese or Guyanese/ Trini meant Indo-Caribbean (Trini being short for Trinidadian); Indian could mean parents or ancestors (in the case of Indo-Caribbeans) from India; and Spanish meant Hispanic. In London they called themselves Hindu, Asian, British Indian, Indo-British, Gujarati, Hindu Asian, black Caribbean, black, mixed race, black British, European, Caucasian, white British, Celtic, and more.

When pressed to explain what their ethnic and racial identities meant, Londoners were most likely to say they didn't know. For example, Kumar, an Indian[12] boy in London, responded to a survey question asking about his ethnic and racial identity with 'Indian'. In his interview I asked him to explain his answer:

> N: *And what does that mean to you? What does it mean to be Indian?*
> R: *I don't know, I'm just proud to be Indian.*
>
> N: *So what does that say about you, to say that you are Indian?*
> R: *Nothing. Just says that I am Indian, that's all.*

---

[11]   Lamont and Molnar (2002, p. 168) define symbolic boundaries as 'conceptual distinctions made by social actors to categorize objects, people, practices, and even time and space.'

[12]   Because almost all of the Caribbean and Indian youth I interviewed were second generation, I only indicate when someone is not second generation.

Joy, an Afro-Caribbean girl in London, told me she decided on her identity by a process of elimination from official forms, rather than a strong sense of identity:

> *N: If someone asked you what's your main identity in terms of race or ethnicity or whatever, what would you call yourself?*
> *R: ... Black Caribbean.*
>
> *N: And what does it mean to you to be Black Caribbean?*
> *R: I don't really know though. I think they ... that's why they ... like when I get the application forms I don't know which one to tick. Black Caribbean or Black British?*
>
> *N: But you choose Black Caribbean?*
> *R: Yeah.*
>
> *N: And why is that?*
> *R: Because ... I don't know. Because then sometimes I put Black British. Like there was a time I did. That's where I am from, but I don't know why I ticked Black Caribbean last time.*
>
> *N: So would you call yourself British too?*
> *R: Yeah.*
>
> *N: What does that mean to be British?*
> *R: I don't know. British Black, where I was born. Where I live. Where I plan to stay I think, and that's about it.*

Rather than having a strong sense of identity in terms of race, nationality, or ethnicity, Joy seems to try to figure out the category that 'they' expect her to choose. Her ambivalence about identity reflects London youth's general lack of emphasis on ethnic and racial identity, in contrast to their American peers.

In contrast, when I asked New Yorkers to explain their ethnic and racial identities they most commonly cited cultural aspects of ethnicity. Arlette, an Indo-Caribbean girl in New York who identified as Indian, associated her ethnic identity with positive cultural values:

> *N: What do you call your main identity in terms of your race? If someone asks you what's your race, or what's your ethnicity, what would you say?*
> *R: ... I think I am more Indian .... I like my culture ... , maybe because ... my past is really a big thing to me, where I came from and everything else. I would*

like my future children to be just like me, you know. Culture is an important part
of your life and who you are, so yeah.

N: So what does it mean to be Indian?
R: ... Maybe the way you dress, the way you act, your family life, everything.
Education wise I think you have to be, you know, in a certain family status (sic).

The association of ethnic and racial identity with culture was not limited
to Indian identity. For example, Barry, a New Yorker whose father is Afro-
Trinidadian and mother is African American, told me that his black identity
affected his style and outlook:

N: How does that make you different from people who are not black?
R: ... The different skin color, the different point of view on different subjects, you
know.

N: Give me an example of that. What things would be different? How would
your ideas be different?
R: Like ... they say this looks better and my point of view is like, "No I don't
[think so]. That would look better." And then you know I have different ideas,
different kind of, way of talking, ... different way, everything that you might have
a different way because you are white or Indian or something like that.

N: So you think people's styles are based on their race?
R: Yeah. Like, like if you go to somewhere, where like most of the Indian peo-
ple are, most of them wear the same thing. You can go to a black [area, and] most
of us wear name brands and stuff like that.

In contrast to American cultural explanations, just one London interview
respondent made reference to culture when explaining his/her ethnic identity.

In addition to ethnic and racial identities, I asked respondents about their
national identities through an interview question: *"Do you consider yourself*
American/British? What does it mean to be American/British?" As with ethnic and
racial identities, New Yorkers had stronger feelings about national identity – just
four New Yorkers said they were 'not sure' if they were American, in contrast
to 14 British interview respondents (23 per cent) saying they didn't know what
it meant to be British, or that it didn't mean anything. When asked to explain
what it means to be American/British, most on both sides of the pond said that
it meant they were born it the country, lived there, and/or were citizens of the
country. However, in the U.S. many also responded with references to the free-
doms available in U.S. society. 15 per cent made references to freedom in

American society. This finding resonates with Patterson's (2006) finding that immigrants are more likely than non-immigrants to define American freedom as having to do with 'rights' (and perhaps by extension the second generation more than children of U.S.-born parents). For example, Tina, an Indo-Caribbean New Yorker, said this:

> *N: So you think of yourself as more American?*
> *R: Yeah.*
>
> *N: What does that mean, to be American?*
> *R: ... You have your own rights, [and] freedom, because some people don't have freedom, like the people in Iraq. And I think basically [you can] do whatever you want, just don't break the law.*

Tina's association of American identity with freedom is clearly related to current events, and American government ideology about U.S. freedom in contrast to its absence in places like Iraq. Others in New York contrasted American freedom to the situation in their parents' birthplaces. For example, Jasmine, a New Yorker whose parents came from Haiti, contrasted the free speech rights in the U.S. with the possible dangers of speaking one's mind in Haiti:

> *N: Do you consider yourself American?*
> *R: Yeah.*
>
> *N: What does that mean to be American?*
> *R: ... Well to be American is, alright – like in Haiti ... you are afraid that they might end up killing you and something like that ... It's easier to have your free speech here.*

This American freedom in contrast to their parents' countries of origins was not always positive. Pradeep, a 1.5-generation Indian who had been involved with violent gangs in New York, told me that American freedom was both good and bad:

> *N: What does American mean to you?*
> *R: For me American? Freedom ... Okay freedom has like two parts, good and bad. So like in India our parents used to watch us. So we never got involved in all that stuff. But now we have freedom over here. We do like all that kinda bad stuff over here.*
>
> *N: Because you have too much freedom?*
> *R: Yeah.*

N: Why do you think your parents are more free with you right now?
R: My parents actually, they don't have time.

N: They don't have time?
R: They don't have time, because they are at work all the time. So when they come home they are, "Yeah what happened in school? Did you do your home-work?" That's all. That's it. That's all they ask.

The change in family life that came with immigration permitted Pradeep to become involved in a dangerous lifestyle (which he acknowledged wanting to change in another part of his interview), in contrast to his life as a youngster in India. Still, freedom was very much tied to American identity for Pradeep and many of his peers. They had strong feelings about American identity, as with their ethnic identities.

British youth expressed weaker feelings about national identity. When asked whether they would call themselves British, most Afro-Caribbean and Indian students in London said yes, but when pressed about what it *means* to be British most said it means having a British passport or having been born in Great Britain, but nothing more. For example, Sonia, a second-generation Indian student, told me what it means to her to call herself British:

N: Would you consider yourself British?
R: Yeah.

N: And what does that mean? What does it mean to be British to you?
R: Nothing. Just I am born here. Nothing. No, it means nothing to me.[13]

Just two interview respondents said they did not identify as British, and four more indicated they weren't sure or didn't know how to define what it means to be British. One white Londoner distanced himself from a culturally British identity that he didn't associate with:

N: Would you call yourself British?
R: I don't really like the term British …

N: Why don't you like 'British'?
R: I don't know because like, when someone says 'British' it is always like, like Union Jack [British flag] and 'God Save the Queen' [British national anthem] and stuff like that. And I don't really think that's me or any of my family because I know it's stupid.

---

[13]   Many white students had similar responses.

Jake not only doesn't identify as British, he also distances himself from cultural associations of British identity. Hence although New Yorkers had stronger feelings about ethnic and racial identities, they also associated *American* identity with more meaning than did Londoners with British identity. Ethnic and racial identities thus did not supplant national identities, but rather in both cities identities were similarly weak or strong. Next I turn to the social markers of groups in both school environments.

Social Groups at School

In this section I present the variables of difference that youth in London and New York used to categorize each other, using interview responses to the question '*If you had to describe what the different social groups are at school, what would you say they are? Who hangs out with whom?*' Rather than assume a salient boundary marker such as ethnicity, I asked youth themselves about the social groups at their schools, to elicit what boundaries they themselves see (Lamont 1992).

Sixty-six per cent of students interviewed in New York described *race* groups when asked to describe the social groups at their school, in contrast to just 20 per cent in London. In addition to using race categories to describe their school's social groups, students in New York also described the social groups by level of popularity (16 per cent) and taste groups (16 per cent), such as punks, hip-hop listeners, etc.[14] Although the New York City Board of Education compiles school statistics according to race and ethnicity categories commonly used by U.S. social scientists, students defined their race and ethnicity categories quite differently from official statistics, as mentioned earlier. They said things similar to Sanjay (below), when asked to describe the social groups at their school:

> Q: *If you had to describe what the different social groups are at school, what would you say they are? Who hangs out with whom?*
> R: *It depends. Some Punjabi people hang out with Punjabi, blacks with blacks, Spanish with Spanish. [Sanjay, Indian male]*

Like many of his peers, Sanjay interpreted a question about social groups to be about ethnicity, suggesting that ethnicity was the most salient group marker in New York.

---

[14]   Many students listed more than one type of social group, and others described groups not listed here; hence, the percentages do not add up to 100%.

Responses in London were more diffuse. Teens in London reported three main categories of social groups at school: (1) gender; (2) proximate groups – their Form Classes and what they did during lunchtime; and (3) consumption groups – tastes in music and style. Twenty-four per cent of London interview respondents named gender groups when asked about their school's social groups. When I began my research in London the gender segregation in students' social patterns struck me. When they could choose seats, inevitably boys would end on one side of the room, and girls on the other. Even students who insisted that their school didn't have social groups that separate said that students did separate by gender. For example, Vimal told me,

> N: If you had to describe the different social groups in this school, what would you say they are? Who hangs out with whom?
> R: Everyone hangs out with each other like, but mostly separated by, boys hang out with mostly boys and girls with girls.

Perhaps this separation resulted from their social groups developing at an early age in Year 7, when the class first comes together (age 11).

In addition to gender, one-third of London students described Form Classes as social groups. Form Classes spent their whole school days together from Year 7 (ages 11–12) to Year 10 (ages 14–15), when science classes became tracked and students began to take electives. Even during Year 10 students spent most of the day with peers from the Form Class, and Year 11 students still had English class with their Form Classes, which most had known since Year 7.[15] Hence, most Form Classes grew to be quite close and fond of each other, even if the occasional inevitable fights developed. One Year 11 Indian girl, Angela, explained how close her Form Class was:

> My class is like, I think it's the only class that love each other. I mean really tight. I don't know we just click. All of us just click with each other ... When we are in trouble, our class always ... stick up for us.

This closeness formed after being together for five consecutive years. Later, Angela told me that she was going to be very sad at the end of the school year, because her Form Class would be breaking up and everyone would be going their separate ways – some to Sixth Form, some to work, and some to college.

---

[15] In addition, tracked classes had about one-third of the pupils from students' Form Classes, and gym classes have all their same-gender Form Class peers.

When asked to describe the school's social groups, some used Form Classes as the unit of division, and others relayed within-class social groups. For example, Frank, a white Year 10 student, said this:

> N: *If you had to describe the different social groups at school, like who hangs out with whom, what would you say?*
> R: *... I don't really know how to explain it, but you know Jason?*

> N: *Yeah.*
> R: *Yeah his table sits like at the back. And then you got my table sitting like right next to his.*

> N: *This is in maths class?*
> R: *Yeah. And then we got all the like people who – geeks, sort of. [They] sit along near the window, near the front of the board.*

> N: *Who would that be?*
> R: *Peter, Jagdish, Bupesh, Sunil and Amarjit.*
> *And then we've got the girls' tables there, and then, like Lucy, Habiba, and Lisa would sit in the middle.*

> N: *And all the other girls at the other tables, right?*
> R: *Yeah.*

> N: *How would you describe those groups? How would you describe your group?*
> R: *My group is just the people who play football ... Depends what classroom it is. Say if it's in maths. I will probably sit with the people who play football, like Derek and John and Vimal. But if I was in a different class, like sociology, I would sit next to Jason.*

Frank's description shows that his social world at school is his Form Class – all of the students he mentions are from his Form Class. Frank bases his social group on his lunchtime activity (football), but when he sits in an elective class and all his classmates are not with him (sociology) he sits with the one student who *is* from his Form Class, Jason. I observed this seating arrangement in many elective classes – students usually sat with peers from their own Form Classes, regardless of taste preferences or ethnicity/race.

In addition to identifying with their Form Classes, students in London broke off into social groups during school breaks, according to their activities during those times – 20 per cent described lunch activities when defining the school's social groups. The entire school had two breaks during the school day, during which time all students were free to eat, play in the large school yard, sit in the

Table 4: Categories listed by interview respondents regarding school social groups[1]

	Social Groups
New York	Race (66%)
	Popularity (16%)
	Taste (16%)
London	Form Class divisions (33%)
	Gender (24%)
	Taste (24%)
	Lunchtime activities (20%)
	Race/ethnicity (20%)

Source: Interview data, n=86[2]

[1] Percentages add up to greater than 100%, because many students mentioned more than one kind of group.

[2] Although there were 120 interview respondents, due to time constraints some were not asked the questions on social groups and popularity, because preliminary interviews with a range of students addressed questions regarding school social groups and peer hierarchies. I did not include preliminary interview data in the final results.

library, or roam the school's hallways, since no classes were in session. Students' activities during breaks influenced their social groups; hence one's activity during breaks was quite important to defining one's school identity.

Finally, London students described taste groups at school (24 per cent). Abe, a 17-year-old white Sixth Form student who had moved to London from the north of England a few years prior, described the school's social groups in terms of music:

> N: *If you had to describe the different social groups at school, what would you say they are?*
> R: *You've got like … I would say you could almost separate it with like music. You've got like people that like more Americanized music like hip-hop and stuff like that. Then you've got people that like garage, proper English garage. And then you've got people who like rock music, and a couple of people that like classical music. And you probably could go to the different groups because you can obviously, you can see them even when they are wearing uniform you can still see them. People would – there is one girl I see and she wears like big boots and she has got pink hair, stuff like that. She likes rock music and there is like kind of people who wear their trousers a bit baggy even if it's uniform and stuff like that, you can see. So I'd say that's how you could separate it.*

Abe points out the congruence in London between style of dress, music tastes, and social groups. After Form Class groups, taste groupings were the most common (along with gender) groups described by London youth in interviews.

Race was significant in London in two ways. First, as in New York, some students named race groups when asked to describe their school's social groups (20 per cent). Second, race was a part of the taste categories named by 24 per cent of London youth, in that groups based on taste preferences were often racialized. For example, although many white and Indian students listened to hip-hop music (like Abe), hip-hop and R&B were seen as 'black' music, for their African American origins. On the other hand, rock and grunge music were seen as 'white' music. Grace, a Year 11 student who lives with her Nigerian mother and white English stepfather but spends a lot of time in the US with her Afro-Caribbean father, told me this:

> N: So if you had to describe the different school groups at school, what are the different groups here?
> R: It's like, there is all black in my group ... There is one mixed race person and there is one white person, but the white person ... she is more, like, you know, black. The way she behaves is like a black person, and she likes black things ... And then you have the all white girls group. It's mixed – it's got, oh you might get one black girl in it. She behaves like more like a white girl ... But then you can get white people that act like black people, black people who act like white people ...

In other words, students defined racial categories in terms of taste and behaviors, rather than by the race of individuals in the group. These socially-defined groups are labeled 'black', and 'white' *because of the cultural heritage of the genre's contents* rather than because of the members of that group, in contrast to New York, where groups were defined *by the ethnicity of the individuals in them*.

Social Interactions

Race and ethnicity were also more likely to be a barrier to social interaction among students in New York compared with those in London. In the survey, 74 per cent of London youth said they 'agree a lot' with the statement *In my school, students feel comfortable talking with students of other racial and ethnic groups.* In contrast, just 42 per cent of their New York counterparts agreed a lot. In addition, New York students were more likely to have close friends of their own ethnicity: when I asked students in interviews to name their closest friends, 82 per cent of those

Table 5: Symbolic Boundaries in Comparison

	Social Groups	'In my school, students feel comfortable talking with students of other racial and ethnic groups' Agree a Lot:	Percentage of closest friends being same ethnicity	Prefer to date own Race/Ethnicity
New York	Race (66%) Popularity (16%) Taste (16%)	42%	82%	54%
London	Form Class divisions (33%) Gender (24%) Taste (24%) Lunchtime activities (20%) Race/ ethnicity (20%)	74%	68%	35%

Sources: Survey data (n=191) and Interview data (n=86)

named in New York were of the same ethnic group, compared with 68 per cent of those named by London interview respondents.[16] Dating preferences also illustrated New York youth's stronger ethnic and racial boundaries: 54 per cent listed their own race or ethnicity in response to an open-ended question asking 'If you were to date someone, what race/ethnicity would you like him/her to be?' In contrast, just 35 per cent in London listed coethnics as a preference for dating.

The greater salience of ethnicity in New York led to same-ethnicity couples in New York who had quite distinct styles and music tastes but shared an ethnic background. For example, in New York Indo-Guyanese Tina wore pink and black converse sneakers to school every day, and black and hot pink jelly bracelets and nail polish to match, signaling her taste for punk and rock music as

[16] Individuals were equalized, so that a student who listed three best friends was weighted the same as those who listed one best friend. Because students in New York identified Indo-Caribbeans and Indians as separate social groups but African Americans and Afro-Caribbeans as one, for this analysis Afro-Caribbean-African American friendships were seen as an in-group friendship, but Indian-Indo-Caribbean friendships were counted as out-group friendships. The results are similar if Afro-Caribbeans are separated from African Americans, or if Indo-Caribbeans are grouped with Indians.

well as skateboarding, all of which she described to me in her interview. I sometimes saw Tina in the hallway with her boyfriend, who wore baggy jeans in a
hip-hop style. During her interview, I asked Tina about the boy I often saw her
with, and found out that he is Indo-Guyanese, like she is. She told me that she
likes 'punk' and 'rock' music, and dislikes 'ghetto' music, in contrast to him,
who she identified as her boyfriend. I asked Tina why she preferred rock:

> N: And so what specifically do you like about rock?
> R: I like the beat and I like that it doesn't talk about, like you know the ghetto
> music, rap, it talks about killing and about girls, and they use girls in a negative
> way. In rock music they don't do that ... I don't really like rap and hip-hop and
> all that stuff ...

Although Tina felt strongly about the portrayal of women in rap music, it
didn't seem to matter to Tina that her partner had different tastes in music:

> N: And so is your boyfriend into punk, too?
> R: He is half ... He is like, he is like both. He is both, a mixture like ghetto and
> punk ... He is like half punk and half ghetto. Like he listens to rap, but he lis-
> tens to rock.

Tina's connection to her boyfriend goes beyond their taste preferences, and she
shares her ethnicity rather than her taste preferences with her boyfriend.

When it came to ethnic markers in their style, however, New Yorkers had to
demonstrate authenticity and not fluidity. For example, Renee, a second generation Barbadian in New York, told me that those around her sanctioned her displays that seemed to contradict her 'real' ethnic identity as a Barbadian:

> N: And so do you feel like anyone ever misunderstands you based on what you
> are wearing?
> R: ... People ask why I have to wear the certain things I wear that, um like, I
> was on the street buying a soda, and this guy asked me why I'm wearing a Puerto
> Rico shirt, if I am not from Puerto Rico.

> N: So he knew you weren't Puerto Rican?
> R: Yeah.

> N: How did he know that?
> R: He used to see me around the way and he knows my mother. He used to go
> out with my cousin actually. And she said nobody from my family is from Puerto
> Rico except one person my uncle is about to marry.

This sanctioning demonstrates the salience of ethnicity in Renee's environs, where showing signs of an ethnicity other than one's own is seen as inauthentic, even if someone in the family has that heritage.

Given these stark differences between London and New York identities and symbolic boundaries, what explains them? I turn to this question next.

Influences on Symbolic Boundaries

A combination of the anonymous structure of York High School (similar to most urban public high schools in the United States); macro-structural racial division in the U.S; and the relative recency of arrival of immigrant families at York High School compared with Long Meadow, led students in New York to have identities and symbolic boundaries marked by race and ethnicity more strongly than in London. In what follows I unpack each of these factors.

School Structures

York High and Long Meadow had quite different school structures, and both were typical for their respective cities. New York City's public schools operate on a semester system, so that classes change not only every September, but also every February. There are no set 'homeroom' or 'registration' classes that travel from subject to subject together; rather, students encounter different configurations of peers in every subject. In addition, as are most, if not all public high schools in Queens, York High is vastly overcrowded, housing over 3,000 students. As a result, the school is forced to educate students in shifts, so that although individual students only attend school for seven to eight periods a day, the school runs for 12 periods a day. Some students start school before 7:30 a.m., and others finish after 4:00 p.m. Related to the overcrowding problem is the lack of morning or afternoon homeroom/registration period–students need to arrive and leave the building as quickly as possible.

Lunchtime poses a great challenge for overcrowded schools. York High School solved this problem through a staggered, optional lunch period. That is, the cafeteria served lunch starting at fourth period (starting at 9:45 a.m.) and continued through eighth period (ending at 1:35 p.m.). Surprisingly, the cafeteria was quite full during fourth period (9:40 a.m.), yet quite empty around the typical lunchtime, noon. When scheduling their classes, students could state a preference to have a lunch period or not (and have seven consecutive classes instead), but this preference was not guaranteed, and the schedule would change (along with the peers encountered during that lunch period) twice a year, with the start of each new semester in September and in February. Some students preferred to have lunch yet did not get one. More commonly, students told me they prefer to go straight through the day with no lunch break – perhaps partly because the food was not tasty, but also to avoid the social anxiety of not knowing anyone during that lunch period.

Many New York students spent their lunch period in the library when they could get in (in addition to often being closed, the library had space limitations). The library was a safe space for students who didn't share their lunch period with any friends, because they could sit quietly and read a magazine, or chat with someone who might have sat at their table. One day in the library I met Tasha, a black student who had arrived at York High School one week prior:

> Tasha wore a short denim dress and wore her hair in a short ponytail. She told me of her mixed ancestry: 'Well, I'm a mixture of everything ... I'm Dominican, Trinidadian, Jamaican, St. Lucian ...' Later in the week I bumped into Tasha in the hallway. The library was closed – as was frequently the case, because meetings were sometimes held there or teachers brought classes in to use the library's resources. Tasha asked me where she could go, since the library was closed. She insisted that she didn't want to go to the cafeteria, and seemed intimidated by the prospect. She asked Dave, the boy I was talking with when I encountered her, where he goes during his lunch period. He told her he goes to help his guidance counselor. Tasha had not yet figured out a strategy for dealing with her lunch period, although eating did not seem like a viable option to her, at least for now. [field notes, May 13, 2004]

Students were not permitted to wander the halls during their lunch period, since classes were in session during all lunch times. There was also no outdoor space for them to play in, since the schoolyard was taken up by trailers that served as makeshift classrooms, another solution to the problem of overcrowding.

Lunchtime illustrates well the dilemma faced by students in large urban high schools: how to deal with anonymity and the lack of opportunities to form strong, trusting friendships, especially with peers who on the surface seem quite different from oneself – for example from different ethnic and race groups. The structure of traditional urban public high schools in the U.S. like York High School leads to this dilemma. The large size (recall that York has over 3,000 students); class structure that mixes students up every period for seven periods, and again every September and February; no homeroom time; and limited lunch breaks, if any, together create a situation in which students have little opportunity to develop close relationships with peers with whom they don't immediately identify. Some recent immigrants from India I met at York High explained to me that when they arrived in the school other Punjabi students noticed them and approached them in the hallway, asking many questions and befriending them – it was an attempt to show them the ropes, perhaps because they knew the student would find little guidance on his or her own. In this anonymous environment, not only immigrants but also U.S.-born students gravitated towards what felt most familiar – their own ethnic and racial groups.

In contrast, in London students developed close ties to Form Class peers with whom they shared all classes during multiple years. Form Classes were groups of 25–30 students who would attend most of their classes together from Year 7 (ages 11–12) to Year 11 (ages 15–16). Even by Year 10, only math classes and up to two electives per day were not with the Form Class group. The Form Class structure led London students to bridge ethnic ties. Nathan, a white English student, explained that racial separation happened only in the early years, before students got to know peers of other groups:

> N: Would you say there are certain groups that are most popular?
> R: Nope, not at all. I'd just say it's by personality. People, sometimes people do gang together with skin color. Though I don't really find that the case very much. That's only in Year 7 when people are just getting to know each other. So in this school, you quickly learn to become friends with all, all nationalities. Or you begin to go into the group which has very few friends.

As Nathan describes, once students have a chance to form close relationships within their Form Classes, they no longer feel the urge to cling to same-race peers. Nathan's description contrasts with the New York context, in which students never have the chance to form those close bonds within a Form Class and hence more often stay in the same-race or same-ethnicity groups that Nathan observed when his class first came together, in Year 7.

In addition, Long Meadow, with just over 1,000 students, could offer lunch to all its students simultaneously. Hence the school had two school-wide breaks during the day, during which time students could eat in the cafeteria, play in the schoolyard, roam the halls, or sit in the library or computer room. Finally, the school day began and ended with a morning 15 minute and afternoon five to ten minute registration period with a Form Tutor, who usually followed the class through their years until age 16, Year 11, and was the first person to whom a subject teacher would complain about a troublesome student. During registration, the Form Tutor would take attendance, sometimes check students' school supplies, make announcements and, when necessary, reprimand students (especially at the end of the day). Every day, a different student in the class was charged with a Daily Record Sheet, which the student took to all his/her classes for teachers to write a short description of how the class had behaved that day; if a particular student was troublesome (or excelled, which was more rarely reported), his or her name would appear on the Daily Record Sheet. When bad behavior was reported on the Daily Record Sheet, individuals or the class would be made to stay after school by the Form Tutor. The Daily Record Sheet created some self-policing and peer-policing by students, especially when a teacher threatened to write negative comments on the sheet. Crucially, however, registration was a time for most classes (besides those with the strictest teachers, or days when the class got too loud) to socialize and chat among peers.

This overall structure of the Form Class and the Form Tutor contrasts with York High's highly anonymous structure. Daily registration periods and two daily school-wide breaks provided time for students to socialize outside of their classes, unlike the schedule at York in which at most students had a period for lunch to socialize, and at the least they had no non-academic time at school (those who didn't have a lunch period). These findings contrast with previous theorists who suggest that urbanization and industrialization lead to the breakup of traditional ties of birth membership (e.g., religion, ethnicity, family) and consequently lead to projects of self-realization as an individual process, achieved through consumerism (Zukin and Maguire, 2004). In fact, I found that the more atomized, bureaucratic school system in New York led to a stronger salience of ethnicity.

Macro-structures: Racialization in US Society and US Residential Segregation

The nature of race in the U.S. versus Britain influences the local dynamics of race relations and racial identity formation among youth in New York and London. Previous scholars have documented the degree to which the U.S. society is racialized, in contrast to Britain, where class defines social groups and even political mobilization more than race and ethnicity do (Gates, 1997; Katznelson, 1973; Modood, 1996). Gates points out that in Britain, for example, an Oxford University education can lead to a posh life and mutes the stigma of being black, unlike in the U.S., where racial stigma trumps class (Gates, 1997).

The United States' preoccupation with race dates back hundreds of years, to a system of slavery that racialized blacks as intellectually and otherwise inferior in order to justify their use as objects in society rather than as individuals with free agency. Even after slavery ended, legalized segregation, especially in the South, continued until just 40 years ago, and school segregation was deemed illegal by the US Supreme Court just 50 years ago in the landmark *Brown vs. Board of Education* decision. The legacy of slavery and subsequently segregation (which continues today in the form of housing discrimination and concentrated poverty experienced by poor urban African Americans) has led to distinct traditions, identities, and perceptions for black and white Americans. Omi and Winant (1986) describe processes of *racial formation* that give meanings to *race*, which operates as 'an autonomous field of social conflict, political organization, and cultural/ideological meaning' in the U.S.

Although Britain's colonial history preceded the immigration of South Asians and West Indians to Britain and black identity has been excluded from British national identity (Gilroy, 1987), the legacy of racialization is weaker in Britain. For example, racial intermarriage among blacks is much more common in Britain. Over 20 per cent of married Afro-Caribbeans (any generation) in Britain have non-black spouses (U.K. Census 2001, Focus on Ethnicity and Identity, Inter-ethnic Marriage); in contrast, of all married blacks in the U.S., less than 7 per cent are married to non-blacks (U.S. Census 2000, PHC-T-19: Hispanic Origin and Race of Coupled Households). Furthermore, Model and Fisher (2002) find that second generation Afro-Caribbean men in Britain are four times as likely to marry whites compared with their U.S. counterparts, and second generation Afro-Caribbean women in Britain are three times as likely to marry whites compared to their U.S. counterparts.

Not surprisingly, residential segregation patterns correlate with intermarriage rates, and can perhaps explain low intermarriage rates for American blacks. Urban America is significantly more segregated than London, especially for blacks (Gates, 1997; Peach, 1996). And, Afro-Caribbeans tend to live where African Americans do (Foner 2005). The highest percentage of Afro-Caribbeans in a single British Ward is 30 per cent (Peach, 1996), in contrast to the hypersegregation of the American inner city. In British schools, the percentage of blacks at schools at the 95th percentile in terms of percentage of blacks is just 20 per cent; for Asians the figure is 30 per cent (Burgess and Wilson, 2004). The greater segregation in New York relative to London means that even if students attend an ethnically diverse schools, the neighborhood lives of youth in New York are more likely to be with mostly coethnics. In contrast to blacks, Asian Indians are slightly more integrated in the U.S. compared to Britain: 8 per cent of married Asian Indian women and 10 per cent of married Asian Indian men in the U.S. are married to non-Asians, as are 6 per cent of married Indians overall in the U.K. (U.K. Census 2001, Focus on Ethnicity and Identity, Inter-ethnic Marriage; Lee, 2005). Still, overall racial division in the U.S. is much higher than in Britain.

The history of racial formations in the U.S. leads to stronger identities in New York – both ethnic and national – compared with London. Other research

(Warikoo, 2004) has documented 'cosmopolitan ethnicities' in New York – ethnicities that are both 'thick', or having strong salience in everyday life (see Cornell and Hartmann's (1998) definition of 'thick' versus 'thin' identities), as well as flexible and sometimes drawing from diverse sources (in the case of this research, both national ideology about freedom as well as parents' cultures).

Patterns of Migration

A greater percentage of New York City's population is immigrants compared to London's (36 per cent versus 27 per cent). The parent populations at my research sites reflected this difference. At Long Meadow in London, 72 per cent of survey respondents' mothers were foreign-born, in contrast to 81 per cent of mothers of York High students in New York. Although most mothers in both cities were foreign-born, just 6 per cent of London respondents were first or 1.5 generation, in contrast to 27 per cent in New York. This relative recency might account for the greater salience of ethnicity in New York, assuming that over time ethnicity's salience and segregation will decrease for an ethnic community. Many scholars have found that, for example, native language usage drops sharply between the first and second generation (Portes and Rumbaut, 2001; Rumbaut, 2004; Zhou and Bankston, 1998). Also, age of arrival matters, even among individuals of the same generation (Rumbaut, 2004). Portes and Rumbaut (Portes and Rumbaut, 2001; Rumbaut, 2005; Rumbaut, 2004) have found that immigrant children's age of arrival (and age of arrival of parents of US-born children of immigrants) influences English and native language proficiency; identification with country of origin; propensity to early childbearing; and experiences with the criminal justice system. They have also found that youth identifying as 'American' or Hyphenated American (e.g., Indian American) had spent longer in the U.S. in comparison to youth identifying with their parents' countries of origin or a panethnic label (e.g., Hispanic) (Portes and Rumbaut, 2001; Rumbaut, 2004). Similarly, U.S.-born youth and U.S. citizens in Portes and Rumbaut's study of children of immigrants in Miami and San Diego were more likely to call themselves some form of American or ethnic American, in contrast to their foreign-born and foreign-national peers, who were more likely to define their ethnic identities through their (foreign) nationality, or a pan-ethnic label. Hence the relative recency of arrival for ethnic communities in the York High School area in contrast to the Long Meadow community may partly explain the greater salience of ethnicity and race among students in New York in contrast to students in London.

Conclusion

In this chapter I have demonstrated the continuing significance of race and ethnicity in the urban American school context, even in multiethnic schools in which no ethnic or racial group predominates. Furthermore, strong racial and ethnic identities did not supplant national identities – New Yorkers in fact also had stronger feelings about 'American' identity than Londoners did about 'British' identity. The contrast with a similar schooling context in London suggests three major influences on identities and symbolic boundaries: contrasting school structures; racialized social structures in New York in contrast to London; and contrasting patterns of migration. Hence traditional immigrant destinations – what Bill Frey has termed '*Melting Pot*' areas of the United States – have, on the one hand, led to greater racial and ethnic integration, especially in schools that serve multicultural student bodies. On the other hand, however, U.S. school structures as well as the historical legacies of racial formation in the U.S. have led to the continuing significance of race and ethnicity in the everyday lives of teens.

References

Alba, Richard D., Denton, Nancy A., Leung, Shu-yin J. and Logan, John R.. (1995) 'Neighborhood Change under Conditions of Mass Immigration: The New York City Region, 1970–1990,' *International Migration Review* vol. 29, no. 3, pp. 625–56.

Cornell, Stephen E. and Hartmann, Douglas (1998) *Ethnicity and Race: Making Identities in a Changing World* (Thousand Oaks, CA: Pine Forge Press).

Fong, Eric and Shibuya, Kumiko (2005) 'Multiethnic Cities in North America,' *Annual Review of Sociology* vol. 31, no. 1, pp. 285–304.

Frey, William H. and Farley, Reynolds (1996) 'Latino, Asian, and Black Segregation in U.S. Metropolitan Areas: Are Multiethnic Metros Different?' *Demography* vol. 33, no. 1, pp. 35–50.

Gates, Henry Louis (1997) 'Black London,' *The New Yorker* (28 April and 5 May) pp. 194–205.

Gilroy, Paul (1987) *"There Ain't no Black in the Union Jack": the Cultural Politics of Race and Nation* (London: Hutchinson).

Katznelson, Ira (1973) *Black Men, White Cities; Race, Politics, and Migration in the United States, 1900–30 and Britain, 1948–68* (London, New York: Published for the Institute of Race Relations by Oxford University Press).

Lamont, Michèle (1992) *Money, Morals, and Manners: the Culture of the French and American Upper-Middle Class* (Chicago: University of Chicago Press).

Lamont, Michele and Molnar, Virag (2002) 'The Study of Boundaries in the Social Sciences,' *Annual Review of Sociology* vol. 28, pp. 167–95.

Lee, C.N. (2005) 'Interracial Dating and Marriage,' *Asian-Nation: The landscape of Asian America*, www.asian-nation.org/interracial.shtml.

Model, Suzanne and Fisher, Gene (2002) 'Unions Between Blacks and Whites: England and the US Compared,' *Ethnic and Racial Studies* vol. 25, no. 5, pp. 728–54.

Modood, Tariq (1996) 'The Limits of America: Rethinking Equality in the Changing Context of British Race Relations,' in B. Wardf and T. Badger (eds.), *The Making of Martin Luther King and the Civil Rights Movement* (New York: New York University).

NYC Department of Education (2004) "School Report Cards." (New York: NYC Department of Education).

Omi, Michael and Winant, Howard (1986) *Racial Formation in the United States: from the 1960s to the 1980s* (New York: Routledge & Kegan Paul).

Orfield, Gary (2004) *Dropouts in America: Confronting the Graduation Rate Crisis* (Cambridge: Harvard Education Press).

Patterson, Orlando (2006) 'Ordinary Liberty: What Americans Really Mean by Freedom and its Implications,' *James Bryce Lecture on the American Commonwealth* (London).

Portes, Alejandro and Rumbaut, Rubén G. (2001) *Legacies: The Story of the Immigrant Second Generation* (Berkeley & New York: University of California Press; Russell Sage Foundation).

Rumbaut, Rubén (2004) 'Ages, Life Stages, and Generational Cohorts: Decomposing the Immigrant First and Second Generations in the United States,' *International Migration Review* vol. 38, no. 3, pp. 1160–1205.

Rumbaut, Rubén G. (2005) 'Turning Points in the Transition to Adulthood: Determinants of Educational Attainment, Incarceration, and Early Childbearing Among Children Of Immigrants,' *Ethnic & Racial Studies* vol. 28, no. 6, pp. 1041–86.

Vertovec, Steven (2006) 'Super-diversity and its implications,' in *Beyond the Multiculturalism Debate: Immigrant Incorporation in the US and Britain.* London www.compas.ox.ac.uk/publications/Working%20papers/Steven%20Vertovec%20WP0625.pdf.

Warikoo, Natasha (2004) 'Cosmopolitan Ethnicity: Second Generation Indo-Caribbean Identities,' in P. Kasinitz, J. H. Mollenkopf, and M. C. Waters (eds.), *Becoming New Yorkers: Ethnographies of a New Second Generation* (New York: Russell Sage Foundation).

Zhou, Min and Bankston, Carl L. (1998) *Growing up American: How Vietnamese Children Adapt to Life in the United States* (New York: Russell Sage Foundation).

Zukin, Sharon and Maguire, Jennifer Smith (2004) 'Consumers and Consumption,' *Annual Review of Sociology*, vol. 30, pp. 173–198.

7
Living Together – Living Apart:
Racial and Ethnic Integration in Metropolitan
Neighborhoods, 1970–2000[1]

David Fasenfest and Jason Booza

Introduction

As the United States became an increasingly urban society in the period following World War II, the nature of its racial and ethnic relations in urban settings
came ever more into focus. It is evident, however, that America is presently
undergoing a major demographic and social transformation. As heretofore-
marginalized urban subpopulations grow in size and gain a larger political voice,
old issues resurrect themselves. That the politics of exclusion should generate
new political and social alliances is an old story. One need only to look back at
the successive waves of ethnic-based political machines (at first Irish, then Italian)
taking power over the last century in cities like New York and Chicago to
understand how the politics of immigration reform in the early twenty-first century is little more than old wine in new bottles.

What makes recent developments in the United States remarkable, however,
is that the new politics is being played out in the arena of race and ethnicity, not
just national origin. Cities with isolated and segregated minority populations are
now more often characterized by greater multi-ethnic neighborhoods and
boundaries are no longer as clearly drawn in the urban landscape. Analysis of the
2000 U.S. Census confirms these observations. Two reports released by the
Brookings Institute show that residential segregation for African Americans continues to decline (Glaeser and Vigdor, 2001) as American cities are becoming
more racially and ethnically diverse with the rapid growth of Hispanic and Asian

[1] A version of this paper was presented at *America's Americans: The Populations of the United States*,
co-organized by the British Library's Eccles Centre for American Studies and the University of
London's Institute for the Study of the Americas, British Library Conference Centre, May 8–9, 2006.
We thank the organizers and participants for helpful comments and suggestions.

populations (Frey, 2006). With these changes in the American landscape come many challenges; our purpose is to address the issue of how to adequately measure these changes and their impact on urban space. Many of the quantitative tools used to understand spatial relationships between groups developed from earlier research that focused on the plight of African Americans living in central cities. While these measures were well suited for a society divided into black and white America, they are inadequate for capturing and documenting the growth of the new multi-ethnic community.

In our earlier work (Fasenfest, Booza and Metzger, 2004), we explored how to capture these changes, and we developed a multiethnic neighborhood typology based on the work of Ingrid Ellen Gould that allowed researchers to examine the interaction between different population groups. Using this metric, we were able to examine how the changing face of America has manifested itself at the neighborhood level.

What follows is the second phase in a multipart study examining patterns, trends and determinants of multi-racial neighborhood transformations. Phase one, which began in 2003, provided a snapshot of increased integration in America using recently released 2000 U.S. Census Bureau data (Fasenfest, Booza and Metzger, 2004). We found that between 1990 and 2000, the ten largest metropolitan areas became more racially diverse as the number of homogeneous neighborhoods (defined below) declined and that of multi-racial neighborhoods increased. Since the initial study we have updated our findings to incorporate a broader timeframe and a larger geographic area. The research presented in this chapter assessed changes over the period from 1970 to 2000 and evaluates the 100 largest metropolitan areas in the United States. In this way we capture the urbanization that has occurred since 1970, we identify the rapid growth and subsequent impact of non-white minority populations on urban residential practices, and we monitor the structure and pattern of neighborhood racial change.

Measuring Integration

Empirical research on racially integrated neighborhoods has been undertaken for several decades. While research on the spatial relationship between racial/ethnic groups in American cities dates back to the early 1900s, it has primarily focused on segregation rather than integration. Dominated by the legacy of the Chicago School of Sociology's invasion–succession model, this research has informed our understanding of neighborhood transition patterns in the United States and was biased towards black/white definitions of spatial racial relations (Schwirian, 1983). Traditional models like the invasion–succession model were used to describe the experience of many eastern and midwestern cities during the early part of the twentieth century as waves of immigrants from Europe and migrants from America's rural South increased urban populations. With the changes instigated by the 1968 Fair Housing Act, many neighborhoods experienced decreased segregation and racial isolation so characteristic of Midwestern cities during the middle of the twentieth century (Wilson, 1987). At the same time, Southern and Western cities experienced a large influx of non-black minority groups, mainly Asians and Hispanics. Traditional models of racial segregation increasingly failed to account for all of these changes and the different residential patterns of minority groups.

There are two schools of thought defining integration, those taking the absolute approach to understanding racial composition and those who view the issue more comparatively. The absolute approach defines integration relative to a predetermined racial composition, or goal, for defining an integrated neighborhood. This is in contrast to the comparative approach that defines integration based on the particular demographic composition of the metropolitan area within which the neighborhood is located. Smith (1998) criticizes the absolute approach as being non-precise, non-grounded, arbitrary and atheoretical. However, Galster (1998) finds that the comparative approach also has its faults. The foremost problem with the comparative approach is that the metropolitan area used as the standard may itself not be integrated. For example, a neighborhood in Salt Lake City-Ogden MSA (Metropolitan Statistical Area) with only 1.0 percent of its population African American is considered integrated because 1.1 percent of the MSA is black, but a neighborhood in Mobile Alabama that is 24 percent black is considered segregated because the overall share of African Americans in the MSA is 27.4 percent.

The second problem with the comparative approach is that it is difficult to make cross-sectional and inter-temporal comparisons within and between urban areas. Not only does the demographic composition of the metropolitan area change over time (a Census definitional change), but also the spatial boundaries change as populations grow, making geographic comparison nearly impossible. To avoid the problems with the comparative approach we have chosen to employ an approach that allows us to compare neighborhoods over both space and time. Furthermore, we agree with Galster (1998) when he argues that an absolute approach implicitly assumes that integration is based upon a nontrivial degree of racial diversity.

One of our central arguments is that the increase of non-black minorities in metropolitan areas, particularly during the 1990s, means that measures of integration that rely on black/white ratios within a neighborhood no longer suffice. In order to take into account the growing role of Hispanics and Asians in neighborhood integration, we use a multiethnic neighborhood typology (Ellen, 1998). This typology categorizes neighborhoods seven ways – three for which a single race is predominant, and four reflecting the degree to which they are racially mixed or integrated. In order to keep the number of descriptive categories within reason, we have decided to classify all non-black minorities (Asians, Hispanics, Native Americans and Pacific Islanders, and those indicating 'other' race) into an omnibus 'other' category. With few exceptions, growth in the 'other' category predominantly reflects growth among the MSA's Hispanic population – though in some cases the changes are driven by growth among Asians, and in a few instances changes among both ethnic groups are important.[2]

We classify neighborhoods as homogeneous when one group predominates within the overall racial/ethnic composition. Thus, there are three types of homogeneous neighborhoods: predominantly white, predominantly black, and predominantly 'other'. If any minority group other than the predominant group represents more than 10 percent of the population in a neighborhood, we classify that neighborhood as mixed. The different threshold levels for blacks and whites, such as those defining homogeneous status (50 percent for blacks, 80 percent for whites – this is clarified in greater detail below), reflect the overall difference in the proportion of blacks and whites in the general population.

Changing National Demographics

A major factor in understanding neighborhood transformation is the demographic changes the United States has experienced between 1970 and 2000. The total population in the United States grew by over 78 million persons, with 84 percent of that growth occurring in the South and West regions (see Table 1). While the non-Hispanic white population is the major component of urban populations, the rapid growth of the Hispanic (268 percent) and Asian (571 percent) populations due to immigration, migration and natural increases are responsible for significant changes in urban neighborhood racial and ethnic composition for the fastest growth metropolitan areas (Frey, 2006). What follows are summary discussions of regional variations on this overall trend.

The Northeast only grew by 9.3 percent, which is the smallest increase of any region during the 1970 to 2000 period. Relocation due to large out-migration

[2]   To isolate each alone would call for too many categories and make the analysis cumbersome. It is certainly the case that detailed examinations of a particular MSA – like that of Los Angeles – benefits from greater differentiation of the 'other' category. To permit national trends to develop we limit ourselves to the three-way racial/ethnic classification of white, black and 'other', and their various combinations.

Table 1: Change in Population by Race and Region Between 1970 and 2000

Region	Total Population		White		Black		Hispanic		Asian	
	Total	Percent	Total	Percent	Total	Percent	Total	Percent	Total	Percent
United States	78,211,748	38.5	25,529,706	15.1	12,118,828	53.8	25,716,602	268.2	8,716,586	571.1
Northeast	4,550,363	9.3	-3,268,224	-7.7	1,766,891	40.8	3,226,978	159.2	1,916,456	944.2
Midwest	7,827,859	13.8	1,480,412	2.9	1,936,713	42.4	2,281,710	270.7	1,071,746	851.9
South	37,443,938	59.6	18,130,139	37.9	7,027,543	58.8	8,798,606	315.6	1,807,784	1,577.2
West	28,389,588	81.6	9,187,379	33.1	1,387,681	82.2	11,409,308	290.2	3,908,291	356.8

Source: US Census Bureau (2002) Historical Census Statistics on Population Totals by Race, 1790 to 1990, and by Hispanic Origin, 1970 to 1990, for the United States, Regions, Divisions, and States.

Source: US Census Bureau (2002) Demographic Trends in the 20th Century.

of residents into the South and West regions and the low birth rates in the Northeast slowed population growth. For the region there was a decline of non-Hispanic whites and low growth rates for African Americans in the urban areas. In fact, no other region had an overall decline of its white population and a smaller growth rate for blacks. While the growth rate among Hispanics in the region was almost enough to compensate for losses of its white population, the overall population change for the region trailed behind the other regions. The largest growth rate in the Northeast was among Asians, which had the second highest rate and total increase in the United States.

The Midwest region is very similar to the Northeast, with the overall population comprising black and white residents, but to a greater degree. More than half of the Midwest's population growth of over 13 percent between 1970 and 2000 is attributable to the influx of Hispanics and Asians. The white population grew by a meager 2.9 percent and the corresponding black population growth was 42.4 percent, overall the second lowest growth rate when compared with other regions. Even with the large influx of non-black minority populations as a share of overall population growth, blacks and whites still comprised 91.5 percent of the regional population in 2000 (see Appendix I).

In contrast to the Northeast and Midwest regions, the South experienced large growth rates across the board. Aided by the in-migration of blacks and whites from the Midwest and Northeast and immigration of Hispanics and Asians, the region's population grew by 59.6 percent, the second highest growth rate and highest overall population change among the regions. The largest single racial group population change in any region occurred in the South as 18 million more whites lived in that region by 2000. Hispanics experienced the second largest growth of any regional group (almost 9 million more) followed by blacks (over 7 million). By 2000, only 65.8 percent of the population in the South was comprised of whites, blacks accounted for 18.9 percent and Hispanics for 11.6 percent. It is this pattern of and magnitude of growth in the South that explains the neighborhood changes that we detail below.

The West region has undergone the most significant demographic changes in the United States since 1970. Its population was 81.6 percent higher in 2000, accounting for over one third of the total U.S. population growth over the 30-year period. The region has the second largest growth rate among whites (33.1 percent) and 53.9 percent of the overall increase was due to the increase in the Hispanic and Asian population (with almost 11.5 million more Hispanics and just under 4 million more Asians). The rate of increase in the number of blacks in the West was significant (82.2 percent) but this still translated into the smallest growth in numbers in any region.. By 2000, although 1.4 million more blacks lived in the West, they still only represented 4.9 percent of the region's population (the same as in 1970). Meanwhile, the large overall increase in the white population did not prevent the white share of the region's population decreasing from 79.6 percent in 1970 to only 58.4 percent by 2000. Hispanics accounted for 24.3 percent of regional population in 2000 and when combined with Asians accounted for one out of every three residents. The West has the largest concentration of non-black minorities in the nation and is likely to be the place where a new type of neighborhood segregation will occur in the future.

While these overall regional changes are themselves interesting, they do not tell us much about the changes within neighborhoods in the urban areas of each region. At times local changes echo the regional shifts, at others moderate overall changes mask drastic local transformations that cancel each other out when aggregating for the region as a whole. It is important to explore urban transformation as the product of patterns of residence to fully understand the changing neighborhood dynamics as a result of the race- and ethnic-based population changes.

Methodological Framework for Neighborhood Transformation

Our study uses U.S. Census data for the 100 largest metro areas in the United States in the period from 1970 to 2000. These 100 metro areas accounted for 54.8 percent of the total U.S. population in 1970 and by 2000 that figure had risen to 61.1 percent of the population, or almost two out of every three residents. They also represent the changing racial and ethnic composition of urban America as only 46.7 percent of non-whites lived in the 100 largest urban centers in 1970 growing to 74.1 percent of the non-white residents in the U.S. population by the end of the century. The findings below offer a good indication of the nature of racial integration in metropolitan areas between 1970 and 2000 for an increasingly urban society.

Units of Geography

The primary unit of geography used in our study is the 100 largest U.S. metropolitan areas according to the 2000 U.S. Census (See Appendix II). Like other geographic units of analysis, metropolitan area boundaries are redefined as new population data become available. Researchers have two options when faced with this dilemma. They can either hold boundaries constant over time (selecting an arbitrary point in time as the reference boundary) to create metropolitan area equivalencies and use corresponding data, or they can accept the boundaries as they were defined in each decennial census making general comparisons. In our earlier study (Fasenfest, Booza and Metzger, 2004), we controlled for boundary changes by using the 2000 boundary definition for 1990 and 2000 data. Our current study presents more of a challenge. First, we cannot obtain 1970 data for 2000 metropolitan boundaries because we also use census tract data in our study, and data at that level was not available prior to 1990 for geography outside of metropolitan areas. The U.S. Census Bureau did not start providing tract level data for the entire United States until 1990.[3] The other option for holding boundaries constant over time is to use 1970 boundary definitions and equate 2000 data to these boundaries since all of the data is available. This option would seriously undermine our study since we would miss out on large portions of newly urbanized areas, we would skew our results towards older neighborhoods, and we would not include the large level of suburbanization that has occurred since 1970. Faced with these two dilemmas, we choose to allow the boundaries to change over time (see Booza, Galster and Cutsinger, 2006).

We are interested in neighborhood level changes of racial composition and so we choose to use census tracts as our secondary level of analysis as proxies for neighborhoods. While tracts are larger than most neighborhoods and their boundaries change over time, census tracts are widely used in studies of racial integration and segregation because they represent the best estimate of neighborhood.[4] Census tracts, like metropolitan areas, change over time. While they are designed to be semi-permanent, the U.S. Census Bureau's Participant Statistical Area Program, which defines boundaries, has allowed for changing boundaries in order to reflect changes in population and physical characteristics of areas.[5] In keeping with other studies, we chose to accept tract boundaries based on original definitions and report our findings in terms of percentages of tracts in order to control for changes in the total number of tracts that are contained within metropolitan areas. Additionally, we further constrained our data by eliminating census tracts with fewer than 500 persons or those in which people living in group-quarters comprised 50 percent or more of the population within that tract. Our methods and subsequent results are similar to previous research on neighborhood change (see Lee and Wood, 1990; Ellen, 1998).

---

[3] As a result, we have no way of obtaining census tract level data for portions of metropolitan areas that were non-metropolitan prior to 1990. This defeats many of the objectives of our study.

[4] The U.S. Census Bureau defines census tracts as population-based statistical entities that are defined by local area and are between 1,500 and 8,000 persons in size with an optimal size of 4,000. Because census tracts are population based, their geographic size varies depending on the density of settlement (U.S. Census Bureau, 2001).

[5] The GeoLytics Neighborhood Change Database contains an additional feature that equates tract boundaries over time through the use of interpolation, but we found this approach to be highly unreliable after viewing the extreme changes that took place in a tract's boundaries in certain metropolitan areas, including those for Detroit, which are worth examining in closer detail.

Data

Our study is based on the classification of neighborhoods according to three racial/ethnic groups. Data for the study was derived from the GeoLytics Neighborhood Change Database (NCDB), which contains U.S. Census Bureau data at the tract level for the 1970, 1980, 1990 and 2000 censuses. For the purpose of this study, we only included data from the 1970 and 2000 end points. The three racial groups that were included are broadly defined as white, black and 'other' with the last category consisting of all non-white and non-black racial and Hispanic groups.[6] Based on these three classifications, we developed a race/ethnic typology of neighborhoods.

Typology

The typology that we employed in this study was first developed by Ellen (1998) and is meant to categorize neighborhoods according to distinct population distribution. The typology allocates neighborhoods into seven categories – three in which a single race is overwhelmingly present and four that are racially mixed or integrated. Therefore, neighborhoods are classified as homogeneous when one

---

[6] Consistently classifying residents by race for this time period posses significant challenges. The 2000 census brought with it changes in the categories from which race is tabulated. For the first time, individuals were able to choose (and be classified by) more than one racial category. When combined with the Hispanic/non-Hispanic classification, the result represents 126 possible mutually exclusive race/Hispanic categories, as opposed to just five such categories found in the 1970 census. Furthermore, Hispanics were not identified separately from the racial categories in 1970 because only a portion of the country was sampled at that time. This leads to comparability issues across racial categories arising because of the multi-racial designation in 2000 and lack of a Hispanic/race cross tabulation in 1970. To address this issue, we define the *white* category in 1970 (78.9 percent) as the total white population minus the Hispanic population. Unlike other studies (Massey & Denton, 1987) that were able to use the 1970 U.S. Census Bureau Summary File 4 to separate out non-Hispanic individuals by race, we did not have this option using the NCDB. As a result, the most appropriate option in our study was to subtract Hispanics from the white population only. For 2000, we defined this category as white, single-race, non-Hispanics (62.6 percent). We define the *black* category as the black population in 1970 (12.8 percent) and as the single-race, non-Hispanic black population in 2000 (13.8 percent). The 'other' category in 1970 (8.2 percent) comprises all individuals that are not classified as within the white or black categories according to the above definition. This group mainly comprises Hispanics (6.7 percent of entire 1970 population in sample) and Asians in our sample. In 2000, this category comprises the Hispanic, single-race population (15.8 percent); non-Hispanic multiracial population (2.0 percent); and the non-Hispanic, single-race populations of the following groups: American Indian/Alaska Native (0.4 percent), Other (0.2 percent), Asian/Native Hawaiian/Other Pacific Islander populations (5.2 percent).

racial group predominates with regard to the residential composition within that neighborhood. There are three types of homogeneous neighborhoods: Predominantly white, black and 'other'. The compositional requirements to be classified as homogeneous are:

- *Predominantly White*: must be at least 80 percent white and contain no more than 10 percent of any single minority group.
- *Predominantly Black*: must be at least 50 percent black and contain no more than 10 percent of any single minority group.
- *Predominantly Other*: must be at least 50 percent non-black minority[7] and be no more than 10 percent black.

When any race/ethnicity group besides the predominant group represents more than 10 percent of the population in a neighborhood, that neighborhood is classified as mixed. The typology consists of four mixed race or integrated neighborhoods identified as: Mixed White and Other; Mixed White and Black; Mixed Black and Other; and, Mixed Multiethnic. The criteria for a mixed neighborhood designation require that it consist of at least two distinct groups and where at least one minority group comprises 10 percent or more of the population. The compositional requirements are as follow:

- *Mixed White and Other*: must have between 10 percent and 50 percent of the population classified as 'other' and less than 10 percent black.
- *Mixed White and Black*: must have between 10 percent and 50 percent of the population classified as black and less than 10 percent 'other'.
- *Mixed Black and Other*: must have at least 10 percent classified as black, 10 percent classified as 'other' and no more than 40 percent white.
- *Mixed Multiethnic*: must have at least 10 percent classified as black and 10 percent classified as 'other' with 40 percent or more white.

One should not forget that this exercise is essentially a comparative static rather than a dynamic look at population change. Particular mixes of white, black and 'other' people define neighborhood types, and so those neighborhoods can change type from 1970 to 2000 for a variety of reasons; for example, an

---

[7] As we have stated, the term 'non-black minority' includes any combination of Hispanic, Asian, Native American and 'other' races in 2000. Native Americans and persons of 'other' races constitute less than 0.6 percent of our sample and these groups are not present in large enough concentrations in our 100 metropolitan areas to impact on our typology. When discussing 'Predominantly Other' neighborhoods, we are effectively referring to concentrations of either Hispanics or Asians (or on occasion both).

Table 2: Neighborhood Typology for All 100 Metropolitan Areas, 1970–2000

	1970		1980		1990		2000		Change		
	Total	Percent	Total	Percent	Total	Percent	Total	Percent	Total	Percent of Type	Percent of Total
Homogenous											
Predominantly White	18,585	75.4	15,398	53.1	13,867	43.2	11,707	30.4	-6,878	-37.0	-45.0
Predominantly Black	2,862	11.6	3,095	10.7	3,302	10.3	3,118	8.1	256	8.9	-3.5
Predominantly Other	134	0.5	1,230	4.2	1,973	6.1	4,014	10.4	3,880	2895.5	9.9
Total		87.5%		68.0		59.6%		48.9			-38.6%
Mixed											
Mixed, white and other	251	1.0	4,501	15.5	6,557	20.4	10,518	27.3	10,267	4090.4	26.3
Mixed, white and black	2,694	10.9	2,432	8.4	2,822	8.8	2,268	5.9	-426	-15.8	-5.0
Mixed, black and other	35	0.	1,385	4.8	2,053	6.4	3,905	10.1	3,870	11057.1	10.0
Mixed, multiethnic	97	0.4	949	3.3	1,557	4.8	2,969	7.7	2,872	2960.8	7.3
All Neighborhoods	24,658	100.0	28,990	100.0	32,131	100.0	38,499	100.0	13,841	56.1	0.0

influx of one or another group can cause the balance to change. The purpose of this study is not to explain these changes but to offer a description of how America's neighborhoods have changed.

Evaluating the changes in neighborhood type according to the distribution of the number of residents of different racial and ethnic origins within the neighborhood warrants some cautionary comments. This evaluation focuses on the what, not the why, of residential patterns. Furthermore, on some level, these designations into neighborhood type are very dependent on the statistical artifact of population levels and densities. However, we can and should use the patterns described below as instructive of some key dimensions of U.S. urban society as an increasingly multi-cultural and multi-racial society.

National Patterns of Neighborhood Transformation

The face of U.S. urban areas has certainly changed over 30 years. Even though cities in 1970 had large numbers of non-white residents, almost nine out of every ten people lived in communities characterized as racially or ethnically homogeneous. Furthermore, urban America was predominantly the home of black and white Americans. Over the three decades that followed, the combination of large population shifts, a massive influx of new residents, and changing residential patters mean that less than one in two residents now live in these homogeneous communities. Instead, people are living in closer proximity to people of other races or ethnic origins, though the very large influx of mostly Hispanic residents has resulted in large numbers of predominantly Hispanic neighborhoods. But unlike whites or blacks before them, this increase has also brought with it a larger number of Hispanics (and at times Asians) living among whites and blacks.

Nationally, there was a dramatic decrease in the percentage of neighborhoods classified as homogeneous. As represented in Table 2, 87.5 percent of all neighborhoods in 1970 were predominantly black, 'other' or most often white. By 2000, this overall classification had dropped to 48.9 percent of all neighborhoods, signifying that metropolitan America had become more diverse. The decline in homogeneous neighborhoods over these three decades is attributable to the decline in the number of predominantly white neighborhoods, which fell from 75.4 percent of all neighborhoods in 1970 to only 30.4 percent by 2000. This represents the largest single change (positive or negative) for any neighborhood type. There was a similar but not so dramatic decline in those neighborhoods classified as predominantly black. Over this same period, however, predominantly 'other' neighborhoods increased from less than 1 percent of the total to 10.4 percent of all neighborhoods by 2000. More diverse neighborhood types replaced homogeneous neighborhoods in the thirty-year period. For the most part those neighborhoods formerly classified as predominantly white or black were replaced by predominantly white/other, black/other and multiracial mixed neighborhoods.

Heterogeneous neighborhoods in U.S. metropolitan areas increased to 51 percent of all neighborhoods by 2000. Of those, white/other neighborhoods had the largest increase of any neighborhood type from a barely existent 1.0 percent in 1970 to 27.3 percent of all neighborhoods by 2000, a drastic increase in the spatial proximity between whites and 'other' groups (Hispanics and Asians). We should recall that the traditional indicator of racial integration measures the degree to which whites and blacks live in close proximity, and these neighborhoods have actually declined in percentage terms between 1970 and 2000. In 2000, less than 6 percent of all neighborhoods could be designated as 'integrated' when considering blacks and whites only.

While other measures, like the index of dissimilarity, show increased interaction between blacks and whites across all neighborhood types (Iceland, Weinberg and Steinmetz, 2002), the number of neighborhoods in which these two groups actually share space is declining. Where, then, are black and whites living? Table 2 shows that blacks, like whites, are more likely to live with 'other' minority groups. Black/other neighborhoods accounted for 10.1 percent of all neighborhoods by 2000. Finally, blacks and whites, if living together, are more likely to live in multiracial neighborhoods. By 2000 almost 8 percent of all neighborhoods were classified as mixed, multiethnic.

Traditional measures of integration, focusing on whether whites and blacks live together, must be understood in terms of new definitions of integrations. No longer is the appropriate indicator exclusively a question of racial balance, but we must consider that ethnicity plays an increasingly important role in patterns of integration. While this may appear to be a positive change, a look at the disparate pattern across regions reveals once again that aggregation often hides as much as it reveals.

Regional Neighborhood Transformations

Much as the overall gains and the structure of changes in the U.S. population give way to different stories of increases and decreases when looking at each region in broad terms (and, as Frey in this volume demonstrates, give way to different narratives underlying each regional change), so do patterns of neighborhood change by region offer us different pictures of how these regions' urban spaces are being transformed. We now examine the changing neighbor-hood structure within each region in turn to highlight these differences.

West Region

The West experienced the most dramatic change of any region in the country. However, the pendulum of diversity swung from a situation in which most neighborhoods were predominantly white in this region in 1970, to one char-acterized by large numbers of predominantly 'other' neighborhoods. At the start of our period 81.6 percent of all neighborhoods were predominantly white, rep-resenting the largest percentage among all the regions in the United States. Metropolitan areas like Orange County, CA PMSA had over 99 percent of its neighborhoods predominantly white. By 2000, the share of predominantly white neighborhoods in the West dropped to 8.1 percent, the largest share change of any neighborhood type in any of the region. By contrast, the second largest change, this time growth, for any category occurred among predominantly 'other' neighborhoods in the West, increasing from 3.8 percent of all neighbor-hoods to 50.9 percent by 2000. During this period predominantly black neigh-borhoods became effectively nonexistent (only 0.1 percent were so designated within the region in 2000).

The consequence of the decline of predominantly white neighborhoods is the increase of heterogeneous neighborhoods, especially for white/other neighbor-hoods that experienced the largest share growth of any category in any region with an increase to 47.1 percent of the total by 2000. Metropolitan areas like Las Vegas, Seattle, Tucson and Ventura went from less than 4 percent white/other in 1970 to over 64 percent by 2000. The influx of Asians and Hispanics to these metropolitan areas resulted in the integration of predominantly white neighbor-hoods. At the same time, this rapid influx led to the creation of predominantly 'other' neighborhoods in the Ventura and Tucson metropolitan areas.

The other significant change among heterogeneous neighborhoods occurred for those classified as white/black and black/other neighborhoods. In 1970, the West had the smallest percentage of white/black neighborhoods in the country. This is not surprising since they also had the total smallest black population (in both total numbers and as a percent of the total). More surprising perhaps is the fact that these white/black mixed neighborhoods were not located in major metropolises, but in secondary metro areas like Riverside-San Bernardino (n=1), Seattle (n=1) and Portland (n=2).

Corresponding to the effective disappearance of black/white neighborhoods is the rise of black/other neighborhoods. Those metropolitan areas with sizable black populations were more likely than other areas to experience the decline of predominantly black neighborhoods and the creation of black/other neighborhoods because of the influx of Asians and Hispanics migrating into these areas. Metropolitan areas like Los Angeles, Oakland, Stockton and Vallejo all had shares of black/other neighborhoods above 20 percent by 2000 and, with the exception of Los Angeles, they had no predominantly black or black/white neighborhoods.

The growth of the Asian and Hispanic population in the Western region since 1970 has heralded the decline of homogeneous white and black neighborhoods through integration as well as the rise of predominantly 'other' neighborhoods. Given the population growth of both of these minority groups, and given the common belief that many western metro areas are multiethnic, we note that the absence of multiracial neighborhoods is surprising when compared to metropolitan areas in other regions. In 1970, 1.5 percent of all neighborhoods in the West were considered multiracial, the highest percentage of any region. San Francisco, Stockton and Oakland had the largest share of multiracial neighborhoods in the country. For reasons that have yet to be determined, these shares either barely grew by 2000, or else they declined in places like Stockton and San Francisco metropolitan areas.

Overall, these changes point to increased integration, especially between whites and non-black minorities, yet other changes may signify that the West is going to become the new segregated region of the country as a result of the unprecedented growth of predominantly 'other' neighborhoods. In the Western region, fully one in four neighborhoods was predominantly 'other' by 2000, and blacks and whites were less likely to live with one another and more likely to live with Hispanic and Asians through the infusion of these groups into formerly white and black areas. Perhaps the fact that in the West few people live in multiracial neighborhoods is an indication of new forms of segregation. Whereas in 1970 the West had the highest percentage of neighborhoods that were considered multiracial, by 2000 that had fallen to represent the smallest percentage in any region; more traditionally segregated regions like that of the Midwest had been surpassed by the West.

South Region

Historically, metropolitan areas in the South region have had large concentrations of African American residents. In fact, the South accounted for 53 percent of all blacks living in the United States in 1970, and this percentage grew to 55 percent by 2000. The persistence and growth of the African American population helps explain the prevalence of predominantly black and mixed white/black neighborhoods in urban centers of this region. However, the large concomitant increase in the Hispanic population within the South has meant that many neighborhoods have become more multiracial. In contrast to the West, non-black minority groups like Hispanics live among other racial and ethnic populations and not within homogeneous Hispanic communities, resulting in more multi-group integration rather than the segregation we find in the West.

In 1970, the South led the nation with the largest percentage of predominantly black neighborhoods (16.8 percent), the lowest percentage of predominantly white neighborhoods (66.5 percent) and, perhaps most important for our analysis, the largest percentage of white/black neighborhoods (16.4 percent). In 1970, two thirds of neighborhoods in the South were predominantly white and the other third were either predominantly black or white/black; Asian and Hispanic residents were nearly nonexistent. By 2000 this landscape had changed. Predominantly white neighborhoods had declined drastically, the second largest decline among this classification after the change in the West, mainly as a result of the influx of Hispanics into the region. The growth of the Hispanic population has had much less of an impact on predominantly black neighborhoods, whose number declined only slightly. No predominantly 'other' neighborhoods existed in the South in 1970, but by 2000 there were 784, accounting for 6.9 percent of all neighborhoods. These homogeneous neighborhoods were located mainly in the Miami, El Paso, Houston and San Antonio metropolitan areas, all of which are known as both historic centers of Hispanic culture and also for the rise in the Hispanic population during the last three decades of the twentieth century. In general, homogeneous neighborhoods in the South declined as a percentage of all neighborhoods; but as we have shown this overshadows the emergence of predominantly 'other' neighborhoods in the region, a pattern similar to that in the West.

The number of the heterogeneous neighborhoods white/other and black/other also increased in the South owing to the growth of the Hispanic population. While the overall changes in these classifications were not as large as they were for other regions, the gain was still significant. Like predominantly 'other' neighborhoods in the South, there were no black/other neighborhoods in 1970. There were 1,103 in the South by 2000, mostly in the Washington DC, Houston and Dallas metropolitan areas, urban centers with historically large black populations that experienced a large influx of Hispanics. The other mixed neighborhood type involving black residents, white/black, declined in the South much as it did in other regions. However, the decline was not the same across the board. Metropolitan areas along the Atlantic coast, including places like

Charleston, Columbia, Raleigh-Durham and Richmond, increased their share to above 30 percent of all neighborhood types as they experienced smaller growth rates among Hispanics.

While the decline of white/black neighborhoods in the South is important, the most telling story to come out of the South is the growth of multiracial neighborhoods. The growth of non-black minority populations in other regions witnessed a residential pattern where these groups lived in previously black or white communities, and led to the growth among white/other and black/other neighborhood classifications (this did occur in the South, but not to the degree we see in the Northeast and West). Instead, the South experienced a rapid increase in the number of multiracial neighborhoods increasing from less than 1 percent of the total in 1970 to over 12 percent by 2000, representing the largest increase in this category within any region. We speculate that this is because of the large share of white/black neighborhoods that already existed in 1970 in the South and Hispanics arriving into the region and moving into these already integrated neighborhoods.

Midwest Region

Similar to the South, the Midwest was largely defined by homogeneous black and white neighborhoods. The Midwest experienced the smallest change among neighborhood categories between 1970 and 2000, though these changes are significant on their own. In 1970, 91.7 percent of all neighborhoods were homogeneous, exclusively white or black. By 2000, this figured had dropped to 67.6 percent but there was a small overall increase in predominantly 'other' neighborhoods appearing by 2000, mainly in the metropolitan areas of Chicago and Milwaukee. This growth of predominantly 'other' neighborhoods was the smallest of any region. Furthermore, the decline of predominantly white neighborhoods was also the smallest of any region and, unlike other regions, predominantly black neighborhoods increased only slightly as a share of all neighborhoods. This trend was not consistent across the region as a whole with highly segregated metropolitan areas like Detroit, St. Louis and Cleveland actually experiencing an increase in the share of predominantly black neighborhoods in their urban areas. Overall, nine out of every ten neighborhoods were homogeneous in 1970 and by 2000 this dropped to only seven in every ten.

The dominance of homogenous neighborhoods in the Midwest reflects the fact that it had the smallest percentage of neighborhoods that were classified as white/other or black/other. By 2000 only 15.2 percent of neighborhoods in this region were white/other and 4.5 percent were black/other. Indeed, white/black neighborhoods (6.7 percent of the total) were more common in the Midwest than were black/other neighborhoods. In the Midwest, Hispanics and Asians were more likely to integrate into white neighborhoods than black neighborhoods.

The final evidence of continued residential segregation in the Midwest is the small growth of multiracial neighborhoods. Similar to the Northeast and South, only 0.1 percent of all neighborhoods were multiracial in 1970. However, by 2000, the other regions had appreciable gains while the Midwest did not. This is partially due to the fact of lower growth rates of groups like Hispanics and Asians in the Midwest. However, even small growth in the numbers of non-black minorities, outside of traditional centers of Hispanic or Asian concentrations like Chicago, is not enough to explain this difference. When considered as a whole, the Midwest is a region largely characterized by distinct black and white neighborhood residential patterns, as was much of the U.S. in 1970. However, while other regions have experienced the emergence of new patterns of neighborhood classification as a result of the growth of their non-black minority populations, the Midwest has largely been untouched by this trend.

Northeast Region

The changes that occurred in the Northeast are much less dramatic than those that occurred in the West and Midwest, but have similarities to both. Like the Midwest, the Northeast has historically been divided between black and white neighborhoods but by 2000 the region had taken on a more heterogeneous look, similar to the one in the West, with the growth in its Asian and Hispanic populations. Homogeneous neighborhoods declined rapidly in the 30-year period. Predominantly white neighborhoods declined dramatically, with a smaller overall decline among predominantly black neighborhoods. As we saw in the South and West regions, the number of predominantly 'other' neighborhoods increased, but mainly centered around the Jersey City and New York metropolitan areas.

Of interest in the Northeast is the significant growth of white/other and black/other neighborhoods, reflecting the second largest and largest growth rates in the nation respectively. Like in the West, white/other neighborhoods increased from less than 1 percent in 1970 to over 22 percent in 2000. The growth mainly occurred in the 'megapolitan' corridor of the New York, Boston, Bergen-Passaic and Jersey City metropolitan areas. In many cases, these new neighborhoods represent the influx of Hispanic and Asian residents. The story is very similar for black/other neighborhoods, which grew significantly in these same metropolitan areas. Unlike the Midwest, where Asians and Hispanics were likely to integrate white neighborhoods only, we find increases for these new arrivals in traditionally black neighborhoods as well as white, increasing the level of over-all integration in this region. As a result of the more diverse residential experi-ence of these new arrivals over 30 years, the Northeast had the second largest percentage of multiracial neighborhoods at the end of the century. This neigh-borhood category grew from 0.1 percent of all neighborhoods in 1970 to 6.7 percent by 2000, mainly due to the increase in the number of this neigh-borhood type within the metropolitan areas of New York and Philadelphia.

Conclusion

The evidence we have outlined confirms what has been well rehearsed in discus-sions of changes in the U.S. population but also raises some new considerations as we move to a much more ethnically and racially diverse society. We confirm, not surprisingly, that the large influx of Hispanic (and to some degree Asian) res-idents in our urban centers has altered the social landscape in urban America. Regional variation notwithstanding, the result has been a greater tendency for white and black Americans to live in increasingly diverse communities. Homogeneous patterns of residence, where people remained in communities populated predominantly by others of the same race, have given way to hetero-geneous neighborhoods in which both whites and blacks live with Asians and Hispanics in increasing numbers.

These results also raise some new questions about how we understand the nature of neighborhood residential patterns. Heretofore, concerns about integra-tion defined as the degree to which a community experiences increasing black and white residential proximity must be reconsidered. We may draw negative conclusions from the fact that the incidence of blacks and whites living within the same neighbor has apparently declined, but this misses an important change. Each group is being exposed to (in general terms – there are some regional dif-ferences to which we shall return momentarily) a more diverse experience as a result of the influx of the Hispanic population into their communities. As a national trend, we might suggest that the question for the future is not how blacks and whites will manage to live together, but what happens as both blacks and whites interact in more diverse and complex communities.

Even as the national trends give us pause about the meaning of integration and some hope that we have entered an era of greater residential diversity, the regional patterns reveal that in some cases segregation has intensified. In some regions Hispanics have only moved into communities with residents like them-selves and, even as homogeneous white or black communities are in decline, a new form of ethnic segregation is taking root. In others the increased diversification is uneven: Hispanics tend to move into black neighborhoods or into white neighborhoods only (and without further analysis we can only speculate on whether and when economic considerations determine which of these two patterns dominates). Finally, in some regions the patterns of racial segregation are so entrenched that over the three decades little changed or there has even been an increase in the number of predominantly black or white neighborhoods.

Clearly, much still needs to be done. On some level the sheer scale of immigration, relocation and natural rates of increase have meant significant changes in the dynamics of racial and ethnic residential patterns. At the same time, old patterns reflecting historical forces still need to be changed – perhaps through legislation, perhaps through increased economic or political activity. What is clear is that change is happening, perhaps at an uneven pace and with different outcomes. But we are confident that the urban landscape in the next 30 years will change much more dramatically than we have seen for the past 30 years.

Bibliography

Booza, J., Galster, G., and Cutsinger, J. (2006) 'Where Did They Go? The Decline of Middle-Income Neighborhoods in Metropolitan America,' *The Brookings Institution – Living Cities Census Series* (June).

Ellen, I. (1998) 'Stable Racial Integration in the Contemporary United States: An Empirical Overview,' *Journal of Urban Affairs* vol. 20, no. 1, pp. 27–42.

Fasenfest, D., Booza, J., and Metzger, K. (2004) 'Living Together: A New Look at Racial and Ethnic Integration in Metropolitan Neighborhoods, 1990–2000,' *The Brookings Institution – Living Cities Census Series* (April).

Frey, W. (2006) 'Diversity Spreads Out: Metropolitan Shifts in Hispanic, Asian, and Black Populations Since 2000,' *The Brookings Institution – Living Cities Census Series* (March).

Galster, G. (1998) 'A Stock/Flow Model of Defining Racially Integrated Neighborhoods,' *Journal of Urban Affairs*, vol. 20, no. 1, pp. 43–51.

Glaeser, E. and Vigdor, J. (2001) 'Racial Segregation in the 2000 Census: Promising News,' *The Brookings Institution – Survey Series* (April).

Iceland, J., Weinberg, D., and Steinmetz, E. (2002) 'Racial and Ethnic Residential Segregation in the United States: 1980–2000,' *U.S. Census Bureau – Census 2000 Special Reports* (August).

Lee, B. and Wood, P. (1990) 'The Fate of Residential Integration in American Cities: Evidence for Racially Mixed Neighborhoods,' *Journal of Urban Affairs*, vol. 12, no. 4, pp. 425–36.

Massey, D. and Denton, N. (1987) 'Trends in the Residential Segregation of Blacks, Hispanics, and Asians: 1970–1980,' *American Sociological Review*, vol. 52, no. 6, pp. 802–825.

Schwirian, K. 'Models of Neighborhood Change,' *Annual Review of Sociology*, vol. 9, pp. 83–102.

Smith, R. (1998) 'Discovering Stable Racial Integration,' *Journal of Urban Affairs*, vol. 20, no. 1, pp. 1–5.

U.S. Census Bureau (2001) 'Census 2000 Summary File 1 Technical Documentation.'

U.S. Census Bureau (2002) 'Historical Census Statistics on Population by Race, 1790 to 1990, and by Hispanic Origin, 1970 to 1990, for the United States, Regions, Divisions, and States.'

U.S. Census Bureau (2002) 'Demographic Trends in the 20th Century.'

Wilson, W. (1987) *The Truly Disadvantaged* (Chicago, IL: University of Chicago Press).

Appendix 1: Population by Race and Region Between 1970 and 2000

Region	Total population 1970	Total population 2000	White (non-Hispanic) 1970	%	White (non-Hispanic) 2000	%
United States	203,210,158	281,421,906	169,023,068	83.2	194,552,774	69.1
Northeast	49,044,015	53,594,378	42,595,486	86.9	39,327,262	73.4
Midwest	56,564,917	64,392,776	50,905,719	90.0	52,386,131	81.4
South	62,792,882	100,236,820	47,797,655	76.1	65,927,794	65.8
West	34,808,344	63,197,932	27,724,208	79.6	36,911,587	58.4

Region	Black 1970	%	Black 2000	%	Hispanic 1970	%	Hispanic 2000	%
United States	22,539,362	11.1	34,658,190	12.3	9,589,216	4.7	35,305,818	12.5
Northeast	4,332,990	8.8	6,099,881	11.4	2,027,109	4.1	5,254,087	9.8
Midwest	4,563,020	8.1	6,499,733	10.1	842,822	1.5	3,124,532	4.9
South	11,954,149	19.0	18,981,692	18.9	2,788,090	4.4	11,586,696	11.6
West	1,689,203	4.9	3,076,884	4.9	3,931,195	11.3	15,340,503	24.3

Region	Asian 1970	%	Asian 2000	%
United States	1,526,410	0.8	10,242,996	3.6
Northeast	202,970	0.4	2,119,426	4.0
Midwest	125,808	0.2	1,197,554	1.9
South	114,623	0.2	1,922,407	1.9
West	1,095,320	3.1	5,003,611	7.9

Source: US Census Bureau (2002) Historical Census Statistics on Population Totals By Race, 1790 to 1990, and By Hispanic Origin, 1970 to 1990, for the United States, Regions, Divisions, and States.
Source: US Census Bureau (2002) Demographic Trends in the 20th Century.

Appendix 2: Metropolitan Areas Ranked by Total Population, 2000

Rank	Metropolitan Area	Total Population in 2000
1	Los Angeles-Long Beach, CA PMSA	9,519,338
2	New York, NY PMSA	9,314,235
3	Chicago, IL PMSA	8,272,768
4	Philadelphia, PA-NJ PMSA	5,100,931
5	Washington, DC-MD-VA-WV PMSA	4,923,153
6	Detroit, MI PMSA	4,441,551
7	Houston, TX PMSA	4,177,646
8	Atlanta, GA MSA	4,112,198
9	Dallas, TX PMSA	3,519,176
10	Boston, MA-NH PMSA	3,406,829
11	Riverside-San Bernardino, CA PMSA	3,254,821
12	Phoenix-Mesa, AZ MSA	3,251,876
13	Minneapolis-St. Paul, MN-WI MSA	2,968,806
14	Orange County, CA PMSA	2,846,289
15	San Diego, CA MSA	2,813,833
16	Nassau-Suffolk, NY PMSA	2,753,913
17	St. Louis, MO-IL MSA	2,603,607
18	Baltimore, MD PMSA	2,552,994
19	Seattle-Bellevue-Everett, WA PMSA	2,414,616
20	Tampa-St. Petersburg-Clearwater, FL MSA	2,395,997
21	Oakland, CA PMSA	2,392,557
22	Pittsburgh, PA MSA	2,358,695
23	Miami, FL PMSA	2,253,362
24	Cleveland-Lorain-Elyria, OH PMSA	2,250,871
25	Denver, CO PMSA	2,109,282
26	Newark, NJ PMSA	2,032,989
27	Portland-Vancouver, OR-WA PMSA	1,918,009
28	Kansas City, MO-KS MSA	1,776,062
29	San Francisco, CA PMSA	1,731,183
30	Fort Worth-Arlington, TX PMSA	1,702,625
31	San Jose, CA PMSA	1,682,585
32	Cincinnati, OH-KY-IN PMSA	1,646,395
33	Orlando, FL MSA	1,644,561
34	Sacramento, CA PMSA	1,628,197
35	Fort Lauderdale, FL PMSA	1,623,018
36	Indianapolis, IN MSA	1,607,486
37	San Antonio, TX MSA	1,592,383

38	Norfolk-Virginia Beach-Newport News, VA-NC MSA	1,569,541
39	Las Vegas, NV-AZ MSA	1,563,282
40	Columbus, OH MSA	1,540,157
41	Milwaukee-Waukesha, WI PMSA	1,500,741
42	Charlotte-Gastonia-Rock Hill, NC-SC MSA	1,499,293
43	Bergen-Passaic, NJ PMSA	1,373,167
44	New Orleans, LA MSA	1,337,726
45	Salt Lake City-Ogden, UT MSA	1,333,914
46	Greensboro–Winston-Salem–High Point, NC MSA	1,251,509
47	Austin-San Marcos, TX MSA	1,249,763
48	Nashville, TN MSA	1,231,311
49	Providence-Fall River-Warwick, RI-MA MSA	1,188,613
50	Raleigh-Durham-Chapel Hill, NC MSA	1,187,941
51	Hartford, CT MSA	1,183,110
52	Buffalo-Niagara Falls, NY MSA	1,170,111
53	Middlesex-Somerset-Hunterdon, NJ PMSA★	1,169,641
54	Memphis, TN-AR-MS MSA	1,135,614
55	West Palm Beach-Boca Raton, FL MSA	1,131,184
56	Monmouth-Ocean, NJ PMSA★	1,126,217
57	Jacksonville, FL MSA	1,100,491
58	Rochester, NY MSA	1,098,201
59	Grand Rapids-Muskegon-Holland, MI MSA	1,088,514
60	Oklahoma City, OK MSA	1,083,346
61	Louisville, KY-IN MSA	1,025,598
62	Richmond-Petersburg, VA MSA	996,512
63	Greenville-Spartanburg-Anderson, SC MSA	962,441
64	Dayton-Springfield, OH MSA	950,558
65	Fresno, CA MSA	922,516
66	Birmingham, AL MSA	921,106
67	Honolulu, HI MSA	876,156
68	Albany-Schenectady-Troy, NY MSA	875,583
69	Tucson, AZ MSA	843,746
70	Tulsa, OK MSA	803,235
71	Ventura, CA PMSA	753,197
72	Syracuse, NY MSA	732,117
73	Omaha, NE-IA MSA	716,998
74	Albuquerque, NM MSA	712,738
75	Tacoma, WA PMSA	700,820
76	Akron, OH PMSA	694,960
77	Knoxville, TN MSA	687,249

78	El Paso, TX MSA	679,622
79	Bakersfield, CA MSA	661,645
80	Allentown-Bethlehem-Easton, PA MSA	637,958
81	Gary, IN PMSA	631,362
82	Harrisburg-Lebanon-Carlisle, PA MSA	629,401
83	Scranton–Wilkes-Barre–Hazleton, PA MSA	624,776
84	Toledo, OH MSA	618,203
85	Jersey City, NJ PMSA	608,975
86	Baton Rouge, LA MSA	602,894
87	Youngstown-Warren, OH MSA	594,746
88	Springfield, MA MSA	591,932
89	Sarasota-Bradenton, FL MSA★	589,959
90	Wilmington-Newark, DE-MD PMSA	586,216
91	Little Rock-North Little Rock, AR MSA	583,845
92	Ann Arbor, MI PMSA	578,736
93	McAllen-Edinburg-Mission, TX MSA	569,463
94	Stockton-Lodi, CA MSA	563,598
95	Charleston-North Charleston, SC MSA	549,033
96	Wichita, KS MSA	545,220
97	New Haven-Meriden, CT PMSA	542,149
98	Mobile, AL MSA	540,258
99	Columbia, SC MSA	536,691
100	Vallejo-Fairfield-Napa, CA PMSA	518,821

★ These metropolitan areas were excluded from the analysis because comparable areas did not exist in 1970.

8
Integrating New Americans

Bill Ong Hing

Introduction

Every day the people of the United States are reminded that their country is a land of immigrants. Most Americans need only walk outside their front door and travel to work to notice the diverse ethnic backgrounds, languages, cultures, customs, and foods that make up America. The 1965 amendments to the nation's immigration selection system, refugee policies, family ties, economic opportunities, and political tensions abroad have all come together to fuel the increased diversity that immigrants and refugees have brought to the United States in the last forty years.

The reaction to newcomer diversity is itself diverse. Many native-born Americans welcome the economic, social, and cultural contributions that new Americans bring, while others fear or even resent the social and economic impact of new arrivals. For some native-born, the reaction varies, depending on the particular immigrant or refugee group considered. Still others may be concerned about being overwhelmed by too many newcomers. A more negative or hostile reaction may also be forthcoming when native-born Americans perceive newcomers as unwilling to learn English or to adopt 'American' customs or values.

Immigrants and refugees themselves have different reactions to their new environment. They are grateful to be in the United States and appreciate the opportunities available to them. Many seek out opportunities to learn English, to learn about their new country, and to participate actively in civic life. Others are overwhelmed by their new foreign environment (especially those refugees who may be suffering from post traumatic stress) and fall back on the comfort or familiarity of enclaves where they are able to speak their native language in a familiar culture. Most are focused on getting their feet on the ground.

Given this diversity of opinion, the integration of newcomers into civic life is positive and important, from the perspectives of both the receiving communities and the newcomers themselves. The early integration and civic involvement of newcomers should be a high priority because that involvement is a key to better social, economic, and cultural integration of both the newcomer and his or her family. And integration is likely to be good for America's national security. Important forms of civic engagement are not predicated on citizenship. Voting may be an aspect of civic participation, but civic participation is broader than voting and should be encouraged soon after arrival into the country.

Demographic Data

As a land of immigrants, Nathan Glazer's 1985 description of the United States as the 'permanently unfinished country' continues to be apt (Glazer, 1985). With the number of foreign-born residents in the United States increasing by 15 million in the past ten years, a primary lesson from demographic data is that our nation continues to be a land of immigrants. The foreign-born population numbers 36 million, about 11 percent of the total. In particular, the census story reveals changes in the past dozen years that reflect increasing numbers of residents of Latin and Asian descent in new parts of the country. Asians and Latinos have reached a stunning 58 percent in population growth rate over the last ten years nationwide (Tira Andrei, 2001, p. 27).

The rise in Latinos outstripped overall population growth throughout the country (Belsie, 2001, p. 1). Data from the 2000 census showed explosive growth in the Latino population outside the nation's urban areas as Latinos helped to fill increasingly available low-wage jobs in the 1990s. They came in droves to work in meatpacking plants in Minnesota and Nebraska, tend crops in Kentucky, and manufacture carpets in Georgia mills (Armas, 2001, p. A7). Half of all Latinos live in Texas and California, and 77 percent (27.1 million) live in seven states: California, Texas, New York, Florida, Illinois, Arizona, and New Jersey. In fourteen other states scattered throughout the country, the percentage of Latinos as part of the overall population doubled in the 1990s (Pugh, 2001). The dramatic surge in the nation's Latino population was due mainly to a 53 percent increase in the number of people of Mexican heritage. Mexican Americans make up 58 percent of the nation's 35.3 million 'Hispanics' (Pugh, 2001).

Asian Americans' growth almost matched Latino growth in the 1990s. Their presence is most visible in Texas, New York, New Jersey, Virginia, Maryland, Illinois, Ohio, and Pennsylvania. They prefer to cluster in huge numbers in these states' capital cities where jobs are available and generally recession-proof (Tira Andrei, 2001).

Immigration-driven growth is not limited to a few states. In fact, the 2000 census showed that in the previous decade the foreign-born population grew far more slowly in states with the largest immigrant populations, such as California, New York and Texas, than in a group of nineteen new growth states (*Growth of California's Foreign-born Population*, 2001). The nineteen new growth states – those with the fastest growing immigrant populations in the 1990s – were Alabama, Arizona, Arkansas, Colorado, Georgia, Idaho, Iowa, Kansas, Kentucky, Maryland, Mississippi, Nebraska, Nevada, North Carolina, Oklahoma, Oregon, South Carolina, Utah, and Virginia. During the 1990s, the foreign-born population grew by a dramatic 95 percent in these states, compared with only 23 percent in traditional immigrant destinations (*Growth of California's Foreign-born Population*, 2001).

Information on particular states suggests that issues pertaining to cultural pluralism, race relations, and defining who is an American are questions in many communities across the nation. Consider these examples.

Colorado's Latino population grew by 73 percent and its Asian population by 68 percent in the last decade of the twentieth century (Seattle Times, 2001). Latinos made up more than a third of Denver's population by 2000. Roughly one-fourth of the state's 724,000 students are Latino. In Denver, Latino and Asian American communities are booming, and businesses in thriving immigrant enclaves do well. Merchants and workers in some neighborhoods find it increasingly necessary to use three languages – English, Spanish, and an Asian language, often Korean. Jeremiah Kong, a native of Seoul, South Korea, owns La Plaza Mexicana, a 26,000-square-foot building that caters to Spanish-language immigrants with 18 shops selling everything from auto parts to furniture. Eight of the shop owners are Korean; the others are Latino, both U.S. born and Mexican immigrants. His workers are also Spanish-language immigrants. So, for Kong to deal with his employees, he tends to use 'Spanglish' – a combination of English and Spanish (Griego, 2001, p. B1; Amaya, 2001, p. B11; Aguilar, 2001, p. C1).

Iowa's Latino population has grown by around 29,000, a leap of roughly 90 percent, since 1990. The 61,500 Latino residents are the state's largest minority group. Iowa's Asian population has grown by 11,300 since 1990, an increase of 44 percent (Beaumont, 2001, p. 1). In all of Iowa's 99 counties, Latino population growth during the 1990s outpaced the overall population rise. Latino growth ranged from Clarke County, up 1,842 percent, to suburban Dallas County right outside Des Moines, up 1,112 percent (Belsie, 2001).

North Carolina led the country in Latino growth, up 394 percent in the last decade of the twentieth century, followed by Arkansas, Georgia, Tennessee and Nevada. In Siler City, North Carolina, Latinos made up 4 percent of the town's

4,808 people in 1990. By 2000, they constituted 39 percent of its 6,966 residents, drawn by jobs at chicken-processing plants and textile mills (Armas, 2001, p. A7).

Kentucky's population increased by nearly 10 percent during the 1990s, topping 4 million for the first time at 4,041,769 (*Population Shifts During the 1990s*, 2001, p. A20). Asian Americans led the way with a 75 percent increase to almost 30,000 and Latino numbers more than doubled to about 60,000 (John, 2001a, p. 4a; Gerth, 2001, p. A1).[1]

Consider, too, these other immigrant-driven statistics in the 1990s: One of every four residents of Arizona is Latino. In Tennessee, the Latino population nearly tripled in ten years and now accounts for 2 percent of the state population. The number of Asians almost doubled. However, the state remains 80 percent white and 16 percent black. The Latino population also tripled in Alabama, Georgia and Minnesota, while at least doubling in states like Utah, Idaho, Indiana, Oregon, Kansas, South Carolina, and Mississippi. In New Hampshire, the Latino population grew by 81 percent and the Asian Pacific Islander community by 74 percent. In Utah, Asians are the second-largest minority group following Latinos. In Massachusetts, the Asian population increased nearly 70 percent, while Latinos grew almost 50 percent. The Asian population doubled in South Dakota. (*Population Shifts During the 1990s*, 2001, p. A20).

The effect of immigration on the census is obvious; the population throughout the country is becoming more diverse. And this immigration-driven growth in diversity will likely continue.

Resentment and Misunderstanding

Lack of accurate information about each other and the absence of opportunities to meet and intermingle have led to misunderstanding and resentment between newcomers and native-born Americans. A typical example might be Hamblen County, in the northeastern section of Tennessee, where the Latino population became 6 percent of the county's residents within a ten-year span (outnumbering the small but longstanding black population). Already bitter about the movement of local jobs to other countries, including Mexico, many white working-class residents viewed the entry of Latinos into the local labor markets as an aggressive threat that added insult to injury. A white woman recounted:

> [S]omeone decided to come up and start telling me – and she didn't
> even know me – that she had just lost her job because of the

---

[1]   Within the Asian American population, Vietnamese grew at the highest rate.

immigrants. I said, 'How do you know that?' She couldn't give me an answer, but I think what it came back to is that the job she had before this, ... that plant had shut down to relocate to Mexico. Then the place where she lost her job just last week had a few immigrants employed there, and when she lost her job she just naturally assumed that was why.

One Latino expressed concern about her white co-workers: 'They view me badly, they don't want me; they hate me' (Smith, 2003).

Latino immigrants also unsettled the dualistic racial hierarchy of black and white in Hamblen County. Most residents sense the intense hostility that some white workers hold toward new immigrants, and black and white residents have observed that Latinos have replaced African Americans as the chief target of white racism.

While some long-term residents are negative about immigrants, others are not. In January 2002, the Morristown-based chapter of the Ku Klux Klan organized a rally at the courthouse in order to protest 'the growing non-white flood of illegals.' Literature promoting the event called for closing the nation's borders 'before American-hating foreigners pollute and destroy our community. We must secure the existence of our people and a future for white children.' The rally attracted more than 50 supporters. However, a counter-demonstration, organized by the National Association for the Advancement of Colored People (NAACP), Jewish anti-defamation groups, and others drew 800 to 1,000 people. In addition, a celebration of diversity at the local high school, supported by the mayor and district attorney, was held to counter the Klan's message of hate.

Yet, the resentment toward immigrants can be chilling, as epitomized by the sentiments of a local labor leader:

> I'll tell you what I hear through the grapevine: we are going to have a real problem here in America. It will probably wind up being racial. I'm not saying anything against the Latino, but I hear there are groups here in the South and the Midwest that is just ready to roll if things don't change. I'm not a fanatic, and I'm not reading this out of any kind of lunatic magazine, but I'm thinking people are really getting down on the politicians more and more ... [T]here is not going to be any kind of move made ... to change anything to benefit the working people. And I think the NAFTA thing and losing jobs – if this economy drops down, I believe [America] is going to be a violent place. (Smith, 2003)

When Things Go Seriously Wrong

Unfortunately, cultural pluralism is under siege in some quarters. The rise in hate violence directed at law-abiding Arab Americans, Muslims, and Sikhs following 9/11 demonstrates that things can go terribly wrong in some neighborhoods. Misguided individuals act against Americans who do not fit a particular, European-descent, image.

Within two weeks of 9/11, these hate incidents were reported:

- A gunman drove to a Mesa, Arizona gas station and fired three shots, killing its Sikh owner. In a wild rampage, the gunman drove to another gas station and shot at the Lebanese clerk, and then fired shots into the home of an Afghan family.
- In Los Angeles, a Pakistani man parked his vehicle at a mall and returned to find it scratched across the right side with the words, 'Nuke 'em.'
- In San Francisco, vandals threw a bag of blood on the doorstep of a center that serves Arabs and the city's large Asian population.
- An Indian American walking in the South Market area of San Francisco was beaten and stabbed by a gang of individuals yelling anti-black and anti-Arab epithets.
- A Huntington, NY, man screamed, '[I am] doing this for my country' as he attempted to drive over a Pakistani woman.
- A shop owned by a Sikh was burned down in Ronkonkoma, Long Island.[2]

Unfortunately, examples of other anti-Asian hate crimes in the United States have been chronicled at a significant rate in the past two decades. One of the most highly publicized incidents was the murder of Vincent Chin. The young Chinese American was beaten to death by two unemployed autoworkers in Detroit who blamed Japanese automakers for their plight and thought Chin was Japanese American (see *United States v Ebens*, 1986).

Hate crimes directed at Latino immigrants are also common. In one of the most outrageous cases, private security guards in Nashville systematically terror-ized Latino residents of several apartment complexes. They kicked residents in the ribs, maced their genitals, and warned, 'I'm going to throw your Spic ass out of the country.' The owner of the security firm encouraged the assaults. 'I'm bored,' he told his staff, 'Let's go down to taco city and f—- with the Mexicans.' (Yeoman, 2000)

Hate crimes directed at immigrants of color are fueled, and perhaps inspired, by anti-immigrant rhetoric. A New York-based group has put up billboards in

---

[2]   From the Asian American Legal Defense and Education Fund's partial list of reported incidents of Anti-Asian, bias-related incidents (2001) *AsianWeek* (Sept. 20–26), p. 9.

twelve states that blame immigrants for inflating the U.S. population. The Washington, DC-based Federation for American Immigration Reform (FAIR) runs ads blaming immigrants for urban sprawl. According to the group's political algebra, immigrants cause population growth and population growth causes urban sprawl. So immigrants cause sprawl. (Navarrette, 2000, p. L-02). FAIR also blames immigrants for a rise in the number of cases of rubella in North Carolina (Parker and McMahon, 2001).

A few years ago in Phoenix, the residents of once solidly white neighborhoods grumbled about Mexican taco trucks and inspired city officials to try to use regulations to create a 'taco-free zone' (Navarette, 2000). Along the border, private vigilante groups, like the Minutemen, have volunteered to help the Border Patrol monitor undocumented border crossers.

In Bybee, Tennessee, more than two-thirds of the town's residents tried to block the opening of a Head Start center for Latino children. And in Lexington, Kentucky, residents circulated a petition opposing efforts to make the city 'a safe place for Hispanics' (Yeoman, 2000). In Marietta, Georgia, a suburb of Atlanta, the city council passed an ordinance prohibiting day laborers and contractors from gathering on city streets to arrange for work (Parker and McMahon, 2001).

Whether such incidents could have been avoided completely by integration efforts is, of course, subject to debate. But certainly, integration efforts could have helped.

Why Civic Integration Programs are Necessary

For all the reasons that native-born Americans should be encouraged to participate in civic life, newcomers should be encouraged as well. Engaging Americans in working to better our communities, schools, and neighborhoods – to work for the common good – is a goal that we must constantly pursue. In the case of newcomers, we also need to encourage civic participation and integration flows because of misinformation about immigrants that at times leads to hate. Integration policies 'generally refer to helping immigrants understand, navigate and participate in the social, economic and political aspects of society' (We the People, 2002, p. 23). These may include efforts to help newcomers understand U.S. law and cultural practices, to assist in starting a business, finding a job or otherwise becoming self-sufficient, while encouraging them to participate in civic organizations and community groups.

State and local governments can play important roles. Compared with community-based organizations, governmental entities have more resources. Immigration and naturalization policy falls largely in the hands of the federal government. However, while federal policies determine how many immigrants and refugees enter the country, state and local governments are presented directly with the challenges and opportunities that newcomers present.

The importance of state and local government leadership in promoting the civic integration of newcomers has been recognized by many governmental entities. California's bi-partisan Little Hoover Commission (LHC) recognizes that the state has a responsibility to ensure that public programs, including education and training, public health and welfare, and economic development services effectively serve immigrants enabling them to contribute to the state (*We the People*, 2002, p. 37). Critical to achieving this goal is recognizing the importance of investing in immigrants. Many immigrants are young and many others come to the United States with limited formal education. The LHC believes 'high quality education and training programs can improve [immigrants'] earning potential and enhance their self-sufficiency' (*We the People*, 2002, pp. 37–38). The LHC emphasizes the importance of this investment, as education and skills, more than any other factor, determine the earning capacity of immigrants (*We the People*, 2002, p. 38). Investing in immigrants is necessary to ensure that they are able to make lasting contributions (*We the People*, 2002, p. 38).

In recognition of the importance of promoting civic integration, the LHC proposed the creation of a California Commission on Immigrants charged with initiating statewide dialogues on immigration, advocating for effective programs and monitoring progress in immigrant integration. The statewide dialogues would 'promote public awareness of the contributions of immigrants and how immigration can support community goals' (*We the People*, 2002, p. 53). The Commission would advocate for improvement in public programs that promote 'immigrant responsibilities to their communities and community responsibilities to immigrants' (*We the People*, 2002, p. 53). The Commission should 'pay particular attention' to community-based organizations that promote integration and citizenship. Further, it would 'identify ways to define and measure immigrant integration and self-reliance and report progress to policy makers and the public' (*We the People*, 2002, p. 53).

Fundamental to the LHC's position is the understanding that California's continued prosperity is dependent on the opportunities and achievements of all its residents – including its immigrants. That is, all of California benefits when immigrants are successful. Conversely, when immigrants are trapped in poverty and isolation, the state bears a higher tax burden for providing these immigrants services. In short, 'California's primary goal [is] to support the ability of all residents, including immigrants, to be safe, health and law abiding, as well as live in safe affordable housing and be economically self-sufficient.' (*We the People*, 2002, p. 65) Immigrants should participate in self-governance and feel they belong and are responsible to their community. The state should also try to influence federal policies to better align federal immigration practices with community goals. The reason is clear. 'Public policies that hinder immigrants' ability to become self-reliant, responsible community members hinder the success of all Californians.' (*We the People*, 2002, p. 65)

Given immigrant-driven demographic changes occurring throughout the country, lessons from California are worth reviewing. In Santa Clara County (home to San Jose and Silicon Valley), officials have recognized the importance of newcomer integration: 'Our collective need to integrate, improve, and transform the lives of all residents of Santa Clara County depends upon our ability to integrate, improve, and transform the lives of immigrants and the need to re-think planning, policies, and practices' (Bridging Borders in Silicon Valley, 2000, p. 21). In line with this, they declared:

> The improvement and transformation of our lives in Santa Clara County is integrally inter-wound with the improvement and transformation of the lives of immigrants in Santa Clara County. To the extent that immigrants are not provided the opportunities to integrate into existing structures, improve their lives, and help transform our lives and structures into a meaningful, productive, well-rounded existence, to that extent our economy, society, and culture will decline. We will slide into a Silicon Valley culture less rich in diversity, in knowledge, in growth, and in meeting human needs and potential. If we seek to blame those who look different than ourselves, act different than ourselves, or immigrated to this area at different times and are therefore seen as competitors rather than adding value, we could spiral downward as a county.
>
> With such a large number, percentage, and diversity of immigrants and a mandate to meet the human needs of all its residents, Santa Clara County needs to engage in long-term, strategic, sustainable, human-needs based planning. In many respects, if the county doesn't have a vision for meeting the human needs of immigrants in the county and individuals in the world, then the county cannot have a vision for meeting the needs of county residents. More than ever, immigrants and U.S.-born county residents have an interlocking common fate. (Bridging Borders in Silicon Valley, 2000, p. 30)

In short, the best interest of the community (and thus the country) is served when all residents, native-born and foreign-born alike, are integrated into civic culture. Marginalization leaves people out; bringing them in encourages contributions and understanding that benefits all.

Examples That Work

Sentiment supportive of immigrant integration and cultural diversity has provided the impetus for a variety of efforts across the country that assist immigrants in their adjustment to American life. In recognition of the mutual responsibility of civic integration shared by the community and the newcomer, these efforts are not simply examples of providing services to immigrants and refugees, but also about encouraging newcomers to uphold their responsibilities to the community. Clear expectations can speed immigrants to personal success, by encouraging them to learn English, develop social networks, and access education and training programs that lead to expanded opportunities.

Consider Nebraska. Metropolitan Area Transit in Omaha has installed informational signs in Spanish and English in the advertising trays of all 131 buses, in recognition of the area's growing Latino population. Bank and cash machines now offer information in two languages, and the State of Nebraska prints several information brochures, including the driver's manual, in Spanish. Sister Angela Erevia, director of a local Catholic ministry, said the effort follows the policy of the region's Archbishop in assisting the growing Spanish-speaking population 'to become an integral part of the community.' 'Many of the new Hispanic immigrants are looking for jobs. They haven't enough money to buy cars, and they are dependent upon public transportation.' (Ivey, 2001)

Omaha is becoming a U.S. Sudanese refugee population center where many refugees find better work, housing and refugee support than in their first destination, Des Moines, Iowa. Refugees have found opportunities and a sense of belonging that was missing in Iowa. Perhaps most important is Omaha's Sudanese Association itself, which former Des Moines refugees say provides the assistance needed for those whose transition to American life is a constant challenge. The Omaha center, which is supported by a mix of grants, offers refugees transportation, interpreters and daily English classes taught by fellow Nuer tribespeople, the southern Sudanese natives most common in the United States. Nebraska gives refugees a few additional months of state assistance (compared with Iowa) to help them get on their feet. The Omaha Sudanese association attempts to create a family atmosphere, translating mail, accompanying them in court, filling out immigration paperwork, searching for jobs. The goal is to bring the Sudanese to self-sufficiency (Rood, 2001, p. 1).

As part of the initiative to attract more immigrants to Iowa championed by Governor Tom Vilsack, the Sioux City New Iowans Center and a similar one in Muscatine are giving immigrants a foothold by helping them find jobs, homes, English classes and even rides to the doctor. As the president of the chamber of commerce notes: 'We're going to have some way to integrate people into our society quickly.' Although Nebraska does not operate anything similar to the New Iowans Centers, an immigration task force supports such centers in Nebraska as well (Morantz, 2001, p. 1). Similarly, in Arkansas, the Northwest Arkansas Multicultural Center, started in 2000, which provides education and information to new immigrants in the area. 'We don't want you to forget your culture, we want you to become part of our culture,' said Fred Patton, Fort Smith Multicultural Commission chairman. Arkansas political leaders promote such programs. In his welcoming remarks at a multicultural conference, Senator Tim Hutchinson, R-Ark., acknowledged the strength that flows from cultural diversity and from the common desire for freedom. To Hutchinson, bigotry, prejudice and violence usually are the result of ignorance (Hughes, 2000, p. B1).

In Kentucky, where the Latino population mushroomed in the 1990s, Project PLOW (People Learning Each Other's Ways) was instituted to bring together white farmers and Latino immigrants to learn each other's language and culture (Navarrette, 2000, p. L-02). Pressed by a growing local need for teachers who can work with foreign students, the University of Louisville has held a special six-week English as a Second Language institute during the summer. Up to 20 teachers from the Jefferson County Public Schools honed skills needed to teach students with limited English and diverse cultural backgrounds. The teachers can take more courses in the fall and spring. Others also are stepping up efforts to pre-pare future teachers to deal with the community's growing diversity, while still others are tailoring courses to reach adults with special language needs. Local uni-versities soon will have to actively recruit Latino high school students to train as teachers. At Jefferson Community College, there was one full-time and one part-time ESL instructor in 1992; by 2000 there were two full-time and 17 part-time instructors, with evening courses to accommodate immigrants' work schedules. Eight years ago only classes in grammar and writing were offered; now courses cover conversation, reading, speech, real estate, human services, philosophy and American history and government (Stahl, 2000, p. 1b).

Non-English language services are needed in other areas of Kentucky life. When Chuk Chiu's Chinese restaurant was robbed, he couldn't find the words to tell police what happened. He didn't speak English. When Jose Rodriguez's car was stolen from outside his apartment, he couldn't understand the officers' questions. He didn't speak English either. Rodriguez said police treated him well and said he didn't expect officers to speak Spanish. He wanted to learn English, but it was difficult to find time while working two jobs to make ends meet. When police asked a victim's friends or family members to act as interpreters, the situation could get awkward, officers said. In one homicide case, for instance, the suspect spoke only Korean, and police had to ask their initial questions through the suspect's relatives. In one move to deal with the problem, Louisville police circulated a questionnaire to learn who on the force was bilingual. Of 718 officers, just six were listed as speaking at least two languages. Two were fluent in Spanish. The fastest-growing population in Jefferson County is the immigrant refugee and migrant students. Jefferson County police have been prompted to put pocket Spanish guides in every cruiser and to require each officer to take several hours of basic Spanish classes (Tangonan, 2000, p. 1b). The city of Louisville, working with several private agencies such as Catholic Charities and Kentucky Refugee Ministries, planned to identify a bank of potential interpreters, and help train and certify them. The interpreters would work through the agencies for a fee – allowing hospitals, medical clinics, home-health providers, legal services, government agencies and other federally funded human-services agencies to contract for interpreters. A city language bank would be a tremendous asset in cases where the language in question was not widely spoken. (John, 2000, p. 1A)

From a different angle, Louisville business leaders and academics also realize that many immigrants are highly skilled, in some cases with professional backgrounds, and should be provided with tools to resume their professional talents to the benefit of their new community (John, 2001b, p. 1A). Louisville also has a Center for Microenterprise Development, which offers a 10-week course that teaches business start-up skills to refugees and other immigrants. The participants have come from strife-torn countries such as Zaire, Russia, Bosnia, Cuba, Vietnam, Sierra Leone and Haiti (Sherrer, 2000, p. 1c).

In Oklahoma, the bulk of jobs held by black and Latino workers are in service industries, while white workers are concentrated in the areas of executive, professional, administrative and sales jobs (Graham, 2001a). The attitude of assistance in immigrant integration that has emerged is typified by the following sentiment:

> Workplace diversity doesn't stop with hiring. The concept extends to
> forging relationships with people of different cultures, backgrounds,
> races and gender. It takes understanding that diversity goes beyond
> what a person can see. It reaches into accepting a person's economic
> status, religion, and even home life. Month-long celebrations at work
> related to education and diversity can help. 'We find this one of the
> easiest and most enjoyable ways to educate people ... Rather than
> always having to go to a class, people can experience something new
> in their normal environment.' Diversity is part of our foundation
> and core values, and it is the right thing to do. 'Wherever we are
> as a community, we need to be doing better ... What diversity boils
> down to is being a good neighbor – being good to each other. It's an
> attitude issue. The values and visions of company leaders are reflected
> in the work force. There are some companies that take on diversity

as a corporate responsibility and don't feel it is a mandate ... Racism is not about black and white. It's about the haves and have-nots, the privileged and not-so-privileged and why that is. To help people understand diversity, we have to define it.' To give diversity meaning, Radious Guess, a diversity consultant, talks about how people have innate prejudices and ways to recognize those. She wants people to talk about their differences, to start working in teams and to go outside their 'comfort zones.' (Graham, 2001a)

A significant increase in Tulsa's Latino population has led companies to look for ways to deal with a language barrier (Graham, 2001a). Advocacy on behalf of Latinos in Tulsa began in 1979 when the city created the Greater Tulsa Area Hispanic Commission, an advisory board with no authority to set policy. A statewide initiative petition in 2000 to ban foreign languages from government services prompted the group to create the Coalition of Hispanic Organizations, an official nonprofit advocacy group that handles social issues brought to the foundation. 'That initiative petition made us realize there was no organization to speak on behalf of political issues ... When we established the Hispanic American Foundation, we never dreamed we were going to be faced with so many issues.' Rev. Victor Orta, president of the Coalition, said the organizations bring together people in the community to understand reasons for immigration and challenges facing immigrants. 'The established Hispanic community has opened up to receive the newcomers,' Orta said. 'We're responding with what we can to make assimilation or resettlement here easier. A newcomer needs to learn the language to pursue their profession or vocation and know the laws and issues facing them. But first and foremost is getting a job.' (Graham, 2001b)

North Carolina, in particular, has engaged in immigrant integration and understanding efforts that are noteworthy. Between 1995 and 2000, North Carolina's Latino population increased by 73 percent, making North Carolina the location of the nation's fastest growing Latino community (*The North Carolina Initiative*). In a state of 7 million people, Latinos now account for more than 4 percent of the population (*The North Carolina Initiative*). Well over half of the recent arrivals are from Mexico (*The North Carolina Initiative*), anticipating greater opportunities for themselves and their families in a state with plentiful work and inexpensive housing. It is estimated that about half of the Mexican immigrants are in the state as undocumented workers. (Yeoman, 2000).

The rapid growth of the new diversity in North Carolina brought problems of its own. The changing demographics immediately impacted the schools, government agencies like the Department of Motor Vehicles, and the police force. It also challenged the cohesion of the different communities affected by the influx of new community members. Schools would receive new students with little or no English skills; agencies would be responsible for communicating requirements or restrictions to Latino clients unable to speak English. Frustrations like these reached a head at the local level when a Democratic county commissioner from Chatham County wrote a heated letter in August 1999 to the Immigration and Naturalization Service requesting help to either document the new arrivals, or send them back home. The county felt strongly that its resources were being 'siphoned from other pressing needs ... to provide assistance to immigrants with little or no possessions' (Yeoman, 2000).

Sensing the potential difficulties facing the state as the immigrant population expanded, the North Carolina Center for International Understanding (NCCIU) began a series of conversations in 1995 with key leaders from universities, foundations, the Latino community and state government. A project of the University of North Carolina, the NCCIU is a 20-year-old program that traditionally focused on community exchanges. The discussions started in 1995 led to the implementation of the Latino Initiative to address the prospective conflicts and public policy needs between the burgeoning Latino population and the people of North Carolina.

One of the primary concerns of the NCCIU was the success of the school system in dealing with the change in its student population. In order to serve the new student population, it was recognized that educators and school administrators should acquire an understanding of the immigrants' culture and family situations. The NCCIU identified the 20 most affected counties across the state from census data and extended invitations to teachers and administrators of the relevant districts to participate in a two-week summer study abroad in Mexico. The program became an annual opportunity for 20–25 educators to spend two weeks in Mexico attending lectures, visiting museums and schools, and staying in the homes of Mexican educators. The NCCIU collaborated with the Mexican organizations like the Universidad Iberoamericana in Mexico City and Ipoderac, an orphanage for street children in Puebla.

The study abroad also invites community and state leaders to participate so that their contribution to emerging public policy will be informed by a heightened understanding of political, social and economic factors driving the decisions behind immigration as well as a first-hand experience with the richness of Mexican culture and family structure. The Latino Initiative also aims to assist leaders to recognize the needs of Latinos and to distinguish the relevant agencies that will provide those needs so that the immigrants can become better incorporated into North Carolina life.

The annual program aims to provide a proactive, sabbatical approach to allow educators and community leaders the opportunity to question their earlier stereotypes as they travel. The program consists of a two-day pre-departure seminar, a two-week visit to Mexico that includes three days in Mexico City, three days in rural schools, and a weekend home stay. The group visits families who have sons, daughters or husbands living in the United States; these families often reside in Mexican states known to be points of origin for many of the immigrants who have traveled to targeted communities in North Carolina. Upon return to North Carolina, a follow-up planning meeting is held to consider appropriate forms for disseminating lessons learned on the trip. The Latino Initiative also holds annual seminars on Latino issues to encourage the development of a network of leaders who can guide public discourse and policymaking on issues surrounding Latino immigration.

Because of his concerns about the increasing misunderstandings and tension felt by the DMV's drivers' license examiners while assisting clients with limited English proficiency, the director of the North Carolina licensing division participated in one of the Latino Initiative trips to Mexico with the Fletcher Foundation. His experience led to the development of cross-cultural training for the state's 350 examiners. The North Carolina DMV contracted with the NCCIU to implement a program geared toward effective communication with Latino customers. The program was implemented through 22 group workshops across the state. The small group format was essential in allowing dialogue rather than lecture alone. As a result of the training, the North Carolina DMV recently was awarded the profession's international award for customer service excellence.

The first trip abroad for policy makers was scheduled for February 2000 and was originally intended exclusively for state-level leaders. The NCCIU received a $20,000 foundation grant. The foundation money fully funded ten participants including six state legislators, representatives of the Department of Public Instruction, the Administrative Office of the Courts, the Co-op Extension Service and the Self-Help Credit Union, a community non-profit organization. An additional five participants from the Governor's Office, AT&T, the North Carolina Rural Economic Development Center, the North Carolina Association of County Commissioners and the University of North Carolina paid their own way to participate in the program.

Unexpectedly, this first trip for state-level leaders was confronted with a request that six civic leaders from Chatham County be included as well. Chatham County was one of the 20 most affected counties already targeted by the NCCIU, and it was in crisis. The county was embroiled in debate over the presence of immigrants sparked by a letter sent from County Commissioner Rick Givens to the INS asking for help in getting the undocumented workers documented or 'routed back to their homes.' The letter had been translated and distributed among the Latino community and county meetings had turned into

screaming matches. One of the cities within county lines, Siler City, was 40 percent Latino. About 50 percent of the enrollment at Siler City Elementary School
was children from Latino families. The county delegation was composed of
Givens, another county commissioner, the Siler City Chief of Police, the sheriff, the vice-chair of the county school system, and a Mexican-born community
educator from a local, Latino-focused community non-profit organization. The
Chatham County group joined the state leaders at the last minute, funded partially by the county, and partially through foundations.

Educators and foundation members who participated in the earlier study
abroad trips had found the experiences 'transforming.' The state leaders, accompanied by the Chatham County delegation, experienced a 'near-miraculous turn
around in attitudes and relationships.' After noting that he was 'going to eat a lot
of crow,' Givens explained how the experience had changed his life and admitted that his earlier judgment of the Latinos was wrong; he also pledged to help
the community in his area. That pledge was challenged only one week after
Givens and the other members of the Chatham County delegation returned to
Siler City from Mexico.

During the trip, the caustic letter Givens sent to the INS had gained a strong
backing, especially among local white supremacists. An anti-immigration rally
was scheduled for the Siler City Hall, featuring the infamous ex-Klansman David
Duke as one of the speakers. The rally intended to make an example of the community to condemn the negative effects of immigration. Givens, the sheriff and
the chief of police quickly mobilized to promote a boycott of the rally. While
the numbers were notably lower than expected, Duke referenced the county
commissioner's new commitment to the Latino community. Threatening to
organize a recall of Givens' commission seat, Duke commented that unless the
law of the land is enforced, 'America will be turned into another Mexico.'

The development of the Latino Initiative to help state and civic leaders understand the issues behind Latino immigration and to inform the development of
sound policy is a model of a public–private–academic collaboration. The
program has facilitated the integration of immigrants into North Carolina communities, and positively educated the communities about the new immigrants to
encourage cooperation at the community level. As one participant commented
upon returning to North Carolina from Mexico, 'the most significant barrier
facing [North Carolina] is the ability to live together and to nurture relationships
across race, religions, and other kinds of diversity. That is the impact this program has had on me – it is making me know that it's possible.' (Yeoman, 2000)

Some short-term initiatives by several states in the late 1990s were launched
to help legal immigrants adversely affected by the 1996 federal welfare law's
restrictions on federal public benefits. For example, the Massachusetts legislature

passed a three-year $2 million initiative in 1997 to fund a Citizenship Assistance Program for low-income immigrant residents. The program matched state funds with contributions from private organizations, foundations and federal agencies. A statewide network of more than 100 community-based organizations provided English and civics classes as well as assistance with citizenship applications. A 24-hour hotline was created to provide information in nine languages on services such as civics and English classes, application assistance, and legal referrals. More than 22,000 Massachusetts residents benefited from the program, and more than 11,000 have become new citizens. When asked their reasons for becoming U.S. citizens, most immigrants in the program said they wanted to vote and help their community. Students participated in Immigrants' Day to get a first-hand look at how government works, meet with legislators, and discuss policies important to their community.

Through the Refugee and Immigrant Citizenship Initiative, Illinois's Bureau of Refugee and Immigrant Services has expended $12 million over the last seven years, contracting with 32 community based organizations to provide lessons in U.S. history, civics, and instruction in English language. More than 90,000 individuals have been served. These contracts serve members of the community through education and by stimulating civic participation. The Coalition of Limited English Speaking Elderly in Chicago developed and tested an innovative curriculum on daily life with a grant from the U.S. Department of Education. Students from Bosnia, Cambodia, China, India, and Korea learned to communicate in English and can now participate in English conversations with family members, grandchildren, and other community residents. The elderly decreased their social isolation and increased their civic participation while they solved real-life problems and learned about their neighborhood and city (Elder, 2004).

The New Jersey Citizenship Campaign was a statewide naturalization effort led by a collaborative partnership of community-based organizations and state and federal agencies. The campaign began in 1997 with support from the Governor and legislature, funded originally at $2 million and later increased to $3 million. Community-based organizations provided in-kind contributions of another $3 million. The campaign initially targeted low-income, elderly and disabled lawful permanent residents and those eligible for New Jersey's State Food Stamp Program. By March 2000, the campaign had provided services to 12,000 individuals, more than 7,100 of whom applied for citizenship (Perez, 2003).

The Maryland Office for New Americans promotes English literacy and civics education by funding participatory English and civics classes. Students are asked to explore the different service agencies and report on the information gleaned in their own visits to these services (Lee, 2001; Briggs, 2001).

The positive effect of modern integration programs on newcomers is readily apparent. In California, Sia Thompson, an immigrant from Sierra Leone, partic- ipated in Santa Clara County's Immigrant Leadership course. With a strong interest in women's rights, she was able to bond with other women participants to lay the groundwork for collaboration during the course. The course also was helpful in providing information on resources available for immigrants generally. She also developed a sense of 'where to go so that our voice will be heard.' But even before she participated in this course, Sia had helped to form a Pan-African women's organization – African Refugee Women Rebuilders (ARWR). She explained part of the reason for forming the organization this way:

> It was so difficult for me to adjust to the American system and I have been through high school. It must be extremely difficult for women [who have no education]. Having experienced trying to get a job, to get connected [to the community], to make myself useful, I wanted to try and continue to work with African women and human rights. When the African women come here and resettle, refugee organizations like Catholic charities, Jewish family services and the International Rescue Committee work with the women for three months. Which in my view it is not a very long time. You are barely stepping your toes on the ground. So we are filling in the gap. Even on the very basic things like: the operation of vending machines, opening a savings account, where you can find the African food market – generally circumnavigating the system. We encourage the women to come in and get assistance.[3]

Churches can also help promote civic participation and integration. Another participant in the Santa Clara County Immigrant Leadership course, Juventino Flores, an immigrant from Mexico, attributes his involvement in civic affairs to his church's leadership program:

> [It] made me aware of the need of the community and helped me become involved in church; to give back. Before I took the course, I went to church, prayed and went home. The course helps every- one take responsibility.
>   I took the class by accident. There was one old lady who was working at the church and told me that the Diocese is offering the course, and asked if I wanted to take it.

---

[3]   Interview with Sia Thompson, December 15, 2004, San Jose, California.

I didn't want to say yes or no – so I said maybe. Then the priest
sent a letter telling me when the orientation was. [I went] and
I liked it. I am fortunate. I have no regrets and [was] very happy to
learn all the stuff.

[The course covered subjects including,] social justice, the
community and things in the church. [It discussed topics like] why
clothes can be cheap in this country and where they are made. It
made you aware of many things. It was interesting and very helpful.
It made me want to get more involved in the community and once
you are there it is hard to get out. When are you sure that you have
done enough – that you have solved all the problems? In this work,
somewhere else there is a need. Once they [the instructors] make
you an activist it is hard to get away and relax.

[In the course they] related faith and the needs in the community.
They make you strong in the faith and then you have to follow Jesus
and Jesus is justice. Sometimes it is hard to sacrifice. It takes time –
to make announcements [and there are] not many volunteers.
[Sometimes] I think to myself that I can take more community
college classes and get better pay and move somewhere else, but then
I would never give anything else to the community. The volunteer
work is part of the faith. I have to give to the neighbors; to my
brothers and sisters; to the society; because according to our beliefs,
if one suffers the other should suffer. It is hard to have more
responsibilities, but you start growing and you take on more and
more. Leadership for the community – helping the community [is]
related to the faith that something better will happen, like Martin
Luther King [and Dolores Huerta]. [4]

Of course, while an ugly side of America has reared its head following 9/11
in the form of hate crimes and intolerance directed at Arab Americans, American
Muslims and Sikhs, efforts at immigrant integration and understanding have also
occurred. In spite of a highly publicized prosecution of an alleged Al-Qaeda
supporter there, the California central valley town of Lodi, is a good example.
The town's population of 57,000 is more than a quarter Latino, and the community also has 2,000 Muslims, mostly from Pakistan (Bell, 2001, p. A23). So
Pakistani men playing cricket on a field across from their mosque and women
wearing *hijabs* – head scarves – walking in the park are a common sight. But
when the mosque was vandalized in the early 1990s, concerned citizens, led by

---

[4] Interview with Juventino Flores, December 15, 2004, San Jose, California.

a Japanese American mayor, came forward to form the Breakthrough Project to combat bigotry. High school students volunteered to help clean up the mosque and police started meeting regularly with mosque leaders. In the wake of 9/11, the pastor of the local United Congregational Christian Church conducted a four-part class on Islam for members of the community to gain better understanding of their Muslim neighbors. Isolated incidents of intolerance have occurred. However, one member of the United Congregational Christian Church who attended the Islam classes hoped that everyone across America was reaching out: 'I came to be supportive of our neighbors so they do not feel persecuted.' (Bell, 2001, p. A23)

Conclusion

Today the time is ripe for renewed civic engagement efforts directed at newcomers to the United States. A century ago, when Italians, Poles and Jews were immigrating in large numbers, there was a vast and vibrant Americanization movement. Everyone – from state governments to local schools to neighborhood YMCAs – took part, promoting love and loyalty for America. The movement fizzled after World War I when new laws dramatically curtailed immigration (Ludden, 2004). Given demographic trends and the potential for newcomers to continue to contribute mightily to the nation – socially and economically – it makes sense to reach out to immigrants and refugees as soon as they arrive so that they might too understand the responsibilities of being an American.

Once Americans recognize that the promotion of civic engagement among newcomers is in their own best interest, they can begin the process in earnest. The examples cited above represent some good thinking on the subject. However, Americans' capacity for creative thinking means that the potential for new, exciting, and innovative ways of promoting civic integration is enormous. While state and local governments should lead the way (including city service agencies and even community policing programs), other institutions have a vital role too. These include schools, daycare centers, local businesses, chambers of commerce, churches, recreation clubs, neighborhood groups, senior groups, and youth groups.

The United States faces a choice between two Americas: one narrow and one broad. One choice is closed-minded, resistant to continuing changes which will continue to breed tension and violence. The other is one that embraces change and encourages integration in the hopes of building a stronger, better community. The choice Americans make, individually, locally, and nationally, will say much about them as a nation, as a community, and as human beings. The goal must be to avoid the pitfalls of division, insular living, and unknowing bias, and instead fully embrace newcomers with open arms to become part of the national community of America's Americans.

Bibliography

Aguilar, Louis (2001) 'Language of Business Binds Cultures: Latino, Asian Markets Thrive,' *The Denver Post* (May 29).

Amaya, Jorge (2001) 'Mexican Immigrants Need to get Involved,' *The Denver Post* (February 21).

Andrei, Mercedes Tira (2001) 'Asians Soar in Number in Big American Cities,' *BusinessWorld* (April 6).

Armas, Genaro C. (2001) 'Hispanic Population Surges in Small Towns, Rural Communities,' *South Bend Tribune* (April 1).

Bell, Elizabeth (2001) 'Fear and Suspicion,' *San Francisco Chronicle* (October 21).

Belsie, Laurent (2001) 'Hispanics Spread to Hinterlands,' *The Christian Science Monitor* (March 26).

Beaumont, Thomas (2001) 'What is Abuse? Cultures Vary,' *The Des Moines Register* (Jan. 2).

Bridging Borders in Silicon Valley: Summit on Immigrant Needs and Contributions (2000) Santa Clara County Office of Human Relations Citizenship and Immigrant Services Program (December 6).

Briggs, Jonathon E. (2001) 'Workers Aim to Ease Language Barriers: Improving Immigrant Aid Discussed at Conference', *Baltimore Sun* (November 9), p. 3B.

Elder, Robert K. (2004) 'One man moving mountains; The local refugee community is small, but a leader with vision is helping establish Chicago as a Cambodian cultural center with the first U.S. memorial to a tragic past,' *Chicago Tribune* (April 8), p. 1.

Gerth, Joseph (2001) 'Bridging a Language Gap: Need for Court Interpreters Grows Quickly,' *The Courier-Journal* (July 31).

Glazer, Nathan (ed.) (1985) *Clamor at the Gates: The New American Immigration* (San Francisco: Institute for Contemporary Studies).

Graham, Ginnie (2001a) 'Celebrating Diversity at Work,' *Tulsa World* (February 16).

Graham, Ginnie (2001b) 'Jump in Hispanics has Advocates Busy: Recent Arrivals Need More Assistance,' *Tulsa World* (May 18).

Griego, Tina (2001) 'Hispanics a Multicultural Nation of our Own,' *The Denver Post* (March 21).

'Growth of California's Foreign-born Population Slows as Immigrants Move to Other States' (2001) News Release, The Urban Institute (January 11).

Hughes, Dave (2000) 'Fort Smith Panel Teaches New, Old Residents: Conference Addresses Matters on Immigration, Diversity,' *The Arkansas Democrat-Gazette* (August 9).

Ivey, James (2001) 'MAT Gets Rolling on Bilingual Effort,' *Omaha World-Herald* (Jan. 17).

John, Butch (2000) 'Breaking the Language Barrier: Pool of Interpreters Being Formed: Federal Law Requires Communication Aid,' *The Courier-Journal* (Sept. 23).

John, Butch (2001a) 'Asian Populations Surge in Kentucky and Indiana,' *The Courier-Journal* (May 20).

John, Butch (2001b) 'Tapping Immigrants' Skills Could Boost Area's Growth: Newcomers Often Can't Use Their Talents,' *The Courier-Journal* (June 29).

Ludden, Jennifer (2004) 'Efforts to help immigrants make easier transitions into American culture,' *NPR Morning Edition* (March 9).

Ly, Phuong (2001) 'Working to Better Aid African Immigrants', *Washington Post* (December 27), p. T3.

Morantz, Dave 'Helping Immigrants in the Midlands: Iowa and Nebraska are Debating How Far They Should Go in Providing Services for Newcomers: Services at New Iowans Centers,' *Omaha World-Herald* (June 28).

Navarrette, Ruben (2000) 'Immigrants are our Most Precious Import,' *The Denver Post* (December 17).

Parker, Laura and McMahon, Patrick (2001) 'Immigrant Groups Fear Backlash Rhetoric, Actions Have Intensified Coast to Coast Since Release of Data from Census 2000, Activists Report,' *USA Today* (April 9).

Perez, Miguel (2003) 'A Landmark for Latinos; Now the Largest U.S. Minority, and Gaining Influence,' *The Record* (June 19), p. A1.

Pugh, Tony (2001) 'U.S. Hispanic Population Surges to 20.6 Million,' *Knight Ridder Washington Bureau* (May 10).

Rood, Lee (2001) 'Sudanese Refugees Abandon Iowa: They're Drawn to a More Viable Support System in Omaha,' *The Des Moines Register* (June 3).

Seattle Times (2001) 'Population Shifts During the 1990s: State-by-State Breakdown of Ups and Downs,' (April 1), p. A20.

Sherrer, Sonja (2000) 'Immigrants Get Helping Hand: Center Offers Language Help, Advice, Money to Start Business,' *The Courier-Journal* (July 25).

Smith, Barbara Ellen (2003) *Across Races and Nations: Toward Worker Justice in the U.S. South* (Memphis: Center for Research on Women, University of Memphis).

Stahl, Linda (2000) 'U of L Offers English Help for Teachers: Rise in Foreign Students Prompts Special Course,' *The Courier-Journal* (May 22).

Tangonan, Shannon (2000) '"It's Really a Challenge For Us": Crisis Workers Hit Language Barrier, Immigrants Often Can't Speak English,' *The Courier-Journal* (March 13).

The North Carolina Initiative: Helping Communities Understand Immigration (2000) (Raleigh, N.C.: Clearinghouse on State International Policies).

United States v Ebens (1986) 800 F.2d 1422 (6th Cir.).

We the People: Helping Newcomers Become Californians (2002) Los Angeles: Little Hoover Commission (June).

Yeoman, Barry (2000) 'Hispanic Diaspora – Drawn by Jobs, Latino Immigrants are Moving to Small Towns like Siler City, North Carolina, Bringing with Them New Diversity and New Tensions,' *Mother Jones*, vol. 25.

9

Demographic Change and Concentrated Poverty in Rural America

Kenneth M. Johnson, Daniel T. Lichter

A preliminary version of this paper was presented at the Conference on *America's Americans: The Populations of the United States*, Institute for the Study of the Americas, University of London, England, May 2006. The authors acknowledge the helpful comments of the co-editors, Philip Davies and Iwan Morgan.

Introduction

A distinctive feature of poverty in rural America is its spatial concentration and persistence over many decades (Beale, 2004; Weber et al., 2005). Rural poverty is heavily concentrated geographically in the foothills of Appalachia, in the lower Mississippi Delta region where cotton production was the lifeblood of the old slave and plantation economy (Parisi et al., 2003), in the Mexican colonias along the Rio Grande River on the Texas–Mexico border (Saenz, 1997), and on Indian Reservations in the northern Great Plains states and in the desert Southwest (Beale, 2004; Ghelfi, 2001). The Economic Research Service of the U.S. Department of Agriculture has defined counties as being persistently poor if 20 percent or more of their populations were poor (by the official government definition) in each of the last four censuses (i.e., 1970, 1980, 1990, and 2000). Over this 30-year period, America's nonmetropolitan counties accounted for 340 of 386 of America's persistently poor counties. The large majority (280) of these counties were located in the South, where racial and ethnic minorities are overrepresented in the rural population (Beale, 2004; Jolliffe, 2004). Indeed, persistently poor counties comprise only 4 percent of the nation's population, but make up significantly higher percentages of the nonmetropolitan population, especially in the South (25 percent).

Previous research on the persistence of spatially concentrated rural poverty has understandably focused on historic deficits in rural education and human capital, market vicissitudes in agricultural production and natural resources (e.g., timber or coal), economic restructuring and globalization, geographic isolation and limited accessibility to labor and capital markets, and racial discrimination (Albrecht et al., 2000; Brown and Warner, 1991; Levernier et al., 2000; Lichter and McLaughlin, 1996). Economic development or job growth is often viewed as a panacea for rural communities. To be sure, economic growth creates new employment opportunities, improves the local and regional tax base, and presumably accelerates upward social and economic mobility among rural people, including the poor. But, as we highlight in this paper, these distal causes are necessarily mediated by changing demographic processes (especially migration) in persistently poor counties (Nord, 1998; Nord, Luloff and Jensen, 1995).

Poverty rates will decline if counties attract more nonpoor people and/or export their poor. A recent study by Fisher (2005), in fact, suggests that rural residence may be endogenous to poverty – that is, the higher poverty rate in rural areas may simply reflect the selection of poverty-prone individuals into rural areas rather than a causal effect of rural residence *per se*. Rural communities may be a collecting ground for poor people – a 'poverty trap' for America's least advantaged and most vulnerable population. Through birth and deaths (i.e., natural increase), the local demographic process of cohort succession may provide ballast to the poverty-producing effects of migration; that is, older and perhaps poorer rural cohorts are being replaced by a new generation who on average are better educated, better prepared for the job market, and therefore less likely to be poor (Lichter et al., 1981).

As we show in this paper, the 1990s clearly marked a period of significant change along several spatial dimensions of rural poverty. We examine recent patterns of population change in persistently poor counties in the United States. Unlike most previous research (Friedman and Lichter, 1998; Albrecht et al., 2000), our analyses focus on the proximate demographic components of population growth and decline. Specifically, we disaggregate recent population change in persistently poor counties into its two key components – net migration and natural increase. A fundamental objective is to highlight persistence and change in America's 'rural ghettos,' that is, counties with long histories of poverty – counties where a disproportionate share of the rural poor live, often in isolation and without a strong political voice in the renewed national discussion over poverty policy (Lyson and Falk, 1991; Brown and Lichter, 2004; Lichter and Jensen, 2002).

Rural Ghettos and Concentrated Poverty

A growing demographic literature has documented the extent and social implications of concentrated poverty in the United States (Massey and Denton, 1993;
Jargowsky, 1997), especially in inner-city neighborhoods of major metropolitan
cities. Recent empirical studies often emphasize the maladaptive behaviors and
values of the urban 'underclass' living in poor and racially segregated neighborhoods or ethnic enclaves (i.e., today's sanitized version of 'ghetto'). Indeed,
urban poverty in America has both a behavioral and spatial component (Cotter,
2002; Voss et al., 2006; Wilson, 1996). At the same time, the 1990s brought significant declines in the number of poor neighborhoods and in the share of the
poor people that live in them (Jargowsky and Yang, 2006). Whether this reflects
the improving circumstances of the poor themselves, or shows that poor people
have simply dispersed spatially is difficult to tell.[1] Urban redevelopment efforts –
the movement of affluent populations back to the city (i.e., 'gentrification') –
may also have played a role (see discussion by Quillian, 1999).

America's so-called 'rural ghettos' have understandably received much less systematic attention (Davidson, 1996; Fossett and Seibert, 1997; Lobao, 2004), and
it is unclear whether post-1990 trends are similar to patterns observed in
America's inner cities. This lack of rural research is nevertheless surprising. Many
rural areas fit the classic definition of 'ghetto' – that is, areas where people from
a specific racial or ethnic background live, are united by common culture (e.g.,
based on shared religion, ethnicity, or economic background), and are isolated
physically from mainstream society. In nonmetro America, over 444 counties, or
almost 20 percent of all nonmetro counties, had poverty rates of 20 percent or
more in 2000 (Beale, 2004). About 28 percent of people living in completely
rural counties were also residing in persistent poor counties (Jolliffe, 2004). This
compares with only 7.5 percent of the population living in the most urbanized
nonmetro counties, those with urban populations of 20,000 or more and adja-
cent to a metropolitan area. Clearly, America's rural poor people and families are
spatially concentrated, geographically isolated, and – like the metropolitan population – are seemingly immune to effective policy interventions (Brown and
Warner, 1991: Partridge and Rickman, 2005).

With the exception of Appalachia, which is overwhelmingly white in racial
composition (Pollard, 2004), persistently poor rural counties also are distinguished
by the heavy concentration of racial and ethnic minority populations. According

---

[1] Among other explanations, Jargowsky and Yang (2006) suggest that the decline in ghetto poverty
is due to decentralized residence patterns (i.e., residential mobility of the poor), such as the growth
in mixed-income developments, the expansion of Section 8 vouchers, and the abandonment of high-
density public housing projects in favor of scattered sites.

to Beale (2004), 210 (47 percent) of the high-poverty counties are black, 74 (17 percent) are Hispanic, and 40 (9 percent) counties reflect the low incomes of Native Americans.[2] For example, in communities on the Pine Ridge Indian Reservation in South Dakota, poverty rates are often in excess of 50 percent (O'Hare and Johnson, 2004; Lichter and Crowley, 2002). Some of America's most impoverished minorities live in remote and economically depressed rural areas, where poverty often is a way of life, passed down from generation to generation by their shared circumstances. Indeed, for rural minorities, parental and filial generations are linked by low education, family instability and out-of-wedlock childbearing, and low aspirations borne of limited opportunities for upward mobility and persistent racial discrimination. While 'rural ghetto' is an apt descriptive term that neatly summarizes both the behavioral and spatial dimensions of rural poverty, it also should be used advisedly. Most ghettos historically had origins that were largely involuntary, the result of forced segregation under apartheid-like conditions (e.g., Jewish ghettos in Eastern Europe during World War II). As we show in this chapter, the population of America's rural ghettos has changed rapidly over the past decade. Rural people are not 'trapped' by current economic circumstances, nor are they necessarily isolated culturally from American mainstream. Rural ghettos are diverse culturally and racially and are dynamic from a demographic standpoint, if measured by the in- and out-movement of both poor and nonpoor people and the changing demographic composition of their population (Nord, 1998).

Indeed, recent research suggests that the 1990s was a period of dramatic change in rural poverty patterns (Lichter and Johnson, 2005). First and foremost, nonmetro poverty rates – both the total and for children – declined more rapidly than metro rates during the past decade. The 1990s also brought large reductions in the number of persistently poor nonmetro counties, and declines in the share of rural people, including rural poor people and minorities, who were living in them. In particular, the number and percentage of rural people living in extremely poor counties (i.e., over 40 percent) declined dramatically over this decade. These patterns of population redistribution among the poor suggest a 'drying up' of America's rural ghettos – at least as they have been defined in the past at the county level – rather than providing new evidence of accelerated spatial inequality in nonmetro America. This has been unexpected news.

At the same time, a disproportionate share of rural blacks and Hispanics continue to live in counties with persistently high poverty rates. Over 50 percent of nonmetro African Americans lived in counties with poverty rates exceeding

---

[2] Minority-defined high-poverty areas are identified when over half of the poor population is a racial minority, or high minority poverty pushes the county's poverty rate over 20 percent (i.e., the white population's poverty rate is less than 20 percent).

20 percent or more, and 45 percent of them lived in persistently poor counties (Lichter and Johnson, 2005). The number of counties with persistently high rates of child poverty far exceeds the number of persistently poor counties overall (602 vs. 340). Any optimism implied by recent declines in concentrated rural poverty may be short-lived if poor children grow up to be poor adults. In fact, the 1990s may be an aberration that reflects America's economic boom and welfare reform revolution (Lichter and Crowley, 2004) rather than a fundamental shift in the spatial distribution and concentration of rural poor people. As we enter the twenty-first century, our study of persistent rural poverty comes at a propitious time, when rural poverty trends are difficult to forecast.

Current Study

The ensuing analysis contributes in two important ways to our understanding of the changing concentration of poverty in nonmetro America over the past decade. First, our primary goal is to increase our understanding of basic demographic processes reshaping population growth patterns in persistently poor counties. Are some rural areas becoming collecting grounds for the poor, attracting and retaining the most disadvantaged population segments of American society? Or are the rural poor – like their urban counterparts – becoming diffused spatially across the U.S. landscape? On the other hand, any resurgence of growth in persistently poor counties may reflect in-migration of nonpoor young adults and their families, a demographic process that masks persistent poverty among the indigenous population that has been left behind. Second, we also highlight important demographic trends among different age and race groups. Rural poverty has a clear intergenerational dimension (Fitchen, 1991; Duncan, 1996). It is important to understand whether current age- and race-specific patterns of net migration and natural increase have built-in momentum for future growth in the rural poverty population. Our analyses serve this goal.

Data and Methods

Data for our analysis come from the 1970 through 2000 U.S. Census Summary Files (1, 3 and 4) and from the 2005 Federal-State Cooperative Population Estimates file. We consider patterns of poverty across all 2,049 nonmetropolitan counties in the United States. The independent cities of Virginia are treated as counties. County equivalents, based on minor civil divisions, are used in the New England states. Counties are classified as metropolitan or nonmetropolitan using the current (2003) metropolitan definition. Nonmetropolitan counties reclassified as metropolitan by 2003 are treated as metropolitan throughout the analysis. A similar practice is used for counties that were metropolitan prior to 2003 but reverted to nonmetropolitan status under the current definition. Adopting a 2003 classification significantly reduces the number of nonmetropolitan counties available for analysis but has the advantage of maintaining a consistent set of counties for comparison over time.

For our purposes, we define the poor population as all individuals who live in families with annual incomes below the official poverty income thresholds. These income thresholds are determined by the Office of Management and Budget and vary by family size and configuration (i.e., adults and children). Family income is measured in the year previous to the year of census enumeration (e.g., 1999 for the 2000 Census). Poverty rates among children are similarly defined.

In this paper, we examine the distribution and concentration of poverty using a typology developed by the USDA Economic Research Service, which classifies counties based on whether poverty persisted over the 1970-to-2000 period. Counties are defined as being persistently poor if 20 percent or more of their populations were living in poverty continuously for the last 30 years (measured by the 1970, 1980, 1990 and 2000 decennial censuses). Using the 2004 classification, there are 386 persistently poor counties in the United States (comprising 12 percent of all U.S. counties and 4 percent of the U.S. population). Some 340 (88 percent) of the persistently poor counties are nonmetropolitan. We also use a new measure of persistent child poverty developed by Johnson (2005).[3] Persistent child poverty counties are identified as having 20 percent or more of the population, aged 17 or younger, that fall below the poverty line in all four of the most recent census years. There are 730 counties with persistent child poverty, of which 601 (82 percent) are nonmetropolitan counties.

For this analysis, we group the 334 counties with both persistent overall poverty and persistent child poverty together. The six counties with persistent overall poverty but not persistent child poverty, were classified as non-poor counties. Thus, to qualify as a persistently poor county for our analysis, a county must be nonmetropolitan and have both persistent overall poverty and persistent child poverty. Using this definition, 1,715 nonmetropolitan counties are classified as not in poverty. Given the stringent requirements to be classified as

---

[3]   William O'Hare of the Annie E. Casey Foundation provided valuable assistance in the conceptualization of the measure of persistent child poverty. Data on child poverty in 1970, 1980, 1990 and 2000 were compiled by the Economic Research Service of the USDA and provided by Tim Parker of ERS.

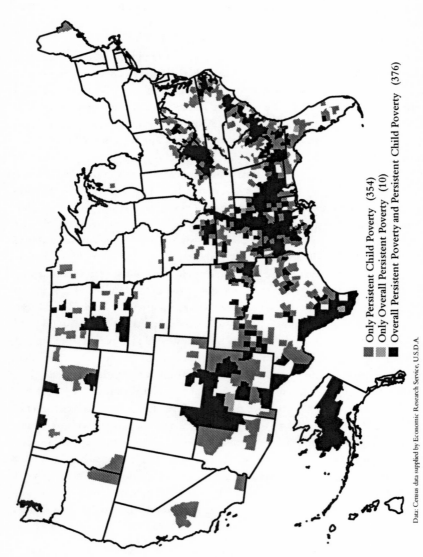

Data: Census data supplied by Economic Research Service, U.S.D.A.

Only Persistent Child Poverty (354)
Only Overall Persistent Poverty (10)
Overall Persistent Poverty and Persistent Child Poverty (376)

Figure 1: Countries with Overall Persistent Poverty and Persistent Child Poverty

persistently poor – at least three decades of high poverty rates – it is important to recognize that some of the counties included in our non-poverty category have experienced some poverty over the last three decades. We also include metropolitan counties for comparison in much of our analysis, but we do not differentiate between poverty and non-poverty metropolitan counties.

Findings

America's poor population is distributed unevenly over geographic space, which arguably magnifies the social and economic impact of poverty (e.g., social service delivery, community social capital and institutional resources) for those communities suffering from high concentrations of poverty. Figure 1 maps the spatial distribution of persistent poverty and persistent child poverty (See Lichter and Johnson, 2005, and Friedman and Lichter 1998 for more in-depth analysis with 1990 data). These data highlight significant concentrations of poverty in Appalachia, the Mississippi Delta, the lower Rio Grande River Valley, and on Indian Reservations in the Southwest and Great Plains. The map also underscores graphically the spatial overlap between persistent poverty and persistent child poverty. These poor regions contrast with other parts of rural America where neither overall persistent poverty nor persistent child poverty exists.

Demographic Trends in Poor and Non-Poor Counties

In general, nonmetropolitan areas enjoyed significant population growth and net migration gain during the rural rebound period of the 1990s and county poverty rates declined, even in persistently poor counties (Johnson, 1999 and 2006; Lichter and Johnson, 2005). The impact of this rural rebound is evidenced in Table 1. Not surprisingly, population growth rates were greater in non-poverty counties (9.5 percent) and smaller in the persistent poverty counties. Moreover, the demographic sources of the growth differed among the county types. Population gains in non-poverty counties came mostly from in-migration, whereas almost all of aggregate county population gains in persistently poor counties came from natural increase – the positive difference between births and deaths. Barely one-half of the persistent poverty counties but two-thirds of the non-poverty counties experienced net in-migration. Such a pattern is suggestive of how the deconcentration of poverty during the 1990s may have occurred. Given that children are at greater risk of poverty than other age groups, the

Table 1: Population Change, Net Migration, and Natural Increase by Poverty and Metropolitan Status, 1980 to 2005

	N of cases	Initial population	Population change			Net migration			Natural increase		
			Absolute change	Percent change	Percent growing	Absolute change	Percent change	Percent growing	Absolute change	Percent change	Percent growing
1980 to 1990:											
All nonmetropolitan	2,049	43,947	812	1.8	42.0	-1,477	-3.4	25.2	2,290	5.2	88.6
Persistent poverty	334	6,233	-125	-2.0	32.9	-586	-9.4	10.0	462	7.4	93.7
Not poverty	1,715	37,714	937	2.5	43.7	-891	-2.4	28.2	1,828	4.8	87.7
Metropolitan	1,089	182,585	21,356	11.7	78.6	6,684	3.7	54.9	14,672	8.0	97.4
Total	3,138	226,532	22,168	9.8	54.7	5,206	2.3	35.5	16,962	7.5	91.7
1990 to 2000:											
All nonmetropolitan	2,049	44,754	4,078	9.1	71.1	2,696	6.0	65.4	1,383	3.1	69.1
Persistent poverty	334	6,108	408	6.7	72.2	80	1.3	53.9	329	5.4	85.6
Not poverty	1,715	38,646	3,670	9.5	70.9	2,616	6.8	67.5	1,054	2.7	65.9
Metropolitan	1,089	203,941	28,639	14.0	91.6	12,963	6.4	81.2	15,676	7.7	92.8
Total	3,138	248,698	32,717	13.2	78.2	15,659	6.3	70.8	17,059	6.9	77.3
2000 to 2005											
All nonmetropolitan	2,051	48,842	1,090	2.2	50.3	549	1.1	42.4	541	1.1	58.9
Persistent poverty	334	6,517	5	0.1	43.7	-138	-2.1	25.5	143	2.2	78.7
Not poverty	1,717	42,325	1,085	2.6	51.5	687	1.6	45.7	398	0.9	55.0
Metropolitan	1,090	232,579	13,863	6.0	83.5	5,753	2.5	71.1	8,110	3.5	90.2
Total	3,141	281,421	14,953	5.3	61.8	6,302	2.2	52.4	8,651	3.1	69.7

Notes: 2003 Metropolitan Status used for all periods.

Initial population and absolute change reported in '000s

Data for 2000–2005 is 4/00 to 7/05.

Source: Census 1970–2000, Federal State Cooperative Estimates and ERS.

disproportionately high rates of natural increase in persistently poor counties may have contributed heavily to the poverty population.

A comparison of the 1990s and the 1980s provides further insights into the impact of overall demographic trends. The 1980s were a difficult economic time for rural America. Population losses were widespread (Fuguitt and Beale, 2001). These population losses were primarily due to net out-migration (Johnson and Fuguitt, 2000). Such migration losses were particularly large from the persistent poverty counties, which experienced a 9.4 percent migration loss during the decade, compared with a loss of 3.4 percent overall in nonmetropolitan counties. Population losses from out-migration were partially offset by a substantial natural increase in the persistent poverty counties. Although our paper focuses on poverty trends during the 1990s, preliminary data for 2000 to 2005 provide insights into the future patterns of demographic change in poverty counties. Persistent poverty counties again experienced significant out-migration during the post-2000 period. However, the substantial natural increase that has historically offset such migration losses has diminished. Recent population growth rates in persistent poverty counties have stagnated as a consequence.

Changes in the Poverty Population

Recent demographic trends in nonmetropolitan areas provide preliminary evidence concerning how the deconcentration of poverty unfolded. However, a fuller understanding of these trends is provided by examining data for the poor population. The poor population in both persistently poor and other nonmetropolitan counties grew more rapidly in the 1980s than the overall population (Table 2). Perhaps ironically, the most rapid gains occurred in the non-poverty counties, although persistent poverty counties continued to have much higher poverty rates. Increases in rural poverty during the 1980s are not linked to population increases – or, presumably, to the in-migration of low-income populations. In persistently poor counties, the poverty rate grew during the 1980s even as the total population declined as a result of the out-migration.

The 1990s, however, provide a striking contrast to patterns observed in the 1980s. Population increases were considerably greater than during the 1980s, and the number of people in poverty either diminished or grew only modestly. The sharpest declines in the poor population occurred in the persistent poverty counties, where the number of poor people dropped by 6 percent. In non-poverty counties, the poverty population grew by 5.3 percent. Significantly, poverty rates fell between 1990 and 2000 for both persistently poor and other counties.

Table 2: Change in Overall Population, Poverty Population and Percent in Poverty 1980 to 2000 by Metropolitan and Poverty Status

	N of cases	Population with known poverty status			Population below poverty line			Percent in poverty		
		Initial Population	Final Population	Percent Change	Initial Population	Final Population	Percent Change	Initial Poverty	Final Poverty	Percent Change
1980 to 1990										
All nonmetropolitan	2,043	42,705	43,349	1.5	6,794	7,494	10.3	15.9	17.3	8.7
Persistent poverty	334	6,109	5,952	-2.6	1,758	1,861	5.9	28.8	31.3	8.7
Not poverty	1,709	36,596	37,397	2.2	5,036	5,633	11.9	13.8	15.1	9.5
Metropolitan	1,089	178,119	198,618	11.5	20,594	24,247	17.7	11.6	12.2	5.6
Total	3,132	220,824	241,967	9.6	27,388	31,741	15.9	12.4	13.1	5.8
1990 to 2000										
All nonmetropolitan	2,049	43,349	47,085	8.6	6,794	6,955	2.4	15.7	14.8	-5.8
Persistent poverty	334	5,952	6,276	5.4	1,758	1,653	-6.0	29.5	26.3	-10.8
Not poverty	1,715	37,397	40,809	9.1	5,036	5,302	5.3	13.5	13.0	-3.5
Metropolitan	1,089	198,618	226,798	14.2	20,594	26,945	30.8	10.4	11.9	14.6
Total	3,138	241,967	273,883	13.2	27,388	33,900	23.8	11.3	12.4	9.4

Notes:

Population reported in 1,000s

Percent change calculated as ((Final − Initial)/Initial) *100

Metropolitan and poverty category as of 2003. Classifications from USDA-ERS.

Five persistent poverty counties without child poverty included in not poverty county.

This decline was a function of the combination of a diminishing poor population and growing overall population in the case of persistent poverty counties, and because population gains overall exceeded growth of the poor population in non-poverty counties. In contrast to nonmetropolitan counties, the poverty rate in metropolitan counties rose sharply in the 1990s as a result of the much more rapid growth in the size of poverty population. Indeed, the number of poor people grew by nearly 31 percent in metropolitan areas between 1990 and 2000. In contrast, the poor population grew by only 2.4 percent in nonmetropolitan counties. Even though the metropolitan population grew considerably faster than the nonmetropolitan population during the 1990s, the growth of the metropolitan poverty population was especially large. As a result, the metropolitan poverty rate grew by 14.6 percent, while the nonmetropolitan poverty rate dropped by 5.8 percent during the 1990s.

The gap between rural and urban poverty rates is now much narrower than it once was. In 1980, the percentage of poor in metropolitan areas was 11.6 compared with 15.9 in rural areas, a gap of 5.3 percent. By 2000, the percentage of poor in metropolitan areas had grown to 11.9 percent, whereas the rural percentage in poverty had diminished to 14.8 percent. Thus, the rural–urban poverty difference was only 2.9 percent in 2000. Poverty rates remain higher in nonmetropolitan than metropolitan areas, but the gap is clearly closing.

Changes in Poverty by Age Group

Poverty rates in America vary by age, with rural children being the most vulnerable populations (Lichter, Roscigno and Condron, 2002). An examination of the changing age profile of poverty between 1990 and 2000 provides additional insights into the contribution of demographic factors to changing poverty concentrations. The focus on children and youth also provides a window to the future, especially in poor children growing up to become poor adults.

Data in Table 3 show that poverty rates are consistently higher among children than other age cohorts. At the same time, poverty rates among children declined in both persistently poor and other counties between 1990 and 2000 (Table 3). This happened because the absolute number of poor children declined rapidly, especially in persistently poor counties (-15.2 percent). Declines in the non-poverty counties were smaller, but still significant. Large reductions in the absolute numbers of poor children in poverty occurred even as the population under age 18 grew or declined modestly. The pattern was distinctly different in metropolitan areas. Declines in child poverty rates occurred because overall growth in the number of children exceeded growth in the population of poor

Table 3: Change in Population, Population in Poverty and Percent in Poverty 1990 to 2000 by Age, Metropolitan and Poverty Status

	N of cases	Population with known poverty status			Population below poverty line			Percent in poverty		
		Initial population	Final population	Percent change	Initial population	Final population	Percent change	Initial poverty	Final poverty	Percent change
Under 18, 1990 to 2000										
All nonmetropolitan	2,049	11,796	12,069	2.3	2,665	2,363	-11.3	22.6	19.6	-13.3
Persistent poverty	334	1,809	1,774	-1.9	731	620	-15.2	40.4	34.9	-13.5
Not poverty	1,715	9,987	10,295	3.1	1,934	1,743	-9.9	19.4	16.9	-12.6
Metropolitan	1,089	50,807	58,856	15.8	8,764	9,385	7.1	17.2	15.9	-7.6
Total	3,138	62,603	70,925	13.3	11,429	11,748	2.8	18.3	16.6	-9.3
Adults 18–64, 1990 to 2000										
All nonmetropolitan	2,049	25,229	28,112	11.4	3,676	3,738	1.7	14.6	13.3	-8.7
Persistent poverty	334	3,364	3,687	9.6	881	849	-3.6	26.2	23.0	-12.1
Not poverty	1,715	21,865	24,425	11.7	2,795	2,889	3.4	12.8	11.8	-7.5
Metropolitan	1,089	124,574	141,497	13.6	12,857	15,128	17.7	10.3	10.7	3.6
Total	3,138	149,803	169,609	13.2	16,533	18,866	14.1	11.0	11.1	0.8
Adults over 64, 1990 to 2000										
All nonmetropolitan	2,049	6,325	6,902	9.1	1,154	857	-25.7	18.2	12.4	-31.9
Persistent poverty	334	779	813	4.4	249	185	-25.7	32.0	22.8	-28.8
Not poverty	1,715	5,546	6,089	9.8	905	672	-25.7	16.3	11.0	-32.4
Metropolitan	1,089	23,237	26,444	13.8	2,627	2,432	-7.4	11.3	9.2	-18.7
Total	3,138	29,562	33,346	12.8	3,781	3,289	-13.0	12.8	9.9	-22.9

Notes:
Population reported in 1,000s
Percent change calculated as ((Final − Initial)/Initial) *100
Metropolitan and poverty category as of 2003. Classifications from USDA-ERS.
Five persistent poverty counties without child poverty included in persistent poverty group.

children. Growth in the number of poor children exceeded 7 percent in metropolitan areas between 1990 and 2000.

For the population aged 18 to 64, poverty rates also declined in both nonmetropolitan county groups. The demographic dynamics that underlay these reductions, however, were somewhat different for 18-to-64-year-olds than for the overall population. Indeed, poverty rates dipped in the 1990s for the working age population because the working age adults in nonmetropolitan areas grew significantly, while the number of poor working age adults either grew slowly (in the case of non-poor counties) or diminished slightly (in the case of persistently poor counties). The case was quite different in metropolitan counties. Here, adult poverty rates grew because the number of poor adults grew faster than the overall working age population.

The most dramatic declines in poverty rates in both metropolitan and nonmetropolitan America were among the elderly. These reductions were especially large for seniors in nonmetropolitan areas, but poverty reductions in metropolitan areas were also substantial. The sharp reductions in elderly poverty rates in nonmetropolitan areas have a simple demographic explanation. They occurred because the number of poor seniors declined by at least 25 percent, even though the total senior population grew. The 1990s reductions in elderly poverty rates were relatively undifferentiated across the rural county types. They were slightly smaller in the persistently poor counties, where the growth of the senior population was comparatively small. The decline in the population of poor seniors in metropolitan areas was only about one-third of declines in rural areas. The population of seniors in metropolitan areas nevertheless grew faster than in rural areas, resulting in a more modest, though still significant decline in the percentage of the urban senior poor population. Despite the substantial declines in the number and rate of poverty in rural areas, the risk of poverty remains higher in rural than in urban areas.

The dramatic reductions in poverty among senior citizens during the 1990s underscores how a societal commitment to reducing poverty through a combination of government programs (social security and Medicare), changes in government policy (i.e., 401K, 403B) and private actions (corporate, government and non-profit pensions) can alter the poverty levels in the nation. It also raises many questions about why such actions have been taken for some groups (senior citizens), but not for others (children). It is quite striking that while the number of poor seniors in rural counties is now down to only 857,000, there were 2,363,000 poor children. In absolute terms, the poverty problem in rural America resides among its children and youth.

Age-Specific Migration Trends

Changes in the number of poor and non-poor people in nonmetropolitan areas are influenced both by migration and by natural increase. Migration is of particular interest because of its potential to rapidly alter the demographic composition of the population. Recent research underscores the important role that age plays in migration (Johnson et.al., 2005). Here we look carefully at the age specific migration patterns to better understand how migration has contributed to recent poverty trends in nonmetropolitan America.

Migration in nonmetropolitan counties with persistent poverty. Our previous analysis suggests that reductions in size and rate of the poverty population have been particularly pronounced in the persistent poverty counties. It also suggested slight declines in population of poor children between 1990 and 2000. Age-specific net migration rates, which are provided in Figure 2, indicate that most of the loss occurred among teenagers. Persistent poor counties lost both whites[4] [EBS1] and blacks in their teens. Although the rate of loss was greater for blacks (data not shown), the actual number of net out-migrants was greater for whites (Figure 2). In contrast, there was an inflow – albeit modest – of teenage Hispanics. Similar patterns are observed among those aged 0–9. Our analysis of historical trends in persistent poverty counties suggests that the outflow of children (both aged 0–9 and 10–17) was more pronounced in the 1980s than during the 1990s, but that the overall age pattern of net migration remained unchanged (data not shown).

Any attempt to assess migration patterns of poor children is speculative at best. However, given that the persistent poverty counties had relatively high rates of natural increase in both the 1980s and 1990s (these would be the groups that were under 18 in 2000), and given that the age-specific migration data reveal that the outflow of children was relatively modest during the 1990s, it is quite plausible that some of the overall reduction in the number of poor children in these counties resulted from some families rising out of poverty. It is also possible that reductions in child poverty also resulted in part from children in their late teens leaving these counties.

Persistent poverty counties experienced substantial population losses of young adults (especially among whites and blacks) and modest population gains at most other ages. The loss of young adults in their 20s, which has been occurring for decades, has two likely impacts on future poverty. First, it reduces pressures on the local labor force, especially where unemployment is high and the local

---

[4]   In this paper all Hispanics are grouped together; therefore, references to whites, blacks or others are to those of non-Hispanic origin. Those who report two or more races are proportionally allocated to the white, black, Hispanic and other categories. See Johnson et al. (2005) for more details on age-specific migration.

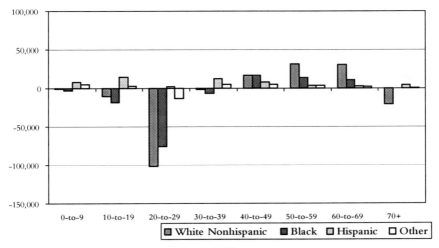

Data: U.S. Census Bureau. Johnson, et al. 2005.
Note: Two or More Races is proportionally allocated among White, Hispanic, Black and Other

Figure 2: Net Migration, 1990 to 2000. Nonmetro with Persistent Poverty

economy is weak. And, second, the decline of young adults also places downward pressure on fertility and the population size of the next generation of rural children. Given the vulnerability of children to poverty, this may have the effect of placing downward demographic pressure on the number of children in poverty in future years. But, of course, this assumes that the most vulnerable young adults are most likely to leave rural areas. Previous research shows instead that young adults with the highest career and educational aspirations and lowest poverty rates typically are most likely to out-migrate. Under this alternative demographic scenario (Kandel and Cromartie, 2004), out-migration of the young is likely to increase rather than decrease poverty rates. Yet our results indicate that poverty is diminishing in persistently poor counties. In contrast to trends among young adults, these counties experienced a modest inflow of adults of all races in their 40s, 50s and 60s. The in-migration of older working age adults to these counties is a recent phenomenon. Generally lower poverty rates among these age groups may have contributed to stable or diminishing levels of adult poverty, despite the overall growth of this population.

Among adults aged 65 and over, there was modest net in-migration for all minority racial groups. However, among whites, there was a net outflow of adults over the age of 70. Modest population gains among the younger older adults, together with 'aging in place' of the long-term resident population, have

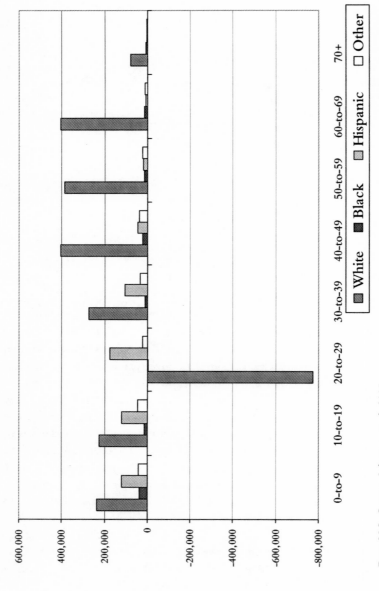

Data: U.S. Census, Johnson, et al. 2005
Note: Two or more races is proportionally allocated to four racial categories

Figure 3: Net Migration, 1990 to 2000: Nonmetro without Persistent Poverty

contributed to relatively more rapid growth of the elderly population. Growth over the longer term, however, will be dampened by the high mortality rates of its aging population. Generational succession – the replacement of older with younger residents – may also reduce the size of the poor population. If history is our guide, older residents of these counties are likely to have less income and resources than the generations that will follow them.

Migration in non-poor nonmetropolitan counties. Patterns of age-specific migration to non-poverty counties contrast sharply with the persistent poverty counties. The number of in-migrants exceeded the number of out-migrants at every age and for every race/ethnic group. Whites in their 20s were the only exception (Figure 3). Hispanic gains are the largest based on rates (data not shown), but the whites gains are considerably larger in absolute terms.

In contrast to the persistently poor counties, which experienced out-migration of both white and black children, non-poverty counties registered significant gains in the number of migrant children, regardless of race. However, most of the absolute increase from migration came from white children, who typically are at low risk of poverty. The gain from less advantaged Hispanic children also was substantial. Growth from the in-migration of children population has occurred over the last thirty years. The inflow of children to such counties has been substantial, but poverty rates for children have declined, a fact that presumably reflects the changing socioeconomic status of their parents.

Perhaps ironically, non-poverty counties were the only nonmetropolitan counties to experience an absolute increase in the number of poor people. These increases occurred mainly among the working-age population. A look at the migration data may help to explain why. The absolute loss of white young adults in their 20s is modest on a rate basis (dwarfed by the net migration gain of Hispanics), but in absolute terms it represents a loss of nearly 800,000 people. In contrast, the Hispanic young adult gain is about 175,000. The loss of young white adults from rural areas reflected in this net outflow of young whites represents a significant loss of human capital. It has been going on for decades. Although the Hispanic gain represents a significant addition to the rural labor force, recent research documents the concentration of Hispanics in relatively low-wage industries (Kandel and Cromartie, 2004). Among older working age adults, an influx of whites and, to a lesser extent, Hispanics offsets the young adult outflow.

The 1990s also ushered in a large net in-migration of adults in their 60s to these non-poverty counties. The largest absolute gains (roughly 400,000) are for whites. To be sure, some of these migrants are relatively affluent retirees moving to the retirement and recreation counties that are common in these new destinations. This pattern, combined with the influence of better pensions and social

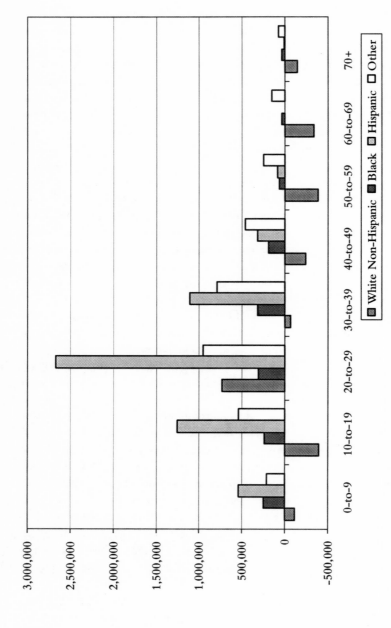

Data: U.S. Census Bureau, Johnson, et al. 2005

Note: Two or more races is proportionally allocated among white, Hispanic, black, and other

Figure 4: Net Migration, 1990 to 2000: Metro

security payments and with differential mortality of the oldest and poorest rural residents, has contributed to the substantial declines in poverty among older rural residents.

Metropolitan migration patterns. While nonmetropolitan poverty generally diminished during the 1990s, both in relative and absolute terms, the situation was different in metropolitan areas. The urban poverty rate increased between 1990 and 2000. The absolute number of poor people in urban areas also increased by 31 percent compared with an increase of 2.4 percent in rural areas. The modest nonmetropolitan absolute gain in the number of poor people can be attributed entirely to gains in the working age poor. Increases in the metropolitan poor population were considerably larger and resulted from gains in both the number of poor children and working-age adults.

Recent migration trends may help us to understand these contrasting patterns. For example, metropolitan areas experienced substantial in-migration of minority children during the 1990s, but lost white children to out-migration (Figure 4). Minority fertility rates were higher than those for whites, which reflects, at least in part, the fact that the minority populations were considerably younger in age than the white population. As a result, the substantial natural increase in metropolitan areas during the 1990s was disproportionately comprised of minority populations. The growth in the number of minority children – with disproportionately high poverty rates – has undoubtedly contributed to unusually rapid increases in the number of metropolitan poor children in the 1990s.

Among working-age adults, metropolitan counties also gained minority residents of all ages through migration, but lost whites of all ages except young adults aged 20–29. The working age minority population is composed primarily of blacks and Hispanics, but also includes a significant number of Asians in some metropolitan areas. Although minority median household incomes are considerably lower than those for whites, this is not the case for Asian households. In this sense, the minority migration streams into metropolitan areas differ from those into rural areas, where Asians are relatively uncommon. Unless the whites leaving metropolitan areas are more likely to be poor than are most white households, which seems unlikely, migration flows between metropolitan and nonmetropolitan areas are likely to place upward demographic pressure on metropolitan poverty. Without definitive data, however, such speculation awaits additional empirical testing.

Metropolitan areas are also losing retirement-age migrants, especially whites, to nonmetropolitan areas. In general, migration rates among the elderly are low, but highly selective. Elderly migrants tend to be younger and more affluent than nonmigrants, and the migration flows for seniors are much more geographically focused than for overall migration. A significant proportion of retirement-age migrants are attracted to rural retirement and recreational areas (Johnson, 2006). The loss of such affluent retirement-age, mostly white migrants may partially explain why recent poverty declines among seniors were lowest in metropolitan areas. The relatively small number of affluent metropolitan seniors moving to rural areas would be expected to have a much larger impact on poverty rates among the smaller rural senior population than it would have on the much larger urban senior population left behind. However, the data show a faster rate of poverty reduction in rural areas and a somewhat slower rate of reduction in urban areas. Urban poverty levels among seniors nevertheless remain significantly lower than those observed in rural areas.

Natural Increase Trends

Most analyses of recent demographic change have focused on net migration because it can rapidly alter the demographic and economic structure of both areas of origin and destination. However, natural increase can also play a significant but less well appreciated role in the demographic transformation of affected areas. In this section, we briefly examine the patterns of natural increase in persistent poverty counties. Historically, rural fertility rates exceeded urban rates for a variety of reasons: different family size preferences and norms; poorer contraception and reproductive health services; and greater exposure to the risk of intercourse (e.g., earlier age at marriage and lower divorce rates). High fertility in rural areas offset the traditional exodus of substantial numbers of rural out-migrants of prime childbearing age to metropolitan areas. Indeed, our analyses of age-specific net migration demonstrated that this net outflow of young adults continued in the 1990s. But, unlike the past, rural–urban disparities in the number of children born per woman no longer exist. Moreover, the historical outflow of young adults from nonmetropolitan areas that has now been sustained for nearly a century has consequences for mortality patterns through the population aging process, i.e., out-migration of young adults accelerates increases in the share of high-mortality age groups (Johnson, 2006).

In nonmetropolitan counties with persistent poverty, the number of children being born diminished between the 1980s and the 1990s (Figure 5). The number of births declined by nearly 9 percent over this period. In absolute terms, there were nearly 100,000 fewer births in the 1990s than in the 1980s. Moreover, the number of deaths increased by nearly 6 percent to 665,000. Thus, the number of children, who are at the highest risk of poverty, declined significantly in the persistent poverty counties. At the same time, deaths to older adults

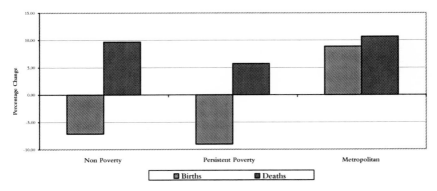

Figure 5: Percent Change in Births and Deaths by Poverty Status, 1980–1990 compared to 1990–2000

increased, especially among the oldest-old with the highest mortality rates. Because the oldest seniors tend to be at the greatest risk of poverty, the overall effect has likely reduced the number of seniors in poverty. We do not have birth and death data for the poor, but the overall trends are consistent with speculation that the number of people at high risk of poverty is diminishing, even in persistently poor areas.

In nonmetropolitan counties without persistent poverty, the trends were quite similar. Births dropped by 400,000, or 7.1 percent, from the 1980s to the 1990s. Deaths, on the other hand, increased in these counties over the same period. Indeed, the 1990s brought 9.7 percent more deaths (370,000) than the 1980s. As in persistent poverty counties, declining natural increase or natural decrease place downward pressure on poverty rates in nonmetropolitan areas – even relatively affluent ones.

The pattern is somewhat different in metropolitan areas, where the number of births increased by 2.7 million (8.8 percent) in the 1990s compared with the 1980s. The number of deaths also increased by 1,724,000, or 10.7 percent. However, the balance of birth and deaths – natural increase – in metropolitan areas likely had the effect of increasing the population at risk of poverty. That is, natural increase probably increased the percentage of the high-risk population (especially children). Our conclusions, of course, remain highly speculative. We do not have the requisite birth and death data by poverty status for definitive answers, but our results nevertheless are suggestive of possible demographic explanations as to why recent reductions in rural poverty have exceeded those in urban areas.

Summary and Conclusion

The primary goal of this study has been to examine the extent and etiology of changing patterns of concentrated rural poverty. Our empirical results indicated that the 1990s marked a significant departure from historical trends in rural poverty. First and foremost, nonmetro poverty rates – even in persistently poor counties – declined during the 1990s (see Lichter and Johnson, 2005). The 1990s also brought absolute reductions in the number of poor people in persistently poor nonmetro counties, even as the rest of the population grew in these areas. In contrast, metropolitan poverty rates and the number of urban poor increased. These changing redistribution patterns among the poor imply a 'drying up' of some of America's rural ghettos – at least as they have been defined in the past at the county level (e.g., Beale and Gibbs, 2006). At the same time, our understanding of demographic processes underlying recent poverty trends remains incomplete. Our study addresses this void.

Specifically, the analyses presented in this chapter provides several lessons about the role of population change – fueled by migration and natural increase – in explaining declining rates of poverty in rural America. For example, our analyses indicated that reductions in poverty in the persistently poor counties resulted both from reductions in the number of poor people and from overall population growth. Reductions in the number of poor people were particularly marked among those under 18 and among seniors in the persistent poverty counties. There was also a slight decline in the number of poor of working age. Clearly, part of the explanation for the decline in the number of poor children is located in reductions in the number of births in persistently poor counties during the 1990s. With fewer children born, fewer were at risk of poverty. The number of deaths also increased in such counties and this also may have contributed to sharp reductions in the number of poor seniors. The oldest of the old are both more likely to be poor and to have higher mortality.

Poverty rates also declined in nonmetropolitan counties without persistent poverty. Here, the slight gain in the population in poverty lagged far behind the overall population gain. The number of children in poverty declined in these counties, as did the number of seniors in poverty. Poverty declines occurred despite the fact that the overall population in each group grew. Among the working-age population, the number in poverty also grew slightly, but the overall population grew more rapidly. As in the persistent poverty counties, an outflow of young adults from rural areas was accompanied by more deaths and fewer births during the 1990s.

The pattern of change was quite different in metropolitan areas, where gains in the number of people in poverty far exceeded overall population gains. As a result, poverty rates increased in the 1990s. Most of the poverty increase occurred among the working age population, but the number of poor children also increased. The number of seniors in poverty declined in metro areas. Our analysis suggested that much of the recent metropolitan population growth was due to net in-migration, although natural increase also played a role. The number of births in metropolitan areas also increased rapidly during the 1990s.

Overall, the reductions of the number and percentage of both children and seniors in poverty in rural areas has placed downward demographic pressure on America's poverty rates. On a less optimistic note, our results showed that child and senior poverty rates remained higher in rural than in urban areas in the 1990s, with persistent poverty counties – surprisingly – being especially disadvantaged. Moreover, recent data also suggest that poverty rates may have turned upwards again after 2000 (O'Hare and Johnson, 2004). And, the number of nonmetro counties with high levels of child poverty that persist over several decades is much higher than the number of persistent poverty counties overall (Johnson, 2005). This is an important demographic disparity, especially if 'concentration' effects prey disproportionately on children and adolescents as they make their way to adulthood and productive adult roles. One implication of our results is that rural children – those still in persistent poor counties – may be more disadvantaged than ever, if we measure disadvantage by the lack of exposure to middle-class role models and environments that promote positive development. In other words, their circumstances may be diverging rapidly from those of most of America's middle-class children (see McLanahan, 2004). Rural children have not been immune to the effects of rapid changes in family structure, especially the growth in single-parent families with high poverty rates (Lichter et al., 2002). Clearly, the harsh residential circumstances of rural poor children jeopardize the likelihood of a successful and productive adulthood. They are more likely than children elsewhere to become poor adults, a life course cycle that reinforces intergenerational poverty and spatially concentrated poverty in forgotten rural areas.

In the final analyses, our study provides only partial answers to the questions of why spatial inequality in rural America is diminishing. Moreover, we cannot determine with our county-level data whether declining concentration of rural poverty is simply masking increasing concentration at the micro-scale level, a pattern of nucleated settlement of the poor *within* counties. Evidence of declines in the concentration of rural poor across poor counties represents only a first step toward a greater understanding of the complex set of demographic, economic, political and social forces that combine to produce the spatial patterns of poverty in rural America.

Bibliography

Albrecht, Don E., Albrecht, Carol M., and Albrecht, Stan L. (2000) 'Poverty in Nonmetropolitan America: Impacts of Industrial, Employment, and Family Variables,' *Rural Sociology* vol. 65, pp. 87–103.

Beale, Calvin L. (2004) 'Anatomy of Nonmetro High-Poverty Areas: Common in Plight, Distinctive in Nature,' *Amber Waves* (February), pp. 21–27.

Beale, Calvin L. and Gibbs, Robert M. (2006) 'Severity and Concentration of Persistent High Poverty in Nonmetro Areas,' *Amber Waves*, vol. 4, no. 1, pp. 10–11.

Brown, David L. and Hirschl, Thomas A. (1995) 'Household Poverty in Rural and Metropolitan- Core Area of the United States,' *Rural Sociology*, vol. 60, pp. 44–66.

Brown, David L. and Warner, Mildred E. (1991)'Persistent Low-Income Nonmetropolitan Areas in the United States: Some Conceptual Challenges for Development Policy,' *Policy Studies Journal*, vol. 19, pp. 22–41.

Brown, J. Brian and Lichter, Daniel T. (2004) 'Poverty, Welfare, and the Livelihood Strategies of Nonmetropolitan Single Mothers,' *Rural Sociology*, vol. 69, pp. 282–301.

Cotter, David A. (2002) 'Poor People in Poor Places: Local Opportunity Structures and Household Poverty,' *Rural Sociology*, vol. 67, pp. 534–555.

Davidson, Osha Gray (1996) *Broken Heartland: The Rise of America's Rural Ghetto* (Iowa City: University of Iowa Press).

Duncan, Cynthia M. (1996) 'Understanding Persistent Poverty: Social Class Context in Rural Communities,' *Rural Sociology*, vol. 61, pp. 103–124.

Economic Research Service (2006) 'Rural Income, Poverty, and Welfare: Rural Poverty,' www.ers.usda.gov/Briefing/IncomePovertyWelfare/HighPoverty

Fitchen, Janet M. (1991) *Endangered Spaces, Enduring Places* (Boulder, CO: Westview).

Fisher, Monica (2005) 'On the Empirical Finding of a Higher Risk of Poverty in Rural Areas: Is Rural Residence Endogenous to Poverty?' *Journal of Agricultural and Resource Economics*, vol. 30, pp. 185–199.

Fossett, Mark A. and Seibert, Theresa (1997) *Long Time Coming: Racial Inequality in the Nonmetropolitan South, 1940–1990* (Boulder, CO: Westview).

Friedman, Samatha and Lichter, Daniel T. (1998) 'Spatial Inequality and Poverty among American Children,' *Population Research and Policy Review*, vol. 17, pp. 91–109.

Fuguitt, Glen V. and Beale, Calvin L. (2001) 'Recent Trends in Nonmetropolitan Migration: Toward a New Turnaround?' *Growth and Change*, vol. 27, pp. 156–274.

Ghelfi, Linda M. (2001) 'Most Persistently Poor Rural Counties in the South Remained Poor in 1995,' *Rural America*, vol. 15, no. 4, pp. 36–49.

Jargowsky, Paul A. (1997) *Poverty and Place: Ghettos, Barrios, and the American City* (New York: Russell Sage Foundation).

Jargowsky, Paul A. and Yang, Rebecca (2006) 'The "Underclass" Revised: A Social Problem in Decline,' *Journal of Urban Affairs*, vol. 28, pp. 55–70.

Johnson, K. M. (1999) 'The Rural Rebound,' *PRB Reports on America* vol. 1, no. 3 (Washington, D.C.: Population Reference Bureau).

Johnson, Kenneth M. (2005) 'Persistent Child Poverty in the United States, 1970 to 2000,' Poster prepared by the Population Reference Bureau (Washington, D.C.).

Johnson, Kenneth M (2006) 'Demographic Trends in Rural and Small Town America,' *Reports on America*, vol. 1, no. 1, pp. 1–35. Durham, NH: Carsey Foundation, University of New Hampshire.

Johnson, Kenneth M. and Fuguitt, Glen V. (2000) 'Continuity and Change in Rural Migration, 1950–1995,' *Rural Sociology*, vol. 65, pp. 27–49.

Johnson, K.M., Voss, P.R., Hammer, R.B., Fuguitt, G.V., and McNiven, S. (2005) 'Temporal and Spatial Variation in Age-Specific Net Migration in the United States,' *Demography*, vol. 42, pp. 751–812.

Jolliffe, D. (2004) 'Rural Poverty at a Glance,' Rural Development Research Report No. 100 www.ers.usda.gov/publications/rdrr100.

Kandel, W. and Cromartie, J. (2004) *New Patterns of Hispanic Settlement in Rural America,* Rural Development Research Report 99 (Washington: Economic Research Service, USDA).

Levernier, William, Partridge, Mark D. and Rickman, Dan S. (2000) 'The Causes of Regional Variations in U.S. Poverty: A Cross-County Analysis,' *Journal of Regional Sciences*, vol. 40, pp. 473–497.

Lichter, Daniel T. and Crowley, Martha A. (2002) 'Poverty in America: Beyond Welfare Reform,' *Population Bulletin*, vol. 57 (June), pp. 1–36.

Lichter, Daniel T. and Crowley, Martha A. (2004) 'Welfare Reform and Child Poverty: Effects of Maternal Employment, Marriage, and Cohabitation,' *Social Science Research*, vol. 33, pp. 385–408.

Lichter, Daniel T., Fuguitt, Glenn V., Heaton, Tim B. and Clifford, William B. (1981) 'Components of Change in the Residential Concentration of the Elderly Population, 1950–1975,' *Journal of Gerontology*, vol. 36, pp. 480–489.

Lichter, Daniel. T. and Jensen, Leif (2002) 'Rural America in Transition: Poverty and Welfare at the Turn of the Twenty-First Century,' in B.A. Weber, G.J. Duncan and L.A. Whitener (eds.) *Rural Dimensions of Welfare Reform* (Kalamazoo, MI: W.E. Upjohn Institute for Employment Research), pp. 113–46.

Lichter, Daniel T. and Johnson, Kenneth (2005) 'Is Rural Poverty Concentrating?' Paper presented at the annual meetings of the Rural Sociological Society (Tampa) (August).

Lichter, Daniel T. and Johnson, Kenneth (2006) 'Emerging Rural Settlement Patterns and the Geographic Redistribution of America's New Immigrants,' *Rural Sociology*, vol. 71, pp. 109–31.

Lichter, Daniel T. and McLaughlin, Diane K. (1996) 'Changing Economic Opportunities, Family Structure, and Poverty in Rural Areas,' *Rural Sociology*, vol. 60, pp. 688–706.

Lichter, Daniel T., Roscigno, Vincent J. and Condron, Dennis J. (2002) 'Rural Children and Youth at Risk,' in David L. Brown and Louis Swanson (eds.), *Challenges for Rural America in the Twenty-First Century* (University Park, PA: Penn State University Press).

Lobao, Linda (2004) 'Continuity and Change in Place Stratification: Spatial Inequality and Middle-Range Territorial Units,' *Rural Sociology*, vol. 69, pp. 1–30.

Lyson, Thomas A. and Falk, William W. (1991) *Forgotten Places: Uneven Development and Loss of Opportunity in Rural America* (Lawrence, KS: University of Kansas Press).

Massey, Douglas S. and Denton, Nancy (1993) *American Apartheid: Segregation and the Making of the Underclass* (Cambridge, MA: Harvard University Press).

McLanahan, Sara (2004) 'Diverging Destinies: How Children are Faring under the Second Demographic Transition,' *Demography*, vol. 41, pp. 607–27.

Nord, Mark. (1998) 'Poor People on the Move: County-to-County Migration and the Spatial Concentration of Poverty,' *Journal of Regional Science*, vol. 38, pp. 329–51.

Nord, Mark, Luloff, A.E. and Jensen, L. (1995) 'Migration and the Spatial Concentration of Poverty,' *Rural Sociology*, vol. 60, pp. 399–415.

O'Hare, William P. and Johnson, Kenneth M. (2004) 'Child Poverty in Rural America,' *Reports on America* vol. 4 (March), pp. 1–19.

Parisi, Domenique, McLaughlin, Diane K., Grice, Steve M., Taquino, Michael, and Gill, Duane A. (2003) 'TANF Participation Rates: Do Community Conditions Matter?' *Rural Sociology*, vol. 68, pp. 491–512.

Partridge, Mark D. and Rickman, Dan S. (2005) 'High Poverty Non-metropolitan Counties in the United States: Can Economic Development Help?' *International Regional Science Review* vol. 28, no. 4, pp. 415–40.

Pollard, Kelvin M. 2004. 'A "New Diversity": Race and Ethnicity in the Appalachian Region,' Series on Demographic and Economic Change in Appalachia (Washington D.C.: Population Reference Bureau and Appalachian Regional Commission).

Quillian, Lincoln (1999) 'Migration Patterns and the Growth of High-Poverty Neighborhoods, 1970–1990,' *American Journal of Sociology*, vol. 105, no. 1, pp. 1–37.

Saenz, Rogelio (1997) 'Ethnic Concentration and Chicano Poverty: A Comparative Approach,' *Social Science Research*, vol. 26, pp. 205–28.

U.S. Census Bureau (1990) Summary Tape File 1 (STF1) and Summary Tape File 3 (STF3) (Washington, D.C.: Bureau of the Census).

U.S. Census Bureau (2000) U.S. Census, Summary File 1 (SF1), Summary File 3 (SF3) and Summary File 4 (SF4). (Washington, D.C.: U.S. Bureau of the Census).

U.S. Census Bureau (1981) Census of the Population: 1980. Characteristics of the Population (Washington, D.C.: U.S. Government Printing Office).

U.S. Census Bureau (1973) Census of Population: 1970. Characteristics of the Population (Washington, D.C.: U.S. Government Printing Office).

U.S. Census Bureau (2006) Federal-State Cooperative Population Estimates, July 1, 2005 (Washington, D.C.: U.S. Census Bureau).

Voss, Paul R., Long, David D., Hammer, Roger B. and Friedman, Samantha (2006) 'County Child Poverty Rates in the U.S.: A Spatial Regression Approach,' *Population Research and Policy Review* vol. 25 (October).

Weber, Bruce, Jensen, Leif, Miller, Kathy, Mosley, Jane M., and Fisher, Monica (2005) 'A Critical Review of Rural Poverty Literature: Is There Truly a Rural Effect?' *International Regional Science Review*, vol. 28, no. 4, pp. 381–414.

Wilson, William Julius (1996) *When Work Disappears: The World of the New Urban Poor* (New York: Alfred A. Knopf).

PART THREE
The Politics and Public Policy of Population Change

10
Social Change, Families and Values: Morality Politics in Contemporary America

Christopher J. Bailey

Moral concerns have assumed a prominent place in contemporary American politics. From efforts to restrict abortion and the availability of contraceptives, to the promotion of sexual education policies espousing abstinence, to debates over same-sex marriages, to proposals to reform divorce law, to attempts to restrict cloning and limit stem-cell research, to controversy over physician-assisted suicide and a right to die, the political agenda is rife with moral issues. Moral concerns have even led politicians to legislate on fashion and cheerleading. In 2005 the Virginia House voted to ban the practice of wearing trousers so low that underwear is visible. Virginians showing too much of their boxer shorts or G-strings could be fined $50. Later that year, the Texas House voted to ban 'sexually suggestive' cheerleading in schools.

Two broad social and political developments underlie this contemporary outburst of moral fervor in the United States. First, social changes and an assertion of group identities over the last four decades have stimulated debate about core values and belief systems (Wuthnow, 1989; Hunter, 1991; Dionne, 1991; Layman, 2001; White, 2003). On one side of this debate are 'traditionalists' who regard rising divorce rates, an increasing incidence of out-of-wedlock births, growing numbers of single-parent households, and the affirmation of gender and homosexual rights as evidence of moral decline. They stress an absolutist set of values based on religious texts that are non-negotiable. On the other side of the debate are 'progressives' who stress a multicultural and largely secular view of morality. They reject the idea that moral 'truths' are derived from transcendent religious texts and champion a more relativist approach to moral authority. Second, changes in party structures and the rise of participatory democracy have given activists with deeply held views opportunities to dominate the political process (Fiorina, 1999, pp. 395–425; Fiorina, 2003, pp. 511–41). Direct primaries, campaign finance reform, the rise of candidate-centered elections, and the increasing use of referenda have provided 'traditionalists' and 'progressives' with the means to exert influence, gain office, and pursue their agendas at all levels of government.

The result of these developments is a contemporary 'morality war' waged largely by issue activists and political elites (Williams, 1997; Fiorina, 2005). Opinion polls not only reveal that moral issues typically have little salience among the general population, but also that the public is not as deeply divided on most of these issues as commonly supposed. Media claims of a polarized nation engaged in a widespread and deep-rooted war over core values are misleading. While a bitter struggle over issues such as abortion, homosexuality, stem cell research and a raft of moral issues is undoubtedly taking place in the United States, there is little evidence that the public is fully engaged in these battles. The majority of Americans have met the social changes of the last four decades with an equanimity and tolerance that belies the vitriolic debate and occasional violence that characterizes the actions of activists and political elites involved in fighting the 'morality war' (Wolfe, 1998).

The Changing Social Fabric of America

Over the last four decades, economic, technological, political, and legal forces have transformed the social fabric of the United States, particularly the structure of American families. The traditional two-parent nuclear family with a breadwinning father, home-making mother, and two or more children under the age of eighteen that dominated the 1950s has gradually given way to a wide variety of family forms as greater economic opportunities or needs, improved contraception, and the securing of sexual and civil rights have re-shaped gender relations. Blended families with children and stepchildren, single-parent families, and co-habiting heterosexual and homosexual couples have become increasingly prevalent. Even contemporary nuclear families differ from their counterparts of the 1950s as more women seek careers outside the home and birth rates fall.

A decline in the marriage rate has been central to the transformation of family structures in the United States. Between 1970 and 2004 the annual number of marriages per 1,000 unmarried adult women fell by nearly 50 percent (Figure 1). Part of the explanation for this decline lies in an increased willingness or need to delay marriage in order to complete university and establish a career. In 2004, the median age of first marriage was 26 for women and 27 men compared with 20 and 23 respectively in 1960. The decline in marriage is also a consequence of a growth in unmarried cohabitation. Between 1960 and 2004 the number of unmarried couples of the opposite sex living together increased more than tenfold from 439,000 to just over 5 million. Approximately one quarter of

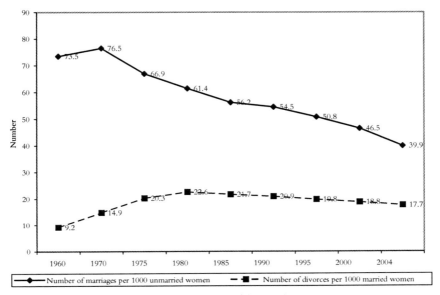

Source: U.S. Bureau of the Census, *Statistical Abstract of the United States: 2006*

Figure 1: Changing Marriage and Divorce Rates

unmarried women aged 25 to 29 currently cohabit with a partner, and another quarter have lived with a partner in the past (Bumpass and Lu, 2000, pp. 29–41). High divorce rates suggest that those marriages that do take place may be unstable. Between 1960 and 1980 the number of divorces per 1,000 married women more than doubled to reach a historical high point before declining slightly over the next two decades (Figure 1). In 2004, 8.2 percent of men and 10.9 percent of women were divorced. The net effect of declining marriage rates and high divorce rates is a fall in the percentage of Americans who are married. In 2004, 55.1 percent of men and 51.7 percent of women were married compared with 69.3 percent and 65.9 percent respectively in 1960.

The increased unattractiveness and fragility of marriages over the last four decades have resulted in substantial and complex changes in children's living arrangements. The decline in marriage and growth in unmarried cohabitation have contributed to a rise in births to unmarried mothers. In 2004 just over one-third of all births were to unmarried women compared with just over 5 percent in 1960. The result has been a fall in the percentage of children living with two married parents from 88 percent in 1960 to 67.8 percent in 2004 (Figure 2). This figure exaggerates the number of children living in traditional family units as it makes no distinction between natural and stepfamilies. The U.S. Census Bureau

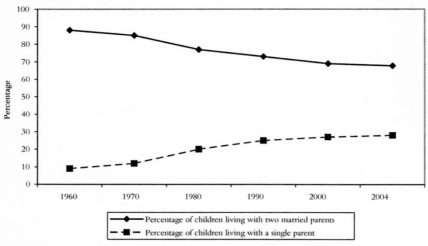

Source: U.S. Bureau of the Census, *Statistical Abstract of the United States: 2006*

Figure 2: Living Arrangements of Children, 1960–2004

estimated that stepfamilies constituted 9 percent of all two-parent families in the mid-1990s (Fields, 2001). In contrast, the number of children living with unmarried cohabiting couples of the opposite sex has risen dramatically from 197,000 in 1960 to just under 1.8 million in 2004. Divorce and a rise in the number of births to single, non-cohabiting women adds further complexity to an account of children's living arrangements in contemporary America. Between 1960 and 2004 the percentage of children living with a single parent, usually the mother, rose from 9 percent to 28 percent (Figure 2).

Changes in the popularity and stability of marriage, and the resultant variation in children's living arrangements, have altered the pattern of household forms in the United States over the last four decades. In 1960 family households made up 84.9 percent of all households, with married couples constituting 74.8 percent of the total (Figure 3). By 2000 the proportion of family households had fallen to 68.1 percent and the proportion of married couples households to 51.7 percent. Female-headed households made up 12.2 percent of the total number of households at the beginning of the new millennium. Non-family households constituted 31.9 percent of all households in 2000. A further change in the pattern of American households has been a growth in the number of gay and lesbian households. Between 1990 and 2000 the number of same-sex partner households increased from 145,130 to 601,209 (Smith and Gates, 2001). This latter figure constituted approximately 0.6 percent of total households in 2000.

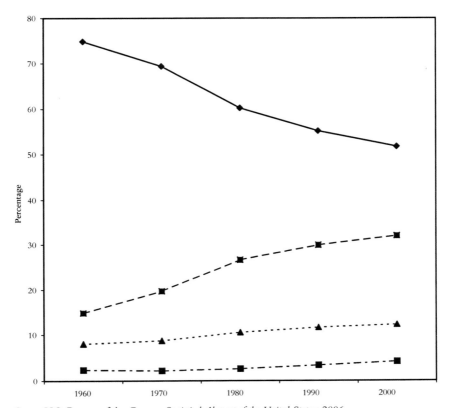

Source: U.S. Bureau of the Census, *Statistical Abstract of the United States: 2006*

Figure 3: Households by Type

The decline in the attractiveness and stability of marriage has been accompanied by a change in gender roles within marriage. An increase in service sector employment, U.S. Supreme Court rulings banning sexual discrimination in the workplace, and a decline in real hourly earnings have provided both opportunities and a need for more women to enter the workforce. The result has been a rise in the number of married women in employment (Figure 4). In 2004, 60.9 percent of married women had jobs compared with 30.5 percent in 1960. The rise in the number of married women with children in employment has been even more dramatic. Between 1960 and 2004 the percentage of married mothers with children aged 6–17 years in employment rose from 30 to 75.6 percent as increasing child-rearing costs and declining real wages required two wage earners to sustain family incomes. Even married women with young children

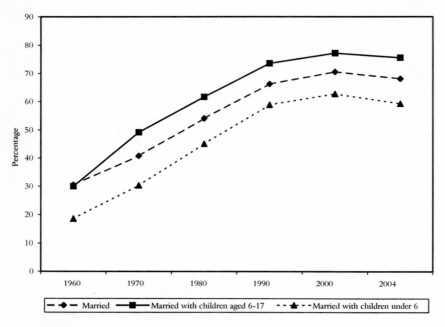

Source: U.S. Bureau of the Census, *Statistical Abstract of the United States: 1970;* U.S. Bureau of the Census, *Statistical Abstract of the United States: 2006.*

Figure 4: Employment Rate of Married Women, 1960–2004

increasingly had jobs. The employment participation rate of mothers with children under age 6 rose from 18.6 percent in 1960 to 59.3 percent in 2004. In just over four decades the archetypical marriage of a working father and a stay-at-home mother had all but disappeared.

An important consequence of this transformation of the social fabric has been a decline in certainty. The diminution of the traditional two-parent family has meant the loss of a central cultural norm and has sparked a debate about what constitutes a 'normal' living arrangement. This debate is particularly fierce because notions of family are fundamental to American identity. Not only do questions about the nature of families raise profound concerns about gender roles, but they also generate disputes about the causes of dysfunctional or errant behavior. Arguments over such emotive subjects as the nature of motherhood, the appropriate roles of husband and wife, and whether non-traditional family structures harm children dominate proceedings. No wonder that political scientist James A. Morone has described the family as 'the ground zero in the struggle for a good society' (Morone, 2003).

Reaction and Counter-Reaction

A bitter debate has accompanied the transformation of the social fabric of the United States with 'progressives' arguing that the changes reflect a commitment to individual rights and self-fulfillment while 'traditionalists' claim they result from hedonism and immorality. 'Progressives' argue that the changing American family is a consequence of women winning greater control over their lives, the granting of rights to previously persecuted groups such as homosexuals, and a greater willingness to allow people to live their own lives. They assert a clear demarcation between the public square and the bedroom that denies govern- ment the right to regulate private sexual behavior between consenting adults. 'Traditionalists' argue that the changing American family is a result of vice and self-indulgence. They deny that there is a distinction between the public and pri- vate spheres, and insist that government has a duty to regulate sexual behavior in order to protect society, families, and children. Each side in the debate seeks to depict the other as radical and 'un-American' (Nolan, 1996, pp. 162–64). 'Progressives' typically use language such as 'hate-mongers' or 'Nazis' to describe their opponents while 'traditionalists' use phrases such as 'immoral' or 'godless'.

Efforts to recast gender relations have been at the forefront of the 'progressive' agenda. An indication of the challenge to traditional sensibilities entailed in these efforts can be seen in the views on marriage contained in the organizing statement of the National Organization of Women (NOW) founded in 1966. NOW declared that: 'A true partnership between the sexes demands a different concept of marriage, an equitable sharing of responsibilities of home and children and eco- nomic burdens.' Equal rights and reproductive freedom were central to this vision of gender relations. Gains were made in both areas. The Equal Pay Act of 1963 mandated equal pay for equal work, the Civil Rights Act of 1964 prohibited dis- crimination at work on grounds of race and sex, and the Education Act of 1972 banned sex discrimination in education and sport. An Equal Rights Amendment (ERA) to the U.S. Constitution passed the U.S. Congress in 1972 but failed to be ratified by the states. The U.S. Supreme Court established the right of married women to acquire and use contraceptives in *Griswold v Connecticut* (1965) and extended this right to single women in *Eisenstadt v Baird* (1972). *Roe v Wade* (1973) and *Doe v Bolton* (1973) established a right to abortion.

Both the campaign to ratify the ERA and the abortion rulings provided a focus for opposition to the 'progressive' challenge to traditional moral and cul- tural boundaries. Groups such as the Eagle Forum and Concerned Women for America formed to oppose ratification of the ERA on the grounds that it appeared to threaten the conventional role of women and families (Matthews and De Hart, 1990). They claimed that the ERA denied gender differences based on biology. Both groups later evolved to campaign against NOW on a range of issues from reproductive rights to homosexual rights. The *Roe* decision had an even greater mobilizing effect than the ERA because it allowed concerns about sexual permissiveness, changing family structures, and new gender roles to be coupled with a highly emotive right-to-life issue (Morone, 2003, p. 488). Pro-life groups such as the National Right to Life Committee formed to challenge the Court's ruling through legislative, legal, and occasionally violent means (Craig and O'Brien, 1993). This opposition to the ERA and *Roe* galvanized 'traditionalists,' particularly evangelical Protestants, who had previously steered clear of direct involvement in politics (Guth, 1983; Smith, 1996). Multi-issue organizations such as the Moral Majority, the Traditional Values Coalition, the Christian Coalition, and the Family Research Council formed to campaign on a wide range of issues that threatened traditional moral and cultural values.

Opponents of abortion initially sought to challenge *Roe* directly by passing a constitutional amendment banning abortion, but their inability to secure the votes to pass such a measure forced a change of tactics. Instead of attacking the *right* to abortion, pro-life groups increasingly campaigned to restrict *access* to the procedure. This campaign had two main components. First, efforts were made to cut off public funding for abortions. The fact that low-income women were more likely to have abortions than those with higher incomes meant that budgetary constraint would have a significant impact on the number of abortions carried out (Jones et al., 2002, pp. 226–35). Second, efforts were made to erect bureaucratic and legal obstacles to abortion. Requirements to have counseling, a waiting period, and parental or spousal consent would make abortions harder to obtain. The pro-life movement hoped that the end result would be the evisceration of *Roe* through a thousand cuts.

The main focus of the anti-abortion campaign has been at the state level. Early efforts by states to restrict access to abortion fell foul of U.S. Supreme Court rulings in *Planned Parenthood of Central Missouri v Danforth* (1976), *Bellotti v.. Baird* (1979), and *Akron v Akron Center for Reproductive Health* (1983), but changes in the composition of the court eventually cleared the way for state laws that prohibit public funding for the procedure, and restrict its availability. Two important U.S. Supreme Court cases established precedents for these restrictions. In *Webster v Reproductive Health Services* (1989) the court upheld a Missouri law that barred the use of public facilities for abortions not necessary to save a woman's life; and in *Planned Parenthood v Casey* (1992) the U.S. Supreme Court upheld a Pennsylvania law that allowed restrictions on abortions as long as they do not constitute an 'undue burden' on the woman. Numerous restrictions on abortion have followed these rulings. In June 2006, 34 states required some form of parental involvement in a minor's decision to have an abortion, 32 states prohibited the use of state funds for abortion except to save the woman's life or if the pregnancy was caused by rape or incest, 28 states required some form of counseling before an abortion, 24 states mandated a waiting period before the procedure is performed, and 12 states prohibited so-called 'partial-birth' abortions. The constitutionality of the majority of these 'partial-birth' bans is open to doubt as the U.S. Supreme Court struck down a similar Nebraska law in *Stenberg v Carhert* (2000) for not having provisions to preserve women's health. The court reaffirmed this need to have provisions to safeguard the woman's health in *Ayotte v Planned Parenthood of Northern New England* (2006) when it ruled that a New Hampshire law requiring a minor to obtain parental consent for an abortion was unconstitutional because it lacked a medical emergency exception.

Federal legislation and executive action has also posed a threat to abortion rights. The Hyde Amendment of 1976 prohibited the use of federal funds for abortion. The U.S. Supreme Court upheld this funding ban in *Harris v McRae* (1980). In 1984 President Reagan withdrew federal funding for overseas organizations that advocated abortions as a method of population control. President Clinton rescinded this 'gagging order' in 1993, but President Bush reinstated the ban in 2001. Bush also approved regulations making fetuses but not pregnant women eligible for health care coverage under the State Children's Health Insurance Program (SCHIP) in 2002. The Partial-Birth Abortion Act of 2003 banned 'partial-birth' abortions, but has been declared unconstitutional by federal district courts in California, New York, and Nebraska, because it lacks provisions to preserve women's health. Two federal appeals courts upheld these rulings in February 2006, and the U.S. Supreme Court subsequently agreed to hear the case. Another important law, the Unborn Victims of Violence Act of 2004, recognized the fetus as a second legal victim in a crime committed against a pregnant woman. The greatest challenge to abortion rights, however, has been President Bush's strategy of appointing anti-abortion judges to the federal courts in the hope of eventually overturning *Roe*. Appointments to federal appeals courts have aroused most controversy, but the appointment to the U.S. Supreme Court of John Roberts and Samuel Alito – both described as ambivalent to *Roe* – also changed the complexion of that body.

These changes in the composition of the U.S. Supreme Court have prompted anti-abortion activists to try new tactics. In March 2006 South Dakota passed a law that banned all abortions except those necessary to save the life of the woman. Opponents of abortion believed that legal challenges to the law would allow the U.S. Supreme Court to overturn *Roe*. South Dakota Governor Mike Rounds claimed that 'The reversal of a Supreme Court opinion is possible' (*The Guardian*, March 8, 2006). In anticipation of such an event, Louisiana enacted a 'trigger law' in June 2006 that would ban abortion if the court overturned *Roe*.

New legislation may not be required, however, to ban abortion in some states. Thirteen states still have pre-1973 abortion bans in place that would become enforceable should *Roe* be reversed.

Homosexuality emerged as a further touchstone issue in the war between 'progressives' and 'traditionalists' in the 1990s. Agitation for homosexual rights began in the late 1960s with campaigns for an end to discrimination. These campaigns provoked conflict but failed to ignite the intense passions associated with abortion. The emergence of AIDS in the 1980s began to raise the temperature of debates about homosexual rights with some 'traditionalists' claiming that the epidemic was a punishment from God for immoral behavior. The Reverend Jerry Falwell claimed, for example, that: 'AIDS is the wrath of a just God against homosexuals.' The spark that ignited a new front in the 'morality war,' however, was a 1993 decision of the Hawaiian Supreme Court that rules prohibiting same-sex couples from marrying violated the state constitution's equal protection clause. This decision conflated homosexual rights with concerns about the American family, and provoked a strong backlash from 'traditionalists.' Rep. Bob Barr (R. GA) claimed that: 'The flames of hedonism, the flames of narcissism, the flames of self-centered morality are licking at the very foundation of our society, the family unit' (White, 2003, p. 110). Anxious that other states would have to recognize any same-sex marriages performed in Hawaii, Congress passed a Defense of Marriage Act (DOMA) in 1996 that defined marriage as a 'legal union between one man and one woman,' denied federal recognition of same-sex marriages, and prohibited states from recognizing same-sex marriages.

The battle over same-sex marriages increased in intensity during the late 1990s and early 2000s. In 1998 the Alaska Superior Court ruled that restrictions on same-sex marriages were unconstitutional. Opponents countered by obtaining passage of an amendment to the state's constitution that overturned the court's ruling. In 1999 the Vermont Supreme Court ruled that same-sex couples were entitled to the same rights as heterosexual married couples. A Vermont law enacted the following year gave same-sex couples legal recognition as 'civil unions' but failed to define these as 'marriages.' Two further court cases propelled same-sex marriages on to the national agenda. In *Lawrence v Texas* (2003) the U.S. Supreme Court ruled that state homosexual sodomy laws were unconstitutional. This ruling removed an obstacle to same-sex marriages and was greeted with horror by 'traditionalists.' The Reverend Pat Robertson declared that '...the Supreme Court has declared a constitutional right to consensual sodomy and, by the language in its decision, has opened the door to homosexual marriages, bigamy, legalized prostitution, and even incest' (Robertson n.d.). The Reverend Louis Sheldon, chair of the Traditional Values Coalition, described the ruling as 'a major wake-up call... This is a 9/11, major wake-up call that the enemy is at our doorsteps' (Fiorina, 2005, p. 81). These fears appeared to be confirmed a few months later when the Supreme Judicial Court of Massachusetts ordered state officials to issue marriage licenses to same-sex couples in *Goodridge v Department of Public Health* (2003). The first same-sex marriages took place in Massachusetts in 2004.

Goodridge prompted a backlash from 'traditionalists' anxious to stop the march towards same-sex marriages. President Bush called for a constitutional amendment to define marriage as a union between heterosexual couples, claiming that 'activist courts have left the people with one recourse' (Bush, 2004). The Federal Marriage Amendment was debated in the Senate in July 2004 but not enough votes were available to invoke cloture. Efforts at the state level to define marriage as a union between heterosexual couples have been more successful. Propositions to ban same-sex marriages were passed by eleven states in the 2004 elections, and a further seven states in the mid-term elections of 2006 (a total of twenty-seven states had adopted marriage amendments to their constitutions by the end of 2006). Numerous legal challenges to these 'mini-DOMAs' have been made in state courts with mixed results. A federal court ruled on same-sex marriages in 2005 when a U.S. District Court declared that Nebraska's marriage amendment violated the U.S. Constitution. 'Traditionalists' seized upon this ruling to press for action on a federal constitutional amendment. Richard Land, president of the Southern Baptist Ethics and Religious Liberty Commission, argued that: 'The only remedy for this kind of imperial judiciary is a federal Marriage Protection Amendment' (Foust, 2005). Republicans made an attempt to get a constitutional amendment through Congress in 2006. The Marriage Protection Amendment was debated in the Senate in June 2006 but the 49–48 vote in favor of the measure failed to achieve the two-thirds majority needed to pass a constitutional amendment.

Whose Values?

The intense struggle over moral issues in the United States has led both activists and commentators to argue that a widespread and deep-rooted 'war' over 'core values' is dividing the nation. James Dobson, head of Focus on the Family, described the conflict over such issues as 'a civil war of values and the prize to the victor is the next generation' (Hunter, 1991, p. 64). Patrick Buchanan told the 1992 Republican National Convention that: 'There is a religious war going on in our country for the soul of America' (White, 2003, p. 126). This notion became the conventional wisdom over the next decade and a half. Linking it implicitly to the Blue State – Red State divide; Republican pollster Bill McInturff claimed in 2001: 'We have two massive colliding forces. One is rural, Christian, religiously conservative. [The other] is socially tolerant, prochoice, secular, living in New England and the Pacific Coast'. Media reports took up the same theme. In the run-up to the 2004 elections, for example, *Newsweek* reported that: 'The culture war between the Red and Blue Nations has erupted again – big time...' (Fineman, 2003). Cartoons published in the wake of 2004 elections portrayed the country as divided between 'blue states' joined with Canadian provinces in the 'United States of Canada' and 'red states' described as 'Jesus land' (see http://politicalhumor.about.com/library/images/blpic-jesusland.htm).

This depiction of a deeply polarized nation engaged in a bitter conflict over moral issues is misleading. Opinion polls suggest that the general public usually has little interest in these issues, and is not as deeply divided as conventional wisdom suggests. They also reveal few significant differences in opinion between the regions on issues such as abortion and homosexuality. The evidence points instead towards a 'morality war' conducted by activists and elites that fails to rouse most Americans. Political scientist Morris P. Fiorina has likened this to those wars in Third World countries where 'unfortunate citizens... try to stay out of the crossfire while Maoist guerrillas and right-wing death squads shoot at each other' (Fiorina, 2005, p. 8).

Opinion polls reveal that moral issues typically have a low salience among Americans. Although one exit poll in the 2004 elections suggested that they were more important to voters than Iraq, the war on terrorism, or the economy in the 2004 elections, no other poll has repeated that finding. A CBS News/ *New York Times* Poll conducted two weeks after the elections found that 4 percent of Americans thought that 'miscellaneous moral values' were the most important problem facing the country compared with the 25 percent who cited the 'War in Iraq' (CBS News/*NewYork Times* Poll, 2004). This finding is consistent with answers to Gallup's 'Most Important Problem' question over the last twenty years. Apart from the years 1998–2001, when the Monica Lewinsky scandal dominated headlines, the percentage of Americans citing 'ethics/moral/religious/family decline' as the most important issue facing the country has ranged between 1–8 percent (Sourcebook of Criminal Justice, 2003). This evidence of low saliency is repeated when specific issues are examined. Gallup Polls reveal that only 1 percent of those polled over the last ten years have cited abortion as the most important issue facing the country, and homosexuality has not been mentioned at all. Other polls confirm these findings. In a *Washington Post*/ABC News Poll conducted in May 2006 only 2 percent cited abortion as 'the single most important issue in your vote for the U.S. House this year', and same-sex marriage did not figure at all (*Washington Post-ABC News Poll*, 2006).

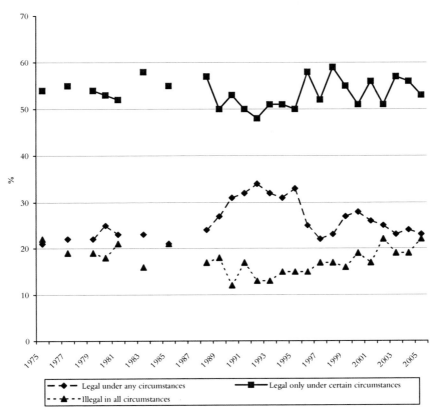

Source: Gallup Poll, 'Gallup's Pulse of Democracy: Abortion', 2006.

Figure 5: Should Abortion be Legal or Illegal?

Poll data also reveals that Americans are not as deeply divided on these issues as conventional wisdom suggests. Although headline figures suggest that the population is divided into a pro-life or pro-choice camp, these figures hide a wide range of attitudes that suggest greater consensus on the issue than commonly allowed (Ginsburg, 1989; Dillon, 1996; Mouw and Sobel, 2001, pp. 913–43). A majority of Americans do not favor making abortion either legal or illegal under all circumstances, but rather believe that the procedure should be available under certain circumstances (Figure 5). Table 1 shows that overwhelming majorities believe that abortion should be legal if the woman's life is endangered (85 percent), the woman's health is endangered (79 percent), or the pregnancy was caused by rape or incest (76 percent). Americans also agree

Table 1: Situations under which abortion should be legal/illegal (percent)

	Should be legal	Should be illegal	Depends	No Opinion
When the woman's life is endangered	85	11	2	2
When the woman's physical health is endangered	79	17	4	2
When the woman's mental health is endangered	63	32	3	2
When the baby may be physically impaired	56	37	4	3
When the baby may be mentally impaired	55	39	3	3
When the pregnancy was caused by rape or incest	76	19	2	3
When the woman/family cannot afford to raise the child	35	61	2	2

Source: Gallup Poll, May 19–21, 2003.

(61 percent) that poverty should not be a reason for abortion. Opinion polls also reveal little support for overturning *Roe v. Wade*. A Gallup Poll in January 2006 revealed that only 25 percent of Americans favored overturning *Roe* while 66 percent did not wish to see the ruling reversed. These sentiments generally hold true throughout the nation (Table 2). Overwhelming majorities in all regions support abortion if the woman's health is seriously endangered, if there is a strong chance of a serious defect in the baby, and if the pregnancy was caused by rape. Only in the case of allowing abortion because of low income is significant variation between the regions apparent. The New England and Pacific Coast states support abortion in such cases while the rest of the country opposes it.

Public attitudes towards homosexual rights reveal a complex range of rapidly changing positions that similarly do not fit easily with notions that Americans divide into two warring armies engaged in a 'civil war over values.' A majority of Americans (51 percent) accept homosexuality as an alternative lifestyle (Figure 6), an overwhelming majority (87 percent) believe that homosexuals should have equal employment rights (Figure 7), but a minority (37 percent) believe that homosexual marriages should be recognized as legally valid (Figure 8). Various recent polls also reveal that a majority of Americans believe that homosexual couples should be able to enter into legal agreements that confer some of the rights of marriage, that homosexual partners should be eligible for health insurance, social security benefits and inheritance rights, and that a plurality believes that homosexual couples should be able to adopt children (AEI Studies in Public Opinion, 2006). Nothing in this jumble of opinion suggests that Americans divide into two immutable and intransigent camps on the issue of homosexuality. Opinion

Table 2: Situations Under Which Abortion is Acceptable, by Region (2000–2006)

Abortion Acceptable if Woman's Health Seriously Endangered

	New England	Middle Atlantic	E. Nor. Central	W. Nor. Central	South Atlantic	E. South Central	W. South Central	Mountain	Pacific	Total
Yes	97.7	90.5	86.4	88.9	89.3	84.0	85.0	89.5	91.8	88.7
No	7.3	9.5	13.6	11.1	10.7	16.0	15.0	10.5	8.2	11.3

Abortion Acceptable if Strong Chance of Serious Defect in Baby

	New England	Middle Atlantic	E. Nor. Central	W. Nor. Central	South Atlantic	E. South Central	W. South Central	Mountain	Pacific	Total
Yes	85.8	80.4	76.6	74.6	77.8	66.3	69.8	80.3	82.0	77.3
No	14.2	19.6	23.2	25.4	22.2	33.7	30.2	19.7	18.0	22.7

Abortion Acceptable if Pregnant as Result of Rape

	New England	Middle Atlantic	E. Nor. Central	W. Nor. Central	South Atlantic	E. South Central	W. South Central	Mountain	Pacific	Total
Yes	88.3	81.6	79.5	79.4	80.6	66.5	71.6	83.3	81.7	79.3
No	11.7	18.4	20.5	20.6	19.4	33.5	28.4	16.7	18.3	20.7

Abortion Acceptable if Low Income – Can't Afford More Children

	New England	Middle Atlantic	E. Nor. Central	W. Nor. Central	South Atlantic	E. South Central	W. South Central	Mountain	Pacific	Total
Yes	63.1	48.1	37.4	37.9	41.4	25.2	32.6	48.9	53.0	42.5
No	36.9	51.9	62.6	62.1	58.6	74.8	67.4	51.1	47.0	57.5

New England: ME, VT, NH, MA, CN, RI; Middle Atlantic: NY, NJ, PA; East North Central: WI, IL, IN, MI, OH; West North Central: MN, IO, MO, ND, SD, NE, KS; South Atlantic: DE, MD, WV, VA, NC, SC, GA, FL, DC; East South Central: KY, TN, AL, MS; West South Central: AR, OK, LA, TX; Mountain: MT, ID, WY, NV, UT, CO, AR, NM; Pacific: WA, OR, CA, AS, HA.

Source: General Social Survey 1972–2004 Cumulative Data File.

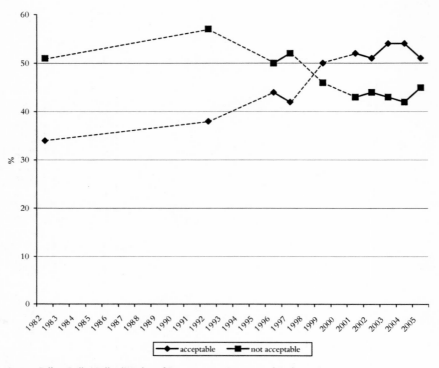

Source: Gallup Poll, 'Gallup's Pulse of Democracy: Homosexual Relations', 2006

Figure 6: Acceptability of Homosexuality as Alternative Lifestyle

in the South is more homophobic than elsewhere, but even in this region evidence of greater toleration has been apparent in recent years.

These findings on the salience and substance of abortion and homosexuality provide little evidence that a 'morality war' is raging among ordinary Americans. Polls conducted by the Pew Research Foundation, in fact, reveal Americans to be tolerant of the views of other Americans (Pew Research Center, 2002). Although 67 percent of Americans believe that the United States is a Christian nation, 84 percent believe that you can be a good American even if you have no religious faith. Such levels of tolerance among the general population contrast sharply with the acrimony and fanaticism that have characterized clashes over abortion and homosexuality policy over the last four decades. A considerable gap is evident between the concerns and actions of political elites and those of the average American (Layman and Green, 2006).

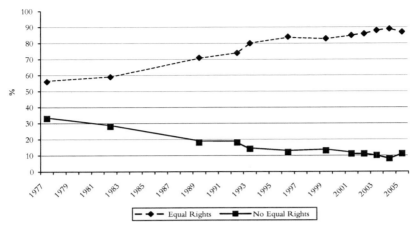

Source: Gallup Poll, 'Gallup's Pulse of Democracy: Homosexual Relations', 2006

Figure 7: Should Homosexuals Have Equal Rights in Terms of Job Opportunities?

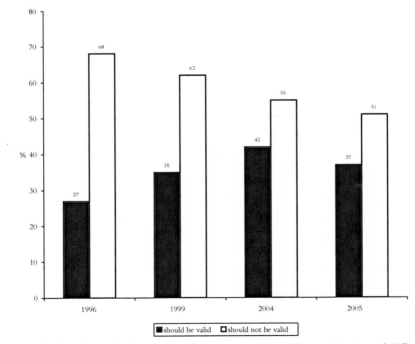

Source: The Pew Research Center, 'Less Opposition to Gay Marriage, Adoption and Military Service', March 22, 2006.

Figure 8: Should Homosexual Marriages be Recognized by the Law as Valid?

The explanation for this gap between political elites and the mass public lies in changes in the party system that allowed issue activists to dominate the political system. In the early 1970s groups representing feminists, homosexuals, and the young secured significant reforms within the Democratic Party that enhanced their role in the presidential nominating process (White, 1973; Shafer, 1984). These reforms undermined the old political establishment and created opportunities for the champions of 'progressive politics' to flourish. Not only did a requirement that state delegations meet targets for the representation of disadvantaged groups institutionalize a 'progressive' voice at the Democratic National Convention, but a greater use of direct primaries to choose presidential candidates also enhanced the power of issue activists and groups in the nominating process by diminishing the role of party leaders in selecting candidates (Ranney, 1978). A need to change state laws to implement direct primaries meant that these reforms also affected the Republican Party's nomination process. The reforms also enhanced the ability of issue activists and groups to play a larger role in party affairs. Opening up party activities allowed new groups to gain control over local party committees and had a major impact on state party politics (Herrnson, 1994, pp. 71–72). Political scientists John C. Green, Mark J. Rozell and Clyde Wilcox (2003), for example, have charted the success of Christian Right groups in seizing control of the grass roots Republican Party. They describe how Christian Coalition activists worked within state and local Republican parties to influence the election of candidates to all levels of government. 'Permeable' parties can easily be taken over by outside interests.

Other reforms provided further opportunities for issue activists and groups to enhance their role in electoral politics. The Federal Election Campaign Act of 1971 (FECA), and its subsequent amendments, changed the nature of campaign financing. By limiting the amount of money that individuals could give to candidates, political parties, and other campaign organizations, FECA enhanced the role of groups in funding federal elections at the expense of the parties (Sabato, 1984). 'Non-connected' Political Action Committees (PACs) representing both sides of the 'morality war' have grown in importance, both as sources of campaign funds for candidates who share their views, and perhaps more significantly as conveyors of political messages in their own right. Between 1990 and 2004, for example, pro-choice PACs such as NARAL contributed approximately $7.5 million to candidates in federal elections, with the vast majority of this money going to Democrats, and pro-life PACs such as the National Pro-Life PAC contributed approximately $3.3 million with virtually all this money going to Republicans (Center for Responsive Politics). PACs fighting the 'morality wars' have also used independent expenditures to influence elections. The

Supreme Court's ruling in *Buckley v Valeo* (1976) that PACs can spend unlimited amounts of money advocating the election or defeat of individual candidates, as long as such spending is completely independent of any other candidate, means that both sides of the 'morality wars' can make direct appeals to the electorate during campaigns. These expenditures give a prominence to single-issue politics, and weaken traditional party organizations by subverting party control over campaign themes.

'Issue advocacy' is another method that issue activists and groups have used to enhance their role in elections. A loophole in campaign finance law means that groups which avoid using 'magic words' such as 'vote for', 'elect', or 'defeat' in their communications can operate outside the purview of FECA entirely. PACs and tax-exempt groups (known as 501(c) and 527 groups depending on their IRS status) have exploited this loophole to engage in 'issue advocacy,' which conveys a political message without *explicitly* advocating the election or defeat of a particular candidate. Groups have also exploited the 'issue advocacy' loophole by distributing 'voter guides' to the electorate that highlight candidates' positions on various issues. Portrayed as non-partisan voter education packages, such guides provide groups like the Christian Coalition with a means to shape political debates and influence the outcome of elections (Sabato and Simpson, 1996).

The end result of these developments has been the transformation of the parties into competing networks of issue activists and groups (Shafer, 1998). This has led to an increased ideological distance between party elites and voters (Layman, 1999, pp. 89–121). A *New York Times*/CBS poll of delegates to the National Conventions in 2000, for example, found that Democratic delegates held more extreme 'progressive' views and Republican delegates more extreme 'traditionalist' views than the average voter (*New York Times*/CBS Poll, 2000). Reflecting partisan polarization, 71 percent of Democratic delegates and 14 percent of Republican delegates were in favor of unrestricted access to abortion, compared with 36 percent of voters. Other studies have revealed a similar distance between the views of politicians and the public. One analysis of voting by members of Congress on homosexual issues not only showed that Democrats supported gay civil rights more than Republicans, but also that both sets of politicians held more extreme positions than the electorate (Lindamen and Haider-Markel, 2002, pp. 91–110). Such findings indicate that public opinion has had little impact on the actions of the political elites waging the 'morality wars.'

The repeal of the South Dakota anti-abortion law in the mid-term elections of 2006 provides further evidence that the contemporary 'morality war' is an elite rather than popular phenomenon. Demands for a strict anti-abortion law in the state had been led by Leslee Unruh, Director of the Alpha Center in Sioux

Falls (a pro-life organization in South Dakota), who argued that the incremental approach adopted by the pro-life movement had reached its limits. 'We'd been there, done that, and it still didn't work,' she claimed (*The Guardian*, October 27, 2006, g2 section, p. 13). Legislation banning virtually all abortions was introduced by Republican state representative Roger Hunt, an ally of Unruh, and passed both chambers of the state legislature with overwhelming majorities. In the wake of Republican Governor Mike Rounds' signature, however, opinion polls began to reveal that most South Dakotans opposed such drastic restrictions on abortion. One poll suggested that 61 percent of South Dakotans opposed the law (Angus Reid Consultants, 2006). Buoyed by such figures, local pro-choice activists easily obtained sufficient signatures to force a referendum on the law in the mid-term elections of 2006. South Dakota's voters subsequently rejected the law by a margin of 55 to 45 percent.

Conclusion

A bifurcated response to social changes has been evident in the United States during the last four decades. While changes in family structures and gender relations have been regarded with a degree of equanimity by most Americans, they have ignited a fierce 'morality war' among issue activists and political elites. Two possible scenarios arise from this disjunction between elite and mass public views on moral issues. The first is that a disjunction of this sort will generate a backlash and force political elites to take action that is more in line with public opinion. Some evidence of a backlash is available with opinion polls suggesting that the public has become less tolerant of the Bush Administration's championing of 'traditional' values (Gallup Poll, 2005). The second scenario is that elite agitation will ignite a widespread 'morality war' that polarizes the country. The social changes of the last four decades have raised questions about core values and provided scapegoats that Jeremiahs may use to ignite popular opinion.

Bibliography

AEI Studies in Public Opinion (2006) 'Attitudes About Homosexuality and Gay Marriage' (Washington, DC: American Enterprise Institute).
Angus Reid Consultants, March 2006.
Bumpass, L. and Lu, H. (2000) 'Trends in Cohabitation and Implications for Children's Family Contexts in the U.S.,' *Population Studies*, vol. 54, no. 1.

Bush, G. W. (2004) 'President Calls for Constitutional Amendment Protecting Marriage,' (February 24), www.whitehouse.gov.

CBS News/*New York Times* Poll (2004) 'What Do You Think is the Most Important Problem Facing this Country Today?' (November 18–21).

Center for Responsive Politics, www.opensecrets.org.

Craig, B. and O'Brien, D. (1993) *Abortion and American Politics* (Chatham, NJ: Chatham House).

Dillon, M. (1996) 'The American Abortion Debate,' in J. Nolan (ed.), *The American Culture Wars* (Charlottesville, VA: University Press of Virginia).

Dionne, E. (1991) *Why Americans Hate Politics* (New York: Simon & Schuster).

Economist 'One Nation, Fairly Divisible, Under God', January 20, p. 22.

Fields, J. (2001) 'Living Arrangements of Children: Fall, 1996,' *Current Population Reports* (Washington, D.C.: US Census Bureau).

Fineman, H. (2003) 'Election Boils Down to a Culture War: Abortion Issue is First Skirmish in the Battle for the White House,' *Newsweek* (October 22).

Fiorina, M. (1999) 'Extreme Voices: A Dark Side of Civic Engagement,' in T. Skocpol and M. Fiorina (eds.), *Civic Engagement in American Democracy* (Washington, D.C.: Brookings).

Fiorina, M. (2002) 'Parties, Participation, and Representation in America: Old Theories Face New Realities,' in I. Katznelson and H. Milner (eds.), *Political Science: The State of the Discipline* (New York: W.W. Norton).

Fiorina, M. (2005) *Culture War? The Myth of a Polarized America* (New York: Pearson Longman).

Foust, M. (2005) 'A First: Federal Judge Strikes Down Neb. Marriage Amendment,' *Bpnews*, www.bpnews.net.

Gallup Poll (2005) 'U.S. Government Loses Public's Blessing to Promote Values,' (October 25).

Ginsburg, F. (1989) *Contested Lives: The Abortion Debate in an American Community* (Berkeley, CA: University of California Press).

Green, J., Rozell, M. and Wilcox, C. (2003) 'The Christian Right's Long Political March,' in J. Green, M. Rozell and C. Wilcox (eds.), *The Christian Right In American Politics* (Washington, D.C.: Georgetown University Press).

Guth, J. (1983) 'The New Christian Right' in R. Liebman and R. Wuthnow (eds.) *The New Christian Right* (New York: Aldine).

Herrnson, P. (1994) 'American Political Parties: Growth and Change' in G. Peele, C. Bailey, B. Cain and B. Peters (eds.) *Developments in American Politics 2* (Basingstoke: Macmillan).

Hunter, J. (1991) *Culture Wars: The Struggle to Define America* (New York: Basic Books).

Jones, R., Darroch, J. and Henshaw, S. (2002) 'Patterns in the Socioeconomic Characteristics of Women Obtaining Abortions in 2000–2001,' *Perspectives on Sexual and Reproductive Health* vol. 34, no. 5, pp. 226–235.

Layman, G. (1999) '"Culture Wars" in the American party system: Religious and Cultural Change Among Partisan Activists Since 1972,' *American Politics Quarterly*, vol. 27, no. 1.

Layman, G. (2001) *The Great Divide* (New York: Columbia University Press).

Layman, G. and Green, J. (2006) 'Wars and Rumours of Wars: The Contexts of Cultural Conflict in American Political Behaviour,' *British Journal of Political Science*, vol. 36, no. 1, pp. 61–89.

Lindamen, K. and Haider-Markel, D. (2002) 'Issue Evolution, Political Parties, and Culture Wars,' *Political Research Quarterly*, vol. 55, no. 1.

Matthews, D. and De Hart, J. (1990) *Sex, Gender, and the Politics of ERA* (Oxford: Oxford University Press).

Morone, J. (2003) *Hellfire Nation* (New Haven, CN: Yale University Press).

Mouw, T. and Sobel, M. (2001) 'Culture Wars and Opinion Polarization: The Case of Abortion,' *American Journal of Sociology*, vol. 106, no. 4.

New York Times/CBS News Poll (2000) (August 14).

Nolan, J. (1996) 'Political Discourses in America's Culture Wars' in J. Nolan (ed.) *The American Culture Wars* (Charlottesville, VA: University Press of Virginia).

Pew Research Center for the People and the Press (2002) 'Americans Struggle with Religion's Role at Home and Abroad' (March 20).

Ranney, A. (1978) 'The Political Parties: Reform and Decline,' in A. King (ed.), *The New American Political System* (Washington, DC: American Enterprise Institute).

Robertson, P. cited at www.pfaw.org/pfaw/general/default.aspx?oid=11421

Sabato, L. (1984) *PAC Power* (New York: W.W. Norton).

Sabato, L. and Simpson, G. (1996) *Dirty Little Secrets* (New York: Times Books).

Shafer, B. (1984) *Quiet Revolution* (New York: Russell Sage Foundation).

Shafer, B. (1998) 'Partisan Elites, 1946–1996,' in B. Shafer (ed.), *Partisan Approaches to Postwar American Politics* (New York: Chatham House).

Smith, C. (1996) *American Evangelicalism* (Chicago: University of Chicago Press).

Smith, D. and Gates, G. (2001) 'Gay and Lesbian Families in the United States: Same-sex Unmarried Partner Households,' A Human Rights Campaign Report (Washington, DC: Human Rights Campaign).

Sourcebook of Criminal Justice Statistics (2003) 'Attitudes Toward the Most Important Problem Facing the Country,' www.albany.edu/sourcebook/

The Guardian (2006) 'State's Abortion Ban Fires First Shot in a Long War Over Women's Rights' (March 8).

The Guardian (2006) 'America's Abortion Battlefield' (October 27).

U.S. Bureau of the Census (2006) 'Statistical Abstract of the United States'.

Washington Post-ABC News Poll (2006) 'What will be the Single Most Important Issue in Your Vote for US House This Year,' *Washington Post* (May 16).

White, J. (2003) *The Values Divide* (New York: Chatham House).

White, T. (1973) *The Making of the President 1972* (New York: Scribner).

Williams, R. (ed.) (1997) *Cultural Wars in American Politics* (New York: Aldine).

Wolfe, A. (1998) *One Nation, After All* (New York: Viking).

Wuthnow, R. (1989) *The Struggle for America's Soul* (Grand Rapids, MI: Eerdmans).

11
Native American Self-Determination: From Nixon to Reagan

Dean J. Kotlowski

The federal government's Native American policy underwent a revolutionary change in the 1970s and 1980s. Beginning in 1970, it ceased efforts to assimilate Indians into Euro-American society. Under the old policy of 'termination,' tribes lost all privileges related to treaties with the federal government; tribal lands – once held in trust by the government – were opened to sale to non-Indians; and Indians became subject to the same laws as other Americans. Under the new policy of 'self-determination without termination,' the federal government promised to respect and to enhance, rather than to destroy, tribal authority and Indian distinctiveness. This change did not occur inside a vacuum. Native American activists, throughout the 1960s and 1970s, used a variety of tactics – lobbying, civil disobedience, and litigation – to reclaim tribal land, fishing, and water rights (see Hertzberg, 1988; Johnson, 1996, pp. 305–23; Nagel, 1996). In response, newly formed Euro-American 'rights' organizations proposed abrogating Indian treaties and eliminating reservations, all the while stressing that both Indians and non-Indians should enjoy the same rights and opportunities as citizens (*Are We Giving America Back to the Indians?*, p. 16).

Such backlash underscored just how much federal Indian policy had shifted in favor of tribes. Furthermore, the United States Supreme Court, during the 1970s, asserted the idea of 'Indian sovereignty,' that is, 'the power of Indian tribes to assert their economic, political, and cultural authority in appropriate spheres' (Kelly, 1988, p. 79). Writing in 1988, historian Lawrence C. Kelly observed that the federal Indian policy had evolved over a century from 'virtual denial of tribal sovereignty to almost full recognition' (1988, p. 80).

For officials at the national level, sentiments at the grassroots, whether for or against tribal self-determination, along with their own convictions, influenced the making of federal Indian policy. During the 1960s, with the legacy of termination still fresh and the Indian movement just underway, Presidents John F.

Kennedy and Lyndon B. Johnson were reluctant to break forcefully with past policies. In the tradition of post-1945 liberalism, both presidents used federal power to advance the civil and economic rights of all Americans, not the specific interests of Native American tribes. Instead, they favored the 'gradual assimilation' of Indians into the American mainstream (Kotlowski, 2002, pp. 23–28; see also Clarkin, 2001). Tribal self-determination received a more sympathetic hearing from Richard M. Nixon, whose presidency coincided with the era of 'Red Power' protest and who was less committed to racial integration than his immediate Democratic predecessors (see Prucha, 1984, pp. 1085–1208; Castile, 1998; Kotlowski, 2001, pp. 188–215). Nixon repudiated termination and asked Congress to pass measures designed to strengthen tribal authority (Prucha, 1984, pp. 1112–13). President Gerald R. Ford continued the policy of his Republican predecessor, as did Jimmy Carter. Yet a rising backlash by non-Indians led Jimmy Carter to approach Native American issues cautiously.

Backlash notwithstanding, Native American self-determination endured even under the most conservative of recent presidents. In 1980 Ronald Reagan affirmed: 'I would support Indian tribal government through the fulfillment of treaty obligations (National Tribal Chairmen's Association). Once Reagan became president, however, the imperatives of governance complicated the task of implementing his promises. Ultimately, Reagan-style conservatism accommodated rather than reversed the thrust of the Native American policy since 1970.

Native American Protest and the Nixon Presidency

The transformation of federal Indian policy originated with an Indian rights movement that was, by the late 1960s, bold, brash, and the focus of popular attention. Native American activists placed – and kept – Indian concerns on the national agenda. The Nixon White House, for its part, responded calmly to unrest at the grassroots and pragmatically in terms of its initiatives. A number of factors, including ideology, personal sympathy, and political expediency, encouraged the president to back Native American self-determination.

Native Americans increasingly demanded 'self-determination,' a concept that carried different meanings for different Indians. To rural, tribal-based organizations, led by the National Congress of American Indians (NCAI), 'self-determination' represented an end to federal efforts to assimilate Indians into white society. In essence, the government would no longer seek to 'terminate' its special relationship with tribes; tribal authority and treaty commitments would be respected; and federal officials would consult tribes before drafting legislation affecting them (Kotlowski, 2003, pp. 201–27). Reservation Indians clung to their federally protected status, refusing 'to swim in a mainstream they largely regarded as polluted' (Cobb, 1998, p. 74). To advance its agenda, NCAI operated within 'the system' by recruiting its members from reservations and by lobbying the government to change its policies. In 1967 an NCAI leader proclaimed, with pride, 'Indians Don't Demonstrate' (Smith and Warrior, 1996, p. 37).

To young, urban Indians, often only loosely affiliated with traditional tribal groups and imbued with the rights-conscious spirit that had inspired African Americans, 'self-determination' meant promoting greater cultural awareness for all Indians, not simply those on reservations, via direct action. Their organization was the American Indian Movement (AIM), founded in 1968; their slogan was 'Red Power'; and their tactics included direct action. The leadership of AIM became famous for visiting a reservation, where their support was usually slight, staging a protest or armed occupation, and then bargaining with federal officials before moving on to other targets (Iverson, 1998, p. 149). Less dramatically, but equally importantly, AIM dispensed financial and legal assistance and established centers to spotlight Indian culture. Unlike NCAI, AIM encouraged civil disobedience (Kotlowski, 2003, p. 205).

Relations between the two branches of the movement proved strained. To AIM, tribal leaders appeared too tied to the federal establishment – that is, the Bureau of Indian Affairs (BIA), which provided benefits only to federally recognized tribes (New York Times, 1972, p. E-2). Resentful of the national publicity garnered by AIM, some tribal Indians mocked that organization as 'Assholes in Moccasins' (Smith and Warrior, 1996, p. 138). Regardless of their differences, Native Americans rejected the integrationist goals of the black civil rights movement. 'In the past,' historian Vine Deloria, Jr. argued, 'they had experienced so many betrayals through policies which purported to give them legal and social "equality" that they distrusted anyone who spoke of either equality or helping them to get into "the mainstream"' (Deloria, 1974, p. 23).

In the Fall of 1969, a group of Native American activists made that point 'perfectly clear,' to borrow a phrase that Nixon himself made famous, when they seized Alcatraz Island in San Francisco Bay. The dispute had actually begun in 1964, when five Sioux Indians briefly occupied Alcatraz and claimed the onetime federal prison under the Fort Laramie Treaty of 1868. The controversy resurfaced in 1969 after Secretary of the Interior Walter Hickel offered to turn Alcatraz into a national park. On November 20, fifty Indians occupied the island and vowed to stay until Hickel ceded it to them. By the end of 1969, more than 100 Indians had made the 'Rock' their home (New York Times, 1969, p. 80; Hoff, 1994, p. 35).

In responding to these events, Nixon's moderate advisers first fumed and then sought compromise. Although Leonard Garment, special assistant to the president, decried the seizure as 'confrontation politics' by 'an irresponsible, but PR-conscious group' (Leonard Garment to John D. Ehrlichman, 1970), he understood that Alcatraz could become 'the biggest political sideshow of 1971' if a single Indian or federal marshal died (Alcatraz Chronology, 1973; Robert Robertson to Indians of All Tribes, 1970; Garment to Ehrlichman, 1970). In the wake of the killing of anti-war protesters at Kent State University in 1970, Nixon agreed to remain patient. In the meantime, the public eventually lost interest in the affair, the Indians squabbled among themselves, and most abandoned the island. Federal marshals removed peacefully the last fifteen holdouts on June 11, 1971 (Ehrlichman, 1971; Patterson, pp. 32–33; Garment, 1997, pp. 224–25; *San Francisco Chronicle*, 1971).

Nixon's domestic policy advisers used the occupation to plead for change in Indian policy. 'The Alcatraz episode is symbolic,' read one unsigned memorandum, 'to the Indians and to us it is a *symbol* of the lack of attention to [their] unmet needs' (undated draft memorandum). Vice President Spiro T. Agnew assumed command by convening, on January 20, 1970, the National Council on Indian Opportunity (NCIO), a panel of tribal leaders and federal officials that, by statute, he chaired (Statement of the Vice President, 1970). The vice president next urged Nixon to disavow termination and to allow tribes, by majority vote, 'to assume complete control' over any federal Indian program. He advised replacing area offices of the Bureau of Indian Affairs – to Indian radicals, a hated symbol of federal wardship – with local centers to ease the 'transition from Federal to tribal control' (Agnew to Nixon). Agnew argued that his proposals would advance the 'New Federalism,' the president's policy to transfer power from federal to local authorities (Bradley H. Patterson to Garment, 1970; Garment to Agnew). It was an argument in favor of advancing tribal self-determination that a later generation of conservatives also would express.

Agnew's reasoning was not a difficult sell, for Nixon sympathized with Native Americans – whom he considered a 'safe' minority to help. Because the Indian movement was just getting underway during the late 1960s, Native Americans proved responsive to presidential gestures. Since they numbered fewer than one million, their problems seemed more manageable than those of African Americans. Popular sympathy favored Indian rights, at least at first, and, unlike liberal African Americans who backed integration, Native Americans welcomed Nixon's opposition to forced assimilation. 'Our overriding aim, as I see it,' Nixon had declared in 1960, 'should not be to separate the Indians from the richness of their past or force them into some preconceived mold of human behavior' (Debo, 1970, p. 341). Such words resembled his later argument against 'forced integration' of blacks and whites. Running for president in 1968, Nixon backed self-determination for Indian tribes and blasted current federal policy as 'unfair,' 'confused,' and 'tragic' (Nixon to National Congress of American Indians, 1968).

Nixon supported Indian rights for many reasons. Here was a way, he reasoned, to appease younger, liberal-minded Americans as well as appeal to the public at large. 'He feels very strongly,' White House chief of staff H. R. Haldeman noted in 1969, 'that we need to show more heart, and that we care about people, and thinks the Indian problem is a good area' (Haldeman to Keogh, 1969). Nixon also acted out of principle. 'There are very few votes involved,' the president privately conceded, but 'a grave injustice has been worked against [Indians] for a century and a half and the nation at large will appreciate our having a more active policy of concern for their plight' (Nixon to Ehrlichman, 1970). Such sentiments partly reflected Nixon's fond memories of his Whittier College football coach, Chief Wallace Newman, a Cherokee (Patterson, 1977).

Nixon and his aides acted to implement tribal self-determination with words and deeds. On July 8, 1970, the White House released a lengthy message on Indian affairs that renounced termination as 'morally and legally unacceptable.' It further asserted that 'self-determination among Indian people can and must be encouraged without the threat of eventual termination.' Nixon then asked Congress to pass a resolution repealing termination as well as eight bills to advance tribal autonomy. Under Nixon's legislation, federal agencies would be allowed to 'contract out' educational and health care services to tribes (*Special Message to Congress*, 1971, pp. 566–67). His statement won wide acclaim among Native American tribal leaders.

In 1970 and 1971 two issues moved to the top of Nixon's Indian agenda: the Taos Pueblo's claim to the area surrounding Blue Lake, in New Mexico, and the land claims of Alaskan natives. Blue Lake had symbolic appeal while the ongoing Alaskan dispute delayed construction of an oil pipeline. The White House settled these matters through new legislation, with the Alaskan Native Claims Settlement Act of 1971 marking the most noteworthy Indian reform passed on Nixon's watch. The act transferred 40 million acres, a record amount of land, and one billion dollars to Alaskan aboriginals. But Nixon's other reforms encountered resistance from westerners on Capitol Hill. Accordingly, the president addressed Indian concerns through administrative actions that established new offices to protect their rights. He also increased federal expenditures for Native American programs and the BIA, and, through an executive order signed in 1972, returned the land around Mount Adams, in Washington State, to the Yakama Nation. (Hoff, 1994, pp. 32–43; Castile, 1998, pp. 153–55; Kotlowski, 2001, pp. 188–221)

Such actions underscored the strengths and weaknesses of Nixon's Native American policy through 1972. By settling land claims, disavowing termination, and courting duly elected tribal leaders, Nixon played to federally recognized tribes, not urban Indians. Moreover, he disappointed radicals by failing to reform the BIA and to renegotiate the government's treaties with Native Americans. The latter issue, raised by the occupiers of Alcatraz, resurfaced during later protests. 'Urban Indians,' one White House staff member accurately predicted in 1971, 'will most likely be creating more confrontations with federal, state, and city authorities over the next two years' (Memorandum for Ed Harper, 1971).

Red Power protest crested early in 1973, when AIM seized at gunpoint the town of Wounded Knee, South Dakota on the Oglala Sioux's Pine Ridge Reservation (Kotlowski, 2003, pp. 211–13). The occupation originated as a dispute among Indians. AIM and its followers had denounced Richard Wilson, the elected head of the Oglala Sioux, as more interested in ruling the tribe by force than in serving its members (Prucha, 1984, p. 1119). The occupiers, for their part, proclaimed an independent Sioux nation, appealed to the United Nations for recognition, and asserted that treaties between the U.S. government and Native American tribes fell within the jurisdiction of foreign policymakers in Washington. In response, U.S. law enforcement personnel cordoned off the hamlet and exchanged sporadic gunfire with its occupiers. After seventy-one days, AIM finally retreated by agreeing to surrender its arms in exchange for an investigation of Wilson's management of the Pine Ridge Reservation. (Kotlowski, 2003, p. 215)

The siege compelled federal policymakers to pay closer attention to Indian concerns. Specifically, the occupiers' demand to discuss 'broken treaties' brought Carl Marcy, a member of the staff of the Senate Committee on Foreign Relations, to Wounded Knee, where Marcy could not believe he was engaging in 'quasi-foreign relations business' (Carl Marcy to Senate, 1973). 'The situation at Wounded Knee,' Senator Warren Magnuson, Democrat of Washington, observed, 'has certainly brought the plight of Indians to the attention of Congress' (Warren G. Magnuson to Peggy A. Robinson, 1973). Indeed, over the following two years, Congress enacted a spate of reforms, proposed earlier by the White House, to promote tribal authority (Kotlowski, 2001, p. 211). It restored the Menominee, a Wisconsin tribe terminated in 1961, to federal trust responsibility, and approved the Indian Financing Act of 1974, Nixon's proposal to lend tribes money via a revolving fund. In 1975 Congress passed the Indian Self-Determination and Education Assistance Act, which expanded Indian control over their schools and allowed federal agencies to contract out services to tribes . In fact, the head of the Association on American Indian Affairs, an advocacy group, lauded the ninety-third Congress as 'perhaps the most constructive

Congress in the field of Indian affairs in our history' (*New York Times*, 1973, p. 14; Prucha, 1984, pp. 1135–38, 1144–46; Congressional Quarterly, 1975, p. 87; Alfonso Oriz to Gerald R. Ford, 1975).

Credit for these advances belongs to many people. Nixon's commitment to the policy of self-determination remained strong; during the siege of Wounded Knee, he told aides that he wanted publicity for his 'remarkably progressive record on Indians' (*Annotated News Summary*, 1989). Tribal leaders and White House staff members conceived the president's reforms, and Congress passed them. Civil disobedience played a major role as well. In June 1973, following the standoff at Wounded Knee, Senator Dewey F. Bartlett, Republican of Oklahoma and a member of the Subcommittee on Indian Affairs, foresaw no trouble passing Nixon's Indian legislation, even though he privately admitted that his committee had ignored most of the president's agenda for two and a half years. The president, after Alcatraz, issued his message on Indian rights, and Congress, following Wounded Knee, began implementing it. Those were the bookends of Nixon's Native American reforms – reforms which set important precedents (Castile, 1998, pp. 104, 166; Dewey F. Bartlett Diary, 1973; American Indian Press Association, 1974).

Indian Policy under Ford and Carter

Three themes defined Native American policy for the duration of the 1970s. First, Presidents Ford and Carter reaffirmed their commitment to Nixon's policy of tribal self-determination. Second, while both White Houses remained wary of any signs of Native American unrest, the public face of the Indian movement was evolving, from urban radicals engaging in civil disobedience – and armed occupations – on federal property to Native Americans working alongside lawyers in court to recover long-lost rights. Their lawsuits shook the foundations of Euro-American society and helped to fuel a backlash against tribal sovereignty. Accordingly, the task of enhancing Indian self-determination became more risky politically, but by no means impossible, for national policymakers.

Gerald Ford, like most presidents since World War II, assumed office with little background in Indian rights.[1] Yet, in this area, Ford had an unmistakably clear precedent to follow and follow it he did. The new president upheld Nixon's Indian policy when he signed the Indian Self-Determination Act of 1975. Ford

---

[1] As a congressman, between 1949 and 1973, from western Michigan, where few Native Americans lived, Ford compiled almost no record on Indian rights. Ford, like Agnew, became acquainted with federal Indian policy during his brief tenure as vice president, while chairing the NCIO. Robert Robertson to Gerald R. Ford, 10 Jan. 1974, box 80, Gerald R. Ford Vice Presidential Papers, GRFL.

called the measure a 'milestone' which gave 'permanence' to the goal of allowing tribes to run many federal programs themselves (see Kenneth R. Cole to
Ford, 1975; Roy Ash to Ford, 1974; John C. Whitaker to Ash, 1974; Statement
by the President). Then, between 1974 and 1975, the president approved additional laws granting parcels of land to such tribes as the Hualapai of Arizona, the
Cheyenne-Arapaho of Oklahoma, and the Sisseton-Wahpeton Sioux of the
Dakotas. He also signed acts giving the U.S. government authority to hold sub-
marginal lands in trust for tribes and to transfer excess federal property to reservations (see Wilfred H. Rommel to Ford, 1974; Cole to Ford, 1975, 1974b and
1974c; and James Cannon to Ford, 1975). Most important, Ford resolved a significant claim when he approved a bill to enlarge Grand Canyon National Park
and add 185,000 acres to the Havasupai Indian Reservation in Arizona (Patrick
E. O'Donnell to Warren Hendricks, 1975; Cole to Ford, 1975; National
Congress of American Indians to Ford, 1975).

At the same time, sporadic unrest, coming a year and half after Wounded Knee,
reminded the Ford administration that it needed to remain sensitive to Native
American concerns. The administration's most bizarre challenge involved the
Kootenai tribe. In 1855 the Kootenai had lost 1.6 million acres in northern Idaho
during a conference at which they had no delegates. To make amends, Congress
in 1974 considered granting the tribe, now with just 67 members, a parcel of land
for use as a reservation. But when the Ford administration refused to send envoys
to Idaho to discuss the matter, the Kootenai declared war on the United States
and assembled roadblocks around Bonners Ferry, Idaho – 30 miles south of the
U.S.–Canadian border. In what might have been a veiled call for AIM volunteers,
the tribe asked for outside help. It also charged motorists a dime to cross their
ancestral lands. When Idaho's governor dispatched seventy state troopers, the
Kootenai rescinded their ten-cent toll, but not their declaration of war (*Declaration
of War*, 1974; *Rocky Mountain*, 1975).

Ford's team used patience and concessions to soothe the protesters. The mat-
ter was serious enough to draw the attention of Ford's cabinet, which discussed
how to prevent 'another' Wounded Knee style 'takeover' (Cabinet Meeting
Notes, 1974). After warning that AIM might seize this opportunity, Bradley H.
Patterson, Jr., who had overseen Native American policy in the Nixon White
House, backed a 'positive response' to 'keep the situation cool' (Patterson to
John G. Carlson, 1974). In that vein, Ford signed a bill transferring 12.5 acres of
federal land into trust status for the Kootenai. The government then placated the
tribe by building a road to its new reservation, awarding the Kootenai $100,000
for a community center, and spending $7,000 per tribal member over a twelve-
month period. Thereafter, this 'crisis' passed (Patterson to Morris R. Thompson
et al., 1974; Cole to Ford, 1974a; *Wall Street Journal*, 1976).

Interestingly, the U.S. government was learning how to master Native American protest just as such unrest was becoming passé. By 1976 a new generation of college-educated activists was filing lawsuits to regain Indian land, fishing, and water rights (*Indian Rights May Haunt Us*, 1976). In Maine, for example, the Passamaquoddy and Penobscot tribes claimed title to over 12 million acres, two-thirds of the state's area. They argued that the transfer of their land to the state was invalid since it had occurred without the consent of the U. S. Congress – a violation of the Indian Non-Intercourse Act of 1790. In 1975 two federal courts ruled in their favor, suggesting that well-prepared lawsuits might shake the moorings of Euro-American society more than armed occupations (George W. Humphreys to Cannon, 1976; Humphreys and Patterson to Ford, 1976). The lawsuits marked the beginning of a prolonged imbroglio, one that Ford gladly passed on to his successor. When, late in 1976, Ford requested a set of options on the Maine claims, Patterson persuaded him to leave the 'problem for the Carter administration' (Patterson to Ronald Nessen, 1976; Humphreys to Cannon, 1976; Patterson handwritten, 1976).

The rise of Euro-American backlash made the task of expanding tribal sovereignty in general, and settling Indian land claims in particular, vexing for national policymakers. Many non-Indians in the West believed that expansion of tribal authority threatened to diminish their fishing, land, and water rights. In 1976 they founded the Interstate Congress for Equal Rights and Responsibilities, an organization that cloaked a policy agenda from the 1950s in the language of civil rights activists from the 1960s (*Declaration of Purpose*). Reviving the idea of termination, the Interstate Congress proposed abrogating all Indian treaties, which it claimed had created 'a most favored citizen unique among all races' (*Are We Giving America Back to the Indians?*, p. 16). As its name suggested, the organization championed equal rights for Indians and non-Indians alike. But, rather than specific lobbying by the Interstate Congress – a small and cash-strapped organization – it was a general sense that Native American demands were going too far that concerned policymakers.[2] A rising number of land claims turned some friends of Indian rights, such as Representative Lloyd Meeds, Democrat of Washington and a former chair of the Subcommittee on Indian Affairs, into foes. In the early 1970s, Meeds explained, 'there was this feeling around the House that [Native American bills] were pretty good civil rights votes. Besides, no one was paying attention to the Indians then.' By 1977, shaken by a court-ordered expansion of tribal fishing

[2]   Members of President Carter's staff greeted a delegation affiliated with the Interstate Congress but considered the organization too radical. Teresa Smith to Marilyn Haft, no date [April 1977], box 86, Public Liaison Office – Jane Wales Files, Jimmy Carter (JCL), Atlanta, Georgia.

rights in his state's Puget Sound, he dismissed Indian claims as 'outrageous' (*Washington Post*, 1977, pp. A1, A8).

Many non-Indians agreed with that criticism. For property-owners in Maine, the claims of the Passamaquoddies and Penobscots unleashed anxiety about the future of their state's economy and revealed a visceral racism. 'Talk that has always been frankly bigoted is now becoming threatening,' a constituent warned Representative William S. Cohen, Republican of Maine (Ron MacKechnie, 1977). Governor James B. Longley of Maine exhibited his bias when he charac-terized property-owners in his state as 'innocent people' mistreated by a federal government beholden to 'special interests,' namely, Native Americans (James G. Longley to Joseph E. Brennan, 1977; Longley to Jimmy Carter, 1978).

Jimmy Carter's uncertainty about Indian issues did little to calm matters. During the campaign of 1976, Carter had backed the Nixon/Ford policy of Indian self-determination, pledging 'full consultation' with tribal leaders and that 'the majority of decisions will be made in the Tribal Council room and not in Washington' (*Carter Views on Indian Affairs*, 1976). Yet Carter had little experi-ence with Native American issues as Georgia, where he had been governor, had no federally recognized tribes. As president, he showed only general interest in the subject and, unlike Nixon, he issued no statement explaining his policy.[3] 'There probably is never a *right* time to do this study,' one Carter aide reckoned. 'Its recommendations will inevitably be unpopular in the West (except with the Indians)' (Handwritten memorandum, 1978).

Not surprisingly, the president seldom became directly engaged in the Maine dispute. Carter's stance derived partly from the explosiveness of this issue. 'Politically, the President can't afford the chaos that will result if the Tribes file their suit and pursue it,' Leo M. Krulitz, the solicitor at the Department of the Interior, explained. 'Neither can he afford a settlement so large that it looks like he "bought off the Indians"' (Leo M. Krulitz to Cecil R. Andrus, 1979). In 1978, speaking in Bangor, Maine, Carter admitted there was no 'advantage in trying to resolve a question of this kind' (*Bangor, Maine*, 1979, p. 341). Over the next three years, Carter, in efforts to settle the Maine claims, named a mediator and then a task force, before Democratic Senator William D. Hathaway of Maine took matters into his owns hands and brokered the outline of an agree-ment (*Bangor Daily News*, 1978; *Statement on Maine Indian Land Dispute*, 1977; William D. Hathaway interview, 2005).

With on-again, off-again involvement by the White House, the Maine settle-ment took almost four years to conclude. Only in 1980 did the tribes and large

---

[3]   Carter rather blandly pledged his 'commitment to protecting the rights of Indians.' Carter to James G. Abourezk, October 2, 1978, box 2, IN, WHCF, JCL.

landowners strike their deal based on congressional appropriation of two trust funds, worth \$27 million and \$54.5 million, for the Passamaquoddies and the Penobscots. The Maine tribes, including the Maliseets, were consequently able to acquire up to 300,000 acres of 'average' woodland from large landowners, chiefly paper companies, in the state's thinly populated northern region (*New York Times*, 1980, p. 6) Congress then passed legislation embodying the settlement and Carter, brandishing an eagle quill, signed it in October 1980, with photographers and journalists looking on. The president's reelection campaign staff had pressed for a 'brief signing ceremony,' arguing that it 'will be well received in Maine' (Stuart Eizenstat and R.D. Folsom to Carter, 1980).

For the White House, however, the dispute represented more than a nettlesome problem transformed by electoral imperatives into a photo opportunity. Determined to regain what they deemed theirs, the Maine tribes had filed a lawsuit that provoked uncertainty, even a crisis, over land titles in their state. The claims became part of the public agenda, compelling officials in Maine, Congress, and the White House to act. It was a lesson not lost on policymakers at the national level, for the late 1970s saw the enactment of further measures to expand political and cultural rights for Indians. Carter's aides helped state leaders in Rhode Island to outline a land settlement bill that transferred 1,800 acres to the Narragansetts (Margaret McKenna, 1978; Prucha, 1984, p. 1174). Carter approved legislation to safeguard Indian religious practices and to expand Indians' control of their schools. He also established, via executive order, an assistant secretary of the interior for Indian affairs, a reform once advocated by Nixon. Most important, Carter's BIA began the Federal Acknowledgment Program, designed to bring unrecognized tribes under federal jurisdiction (Prucha, 1984, pp. 1123–24; Kelly, 1988, p. 79). To be sure, none of these initiatives affected Euro-Americans directly, and they thus sparked none of the emotional backlash wrought by such issues as the Maine claims. Nevertheless, by undertaking them, federal officials acknowledged that the sentiment for tribal self-determination was at least as tenacious as, and perhaps more justifiable than, the backlash that had surfaced in reaction against it.

Native American Self-Determination, Reagan-Style

Ronald Reagan's Native American policy represented a work in progress. At first the White House seemed captive to a budget-slashing mindset, which targeted Indian programs, and to Euro-American backlash, especially concerning tribal land claims. The administration, however, found Native American activists to be vocal adversaries. Over time, moreover, Reagan and his team found philosophical, political, and practical reasons to reaffirm and extend the policy of tribal self-determination.

Reagan's budgetary policy, from the outset, offended Indian leaders. During his first year in office, the president on two separate occasions proposed sizeable reductions in funds for programs affecting Indians, including a cut of 19 percent for all projects funded by the BIA (John R. McClaughry to Martin Anderson, 1981). Ronald Andrade, executive director of the National Congress of American Indians, charged that Indians were being made to pay 'a *disproportionate* price for saving the economy' during a period of recession (Ronald Andrade to Tribal Chairmen, 1982). The White House abraded matters by not consulting Indians before announcing the budget cuts (McClaughry to Anderson, 1981). Throughout the spring and summer of 1981, the leaders of the National Tribal Chairmen's Association (NTCA), an organization founded during Nixon's presidency, pressed for a statement on the administration's Indian policy as well as a 'high level' meeting with officials at the White House. Rebuffed on all fronts, the NTCA lashed out by picketing the White House and by lobbying members of Congress to restore the lost dollars (McClaughry to Anderson, 1981).

Slashing federal programs for Indians scarcely dented the growing annual budget deficit.[4] However, the proposed cuts enabled Democrats – and one powerful Republican – to claim the high ground. After majorities in the House and Senate restored the reductions, Republican Senator Barry M. Goldwater, whose home state of Arizona had a large Indian population, threatened to introduce an amendment to all future foreign aid bills granting $1 billion to Native Americans. Goldwater's purpose was to remind all Americans of the 'poor, squalid conditions' in which many reservation Indians lived (*Washington Post*, 1983). He was probably the only Republican to gain any political mileage from the debate on Reagan's Indian budget.

Land claims were another area where Reagan proved hostile to tribal concerns. Here, the president felt the greatest pressure from anti-Indian backlash in Congress. For example, Representative Kenneth L. Holland, Democrat of South Carolina, assailed as 'ransom' a claim by the Catawbas to 144,000 acres in his state (*The State*, 1979). The Cayugas's claim to 64,000 acres in New York State led Representative Gary A. Lee and Senator Alfonse M. D'Amato, both Republicans, to draft legislation to ratify all transactions between Indians and non-Indians in the states of New York, South Carolina, and Connecticut (where the Western Pequots also sought the return of lost land). Their bill empowered

---

[4] Federal programs for Native Americans comprised $2.75 billion out of a total budget of $744 billion in 1981. Maddux, Thomas R. (1999) 'Ronald Reagan's Indian Policy Statement of 1983: Conservative Self-Determination,' (8 Oct.), unpublished paper, RRL, pp. 3–4.

the Secretary of the Interior to determine the merits of claims and the Indians to sue the federal government in the U. S. Court of Claims. Cash from the federal treasury was to be the only form of compensation, however (*Ancient Indian Land Claims Act*, 1982).

The White House could not ignore this Republican-backed bill but was aware of its historic significance. As leaders of the Indian Law Resources Center warned, it would represent the 'first major anti-Indian legislation to receive White House endorsement since the infamous Indian Termination era of the early 1950s (Robert A. McConnell to Eugene W. Taylor, 1982; Indian Law Resource Center, 1982). Lee's measure consequently provoked a lively debate among Reagan's team. Concern for the 'thousands of innocent landowners' who feared loss of their property induced Secretary of the Interior James Watt to endorse it as 'an expedient and equitable resolution (Secretary of the Interior to Gary A. Lee). Reagan aides in the domestic policy and legal fields took a different perspective. John R. McLaughry, senior White House adviser for policy development, protested that Lee's intent to extinguish tribal land claims was 'unconscionable' and warned of 'a lot of bad press' if the president backed it (McClaughry to Ed Gray, 1982). White House Counsel Fred Fielding advised 'careful' resolution of tribal land claims through talks instead of 'endorsing a measure that many may attack as unfair, "anti-Indian," and "further evidence" of the President's supposed "insensitivity" to minorities' (Fred F. Fielding to Richard G. Darman, 1982). As with Nixon, displaying sympathy for Indian concerns – or 'showing more heart' – represented one way to counterbalance the criticism frequently voiced by African American leaders against Republican presidents.

Facing competing pressures, the Reagan administration endorsed a revised version of Lee's bill (McConnell to Taylor, 1982). William Coldiron, the solicitor at the Department of the Interior, backed the measure but advised the Senate Select Committee on Indian Affairs that state governments must contribute 'a portion' of the cost toward any land claims settlement (William Coldiron to Barry M. Goldwater, 1982). This weakened support for the principles of the Lee bill because some conservatives opposed placing any 'undue burden' on state resources (Strom Thurmond et al. to Goldwater, 1982). Moreover, Republican moderates, such as Senators Cohen of Maine and Richard G. Lugar of Indiana, rejected Lee's bill as too 'sweeping', as did Representative Morris K. Udall, a Democrat and chair of the House Committee on Interior and Insular Affairs, who never released it from his committee (Richard G. Lugar to Will H. Hays, 1982; *New York Times*, 1982, p. 26). Although the Ancient Indian Land Claims Settlement bill failed to become law, the debate over it influenced federal policy. The Reagan White House, determined to curtail domestic spending, insisted that it would no longer 'bail out' states and localities with federal dollars, alone, to resolve Indian land disputes (*Lee Bill Appears Dead*, 1982). The age of resolving tribal claims with sizeable tracts of land and trust funds provided by Congress had come to a close.[5]

Despite the administration's budget-slashing and its responsiveness to the backlash against tribal land claims, Reagan was not hostile toward Native Americans personally. In 1983 the president demonstrated his empathy by affirming, in a formal statement, his commitment to tribal self-determination. The issuance of a message partly reflected pressure by the NCAI and NTCA (Maddux, 1999, p. 6). Morton C. Blackwell, White House liaison to Native Americans, also sensed 'a growing need for action' (Morton C. Blackwell to Kenneth Smith, 1982). But the statement also derived from philosophical considerations, for aspects of Reagan's conservative thought corresponded with some of the aims espoused by Indian activists (Maddux, 1999, pp. 2–3). These included a suspicion of federal power, a desire to lodge decision-making as close to those affected as possible, and a willingness to turn federal services over to local governments, of which Indian tribes were one example. In September 1982 Reagan listened to a report from a White House working group on Indian policy and decided to act (Morton C. Blackwell exit interview, 1984). As the Indian message took shape, Assistant Secretary of Interior Kenneth Smith stressed its 'philosophical thrust' (Smith to Members, 1982).

The ideology of enhancing local versus federal authority, which in part shaped Nixon's Indian policy, pervaded Reagan's message. 'This Administration believes,' the statement opened, 'that responsibilities and resources should be restored to the governments which are closest to the people served. This philosophy applies not only to state and local governments, but also to federally recognized American Indian tribes.' The president pledged to enhance tribal authority by 'removing the obstacles to self-government and by creating a more favorable environment for the development of healthy reservation economies.' The administration offered reservations greater leeway in developing their economies and natural resources, aided by private investment – but in ways 'consistent' with their federal trust status. In other words, the era of termination, in which tribes had lost their federally protected status, was not to return under the guise of capitalism. The statement affirmed a 'government-to-government relationship' between federal authorities, the states, and federally-recognized tribes. Most notably, Reagan's message, like Nixon's, urged Congress to repeal

---

[5]   The administration of George Bush, for example, evaded the Sioux's claim to the Black Hills in South Dakota. See Phil Stevens et al., to George Bush, 13 Feb. 1991 and Mary McClure to Stevens, 22 Feb. 1991, ID# 213678, box 2, WHORM: Subject File, George Bush Library (GBL), College Station, Texas.

House Concurrent Resolution (H.C.R.) 108, a measure passed by the Republican-controlled Eighty-third Congress in 1953 that 'established the now discredited policy of terminating the federal-tribal relationship' (*Statement by the President*, 1983).

Interestingly, Reagan's statement never received the praise it deserved, partly because of poor public relations by a White House famous for its mastery of political stagecraft. The difficulty stemmed in part from the fact that although most Republicans, by the 1970s, had accepted tribal self-determination, some of them continued to believe, as in the 1950s, that enhancing the rights of individual Native Americans involved termination – freeing Indians from all federal control by ending the trust relationship between tribes and the national government. Public comments by Secretary of the Interior Watt proved especially troublesome (*Los Angeles Times*, 1981). Watt unleashed a firestorm in January 1983 – five days after the release of the Indian message – when he described Indians as 'incompetent wards' of the government and reservations as examples of 'the failures of socialism,' ridden by drug abuse, unemployment, alcoholism, adultery, divorce and venereal disease (News Release by Richard Viguerie). Since Watt's remarks called into question the legitimacy of the entire federal trust relationship with tribes, Native American leaders strongly denounced them (LaDonna Harris to Ronald Reagan, 1983; *USA Today*, 1983).

Watt was not alone. Five years later, at a question and answer session at Moscow State University, Reagan expressed regret that the federal government had chosen to 'humor' Native Americans by allowing them to retain their 'primitive lifestyles.' The better course, he ventured, might have been to invite them to 'join us' and 'be citizens along with the rest of us.' (*Arizona Republic*, 1988, p. A1) Tribal leaders again exploded (*New York Times*, 1988, p. A13). Reagan's 'patronizing' tone aside, talk of integrating Indians into the mainstream harkened back to the much-despised policies of the 1950s and 60s, not the tribal-friendly trends of the 1970s and 1980s (Gloria Probst to Editor, 1988). Although Reagan was making unscripted personal observations, his remarks were, a correspondent for *Indian Country Today* remembered, 'wildly misguided' (*Indian Country Today*, 2004, p. B2).

White House aides scrambled to limit the damage caused by such ill-judged remarks. Rick J. Neal, assistant to the president for intergovernmental affairs, pointed out that Watt had attacked past policies of paternalism, not the decade-old policy of tribal self-determination and that the course outlined in Reagan's Indian statement 'will go a long way' in solving the problems listed by Watt (Rick J. Neal to Cheryl Coleman, 1983). Regarding the president's comments, Cristena L. Bach, Neal's successor at intergovernmental affairs, assured one tribal leader 'that President Reagan stands firmly behind his Indian Policy Statement of 1983' (Cristena L. Bach to Anthony Drennan, 1988). Such actions suggested that Reagan's message served as a sort of cover where administration officials might find refuge or as a blanket useful for beating down the embers of Indian discontent.

Reagan's message was something more than that. It was, on one level, a guide to completing Nixon's Indian agenda. Congress, under Reagan, approved three measures that harkened back to the Nixon era. Thirteen years after the federal government restored the once-terminated Menominees to trust status, Congress passed and Reagan approved legislation reinstating the Klamaths, an Oregon tribe that had been terminated, as a federally-recognized tribe (Charles E. Kimbrol and Karen Ray to Reagan, 1986). In 1988, the House of Representatives buried termination when, as recommended by both the Nixon and Reagan Indian messages, it repealed HCR 108 (*Statement by Ross Swimmer*, 1988). In the same year Congress enacted, with presidential support, amendments to the Indian Self-Determination Act of 1975 that removed restrictions on contracting out federal services to tribes and provided federal dollars to cover the indirect costs of such contracts (James C. Miller III to Reagan, 1988). These changes embodied the spirit of the Nixon and Reagan messages, which promised tribes more control over their affairs.

On another level, Reagan and Congress pushed Nixon's policy of self-determination into new areas, such as permitting gaming on reservations. For Reagan, the road to gaming started with his Indian message, which offered to develop reservations economically. In truth, however, a dramatic shift in reservation economies was already underway. By 1985 approximately 120 tribes were operating bingo games, drawing non-Indian patrons from hundreds of miles away. Since state laws do not apply to federally recognized tribes, reservations faced no limitations on their jackpots. The result was an inviting and potentially lucrative source of revenue for tribes – and for Euro-Americans (*New York Times*, 1985, p. A30).

The Reagan administration came to recognize the importance of gaming to reservations. Initially, the president's team stressed that these enterprises had to be well regulated to prevent penetration by organized crime (United States Department of the Interior, 1986). In 1986 the White House went further by sponsoring legislation to permit tribal games of a ceremonial nature to go unregulated; to authorize and to regulate, via a federal panel, bingo on reservations; and to empower states to monitor all other Indian gaming (*Comparison of Pending Indian Gambling Legislation*, 1986). Ultimately, congressional action led the administration to accept Indian gaming. In 1986 Representative Morris Udall proposed a bill that divided gambling into three classes: social and ceremonial; bingo, lotto, and games having cancelled numbers; and all other forms, including casinos. The federal government would legalize all three types of gambling and oversee the latter two through a 'National Indian Gaming Commission' (*Comparison of Pending Indian Gambling Legislation*, 1986). Udall's bill was popular among Native Americans and on Capitol Hill, and both houses, by wide margins, passed a revised version of it in 1988 (Twinkle Thompson to Senator Goldwater, 1986; Miller to Reagan, 1988). White House staff members, at that point, urged Reagan to sign it for practical reasons – the administration's bill had 'attracted almost no congressional support,' negotiating a new agreement among tribes, states, and Congress would take too much time, and gaming would meanwhile proceed unregulated. They also asserted a philosophical reason, in tune with the president's Indian message, for supporting the bill: the need to 'preserve the sovereign rights of Indian tribes.' The strength of these arguments ensured that the president duly signed the measure (Miller to Reagan, 1988).

Reagan's approach to reservation economies and gaming exemplified aspects of his Native American policy. The president at times exhibited a lack of understanding of tribal concerns and an ability to lose the initiative to Congress. Yet Reagan and his team learned on the job, affirmed the policy of self-determination, and then tailored their principles to suit emerging issues such as gaming – which a reporter for *Indian Country Today* in 2004 (p. B2) lauded as 'a godsend for Indian country.' By accepting tribal control of gaming, Reagan added another chapter to the struggle for self-determination.

The Durability of Native American Self-Determination

By the late 1980s, the policy of tribal self-determination had withstood attacks by some Euro-Americans as well as the diffidence, and at times hostility, of policymakers in Congress and in the White House. The result was plain. 'Existing tribal governments,' historian Roger L. Nichols argued in 1988 (p. 71), 'exercise more direct and a wider variety of authority than at any other time in this century.' And the president most responsible for initiating this change harbored no regrets. 'As President,' Nixon reflected in 1989, 'I took special pride in supporting the policy of "Self-Determination Without Termination," whereby my Administration endorsed Indian control and responsibility over government service programs' (Nixon to Dennis DeConcini, 1989).

National policymakers found many reasons to support the aspirations of Native Americans. The emerging, evolving, and maturing Native American movement used a host of devices – including armed occupations, high-profile lawsuits, and vocal criticism – to reclaim, expand, and protect the authority of tribes. Such tactics forced Presidents Nixon, Ford, Carter, and Reagan to do more than just listen and respond in token fashion. The movement encouraged these leaders and their aides to become engaged with past injustices and to adapt their ideas and agendas to Native American issues. Nixon himself spoke privately of the 'grave injustices' inflicted on Indians. Most important, the White House, especially under Nixon and Reagan, perceived the demands for tribal self-determination as an extension of its own efforts to strengthen local over federal authority. However self-serving, it provided an additional ideological motive for this policy.

Such arguments no doubt strengthened the policy of self-determination, for the gains of the Native American movement proved difficult to reverse. The backlash against Indian rights, for example, accomplished little beyond halting, often only temporarily, the settlement of tribal land claims. The 'rights revolution' of the 1960s, moreover, removed barriers to political rights and economic opportunity for individual African Americans, Native Americans, women, and gays, among other groups. It also helped foster a collective sense of group identity and group rights that, as the struggle for Native American self-determination illustrated, has become embedded in and reinforced by federal policy. As non-Indians could attest, it was a force not easily undone.

Bibliography

Spiro T. Agnew to Richard M. Nixon, no date, box 67, Bradley H. Patterson, Jr. Files, Nixon Materials, NA.

'Alcatraz Chronology,' 3 Aug. 1973, Box 33, Leonard Garment Files, Nixon Materials, NA.

American Indian Press Association news release, 9 Aug. 1974, Box 9, Patterson Files, Nixon Materials, NA.

'Ancient Indian Land Claims Act of 1982,' no date, box 1, Series 16: Harjo Records, NCAI Papers, NAA, SI.

Ronald Andrade to Tribal Chairmen, 17 March 1982, box 91, Series 4: Tribal Files, NCAI Papers, NAA, SI.

'Annotated News Summary (19 March 1973),' in Joan Hoff-Wilson (ed.) (1989), *Papers of the Nixon White House* (Lanham, MD.: University Publications of America), pt. 6, fiche 231.

'Are We Giving America Back to the Indians?' Interstate Congress for Equal Rights and Responsibilities, no date, folder 9, box 4, Kenneth McLeod Papers, Accession #2487–005, University of Washington (UW) Libraries, Seattle.

Arizona (Phoenix) *Republic*, 1 June 1988.

Roy Ash to Ford, 31 Dec. 1974, folder: S 1017, box 21, Legislation Case Files, GRFL.

Cristena L. Bach to Anthony Drennan, Sr., 24 June 1988, ID# 572375, SP1263, Speeches (SP), WHORM: Subject File, RRL.

Bangor Daily News, 17 Feb. 1978, box 6, series 16: Harjo Records, NCAI Papers, NAA, SI.

Bangor, Maine: Remarks and a Question-and-Answer Session at a Town Meeting (17 Feb. 1978),' (1979) *Public Papers of the Presidents: Jimmy Carter (1978), Book I* (Washington, D.C.).

Morton C. Blackwell to Kenneth Smith, 5 April 1982, file OA9726, box 3, Neal Files, RRL.

Dewey F. Bartlett Diary, 26 June 1973, box 66, Dewey F. Bartlett Collection, Carl Albert Center, University of Oklahoma, Norman.

Morton C. Blackwell exit interview, 26 Jan. 1984, RRL.

Cabinet Meeting Notes, 17 Sept. 1974, box 3, Kenneth R. Cole Files, GRFL.

James Cannon to Ford, 15 Oct. 1975, box 31, in Legislation Case Files, GRFL;

'Carter Views on Indian Affairs,' *Indian Record* (December 1976), box 82, Public Liaison Office – Wales Files, JCL.

Castile, George Pierre (1998) *To Show Heart: Native American Self-Determination and Federal Indian Policy, 1960–1975* (Tucson: University of Arizona Press).

Clarkin, Thomas (2001) *Federal Indian Policy in the Kennedy and Johnson Administrations, 1961–1969* (Albuquerque: University of New Mexico Press).

Cobb, Daniel M. (1998) 'Philosophy of an Indian War: Indian Community Action in the Johnson Administration's War on Indian Poverty,' *American Indian Culture and Research Journal*, vol. 22, no. 2.

William Coldiron to Barry M. Goldwater, 27 Aug., 1982, box 9, General Office ("O") Files, Barry M. Goldwater Papers, Arizona Historical Foundation, Hayden Library, Arizona State University (ASU), Tempe.

Cole to Ford, 17 Oct. 1974a, folder: S 634, box 10, Legislation Case Files, GRFL.

Cole to Ford, 18 Oct. 1974b, folder: S 1327, box 11, in Legislation Case Files, GRFL

Cole to Ford, 30 Dec. 1974c, box 1, IN, WHCF, GRFL.

Cole to Ford, 1 Jan. 1975, folder: S 521, box 18, in Legislation Case Files, GRFL

Cole to Ford, 2 Jan. 1975, folder: S 1296, box 20, Legislation Case Files, GRFL.

Cole to Ford, 2 Jan. 1975, folder: S 1017, box 21, Legislation Case Files, GRFL.

'Comparison of Pending Indian Gambling Legislation (no date),' attached to Twinkle [Thompson] to Senator [Goldwater], 17 June 1986, box 13, Indian Affairs Files, Goldwater Papers, ASU.

Congressional Quarterly (1975) *Congressional Quarterly Almanac: 93rd Congress, 2nd Session [...] 1974* (Washington, D.C.).

Debo, Angie (1970) *A History of the Indians of the United States* (Norman: University of Oklahoma Press).

'Declaration of Purpose: "Interstate Congress for Equal Rights and Responsibilities,"' no date, box 3, McLeod Papers, Accession #2487–005, UW.

'Declaration of War,' 20 Sept. 1974, box 4, John G. Carlson Files, GRFL.

Deloria, Jr., Vine (1974) *Behind the Trail of Broken Treaties: An Indian Declaration of Independence* (New York: Delacorte Press).

Ehrlichman handwritten comments on Memorandum, Garment to Ehrlichman, 21 Jan. 1971, box 34, Garment Files, Nixon Materials, NA.

Stuart Eizenstat and R.D. Folsom to Carter, 3 Oct. 1980, box 2, IN, WHCF, JCL.

Fred F. Fielding to Richard G. Darman, 14 April 1982, ID# 044435, box 2, IN, WHORM: Subject File, RRL.

Garment to Agnew, no date, box 105, Garment Files, Nixon Materials, NA.

Leonard Garment to John D. Ehrlichman, 28 July 1970, box 10, Egil M. Krogh Files, Richard M. Nixon Presidential Materials, National Archives (NA), College Park, Maryland.

Garment to Ehrlichman, 14 Dec. 1970, box 1, Leonard Garment Papers, Manuscript Division, Library of Congress, Washington, D.C. (quotation).

Garment, Leonard (1997) *Crazy Rhythm: My Journey from Brooklyn, Jazz, and Wall Street to Nixon's White House, Watergate, and Beyond* (New York: Times Books).

H.R. Haldeman to James Keogh, 13 Jan. 1969, box 10A, Arthur F. Burns Papers, Gerald R. Ford Library (GRFL), Ann Arbor, Michigan.

Handwritten memorandum, 13 March 1978, box 165, Domestic Policy Staff – Stuart Eizenstat Files, JCL.

LaDonna Harris to Ronald Reagan, 20 Jan. 1983, ID# 120869, box 5, IN, WHORM: Subject File, RRL.

William D. Hathaway interview with the author, 14 May 2005, McLean, Virginia, in the author's possession.

Hertzberg, Hazel Whitman (1988) 'The Indian Rights Movement,' in William E. Sturtevant and Wilcomb E. Washburn (eds.), *Handbook of North American Indians: History of Indian-White Relations* vol. IV (Washington, D.C.: Smithsonian Institution).

Hoff, Joan (1994) *Nixon Reconsidered* (New York: Basic Books).

George W. Humphreys to Cannon, 19 Oct. 1976, box 13, George Humphreys Files, GRFL.

Humphreys and Bradley Patterson to Ford, 15 Nov. 1976, box 2, IN, WHCF, GRFL.

Indian Country Today, 2 June 2004.

Indian Law Resources Center (1982) News release (9 Feb.), box 1, Series 16: Harjo Records, NCAI Papers, NAA, SI (quotation).

'Indians' Rights May Haunt Us,' News Clipping, 9 Feb. 1976, box 35, Marrs Files, GRFL.

Iverson, Peter (1998) *"We Are Still Here": American Indians in the Twentieth Century* (Wheeling, IL.: Harlan Davidson).

Johnson, Troy R. (1996) *The Occupation of Alcatraz Island: Indian Self-Determination and the Rise of Indian Activism* (Urbana: University of Illinois Press).

Kelly, Lawrence C. (1988) 'United States Indian Policies, 1900–1980,' in E. Sturtevant and W.E. Washburn (eds.), *Handbook of North American Indians: History of Indian-White Relations* vol. IV (Washington, D.C.: Smithsonian Institution).

Charles E. Kimbrol and Karen Ray to Reagan, 28 Aug. 1986, ID# 423955, box 11, IN, WHORM: Subject File, RRL.

Kotlowski, Dean J. (2001) *Nixon's Civil Rights: Politics, Principle, and Policy* (Cambridge, MA.: Harvard University Press).

Kotlowski, Dean J. (2002) 'Limited Vision: Carl Albert, the Choctaws, and Native American Self-Determination,' *American Indian Culture and Research Journal*, vol. 26, no. 2, pp. 23–28.

Kotlowski, Dean J. (2003) 'Alcatraz, Wounded Knee, and Beyond: The Nixon and Ford Administrations Respond to Native American Protest,' *Pacific Historical Review*, vol. 72, no. 1.

Leo M. Krulitz to Cecil R. Andrus, 23 July 1979, box 2, IN, WHCF, JCL.

'Lee Bill Appears Dead, Backers Say' (1982) News clipping (24 June), box 1, Series 16: Harjo Records, NCAI Papers, NAA, SI.

James G. Longley to Joseph E. Brennan, 20 July 1977, box 82, Commissioners Series, James G. Longley Papers, BC (first quotation).

Longley to Jimmy Carter, 12 Jan. 1978, box 1, IN, WHCF, JCL (second quotation).

Los Angeles Times, 31 May 1981, box 2, Series I: Memoranda File, James A. Baker III Files, RRL.

Richard G. Lugar to Will H. Hays, Jr., 13 Aug. 1982, box 10, series 16: Harjo Files, NCAI Papers, NAA, SI.

Ron MacKechnie to William S. Cohen, 22 Feb. 1977, box 9, House: Legislation Series, William S. Cohen Papers, University of Maine Library, Orono.

Maddux, Thomas R. (1999) 'Ronald Reagan's Indian Policy Statement of 1983: Conservative Self-Determination,' unpublished paper, RRL, pp. 3–4.

Warren G. Magnuson to Peggy A. Robinson, 1 June 1973, box 62, Warren G. Magnuson Papers, Accession #3181–5, UW.

Carl Marcy to Senate Foreign Relations Committee, 28 March 1973 and 2 March 1973 (both quotations), box 2004, U. S. Senate: Senate Office Series, Edmund S. Muskie Papers, Edmund S. Muskie Archives and Special Collections Library, Bates College (BC), Lewiston, Maine.

John R. McClaughry to Martin Anderson, 16 Oct. 1981, file OA6389, box 7, Elizabeth H. Dole Files, Ronald Reagan Library (RRL), Simi Valley, California.

McClaughry to Ed Gray, 16 Feb. 1982, file OA11960, box 12, Danny J. Boggs Files, RRL.

Robert A. McConnell to Eugene W. Taylor, 29 June 1982, ID# 080210CU, box 3, IN, White House Office of records Management (WHORM): Subject File, RRL;

Margaret McKenna (1978) Memoranda for the File (1 Feb. and 6 March), box 142, Counsel's Office – Margaret McKenna Files, JCL.

Memorandum for Ed Harper, 24 June 1971, box 8, Garment Files, Nixon Materials.

James C. Miller III to Reagan, 29 Sept. 1988, ID# 60105855, box 13, IN, WHORM: Subject File, RRL.

Miller to Reagan, 11 Oct. 1988, ID# 601142, box 14, IN, WHORM: Subject File, RRL.

Nagel, Joane (1996) *American Indian Ethnic Renewal: Red Power and the Resurgence of Identity and Culture* (New York: Oxford University Press).

National Congress of American Indians to Ford, 2 Jan. 1975, National Congress of American Indians folder, WHCF: Name File, GRFL.

National Tribal Chairmen's Association press release, no date, box 1, Series 16: Records of Suzan J. Harjo, National Congress of American Indians (NCAI) Papers, National Anthropological Archives (NAA), Smithsonian Institution (SI), Museum Support Center, Suitland, Maryland.

Rick J. Neal to Cheryl Coleman, 9 March 1983, file OA9724, box 2, Neal Files, RRL.

News release by Richard Viguerie, Executive Producer, National Television Corporation, no date, box 5, Morton C. Blackwell Files, RRL.

New York Times, 30 Nov. 1969.

New York Times, 12 Nov. 1972.

New York Times, 17 March 1973.

New York Times, 15 March 1980.

New York Times, 11 Sept. 1982.

New York Times, 22 Oct. 1985.

New York Times, 1 June 1988.

Nichols, Roger L. (1988) 'Indians in the Post-Termination Era,' *Storia Nordamericana*, vol. 5, no. 1.

Nixon to National Congress of American Indians, 27 Sept. 1968, box 1, IN, White House Central Files (WHCF), Nixon Materials, NA.

Nixon to Ehrlichman, 30 Nov. 1970, box 12, H. R. Haldeman Files, Contested Documents File, Nixon Materials, NA.

Nixon to Dennis DeConcini et al., 26 Jan. 1989, casefile #018256, box 1, IN, WHORM: Subject File, GBL.

Patrick E. O'Donnell to Warren Hendricks, 2 Jan. 1975, box 20, Legislation Case Files, GRFL

Alfonso Oriz to Gerald R. Ford, 23 Jan. 1975, box 34, Theodore Marrs Files, GRFL.

Patterson to Garment, 2 April 1970, box 105, Garment Files, Nixon Materials, NA.

Bradley H. Patterson Jr., 10 Sept. 1974, exit interview, pp. 32 and 33.

Patterson to John G. Carlson, 17 Sept. 1974, box 4, Carlson Files, GRFL.

Patterson to Morris R. Thompson et al., 26 Sept. 1974, box 4, Carlson Files, GRFL.

Patterson to Ronald Nessen, 18 Oct. 1976, box 4, Bradley H. Patterson Files, GRFL.

Patterson handwritten comments on Cannon to Philip Buchen and Patterson, 3 Dec. 1976, box 4, Patterson Files, GRFL (quotation).

Bradley H. Patterson, Jr. interview with A. James Reichley, 11 Nov. 1977, box 1, A. James Reichley Interview Transcripts, GRFL.

Gloria Probst to Editor (1988) *Spokane Spokesman-Review* (14 June), ID#584690, SP 1268, Speeches (SP), WHORM: Subject File, RRL.

Prucha, Francis Paul (1984) *The Great Father: The United States Government and the American Indians* (2 vols.) vol. II (Lincoln: University of Nebraska Press), pp. 1085–1208.

Robert Robertson to Indians of All Tribes, 31 March 1970, box 1, Indian Affairs (IN), White House Central Files (WHCF), Nixon Materials, NA.

Rocky Mountain (Denver) *News*, 2 June 1975, box 35, Marrs Files, GRFL.

Wilfred H. Rommel to Ford, 23 Dec. 1974, box 17, in Legislation Case Files, GRFL

San Francisco Chronicle, 11 June 1971, box 34, Garment Files, Nixon Materials, NA.

Secretary of the Interior to Gary A. Lee, Draft Letter, no date, box 2, Martin Anderson Files, RRL.

Smith to Members (1982) White House Working Group on Indian Policy (18 May), file OA9726, box 3, Neal Files, RRL.

Smith, Paul Chaat and Warrior, Robert Allen (1996) *Like a Hurricane: The Indian Movement from Alcatraz to Wounded Knee* (New York: New Press).

'Special Message to Congress on Indian Affairs (8 July 1970),' (1971) *Public Papers of the Presidents: Richard Nixon (1970)* (Washington, D.C.: Government Printing Office).

'Statement on Maine Indian Land Dispute,' (1977) White House press release (8 Oct.), box 1, IN, WHCF, JCL.

'Statement by the President,' no date, folder: S 1017, box 21, Legislation Case Files, GRFL.

'Statement by the President' (1983) White House Press Release (24 Jan.), file OA12749, box 3, Cristena L. Bach Files, RRL.

'Statement by Ross Swimmer, Assistant Secretary – Indian Affairs, Regarding President Reagan's Recent Remarks About Indians,' (1988) *United States Department of the Interior Press Release* (10 June), folder: POTUS Moscow State University, file OA18333, Bach Files, RRL.

'Statement of the Vice President, National Council on Indian Opportunity,' 26 Jan. 1970, box 5, William C. Schaab Papers, Taos Blue Lake Collection, Seeley G. Mudd Library, Princeton University (PU), Princeton, N.J..

The State (Columbia, South Carolina), 22 March 1979, p. 19-B.

Strom Thurmond, Alphonse M. D'Amato and Lee to Goldwater, 18 Aug. 1982, box 9, Indian Affairs Files, Goldwater Papers, ASU.

Twinkle [Thompson] to Senator [Goldwater], 17 June 1986, box 13, Indian Affairs Files, Goldwater Papers, ASU.

Undated draft memorandum, box 105, Garment Files, Nixon Materials, NA.

United States Department of the Interior News Release, 14 April 1986, box 13, Indian Affairs Files, Goldwater Papers, ASU.

USA Today, 20 Jan. 1983, file OA9595, box 6, Carlson Files, RRL.

Wall Street Journal, 16 Sept. 1976, box 35, Marrs Files, GRFL.

Washington Post, 9 Oct. 1977.

Washington Post, 18 Aug. 1983, file OA9724, box 3, Rick Neal Files, RRL.

John C. Whitaker to Ash, 27 Dec. 1974, folder: S 1017, box 21, Legislation Case Files, GRFL.

12

Race, Class, Age and Punitive Segregation: Prisons and Prison Populations in the Contemporary United States

Vivien Miller

The incarcerated population of the United States more than quadrupled in the quarter-century from 1980 to 2005. According to U.S. Department of Justice statistics, the total estimated correctional population of the United States in December 2004 was nearly seven million (6,996,500) which included 2,135,901 persons in state and federal prisons and jails (both state and privately-operated facilities) and nearly five million on probation or parole. The national average incarceration rate for 2004 was 724 per 100,000 U.S. residents, rising from 313 in 1985 and 601 in 1995. Seven of the ten states with the highest incarceration rates are in the southern tier of the United States, including the District of Columbia at 1600 per 100,000 residents (the highest) and California with 489 per 100,000 (ranked tenth). The states with the highest prison populations are: California, Texas, New York and Florida, which are of course the states with the highest overall populations. However, recent growth in the federal prison population outstripped that of state prison and local jail populations. The annual average percentage increase from 1995 to 2004 was 7.4 percent for the federal prison population, 2.6 percent for the states, and 3.9 percent for local jails. It costs roughly $41 billion a year, or $20,000 per prisoner, to maintain this carceral population, but inevitably there are marked differences in cost according to state and region.[1]

---

[1]   Human Rights Watch provides the following incarceration figures for 1999–2000:
DC 1600, LA 763, TX 704, OK 653, MS 613, SC 550, AL 524, GA 524, NV 518, CA 489.
See Human Rights Watch (2000) *United States – Punishment and Prejudice: Racial Disparities in the War on Drugs* (May), www.hrw.org/reports/2000/usa/Rcedrg00–05htm
The following information comes from the online *Sourcebook of Criminal Justice Statistics*:
Table 6.28.2004 Number and rate (per 100,000 residents) of sentenced prisoners under jurisdiction of state and federal correctional authorities on Dec 31:
2004 = 1,433,793 which includes 1,337,668 men and 96,125 women.

As sobering as these prison numbers appear, they contain some startling racial and gender disparities. Non-whites are much more likely than whites to be stopped by police, searched, arrested, defended by a public defender with a huge caseload, convicted, and imprisoned. Over 50 percent of new admissions to U.S. prisons at the dawn of the twenty-first century are African American, another 15 to 20 percent are Latino, and Native Americans are also vastly overrepresented (Sabo et al., 2001, p. 20). Figures from the mid-1990s show that African American males comprised less than 7 percent of the total population but nearly half of the total jail and prison populations. Another nine percent were Hispanic males, also disproportionate to their percentage of the prison populations. One-third of all young black men (ages 20–29) were either in prison or directly under the control of a state or federal correctional system. For Hispanic males, the figure was one in eight (Mauer, 2001a, p. 49). But black women, a majority of whom are arrested for drug-related offences, constitute the most rapidly expanding of all imprisoned population, rising from 12,331 sentenced prisoners in state and federal prisons in 1980 to 96,125 in 2004 (Davis, 2001, pp. 35–45). Black women were more than eight times as likely as white women to be in prison in 1997 (Human Rights Watch, 2000, p. 3).

There were also significant rises in the numbers of non-citizens in state and federal prisons between 1998 and 2003. The number of non-citizen federal prisoners increased from 27,682 in mid-1998 to 34,456 in mid-2003, and the number of non-citizen state prisoners increased from 49,417 to 56,244 in the same period (*Sourcebook of Criminal Justice Statistics*, 2003, p. 509). While some of this increase is linked to the post-9/11 war on terror, the majority of these prisoners are serving time for immigration or drugs offences. For example, California currently holds approximately 5,000 illegal immigrants under federal detention (*California's Prisons*, 2006, p. 37). One consequence of the post-1982 'war on drugs' has been the internationalization of the U.S. prison population. The low level 'mules' (often female) carrying drugs into the United States have been incarcerated in ever-increasing numbers. As a result, Goldberg and Evans (2004)

See www.albany.edu/sourcebook/pdf/t6282004.pdf.

Table 6.1.2004 Adults on probation, in jail or prison, and on parole:

Total estimated correctional population in 2004 = 6,996,500 which includes 4,151,125 on probation, 713,990 in jail, 1,421,911 in prison, and 765,355 on parole.

See www.albany.edu/sourcebook/pdf/t612004.pdf.

Table 6.13.2004 Number and rate (per 100,000 residents) of persons in state and federal prisons and local jails:

2004 total in custody = 2,135,901 which includes 170,535 in federal prisons, 1,244,311 in state prisons, 713,990 in local jails.

See www.albany.edu/sourcebook/pdf/t6132004.pdf.

note that, 'At least 25 percent of inmates in the federal prison system today will be subject to deportation when their sentences are completed' (Goldberg and Evans).

Analysis of sentenced prisoners according to race, ethnicity, gender and age reveals further startling differences, and underlines the racial disparities in current sentencing practices. The bulk of sentenced prisoners are aged between 20 and 44 years, but there are of course significant populations of teens and older prisoners. In 2004 the rate of white non-Hispanic male sentenced prisoners aged 20–24 per 100,000 of those residents was 886, but 6,217 for black non-Hispanic men in the same age group, and 2,357 for Hispanics. The sentencing rates were just as disproportionate in succeeding age categories. For example, the rate of white non-Hispanic male sentenced prisoners aged between 25 and 29 years was 1,172 per 100,000 of those residents, but 8,367 for black non-Hispanic men, and 2,480 for Hispanic men in this age group. Such patterns were also evident in the female prison populations. For example, the rate of white non-Hispanic female sentenced prisoners aged between 20 and 24 years was 86, but 272 for black non-Hispanic women and 128 for Hispanic women. The rate of white non-Hispanic female sentenced prisoners aged between 25 and 29 years was 110, but 404 for black non-Hispanic women and 160 for Hispanic women.[2] In 2004, in every age group, more African American and Hispanic men and women were in jail or prison than white non-Hispanics.

This essay explores the reasons for the 'blackening' and 'browning' of the state and federal penal systems. It begins with an overview of the relationship of the 'war on drugs' to racialized rates of incarceration. It is the systematic imprisonment of young urban black men and women that has under-girded the shift to mass incarceration (Garland, 2001, p. 6), a process tied directly to the 'war on drugs' which has been waged disproportionately in poor, urban and non-white areas (Goldberg and Evans; Parenti, 1997). Media and political attention on the U.S. drugs problem has helped shape the racialized and gendered images of drugs abuse and abusers. Far more whites use both powder and crack cocaine than blacks, but the image of the drug offender that dominates media stories is 'a black man slouching in an alleyway, not a white man in his home. When asked to close their eyes and envision a drug user, Americans overwhelmingly picture a black person' (Human Rights Watch, 2001). The essay then goes on to consider the impact of major sentencing changes on the shift to mass incarceration and finally the consequences, most notably the 'graying' of the U.S. prison

---

[2] Table 6.33.2004 Rate (per 100,000 U.S. resident populations in each group) of sentenced prisoners under jurisdiction of state and federal correction authorities. See www.albany.edu/sourcebook/pdf/6332004.pdf.

population. The elderly prisoner (age 55 and over) is the fastest growing age group in the twenty-first century U.S. prison system. In 2000, more than 44,200 inmates age 55 and over were in state and federal prisons, compared with less than 7,000 in 1980. In addition, there were nearly 60,000 prisoners between 36 and 54 years of age serving an average sentence of almost 24 years. The majority of older offenders are non-Hispanic white males, but there are disproportionate numbers of older African American inmates (Aday, 2005, p. 3).

The Arrival of Late Modernity and the War on Drugs

Crime rates in the United States rose sharply from the 1960s, and peaked in the early 1980s when rates were three times those of 1950. The period 1965 to 1973 saw the biggest increases on record in all main offence categories, including property crime, violent crime and drug offending. Mass incarceration emerged in the 1980s and by the 1990s had reached an unprecedented scale for a modern democracy. David Garland locates the increased susceptibility to crime and the penal response within the new social, economic and cultural arrangements generated by major structural changes and the 'new patterns of mentalities, interests and sensibilities' of 'late modernity' in the post-1960s United States (and United Kingdom). From the 1980s, neo-liberalism and social conservatism shaped the ideological environment in which criminal justice decisions were made (Garland, 2002, pp. 90, 134).

The shift from welfarism to conservative neo-liberalism – 'the effort to replace social welfare with social control as the principle of state policy' – has given rise to new conceptualisations of 'dangerousness' and dangerous populations over the past thirty years that, in turn, have led to an ever-increasing penal population. In the same period, faith in the rehabilitative ideal waned and the authority of penal experts eroded as the gulf widened between the public and the bureaucrats who administered prison policy (see Pratt, 1998, p. 509; Garland, 2000, pp. 347–75; Garland, 2001). Americans believed wrongly that crime rates were rising and supported the building of more prisons. The deployment of 'emotive and ostentatious punishments' such as chain gangs, boot camps, and 'three strikes' laws were designed to give vent to human emotion and to deliberately humiliate or brutalise the offender. As U.S. politicians and their supporters engaged in a process of dehumanizing and distancing themselves from inmates, the prison became a warehouse for storing and isolating the poor, racial and ethnic minorities, immigrants and dislocated urban residents – in other words, ungovernable, dispensable and undesirable populations. Thus, in a relatively short period of time, high prison populations became politically popular and economically acceptable (Garland, 2002; Mauer, 2001b, pp. 9–15; Pratt, 1996, pp. 243–64).

Joseph Hallinan credits the federal courts with setting in motion a national prison boom. By the early 1990s, overcrowding and atrocious living conditions meant that 'prisons in over forty states were operating under federal court orders mandating reform of unconstitutional conditions.' By ordering costly improvements, including massive prison building programs, the federal government helped redefine the place and purpose of the prison in society, and was able to draw on public and taxpayer support amid a backlash against inmates' rights which had undergone considerable change since the late 1960s (Hallinan, 2003, p. 30).

Beginning in the 1970s, the use of determinate sentencing started to inflate prison numbers. This dynamic continued throughout the 1980s when the Reagan Administration 'invoked an image of crime that linked violent street crime to welfare, to liberal social policies, and to declining respect for traditional moral values' (Mauer, 2001, pp. 9–15). In 1982 President Reagan declared a national war on drugs, even though reported incidence of drug use in the U.S. was declining (Beckett, 1997, p. 14). The appearance of crack cocaine in urban areas in the mid-1980s, along with illegally-armed young men protecting their markets, fuelled fears of drug-related violence. An aggressive 'war on drugs' complete with a new set of mandatory sentencing penalties produced an almost limitless supply of arrestable and imprisonable offenders, who were overwhelmingly non-white. The 'war on drugs' was in effect a war waged against inner-city poor and minority residents (Simon, 2001, pp. 21–33). It continues despite mounting evidence that drug use is not regulated or decreased by criminalization because 'the groups most adversely affected lack political power and are widely regarded as dangerous and undeserving; because the groups least affected could be assured that something is being done and lawlessness is not tolerated; and because few politicians are willing to propose a policy [of decriminalization or retreat] when there is so little political advantage to be gained by doing so' (Garland, 2002, p. 132).

Throughout the 1990s, more than 100,000 drug offenders were sent to prison annually. There were more than 1.5 million prison admissions on drug charges between 1980 and 2000 (Human Rights Watch, 2000, p. 2). In the first state-by-state analysis of the impact of drug control policies on the admission to prison of blacks and whites, published in 2000, Human Rights Watch found for example 'that blacks comprise 62.7 percent and whites 36.7 percent of all drug offenders admitted to a state prison' even though there are reportedly five times more white drug abusers than black ones in the United States. Thus, 'relative to population, black men are admitted to state prison on drug charges at a rate that is

13.4 times greater than that of white men.' Further, in seven states, blacks constituted between 80 and 90 percent of all drug offenders sent to prison and in at least fifteen states, black men are admitted to prison on drug charges at rates that are from 20 to 57 times greater than those of white men. There are important mandatory sentencing differentials for offences involving powder and crack cocaine, and about 90 percent of crack arrests are of African Americans, while 75 percent of powder cocaine arrests are of whites. Federal law mandates higher sentences for offenses involving crack cocaine than for powder cocaine.[3]

Street-level research on drug sellers in Washington, D.C., and Milwaukee, Wisconsin, has demonstrated that, for most young men engaged in the business, selling drugs was a form of 'moonlighting' to supplement meagre wages earned in the legitimate economy. Given that men going to prison often have only marginal relationships with the legitimate economy to begin with, the stigma attached to the prison experience and the limited skill training available in prison create additional disadvantages when prisoners are released (Mauer, 2001a, p. 51). Rehabilitation within the legitimate economy became harder as the shift to a post-industrial economy saw U.S. employment growth move from manufacturing to the broader service economy with its less secure, lower paid, and increasingly 'feminized' job market.

The non-white working classes were particularly hit by the downsizing of manufacturing industries and relocation of firms from city centres to suburbs or overseas. Post-industrialization and 'technological upgrading' consigned large numbers of 'uneducated blacks to economic redundancy,' while the 'peculiar institutions' of the hyperghetto and the prison stigmatized, controlled, and perpetuated the socioeconomic marginalization and legal incapacitation of the 'urban black subproletariat' (Wacquant, 2001, pp. 96–105). An April 2006 report by the National Urban League showed that the unemployment rate of black men in their twenties who lacked a high school diploma was 72 percent, and there were 190,000 more black men in jail than in college.

According to Loic Wacquant, a 'symbiosis between ghetto and prison' has emerged since the 1970s. For example, public housing resembles the architectural form and embodies the technologies of surveillance associated with the prison. Public schools with their rundown buildings and equipment have become intuitions of confinement, custody and control as children are hidden behind locked doors, fences and walls, and pass through metal detectors on their way in. For Wacquant, 'the carceral atmosphere of schools and the constant presence of armed guards in uniform in the lobbies, corridors, cafeteria, and

---

[3]   Under federal law, it takes only 5 grams of crack cocaine but 500 grams of powder cocaine to trigger a five-year mandatory minimum sentence.

playground of their establishment habituates the children of the hyperghetto to the demeanor, tactics, and interactive style of the correctional officers many of them are bound to encounter shortly after their school days are over.' Further, the fusion of ghetto and prison culture is expressed also in language, dress, music, graffiti and body art. (Wacquant, 2001, pp. 105, 116) Social commentators routinely denounce urban hip-hop gangsta culture for its celebration of violence, drugs and promiscuity.

By the late 1990s, African Americans as a whole represented the majority of state and federal prisoners, and as black incarceration rates continued to rise, Angela Davis warned, 'the racial composition of the incarcerated population is fast approaching the proportion of black prisoners to white during the era of the southern convict lease and county chain gang systems' (Davis, 2001, p. 41). The number of people of colour imprisoned increases with each security level until, in a super maximum security unit, where prisoners remain in their cells nearly twenty-four hours per day, people of colour constitute an overwhelming majority. More than 90 percent of the 'supermax' population in some state systems is black. And 40 percent of the occupants of death rows in the thirty-eight states and federal system that retain capital punishment are African American. In 1997 an official report assessed the lifetime likelihood of ending up in prison for different racial groups. For white men, the odds were one out of every twenty-five, but one in six for Hispanic men and higher than one in four for black men (U.S. Department of Justice, 1997; quoted also in Hallinan, 2003, p. 45).

More recently, brown Americans have come under the punitive segregation and crime control spotlights. Spring 2006 saw hundreds of thousands of legal and illegal immigrants and their supporters take to the streets in more than a hundred U.S. cities to protest against Congressional proposals to criminalize and deport illegals. In December 2005, the Republican-dominated House of Representatives overwhelmingly passed a bill, HR 4437, sponsored by Republican James Sensenbrenner of Wisconsin. The bill proposed to upgrade illegal residence from a civil offence to a criminal felony with a mandatory prison term. Those helping illegal immigrants would also be subject to imprisonment. Illegal immigrants would be automatically deported following arrest, and employers hiring illegals would face stiff fines. The racial overtones were obvious, underlined by the additional proposal to build a 700-mile fence at vulnerable parts of the U.S.–Mexican border. A compromise bill with bipartisan sponsorship in the Senate – which included a guest worker programme and pathway to citizenship for illegal immigrants who would be subject to fines and taxes – was 'scuppered by obstructionists' in both the Democratic and Republican parties (*Not Criminal, Just Hopeful*, 2006, pp. 49–50; *More Marches, a Growing Backlash*, 2006, pp. 51–52). Even if illegal residence became a misdemeanour rather than a felony, any crackdown on illegal immigration would kindle the 'browning' of the federal and state prison populations across the nation.

Truth in Sentencing, Exile in Prison

The majority of prisoners are released back into free society at the end of their sentences, but a growing number of men and women will spend the rest of their lives behind bars. In May 1980 a drunk Phil Seritt Jr., had four previous convictions for selling drugs to an undercover officer when he robbed an Alabama motel manager at knifepoint of $200. This made Seritt a five-time offender under Alabama's recently enacted habitual offender law, which requires a life without parole sentence for a fourth Class A felony conviction. Like one in 20 inmates in a state prison, he will die behind bars. It will cost Alabama's taxpayers $20,000 a year to keep Serritt in prison, for a $200 robbery (Roberts, 1996, 1A).

These laws were part of a significant national transformation of sentencing laws in the 1980s and 1990s whereby sentencing has changed 'from being a discretionary art of individualized dispositions to a much more rigid and mechanical application of penalty guidelines and mandatory sentences' (Garland, 2002, p. 18). The Sentencing Reform Act of 1984 eliminated parole for all federal crimes committed on or after November 1 and reduced judges' discretion in setting terms. The Anti-Drug Abuse Act (1986) and Anti-Drug Abuse Amendments Act (1988) set mandatory minimums for drug dealing and possession (Hallinan, 2003, pp. 38, 40). These reforms reflected the incorporation of new managerialism and working practices by a crime control establishment which has to balance assuaging public fears with the need to target resources, implement risk assessments, and remain cost conscious.

Mandatory sentences, 'three strikes,' sexual predator statutes and 'truth in sentencing' together with Megan's Law and paedophile registers, the reintroduction of chain gangs and children's prisons are 'designed to be expressive, cathartic actions, undertaken to denounce the crime and reassure the public' (Garland, 2002, pp. 133–34). Yet these expressive actions have very real impacts. By 1994, 30 states had adopted variations of 'three strikes' laws at the centre of the 1994 federal crime bill. Other changes include extended prison terms without benefit of parole and life without parole (LWOP), truth-in-sentencing laws, and the abolition in some states of discretionary parole board release in favour of rigid statutory provisions. By the end of 2000, 29 states and the District of Columbia had adopted the federal truth-in-sentencing standard which required violent offenders not under life or death sentence to serve at least 85 percent of their sentence before becoming eligible for release.

Prisons across the nation, especially the larger states, report the effects of sentencing changes in the 1980s and 1990s. In California, which has 172,000 prisoners in 33 prisons, tougher mandatory sentencing including the infamous but extremely popular 'three strikes' law means that more than 30,000 inmates are serving life terms (*Hotel California*, 2005, pp. 49–51). California's prison population is projected to rise by a further 21,000 over the next decade. Georgia's 1994 'two strikes' law established a mandatory ten-year sentence without parole for anyone convicted of armed robbery, kidnapping, rape, sodomy or aggravated sexual battery. A second violation of any of these six felonies or murder results in a mandatory life sentence without parole. These changes added 3,000 offenders to Georgia's prisons in ten years. In addition, in 1998 Georgia's Board of Pardons and Paroles required inmates convicted of 20 additional violent crimes to serve at least 90 percent of their sentences. In 2000, over 40 percent of the prison populations of Alabama, Arkansas, Oklahoma and Tennessee were natural lifers (LWOP), lifers (life with possible parole), and inmates serving 20 or more years (Aday, 2005, pp. 11–12).[4]

Overcrowding and deteriorating conditions inevitably exacerbate racial, ethnic, class and generational tensions; increase the incidence of prisoner-on-guard, guard-on-prisoner, and prisoner-on-prisoner violence; make rehabilitation impossible and recidivism inevitable; and undermine the stability of all types of correctional facilities. Gangs also thrive in overcrowded prisons. These include national collectives such as the Crips, the Vice Lords, and Gangster Disciples. Gang membership is based on race and most inmates will belong to racially exclusive or supremacist groups such as Aryan Nation or El Rukns. In recent years *The Economist* has included several articles on California's prison system. An August 2006 report begins with a stark overview:

> Some of the 172,000 inmates are crowded into institutions – from
> the state's 33 prisons to its 12 'community correctional facilities' –
> that are meant to house fewer than 90,000. Drug abuse is rampant;
> so too are diseases such as HIV and hepatitis C. Race-based gangs
> pose the constant threat of violence, riot and even murder. And with
> more than 16,000 prisoners sleeping in prison gymnasiums and class-
> rooms, rehabilitation programmes are virtually non-existent – which

[4]   Between 1986 and 1997, average prison sentences (in federal prisons) increased from 39 months to 54 months. By 2004, almost 10 percent of all inmates in state and federal prisons were serving life sentences, an increase of 83 percent from 1992. In two states, New York and California, almost 20 percent of inmates were serving life sentences. See Butterfield, Fox (2004) 'Almost 10% of Prisoners Are Serving Life Terms,' *New York Times* (May 12), www.nytimes.com. Parole violators also make up an increasing segment of prison populations. Eleven percent of California's prison population consists of parole violators, often back behind bars for relatively minor violations.

helps to explain why two-thirds of California's convicts, the highest rate in the country, are back in prison within three years of being released. (*California's Prisons*, 2006, p. 37)

Yet, many state and national politicians repeatedly call for an end to the molly-coddling of prisoners and reiterate the view that the primary purpose of prison is punishment and not a prolonged period of relaxation in a sort of penal country club with unlimited air conditioning, television and weight room access. Governor Arnold Schwarzenegger's assessment of the state penal system was damning: it is 'falling apart in front of our very eyes' (*California's Prisons*, 2006, p. 37).

So, have longer sentences, more people behind bars and truth in sentencing restored public confidence in state and federal crime control? Attitudes regarding crime and punishment in the U.S. are inextricably bound up with race and racial attitudes. White Americans generally, and white Southerners in particular, have historically been more supportive of punitive anticrime measures, and 'racist attitudes continue to be the main determinant of white punitiveness.' It is not clear how the changing racial makeup of the United States will impact on existing policies. However, Gallup polls show that Americans have very mixed attitudes toward crime and punishment: the belief that offenders should be severely punished coexists with support for policies aimed at rehabilitation. Gallup poll data showed that Americans' worries over crime, fear of terrorism not withstanding, had been declining in the first years of the twenty-first century. In mid-October 2004, 13 percent of those interviewed described the problem of crime in the United States as 'extremely serious' and 29 percent as 'very serious.' This 40 percent was significantly less than the 54 percent reported in 2003 and 60 percent in 2000. Interviewers found also that Americans were 'much more positive about the crime in their local communities than they were about crime nationally.' Eight percent thought crime local to them was 'extremely' or 'very serious' (compared with 11 percent in 2003 and 12 percent in 2000). However, 53 percent of those interviewed thought there was more crime in the U.S. in October 2004 than in the previous year, compared with 62 percent in 2002 and 60 percent in 2003 (but less than 50 percent in 2000 and 2001) (see Carroll, 2005).

Growing Old and Sick Behind Bars

The U.S. prison population continues to grow – although there is evidence that it is stabilizing, it is graying even faster. The combined effects of mandatory minimum sentencing, longer sentences and increased numbers of lifers, together with more stringent parole policies, has led to a dramatic increase in the numbers of middle-aged (34 to 54 years) and older and elderly prisoners (aged over 55 years). When Robert Hershberger first went to prison in 1945 for breaking and entering a store to steal cigarettes and money, there were few inmates over the age of 55. In 2002, Hershberger was 74 years old and serving a life sentence in Georgia for killing his second wife in the early 1970s. Creed Warren then 90 years old, was halfway through a 20-year sentence for rape and expected to die in the Kentucky State Reformatory (Elderly Inmates Swell Georgia's Prison Rolls, 2000).

By the late 1990s, almost 500,000 people aged 50 years and over were arrested every year in the United States – 18 percent of them for involvement in serious felonies. Between 1995 and 2000 there was a 38 percent increase in the numbers of inmates in this age group, including repeat or chronic offenders and new offenders. By January 1, 2002, prisoners aged 50 and above accounted for 8.2 percent of the total inmate population (11 percent in the federal system). However, there is no evidence of a 'geriatric crime wave.' In essence the growing numbers of older offenders reflect the general aging of the population. Sunbelt migration patterns also mean that states such as California, Texas and Florida are more directly affected than others. In fourteen states in 2002, at least 8 percent of the prison population was in the 50 and over age group, which is estimated to comprise 14 percent of Florida's total inmate population by 2011. (Aday, 2005, pp. 11, 12, 39)

Prisoners are getting older, sicker and more costly to care for (Shreiber, 1999). Corrections officials recognize that the cost of maintaining older prisoners is triple that of other inmates ($70,000 to $22,000) largely due to the expense of health care. It may be the health costs for this group that provide the final straw. A late 1990s study of Georgia's prison system found that older prisoners represented 6 percent of the prison population but consumed more that 12 percent of the annual inmate health care budget (Kinney, 1999; Johnson, 2004). Health care needs specific to older offenders include dementia, cancer, stroke, incontinence, chronic conditions such as arthritis and hypertension, and mental illness, as well as menopause and osteoporosis for older female offenders. Pelosi highlighted the case of one inmate at the McCain Correctional Hospital in North Carolina who was costing the state $200,000 each year in the 1990s. He had received open-heart bypass surgery, angioplasty, and treatment for a stroke that immobilized him. He required speech and physical therapy and drugs for his heart disease, diabetes and hypertension. (Pelosi, 1997, pp. 15–18) In 2000, 83-year old Woodrow Wilson Sexton was serving a ten-year sentence for rape at the Men's State Prison near Hardwick, Georgia, and was confined to a wheelchair after years of high blood pressure culminated in a stroke. It was reported that, 'Beside Sexton's bed are his heart pills and a bundle of adult diapers for times when his digestive system acts up' (Elderly Inmates Swell Georgia's Prison Rolls, 2000).

Aday notes that there has been widespread debate over the medical care and treatment of inmates and the amount of resources that should be allocated. Prison officials cannot give the impression that they are coddling offenders but are legally mandated (under *Estelle v. Gamble* 1976) to attend to the medical needs of their charges. Prisoners generally do not constitute a healthy population. Inmates have greater rates of chronic and infectious disease than persons of the same age in the non-prison population. There is high prevalence of tuberculosis, Hepatitis C and Hepatitis B, psychiatric disorders, trauma, sexually transmitted diseases (including HIV), drug and alcohol abuse, and poor oral hygiene exacerbated by the frequency of cigarette smoking. Elderly prisoners are particularly susceptible to tuberculosis as they are integrated into rather than segregated from the general prison population (Aday, 2005, pp. 58, 89, 98; Sidoti, 2002).

Elderly prisoners are also vulnerable to increased harassment, exploitation and victimization but most seem to make a successful transition or prison life. Aday notes, that for some the experience can bring unexpected results. 'Coming from a lifestyle filled with poverty and lacking access to health care, older inmates are frequently unaccustomed to the regular food, medicine, housing, and clothing now readily available. For many, prison life can actually be a significant improvement in their standard of living' (Aday, 2005, p. 117). This, of course, is not what conservative supporters of 'prison works' want to hear. However, release can pose many challenges for these offenders. Older women in prison remain one of the most neglected groups, yet they often have much greater physical and mental health care needs than male inmates. A special unit for this group recently opened in Florida. Volunteers attend to the special needs of older female inmates, including coping with depression, illness and menopause; providing information on nutrition, personal health and exercise; and teaching life skills.

Advocacy groups such as Project for Older Prisoners (POPS) contend that poor living conditions in prison, inadequate medical treatment, and prior lifestyles (which accelerate aging and medical conditions) make older prisoners a unique population with special pre-release considerations. Proposed solutions include the establishment of private medical prisons; early release of non-violent, low-risk older offenders; and the exploration of alternatives to incarceration. While Californian legislators have resisted pleas from prison officials to pass laws mandating early release for infirm prisoners, Georgia's Board of Pardons and Parole quietly adopted a 'medical reprieve' plan, which allows a supervised parole with medical care for select elderly inmates (Jonsson, 2003). Victims' rights groups oppose such developments.

Most states plan to extend the prison nursing home and hospice programmes set up in the 1990s to deal with the AIDS/HIV, TB and Hepatitis C epidemics, the most well-known at Angola, Louisiana (Krauss, 2005; Polych and Sabo, 2001, pp. 173–83; Stolberg, 2001). Alternatively they will build new or convert existing facilities for geriatric prisoners. Examples include the 60-bed geriatric centre at the W. J. Estelle prison in Huntsville, Texas and the 650-bed Men's State Prison near Hardwick, Georgia (Schreiber, 1999). Governor Schwarzenegger's $5.8 billion prison reform plan includes construction of prison hospitals. Prison hospices and nursing homes are nonetheless sites of potential confrontation between medical providers' care and compassion and the security concerns and emphasis on control of corrections staff. Dying in prison, alone and amid indifference, still carries enormous stigma.

'Prison Works' – But for Whom?

Human Rights Watch notes that, 'No functioning democracy has ever governed itself with as large a percentage of its adults incarcerated as in the United States' (Human Rights Watch, 2000, p. 5). Katherine Beckett predicted in 1997 that, 'If prison construction and the incarceration rate continue to increase at the present rate, two out of three young black men and one of four young Hispanic men will be in prison by the year 2020, (Beckett, 1997, p. 106; also see Donziger, 1996). Nearly one of every 167 Alabamians older than 14 is in a state prison, at a cost of $57 per Alabamian (Roberts, 1996). How long can the trend toward over-incarceration continue? And who benefits?

The 'merger of punishment and profit' is explored by Joseph Hallinan in his Pulitzer-winning late 1990s tour of a growing and ever-powerful prison industry or 'prison-industrial complex.' Hallinan highlighted the keenness of former coal, steel and manufacturing towns to attract prisons. These 'job-hungry towns, desperate for something to keep their young people from leaving, compete for prisons the way they had once for industries, offering tax abatements and job training and all sorts of municipal goodies.' Politicians courting votes promised their constituents wealth and security via the prison boom. Hallinan described the supermax facility at Wallens Ridge, Virginia as 'the perfectly evolved American prison. It was both lavishly expensive and needlessly remote, built not because it was needed but because it was wanted – by politicians who thought it would bring them votes, by voters who hoped it would bring them jobs, and by a corrections establishment that no longer believed in correction.' Rural employees were lured to prison work by the prospects of a good working-class job that offered steady work, decent pay, health insurance and free meals to men and women from communities like Polk County, Texas with high rates of poverty and low rates of home ownership and educational opportunity. As well as guards and administrators, and teachers providing inmates with basic educational skills, 'a prison needs the same workers a regular city needs: doctors and nurses and janitors and cooks, secretaries and social workers and people to fix the computers.' Counties such as Fremont in Colorado have turned themselves into 'prison hubs' with obvious economic and political benefits. Fremont County has thirteen prisons including ADX Florence (Hallinan, 2003, pp. xii, 18, 85, 203).

In New York, the export of black inmates from New York City provided jobs for whites upstate. Nearly half of the state's prisons are located in the overwhelmingly white, rural, upstate districts but are mostly populated by inner-city non-whites. Transportation difficulties and the general inaccessibility of many rural prisons exacerbate inmates' isolation from family, friends and outside support networks. There are also significant political consequences. Upstate New York is represented by four Republican state senators. Tilove notes that, 'While the inmates cannot vote, their numbers count as population for redistricting and augment the leverage of the senators in whose districts they are incarcerated.' This in turn means political power is distributed away from non-white urban communities (Tilove, 2002). The political clout of prison guards' unions has also increased significantly. In California, this organization is a major contributor to electoral campaigns and actively lobbies for specific penal policies (Tonry and Petersilia, 1999, p. 12).

Despite low unemployment levels, a reasonably healthy economy, rising standards of living and stabilizing (although with variations) crime rates, punitive segregation and the crime control state are here to stay. If mass incarceration is tied to the conditions of late modernity, then the prison-industrial complex will remain an integral feature of the U.S. social, economic, political and penal landscape for the foreseeable future. As long as inmates are drawn from classes and racial groups that have become politically and economically problematic, there is little impetus for change. Economic calculation may become a driver for change because the financial burdens of mass incarceration have begun to take their toll as prison costs outstrip tax revenues. Politicians in some states do indeed talk of moderating the 'get-tough-on-crime' legislation of the 1980s and 1990s for this reason. However, repeal is not an issue for consideration. In the absence of real change, the demographic composition of the prison population will continue to challenge America's cherished belief in itself as the exemplar of democratic values. As Garland concludes, 'A government that routinely sustains social order by means of mass exclusion begins to look like an apartheid state' (Garland, 2002, p. 204).

Bibliography

Aday, Ronald H. (2005) *Aging Prisoners: Crisis in American Corrections* (Westport, CN and London: Praeger).

Beckett, Katherine (1997) *Making Crime Pay: Law and Order in Contemporary American Politics* (New York: Oxford University Press).

'California's Prisons: Packing Them In' (2006) *The Economist* (August 12).

Carroll, Joseph (2005) 'Crime in the United States: American Public opinion About Crime in the United States' (March 15), http://poll.gallup.com.

Davis, Angela Y. (2001) 'Race, Gender, and Prison History: From the Convict Lease System to the Supermax Prison,' in Don Sabo, Terry A. Kupers and Willie London (eds.), *Prison Masculinities* (Philadelphia: Temple University Press).

Donziger, Steven R. (1996) *The Real War on Crime: The Report of the National Criminal Justice Commission* (New York: Harper Perennial).

'Elderly Inmates Swell Georgia's Prison Rolls, Add to Medical Costs,' (2000) *Athens Banner-Herald* (GA) (December 3), www.onlineathens.com/stories/120400/new_1204000018.shtml.

Garland, David (2000) 'The Culture of High Crime Societies,' *British Journal of Criminology*, vol. 40 (Summer).

Garland, David (ed.) (2001) *Mass Imprisonment: Social Causes and Consequences* (London: Sage).

Garland, David (2002) *The Culture of Control: Crime and Social Order in Contemporary Society* (Oxford and New York: Oxford University Press).

Goldberg, Eve and Evans, Linda [prisoners' rights activists] (2004) 'The Prison Industrial Complex and the Global Economy,' www.prisonactivist.org/crisis/evans-goldberg.html.

Hallinan, Joseph T. (2003) *Going Up the River: Travels in a Prison Nation* (New York: Random House).

'Hotel California,' (2005) *The Economist* (February 26).

Human Rights Watch (2000) *United States – Punishment and Prejudice: Racial Disparities in the War on Drugs* (May), www.hrw.org/reports/2000/usa/Rcedrg00–05htm.

Human Rights Watch (2001) 'Prisons', p. 3. See www.hrw.org/prisons/united_states.html.

Johnson, Joe (2004) 'Jailers: Suicide, Attempts Point to Need,' *Athens Banner-Herald* (February 15), www.onlineathens.com/stories/021504/new_20040215122.shtml.

Jonsson, Patrik (2003) 'As Prisoners Age, Should They Go Free?' *Christian Science Monitor* (September 5), www.globalaging.org/health/us/prisoners.htm.

Kinney, David (1999) 'Private Prisons Turn Profit Caring for Sick Inmates,' *Athens Banner Herald* (June 7), www.onlineathens.com/sotires/060799/new_0607990006.shtml.

Krauss, Clifford (2005) 'A Prison Makes the Illicit and Dangerous Legal and Safe,' *New York Times* (November 24), www.nytimes.com.

Mauer, Marc (2001a) 'Crime, Politics, and Community since the 1990s,' in Don Sabo, Terry A. Kupers and Willie London (eds.), *Prison Masculinities*, (Philadelphia: Temple University Press).

Mauer, Marc (2001b) 'The Causes and Consequences of Prison Growth in the United States,' *Punishment & Society*, vol. 3.

'More Marches, a Growing Backlash' (2006) *The Economist* (May 6), pp. 51–52.

'Not Criminal, Just Hopeful' (2006) *The Economist* (April 15), pp. 49–50.

Parenti, Christian (1997) *Lockdown America* (London: Verso).

Pelosi, A. (1997) 'Age of Innocence: A Glut of Geriatric Jail Birds,' *New Republic* vol. 216, n. 18 (1997).

Polych, Carol and Sabo, Don (2001) 'Sentence – Death by Lethal Infection: IV-Drug Use and Infectious Disease Transmission in North American Prisons,' in Don Sabo, Terry A. Kupers and Willie London (eds.), *Prison Masculinities*, (Philadelphia: Temple University Press).

Pratt, John (1996) 'Reflections on Recent Trends Towards the Punishment of Persistence,' *Crime, Law & Social Change*, vol. 25.

Pratt, John (1998) 'Towards the "Decivilizing" of Punishment?' *Social and Legal Studies* vol. 7 (Dec.).

Roberts, Chris (1996) 'Population Explosion Since 1980, the Number of People Behind Bars has More than Tripled, Yet Crime Rates Haven't Blinked,' *Birmingham News* (AL) (March 17).

Sabo, Don, Kupers, Terry A. and London, Willie (eds.) (2001) *Prison Masculinities* (Philadelphia: Temple University Press).

Schreiber, Chris (1999) 'Behind Bars: Aging Prison Population Challenges Correctional Health Systems,' Nurseweek (July 19), www.nurseweek.com/features/99–7/prison.html.

Sidoti, Liz (2002) 'Deeper Meaning to "Lifer",' *Athens Banner-Herald* (January 10) www.onlineathens.com/stories/011102/new_0111020010/shtml.

Simon, Jonathan (2001) 'Fear and Loathing in Later Modernity: Reflections on the Cultural Sources of Mass Imprisonment in the United States,' *Punishment & Society*, vol. 3, no. 1.

Stolberg, Sheryl Gay (2001) 'Behind Bars, New Effort to Care for the Dying,'
New York Times (April 1), www.nytimes.com.

Sourcebook of Criminal Justice Statistics (2003 – published online).

Tilove, Jonathan (2002) 'Minority Prison Inmates Skew Local Populations as
States Redistrict,' *Newhouse News Service*, www.newhousenews.com/archive/
story1a031202.html.

Tonry, Michael and Petersilia, Joan (1999) 'American Prisons at the Beginning
of the Twenty-First Century,' *Crime and Justice*, vol. 26, no. 1, p. 12.

U. S. Department of Justice, Bureau of Justice Statistics (1997) *Lifetime Likelihood
of Going to State or Federal Prison*, NCJ 160092 (March).

Wacquant, Loic (2001) 'Deadly Symbiosis: When Ghettos and Prison Meet and
Mesh,' *Punishment & Society*, vol. 3, no.1.

13
The Shifting Politics of Immigration Reform

Andrew Wroe

For several decades the United States has struggled to control its borders. In particular, it has wrestled to curtail the flow of illegal immigrants into its territory while permitting up to one million legal immigrants to settle each year. The 1977 U.S. Select Commission on Immigration and Refugee Policy was tasked with investigating the problem of illegal immigration and producing workable reforms. After many false starts and much partisan and interest-group wrangling, Congress eventually passed and President Ronald Reagan signed the Immigration Reform and Control Act of 1986. IRCA had three main strands: better border security to prevent illegal entry; tough measures to prevent firms employing illegal workers; and an amnesty, in the form of legal residency and later citizenship, for most illegal immigrants already resident in the U.S. The amnesty was designed as a one-off practical and humanitarian response to the problem of tearing millions of people away from their families, homes and jobs. There would, the thinking went, be no need for another amnesty because employer sanctions and improved border security would halt further undocumented migration.

In one sense IRCA was a notable success. A relatively smooth bureaucratic operation saw nearly three million previously undocumented persons granted legal residency, many of whom later went on to become citizens. However, it failed to stem illegal entry into the U.S., especially from Latin America and Mexico in particular. The employer sanctions were never fully implemented. The federal government was reluctant to prosecute firms employing illegal labor, undocumented workers found good-quality fake documents – especially green cards and social security numbers – easy to come by, and the significant disparity in wealth between Latin America and the U.S. and established sending and receiving communities all ensured that large-scale illegal migration continued (Durand et al., 2000, pp. 1–15). Moreover, 40 percent of illegal immigrants actually enter the country legally, on tourist or student visas for example, but overstay. While it is intrinsically difficult to measure precisely the number of illegal residents in the U.S., estimates put the number at around 2.2 million in 1988 after the IRCA legalization, but this quickly rose to 5 million in 1996, 7 million in 2000 and about 12 million in 2006. About half came from one country: Mexico.

Partly in response to the large increase in the number of undocumented residents, the 1990s witnessed a sharp turn in popular opinion against illegal immigration. Anti-immigrant activists in California wrote and qualified for the November 1994 ballot a direct democracy initiative to expel undocumented children from public schools, deny illegal immigrants access to most public services, and require state officials such as school teachers to report to the authorities persons 'suspected' of being illegally resident in the U.S.. Proposition 187 won overwhelming approval by 59 percent to 41 percent of the votes cast. It also helped incumbent California Governor Pete Wilson win a second term in a famous come-from-behind victory. This outcome inspired the 104th Congress, the first under Republican control in forty years, to push ahead with the immigration reform agenda. The debate during the mid-1990s was dominated by conservative, anti-immigration forces. Liberal voices, promulgating the benefits of immigration and an inclusive message, struggled to be heard. There was serious talk of excluding undocumented children from public school and of revoking the birthright citizenship clause of the Fourteenth Amendment, which awarded citizenship to all persons born on U.S. soil regardless of their parents' legal status. And Congress very nearly slashed the number of legal immigrants permitted to enter the U.S., which would have been the first significant reduction since the nativist Quota Acts of the 1920s excluded southern and eastern Europeans. Bob Dole, Republican presidential nominee in 1996, ran on a loud anti-illegal-immigration ticket, buffeted from the right by the even more bombastic anti-immigrant rhetoric of populist Pat Buchanan. President Clinton and others in his administration also spoke the language of the zeitgeist, promising to 'shut the door on illegal immigration' (Reno, 1994, p. A-1; New York Times, 1994, p. A-1).

Given the tone of the debate in the mid-1990s, it is remarkable that in the first decade of the new millennium President George W. Bush backed a guest-worker program and a 'path to citizenship' – an amnesty in the language of the 1980s – for most of America's 12 million undocumented residents. Of course, it would be wrong to suggest that the opposition to illegal immigration has disappeared. It has not. It is still alive and strong, as witnessed by legislative activity in the House of Representatives, but it is important to recognize that the locus of debate has shifted significantly. Guest-worker programs and paths to citizenship are firmly on the political agenda, even if they have not yet been enshrined in law. During the Democratic presidency of Bill Clinton, pro-immigration activists could not have imagined that such ideas would constitute a serious and central part of the contemporary political discourse. The shifting politics of immigration reform largely reflects a change in the electoral calculus of key Republican politicians in response to two main factors. The first is America's changing demography, specifically the explosive growth of the Latino population and the relative decline of the white population. Whites are already a minority in California and are predicted to be so in the wider U.S. by the middle of the twenty-first century. Latinos constituted just 6 percent of the population in 1980. Today they make up around 15 percent, and by 2050 one in every four Americans will be Latino (*U.S. Census Bureau*). As their numbers increase, so does their political power. The second factor is that Latinos are more politically active, largely in response to the perception that their interests were threatened by Republican machinations in the 1990s (Wroe, 2007).

The aim of this chapter is to chart how the politics of immigration reform has changed over the past decade. It will explore the anti-immigrant episode of the 1990s, examining the reasons for its rise, focusing in particular on the political calculus of key Republican politicians who chose to use the immigration issue for electoral gain. It will also explain how that calculus changed as the Latino population grew and became more politicized.

The 1990s: The Wilson Model

The 1990s witnessed a significant backlash against illegal immigration. Its roots lay in California in the early part of the decade.[1] There was a significant amount of hostility toward illegal aliens, in part engendered by their increasing numbers but also by a particularly long and deep recession. Many Californians thought that undocumented workers took the jobs of native workers, paid little tax and heavily used public services at a time when a stagnating economy could least support their presence. Others worried that Latinos posed an increasing threat to the white majority's political and economic power. Unsurprisingly, some politicians began to speak out against illegal immigrants and blame them for California's ills. One such high-profile leader was California Governor Pete Wilson. Facing reelection in November 1994, Wilson was in a precarious electoral position because of the recession and a natural Democratic advantage in the state. Moreover, he was unpopular with his own party activists after raising taxes early in his first term. His approval ratings were the lowest of any governor in California history and opinion polls indicated he was trailing potential

---

[1] For a more comprehensive version of this argument, see Wroe, *The Republican Party and Immigration Politics*.

Democratic challengers by large margins with the election only a year away. He needed to find an issue that would boost his popularity and around which he could construct a winning electoral coalition. In August 1993 he turned his attention to illegal immigration. In an open letter to the federal government he proposed denying U.S. citizenship to children born to undocumented parents, excluding undocumented children from public school, and introducing a 'legal residency' card to prevent undocumented persons taking jobs and receiving welfare and healthcare benefits. The result was immediate and marked. His poll ratings jumped significantly, from minus 33 percentage points in October 1992 and minus 29 points in March 1993 to just minus 8 points in September 1993.[2] Moreover, his focus thrust illegal immigration toward the top of the political agenda. Previously, never more than 3 percent of Californians had identified illegal immigration as the most important problem facing their state – despite the recession and large number of undocumented persons in the state – but in September 1993, 16 percent did so, a dramatic increase in intensity.[3]

At the same time as Wilson began to focus on illegal immigration, grassroots anti-immigrant activists based in Orange County, California, came together to discuss what they could personally do about the perceived problem. Their answer was to write and qualify for the ballot, a direct democracy initiative. In an impressive mobilization of activists and with only minimal help from a professional signature-gathering firm, Proposition 187 qualified with time and signatures to spare. During qualification and the campaign proper, Governor Wilson provided no direct monetary help, but the California Republican Party and other individual Republican politicians made some significant monetary and non-monetary contributions. However, much more important was the oxygen of free publicity provided by the governor's continuing focus on the illegal immigration issue, which raised the initiative's profile. He reinforced the issue's central position in the political agenda by running anti-illegal immigration TV ads, by engineering clashes with the Democrat-controlled state legislature on illegal immigration, and by suing the federal government to reimburse billions of dollars allegedly owed California for the cost of incarcerating, educating and providing healthcare to undocumented persons. In turn, Proposition 187 further increased the salience of illegal immigration and Wilson's campaign against it. This symbiotic relationship benefited both sides handsomely.

Wilson's use of illegal immigration highlighted once again the electoral efficacy of wedge politics. It helped propel him back to the Governor's mansion and

---

[2] Figures represent percentage approving of Wilson's performance minus percentage disapproving.
[3] See *Los Angeles Times Poll*, 20–23 October 1992; *Los Angeles Times Poll*, 20–22 March 1993; *Los Angeles Times Poll* 10–13 September 1993.

establish him as a potential Republican presidential candidate for 1996. Wilson's strategy enabled him to win over some moderate white Democrats and a majority of independents while reinforcing his support among, and turnout of, white conservative voters. The salience of the illegal immigration issue and the triumph of the Wilson model of electoral politics encouraged Newt Gingrich and other Republicans to take up the same cause after the GOP's spectacular 1994 midterm congressional victory. Even though the Contract with America did not mention immigration and the new Speaker had long staked out a pro-immigration position, Gingrich believed that immigration was a winning issue for his party. Electoral considerations aside, his conversion to the cause also reflected his desire to reform the welfare system. He saw an opportunity to reduce welfare costs and enhance his party's popularity by cutting benefits to immigrants. Gingrich's problem was that undocumented immigrants, despite the rhetoric, actually received relatively little welfare support from the federal government. The bulk of their cost to government − for education and incarceration − was largely shouldered by states and localities and was difficult to cut because of political and constitutional constraints. Gingrich's solution was to widen the net and cut legal immigrants' benefits as well. Electoral and policy considerations, then, produced the 1996 Personal Responsibility and Work Opportunity Reconciliation Act, better known as the 'welfare reform' act. This made swingeing cuts to legal immigrants' benefits, making them ineligible for Temporary Aid to Needy Families (AFDC's replacement), SSI and food stamps. It also permitted individual states to cut immigrants' Medicaid benefits.

Other key GOP congressional leaders, especially Lamar Smith (Texas) and Alan Simpson (Wyoming), respectively the new chairs of the House and Senate immigration subcommittees, were more ideologically committed than Gingrich to the anti-immigration agenda. They regarded the approval of Proposition 187 as a vanguard for their proposals to reduce the level of legal immigration, which were backed by the second report of the U.S. Commission on Immigration Reform − otherwise known as the Jordan Commission after its chair, Barbara Jordan. Moreover, such was the anti-immigration climate, the report won even President Clinton's approval.[4] One lobbyist noted:

> In the spring of 1995, we didn't think we could turn the restrictionist tide, could stop the reform juggernaut, and it looked like something close to zero immigration was on the verge of being enacted. The

---

[4] U.S. Commission on Immigration Reform, *Legal Immigration: Setting Priorities*, June 1995. The first report on illegal immigration was *U.S. Immigration Policy: Restoring Credibility*, September 1994. The commission was established by the Immigration Act of 1990.

current system would be gutted, the safety net for legal immigrants would be shredded, and a national work verifications system would be imposed. (Quoted in Gimpel and Edwards, 1999, p. 225)

However, the attempts of Smith and Simpson to reduce the level of legal immigration were thwarted by an unholy alliance of business interests and civil rights organizations and the skillful manoeuvring of Democratic Senator Edward Kennedy (Massachusetts) and Republican Senator Spencer Abraham (Michigan) (see *Congressional Quarterly*, 1995 and 1996; Gimpel and Edwards, 1999). The Senate consequently failed to approve the House provision to exclude undocumented children from public school, the Gallegly amendment authored by Representative Elton Gallegly (California). Nonetheless, the 1996 Illegal Immigration Reform and Individual Responsibility Act significantly enhanced border enforcement by authorizing the doubling in size of the border patrol from 5,000 to 10,000 agents and building and reinforcing border fences. It also increased the penalties for document fraud and alien smuggling, expedited deportation procedures, introduced several new programs for employers to check potential employees' immigration status, increased and tightened income requirements of sponsors, and excluded illegal aliens from most public welfare benefits and services.

The Republicans' anti-immigration agenda and wedge strategy forced the Clinton administration to ratchet up its own rhetoric and produce policy proposals to assuage popular opinion. The president did not want House Republicans setting the agenda. He was especially concerned that Pete Wilson would win the Republican presidential nomination and put California's 54 electoral-college votes out of his reach. Clinton could not support Proposition 187 but he made serious overtures to voters on the hot-button issue of illegal immigration. In his 1995 state of the union address, he declared:

All Americans, not only in the states most heavily affected, but in every place in this country, are rightly disturbed by the large numbers of illegal aliens entering our country. The jobs they hold might otherwise be held by citizens or legal immigrants. The public services they use impose burdens on our taxpayers. That's why our administration has moved aggressively to secure our borders more by hiring a record number of new border guards, by deporting twice as many criminal aliens as ever before, by cracking down on illegal hiring, by barring welfare benefits to illegal aliens.

In the budget I will present to you we will try to do more to speed the deportation of illegal aliens who are arrested for crimes, to

better identify illegal aliens in the workplace as recommended by the
commission headed by former Congresswoman Barbara Jordan.
     We are a nation of immigrants. But we are also a nation of laws.
It is wrong and ultimately self-defeating for a nation of immigrants
to permit the kind of abuse of our immigration laws we have seen in
recent years, and we must do more to stop it. (State of the Union
Address, 1995)

Wilson did not win his party's presidential nomination, but Clinton's eventual
opponent, Bob Dole, also promulgated a stark anti-illegal immigration message
during the primaries. He frequently reiterated his support for Proposition 187
and the Gallegly amendment in the hope that it would protect his right flank
from Pat Buchanan and thereby deter the threat of a third party candidacy on
the part of this maverick.[5] Indeed, Dole was so effective that Buchanan commented, 'It appears Senator Dole is making an effort to reach out to our people... [He's] sounding like us... I'm gonna sue that fella for copyright violations'
(*Los Angeles Times*, 1996a, p. A-1). Even after securing the presidential nomination by winning the California primary in March 1996 and resigning from
Congress in June 1996 to campaign full time, Dole continued to lobby GOP
leaders to include the Gallegly amendment in the final immigration bill. His goal
was to draw a veto that would expose the president to attack that he was not
serious about illegal immigration reform. Strangely, Clinton hit back not by
claiming that Dole was an extremist on immigration reform but by arguing that
he was not as tough as he liked to portray. In particular he lambasted Dole for
previously voting against excluding undocumented children from public schools
and in favor of IRCA (*Los Angeles Times*, 1996b, p. A-16).
     In the mid-1990s, then, an anti-illegal immigration discourse dominated the
immigration reform agenda. Following the Wilson model, many Republicans
sought to use the issue to splinter the Democratic coalition and mobilize the
conservative base. For Dole, however, the strategy was a failure, or at least it did
not allow him to overcome his many failings as a candidate. Too few moderate
white voters split from the Democratic Party and too many Latinos bolted from
the Republican Party. Four years earlier George H.W. Bush had won 48 percent of the white vote and 35 percent of the Latino vote. Dole won a similar
slice of the white vote at 49 percent but Latino support dropped dramatically to
just 22 percent. Another way to think about the Republicans' collapse among

---

[5]   Another element of Dole's wedge strategy was affirmative action. He thus expressed his support
for California's initiative *de jour*, Proposition 209, to end state-sponsored affirmative action programs,
and introduced similar legislation into the Senate during the primaries.

Latinos is to compare the ratio of white to Latino support. Taking the four presidential elections between 1980 and 1992, Republican candidates won 1.5 white votes for every Latino vote. Dole by contrast won 2.3 white votes for each Latino one (National Election Study). The drop off in Latino support for Republican candidates was even more pronounced in California. While Bush Sr. won 1.2 white votes for each Latino one in 1992, Dole needed 2.7 whites for every Latino four years later (National Election Study, 1992; Los Angeles Times Exit Poll, 1996). Perhaps unsurprisingly, given his close association with Proposition 187, Wilson saw his Latino vote share decline from 35 percent in 1990 to 26 percent in 1994. Four years later, Republican gubernatorial nominee Dan Lungren took 24 percent, despite running a Latino- and immigrant-friendly campaign and working hard to distance himself from Proposition 187, which he supported in 1994 when running for attorney general. The 2002 Republican gubernatorial candidate, Bill Simon, did little better in winning just 27 percent of the Latino vote while carrying a majority of the white vote. The message was clear: Republican candidates were losing close elections because of a precipitous decline in support among Latino voters turned off by the party's close association with anti-immigrant policies. While Wilson had compensated for the drop off by winning more white votes, the strategy did not seem to be working for other Republican candidates in California and nationwide. Moreover, in California, even candidates who made a determined effort to win over Latino voters – such as Lungren and Simon – failed to return to pre-1994 levels of support.

The 1990s: The Bush Model

While most Republican voters and politicians expressed strong support for Proposition 187, not all did. Jack Kemp and William Bennett, co-directors of the Empower America think tank, were the first national Republican figures to oppose it. Kemp, previously George H.W. Bush's Housing and Urban Development Secretary, and Bennett, Ronald Reagan's Education Secretary, warned the GOP in 1994 that adopting an anti-immigrant agenda would push Latinos and Asians firmly into the Democratic Party's coalition, just as the Republican Party's hostility to:

> ... the last generation of immigrants from Italy, Ireland and the
> nations of Central Europe... helped to create a Democratic base in
> many of America's cities... Can anyone calculate the political cost
> of turning away immigrants this time? (Los Angeles Times, 1994a,
> p. A1)

> [The anti-immigrant agenda will] turn the party inward to a
> protectionist and isolationist and more xenophobic party... We are
> willing to concede that tossing logs onto the anti-immigrant fire
> might result in short-term gains, but believe that in the medium and
> long term, this posture is a loser. (*Los Angeles Times*, 1994b, p. A-1)

The dismal performance of Bob Dole and the fate of post-Wilson Republican hopefuls in California, as outlined above, made the Kemp–Bennett warning seem particularly prescient. Ironically, Dole chose Kemp as his 1996 running mate in a late effort to liberalize the ticket and appeal to moderates, but it is unlikely that anything could have been done to save his campaign. Governor George W. Bush of Texas was another Republican who eschewed the Wilson model in the mid-1990s. Bush's electoral strategy to win both the state house and the White House was in most respects classically conservative, emphasizing family values, religion, abortion and economic individualism. However, one aspect of the strategy was distinctively liberal. Bush's political Svengali, Karl Rove, had long recognized the increasing political significance of the growing Latino population and sought to construct a majority governing coalition by marrying the Republican Party's traditional advantage among white voters to a significant slice of the Latino vote. One way of doing so, which put no strain on the conservative strategy, was to promote Bush as the friend of instinctively socially and economically conservative Latinos and Asians. The other way, which created the contradiction at the heart of the Bush model, was to pursue a distinctively liberal, pro-immigration position. This meant not only supporting high levels of legal immigration but also treating all immigrants, even those who entered the U.S. illegally, with respect. Bush's pro-immigration message was not merely a hard-nosed electoral calculation, however. He genuinely believed that immigration was a force for good.

Bush was one of the very few high-profile Republican politicians facing reelection in 1994 to come out against Proposition 187. His reward was a significant proportion of the Latino vote in the Texas gubernatorial election and a victory over the popular incumbent Democratic governor, Ann Richards, in a close contest. His comfortable reelection victory in 1998 with nearly 70 percent of the vote, including half the Latino vote, plus his name recognition, folksy image and impressive fundraising ability, convinced many Republicans that the former president's son was the party's future. As its prospective and actual presidential candidate, Bush made several trips to California in 2000 to raise funds and campaign but snubbed Pete Wilson, meeting him neither in public nor in private. Only four years earlier Dole had appointed Wilson chair of his California campaign, but Bush's strategists did not want to risk damaging their charge's reputation among Latinos by communing with the now demonized former governor. Bush's target in an April 2000 speech to the National Hispanic Women's Conference was unspoken but clear:

> It's so important to have leadership that tears down political barriers, leadership that offers a future hopeful for everybody, leadership that rejects the politics of pitting one group of people against another, leaders that stand up and say we will not use our children, the children of immigrants, as a political issue in America. (*Los Angeles Times*, 2000, p. A-10)

Moreover, in contrast to the very 'white' and conservative 1996 Republican convention, Bush's team ensured that the 2000 gathering was a model of diversity and inclusion with Latinos and African Americans speaking in several primetime slots. Bush's pro-immigration and pro-Latino stance was rewarded in the election when he took an impressive 35 percent of the Latino vote. Four years later that improved by nine points to 44 percent, while his support among whites, Asians and African Americans increased by four, three and two points respectively.[6]

Bush's First Term

Early in his first term Bush tried to make it easier for undocumented residents to apply for permanent residency and citizenship, but his attempts to liberalize immigration laws were thwarted by the political fallout from 9/11. Immigration issues became closely tied to national security when it emerged that the terrorist pilots involved in the attacks on New York and Washington DC were trained at U.S. aviation schools and that 13 of the 19 hijackers had entered the U.S. legally. In response, the Bush administration reorganized the various immigration-related federal agencies spread across several executive departments into the new Department of Homeland Security (DHS) in 2003. It returned to immigration reform in January 2004 with a plan for a 'temporary worker program,' which would 'match willing foreign workers with willing U.S. employers' but only after employers had made 'every reasonable effort' to find an American worker. Bush hoped privately that this would help him court Latinos in the

---

[6] 2004 data from *National Election Pool* poll conducted by Edison/Mitofsky for Associated Press, ABC, CBS, CNN, Fox and NBC. 2000 data from *Voter News Service*, which was replaced by NEP. The *Los Angeles Times* national exit poll put Latino support for Bush at 38 percent in 2000 and 45 percent in 2004, an increase of seven points. Whatever the precise percentages, the trend is clear.

upcoming presidential election, but argued publicly that it would promote economic growth and homeland security. He denied adamantly that the program was an amnesty, even though persons illegally resident in the U.S. would be able to apply for guest-worker status and then permanent legal residency (Office of the Press Secretary, 2004a and 2004b). Bush's plan attracted opposition from conservatives suspicious about the reform's security implications and that it was an amnesty in disguise, and from Democrats worried that guest-workers could be exploited by unscrupulous employers. While the plan was not written up as a congressional bill, Bush used it to good effect in his reelection campaign. It formed the core of his message in his Spanish-language media ads and was touted widely when addressing Latino audiences, but not white ones. The strategy helped to deliver an increased and large share of the Latino vote in November. Bush also increased his share of the vote nationally and in the Electoral College and saw the Republicans' majorities increase in both the House and Senate. He planned to use these advantages to push his immigration reform agenda during the 109th Congress.

Bush's Second Term

The first session of the 109th Congress saw much action on immigration reform, but not all of it to the President's satisfaction. Led by the Republican chair of the Judiciary Committee, James F. Sensenbrenner (Wisconsin), the House approved the 'Real ID' act (HR1268) on 10 February 2005, 'to prevent another 9/11-type terrorist attack by disrupting terrorist travel.'[7] The law sought to improve the security of drivers' licenses and personal identification cards issued by the states. Only drivers' licenses that meet strict, uniform national standards can be used for federal purposes such as air travel, and they cannot be issued by states to undocumented residents. The act also tightened up asylum procedures and gave the DHS the authority to build border fences, regardless of federal or local laws. The provision was designed to force the completion of a 14 mile border fence near San Diego (mandated by the 1996 Immigration Act) that had stalled for environmental reasons. While a successful Senate amendment increased modestly the number of temporary non-agricultural workers allowed to enter the U.S., the measure did not include a guest-worker program (Democratic and Republican amendments to add one failed). It received Senate approval on 10 May and Bush signed it into law (PL 109–13) the next day, despite the absence of the

---

[7]   Sensenbrenner quoted in *Congressional Quarterly Almanac Plus* (2005) vol. LXI (Washington D.C.: Congressional Quarterly Inc.), p. 13–3.

guest-worker provision, because he was keen to signal to House Republicans that he would work with them on immigration reform. He hoped his support for the enhanced security measures would engender movement on his favored reforms later in the legislative session (*Congressional Quarterly Almanac Plus*, 2005, p. 13.3; see also *Congressional Research Service*, 2006, pp. 2–5).

House Republicans, however, did not deliver their side of Bush's imagined *quid pro quo*, in part because the 90-strong conservative Immigration Reform Caucus led by Colorado House Republican Tom Tancredo was increasingly vocal and dominant. Under pressure from Tancredo, Sensenbrenner authored and sponsored and his Judiciary Committee approved HR4437, the Border Protection, Anti-Terrorism and Illegal Immigration Control Act, on 8 December. It was an 'enforcement-only' act that snubbed Bush's two key wishes: the guest-worker program and a path to citizenship for undocumented residents (also known as amnesty or legalization, depending on one's political position on immigration reform). The bill, which the full House approved by 239 votes to 182 on 16 December, constituted the first real fissure between the White House and its previously loyal lieutenants in the House. It received support from 203 Republicans, who were joined by 36 Democrats, while just 17 Republicans voted with 164 Democrats in opposition. The measure included four especially controversial provisions. It would: make 'unlawful presence' in the U.S. a criminal rather than civil offense punishable by a year's prison sentence (the length of sentence made it a felony rather than a misdemeanor); criminalize with up to five years' imprisonment people 'assisting' illegal aliens 'knowingly or in reckless disregard' of their immigration status; increase the penalties for hiring undocumented workers and mandate employers to verify employees' social security numbers against a DHS national list; and require state and local law enforcement agencies to enforce federal immigration law or lose federal funds. To Tancredo's disappointment, the bill did not end birthright citizenship, but it did appropriate funds for an extra 700 miles of high-security fencing on the U.S.–Mexico border, abandon the so-called 'catch and release' policy, and eliminate the 50,000 'diversity' visas (*Congressional Quarterly Almanac Plus*, 2005, pp. 13.8–13.9).

Importantly, the provision criminalizing illegal immigrants survived a Sensenbrenner-sponsored amendment to his own bill to reduce the penalty of illegal residency in the U.S. from a felony to a misdemeanor punishable by six months in prison. The Judiciary Committee chair recognized, too late as it happened, that the provision appeared mean-spirited and would serve to alienate immigrants, immigrants-rights advocates and many in the Latino and Asian communities. Even though his amendment would have liberalized the bill, only eight Democrats voted in favor while 191 voted against and were joined in opposition by 65 Republicans who wanted to maintain the felony penalty. Minority Leader Nancy Pelosi's spokesperson, Jennifer Crider, explained, 'The Democrats were not going to do anything to make it easier for Republicans to pass an atrocious bill' (quoted in Weisman, 2006c, p. A1). And, if it did pass, the Democrats looked to highlight the felony provision as evidence of the Republicans' extremism. In response, House Speaker Dennis Hastert (Illinois) and Senate Majority Leader Bill Frist (Tennessee) tried to argue that it was the Democrats who were responsible for the provision making illegal residency a felony because they had failed to back the Republican amendment to reduce it to a misdemeanor. Pursuing the same logic, the Republican National Committee ran ads on Spanish-language TV in April 2006 blaming Senate Minority Leader Harry Reid (Nevada) and his Democratic colleagues for criminalizing immigrants. One ad claimed, 'Reid's Democrat allies voted to treat millions of hardworking immigrants as felons, while President Bush and Republican leaders work for legislation that will protect our borders and honor our immigrants.' A Washington Post editorial responded: 'It takes a pile of cynicism to spin this one as *Democratic* callousness' (*Honor our Immigrants*, 2006, p. A16).

Republicans and Democrats who opposed the Sensenbrenner bill were confident that it could not win the Senate's approval (*Congressional Quarterly Almanac Plus*, 2005, pp. 13.8–13.9). As expected, the bill, and particularly the felony provision, caused outrage. As senators battled over the measure, hundreds of thousands of people came out onto the streets to protest, encouraged to mobilize by church groups and the foreign-language media. The police estimated that the crowd in downtown Los Angeles on 25 March 2006 was 500,000 and the organizers said one million. In Denver, Colorado, home state of Tom Tancredo, over 50,000 protested against a ballot proposal to deny illegal immigrants access to government services (Watanabe and Becerra, 2006).

While House members were especially concerned about how immigration reform would affect their reelection prospects in the 2006 midterms, the debate in the Senate was more closely tied to presidential politics. Judiciary Committee chair Arlen Specter (Pennsylvania) favored both enhanced border security and a guest-worker program with legalization prospects, but was put under pressure by the majority leader and presidential hopeful, Bill Frist, to produce a bill quickly. If he could not, Frist promised to introduce his own bill without the guest-worker program, which would appeal to the more conservative Republican primary electorate. John McCain (Arizona), looking to mitigate his maverick tag, win over establishment Republicans and play to general election moderates and Latinos, supported a guest-worker program and a path to citizenship, along with increased border security. Meanwhile, Senate Minority Leader Harry Reid threatened to sink any bill that did not include a guest-worker provision. In the event, Specter managed to deliver a bill (known as the chairman's mark) by Frist's deadline. However, the Majority Leader still brought his own measure (S2454) – based on the chairman's mark but without the guest-worker or citizenship provisions and with a provision making illegal residency a criminal offense (a misdemeanor for a first-time offense and felony subsequently)[8] – to the floor for several hours of debate. He eventually allowed debate on Specter's bill, but drew fire from both Republicans and Democrats that his presidential ambitions had trumped his institutional and party responsibilities.[9] After a further two weeks of debate and about to leave Washington for a two-week recess, Republican senators finally agreed on a bill that included both a guest-worker program and the prospect of citizenship for illegal residents. However, Harry Reid prevented a vote on the Republican bill until the Senate considered even more immigrant-friendly measures proposed by Democrat Edward Kennedy and Republican John McCain (Weisman, 2006a, p. A18).

The impasse was broken when McCain announced his support for another compromise bill (S2611) authored by two Republican Senators, Mel Martinez (Florida) and Chuck Hagel (Nebraska). Frist and Kennedy also indicated their support, as did about two-thirds of senators. The Martinez-Hagel bill included both the guest-worker program and path to citizenship. Undocumented residents of five or more years (estimated to number about 8 million) could apply for a work visa and, five years later, citizenship. Immigrants resident between two and five years (estimated at 3 million) could apply for one of 450,000 green cards at a designated port of entry, while those resident less than two years (an estimated 1 million) would not be allowed to stay. There would be a further 325,000 guest-worker visas for those applying from outside of the U.S. The bill included the now usual provisions beefing up the border, secure social security cards and more stringent penalties for employing undocumented workers, but it did not make unlawful presence a criminal offense like the Frist and Sensenbrenner bills (Weisman, 2006b, p. A1).

However, partisan disagreements soon surfaced to prevent a vote on the compromise bill, even though there was enough Democrat (almost solid) and GOP support (about half) to pass it. Republicans complained that Harry Reid was

---

[8] The original draft of Specter's bill did, like Frist's, make illegal presence a criminal offense (first offense misdemeanor; second a felony), but it was not included in the version of the bill approved by his judiciary committee. See *Congressional Research Service* (2006) 'Immigration Legislation and Issues in the 109th Congress,' (12 May), pp. 15–16.

[9] Critics also pointed out that he had sought to please primary voters by declaring, after watching a home video, that Terry Schiavo was not brain-dead and by opposing the takeover of several U.S. ports by a Dubai corporation. Charles Babington, 'Senate GOP Fears Frist's Ambitions Split Party', *Washington Post*, 30 March 2006, p. A4.

preventing them voting on amendments to the bill, such as one that would postpone the introduction and legalization of the guest-worker program until the DHS had verified the border was secure. Reid was concerned that Frist was pandering to Republicans opposed to the guest-worker and legalization provisions and that the amendments would strip the heart out of the bill. He also feared that House conservatives would reject the Senate bill. McCain tried in vain to break the new deadlock, unsuccessfully, by claiming he had enough support to vote down any attempt to strip the bill. He also promised that he and his supporters would not accept a bill torn apart in conference by House conservatives. Conservatives themselves worried that the Senate bill would repeat the failures of IRCA but on a grander scale (Swarns, 2006). Some Democrats also wavered when several unions, including the AFL-CIO, came out against the guest-worker program. If conference did strip out the liberal provisions, leaving an enforcement-only bill, most Democrats would vote against it but in doing so would put themselves in opposition to the majority of Americans who wanted tough border control. On the other hand, most Americans also favored guest-worker and legalization programs.[10] Thus, if the Senate's comprehensive reform failed and the Republican position was defined by the House bill, the GOP could look extreme in the November elections. Such partisan difficulties and suspicions prevented the bill coming to a vote (Brownstein, 2006).

A second large demonstration against the immigration reform agenda took place on 1 May 2006. The 'Day Without an Immigrant' attracted 250,000 and 400,000 to two marches in LA and thousands of others to marches around the country, where many protesters carried signs in Spanish reading 'Today We March, Tomorrow We Vote.' The effects of the protests were far from straightforward. In response to the scale of the first demonstration in March and the prospect that the Republican focus on immigration was mobilizing both immigrants and ethnic voters against the GOP, Hastert and Frist signaled that they

---

[10] For example, in a *Los Angeles Times*/Bloomberg national poll (#527, 21–27 April 2006), 54 percent supported and 21 percent opposed a guest-worker program; 66 percent to 18 supported a path to citizenship; 42 to 35 supported the House proposal to fence off the border and criminalize illegal residency. There were few differences across ethnicity or party ID, except on the enforcement-only proposals, which Republicans favored significantly more. These findings are broadly supported by a 5–7 May 2006 Gallup poll, which showed 74 percent of Americans thought halting the flow of illegal immigrants was 'extremely' or 'very important' and 71 percent thought it was 'extremely' or 'very important' to develop a plan to deal with those already illegally resident. When asked to prioritize halting the flow or dealing with illegal residents, a small majority favored the former (52–43), but a significant majority (61) favored allowing existing illegals to remain in the U.S. and become U.S. citizens over giving them temporary guest-worker status (15) or deporting them (21). Majorities also thought in order to gain citizenship applicants must have lived in the U.S. for five years (74–24), pay a fine (57–40) and learn English (89–10).

might drop the provision making illegal residence a felony. It seemed that the tide was turning against the original House bill, which the Republicans had orig- inally expected to help them in the November 2006 midterms. Similarly, some of the 36 Democrats who voted yes on the bill in December 2005 had by April 2006 begun to question the wisdom of their decision. While a yes vote initially appeared to offer protection against potential Republican attacks of being soft on border protection, support for the bill increasingly looked like a political liabil- ity as the size of the marches against it increased in frequency and size through 2006. Commentators even began to suggest that the House bill and the debates in the Senate could help engender a new civil rights movement (Weisman, 2006c, p. A1). However, the 1 May demonstrations led some observers and politicians to question whether they could be counterproductive. Passions on both sides were inflamed, politicizing the issues and making compromise more difficult to reach. Republican Mel Martinez, whose comprehensive immigration bill was the Senate's main focus, argued that the 'Boycotts, walkouts or protests are not going to get this done. This is an issue that isn't going to get fixed on the streets. It's going to take thoughtful action by Congress' (Watanabe and Gaouette, 2006). Bush spokesman Scott McClellan made public the president's opposition to the boycotts, while the anti-immigrant Minutemen Militia claimed that volunteers, donations and website traffic had all increased dramati- cally during the March, April and May protests. National polls also suggested that a majority of Americans had a negative view of the demonstrations (Watanabe and Gaouette, 2006; Gorman et al., 2006).

The White House meanwhile came under growing pressure from Senate Republicans, especially Arlen Specter, to take a lead in the immigration debate and help break the deadlock in the upper house. However, Bush was reluctant to tie his credibility to a specific piece of legislation only to see it stripped out in conference or lose in a vote. His strategy throughout his presidency was to set out his broad aims, allow Congress to debate and settle the specifics, and then step in at the end, if required, to broker a final compromise between different factions. Bush was in a particularly difficult position on immigration reform on which intra-party battles were more important for him than inter-party ones. The Bush model mandated reaching out to Latinos and immigrants without alienating his conservative base. While the president managed to do this with some success in the 2004 election by talking about different issues to different audiences, it was much more difficult to compartmentalize when governing than when running for office. With the GOP split between harder-line conservatives promoting an enforcement-only solution and moderates wanting a more inclusive, holistic one, it was inevitable that Bush's attempt to pursue reform would highlight, and indeed promote, division. The ideological splits were exacerbated by the concentration of conservatives in the House, creating tension between the two chambers and making Bush's brokering job more problematic. Each chamber had different electoral imperatives. Facing reelection every two years as well as a possible primary challenge, House members were more pre-occupied with short-term factors than senators with their six-year terms and presidential ambitions. They had little time or reason to think about building long-term, nationwide majority coalitions. Even though national polls showed a majority of Americans in favor of the comprehensive Senate approach, the House Republicans' electoral strategy depended on getting the conservative base to vote by appealing to its core values. With pre-election polls suggesting a notable decline in support for Bush among previously loyal conservative voters, in part because of dissatisfaction with his record and positioning on immigration, it made little electoral sense to back the president's reform agenda. Thus, while Bush's popularity helped many representatives secure reelection in 2002 and 2004, it looked likely in 2006 that any close association with the president would prove a handicap.

Despite these problems, and perhaps unwisely, Bush was determined to push forward on immigration reform, convinced that he could overcome the divisions. Guided by new chief of staff Joshua Bolten, who was brought on board to give the administration new focus and direction, he raised the ante by taking his case directly to the American people in a televised national address, his first on a domestic issue, on 15 May 2006. The president called for a temporary worker program and path to citizenship but pushed more forcefully the administration's enforcement credentials. He sought to appeal to conservatives by emphasizing his plans to assimilate immigrants and to cut off the supply of illegal immigration by securing the border with enhanced fencing and technology, biometric ID cards for legal foreign workers, ending catch and release, more detention beds, yet more border guards and, controversially, deploying the National Guard to help patrol the border. This focus on enforcement was intended to mollify both House Republicans and the movement conservatives whose high turnout was electorally critical. Addressing a key GOP concern, he explained that his plan was not an amnesty because it did not include an automatic path to citizenship. Rather, illegal residents would have to meet strict criteria, pay a fine and back taxes, learn English and get in line behind existing citizenship applicants (IRCA had fast-tracked applications). Sensenbrenner was unimpressed: 'Regardless of what the president says, what he is proposing is amnesty' (Gaouette, 2006a). The administration clearly had a hard sell on its hands. Thus, in the days after the address, Vice President Dick Cheney was dispatched to Rush Limbaugh's radio show, Karl Rove met privately with House Republicans, and the President again spoke by telephone with Hastert and Frist to persuade them of his proposal's

merits. These efforts were ill rewarded, despite the large amount of political capital spent by the President. He pleased neither conservatives nor liberals. Perhaps
unfairly, a *New York Times* editorial portrayed the speech as a 'victory for the
fear-stricken fringe of the debate' and the President as 'Minuteman in chief'
(*Border Illusions*, 2006).[2]

Despite the hostility to Bush's proposals from all sides, his intervention did
invigorate debate in the Senate, which took up S2611 again in mid-May. The
political dynamics had changed in just one month. The Republican leadership
and most Democrats recognized that the conservatives had the upper hand.
Thus, while a bipartisan coalition of Democrats and moderate Republicans was
able to beat back conservative efforts to strip out the guest-worker and citizenship provisions, many of the same moderate Republicans and some of the
Democrats also backed and sponsored several amendments to enhance the security aspect of the bill with the aim of making it more attractive to House conservatives. Successful amendments included: building 370 miles of fence along
the U.S.–Mexico border; excluding illegal immigrants convicted of three mis-
demeanors or one felony from the guest-worker program and citizenship
process; requiring certification from the Department of Labor that there was no
domestic worker available to do a job offered to a foreign worker; and preventing guest-workers self-petitioning for citizenship – instead, affidavits would be
required from employers (Gaouette and Simon, 2006). Perhaps the most controversial change was making English the 'national language' of the U.S. Such
amendments alienated some immigrants-rights organizations and liberal
Democrats, but had the desired effect of moving the two chambers closer
together and increasing the prospect that the House would not reject the Senate
bill out of hand. In the event, the Senate passed comfortably its comprehensive
reform bill on 25 May by 62–36. Significantly, however, 32 Republican senators voted against and only 23 voted for. Conversely, only four Democrats voted
no, while 38 supported it. The lone independent, Jim Jeffords (Vermont), also
gave the bill his support.

As the Senate was due to vote on its immigration bill, Bush and Rove once
again met with House Republicans to persuade them of the merits of comprehensive reform, but failed to move them. 'The basic difference of opinion that
we have seen on this issue between the House and Senate and the White House
is real, it is honest, and it was exhibited on this meeting,' said House Majority
Leader John Boehner (Ohio) (Gaouette, 2006b). Some House Republicans,
including Sensenbrenner, said that they may be open to a guest-worker program
but not legalization. However, the prospects for a deal looked remote when
Speaker Hastert reiterated that he would only bring an immigration bill to the
floor of the House if it met the usual 'majority of the majority' criteria – in other

words, if it could win the support of at least half the 231-strong Republican caucus. Thus, although the Senate bill might have won a majority of the whole House, with most Democrats and some Republicans in favor, it was not allowed the opportunity to do so because it failed the partisan hurdle. Moreover, the House leaders prevaricated on naming members of the conference committee.

Two further blows to Bush's reform agenda were struck in June. The first was the outcome of a special election for an open seat (to replace disgraced Republican Randy 'Duke' Cunningham) in California in June. In a close race, Republican Brian P. Bilbray took the seat running on a strong border security platform and against guest-worker and citizenship programs. This convinced House conservatives that any policy other than enforcement-only was electorally dangerous (Nogourney et al., 2006). Hastert then revealed on 20 June that the House planned to hold 21 'immigration hearings' in 13 states over the summer recess. House leaders claimed publicly that the hearings would tap public opinion and ideas on immigration matters, but they were in effect little more than a direct attack on the Senate bill and the president's position. One session was entitled, 'Whether Attempted Implementation of the Senate Immigration Bill Will Result in an Administrative and National Security Nightmare.' The hearings represented a remarkable breakdown of partisanship, which had served the GOP so well over the preceding decade. Moreover, they sidelined congressional discussion on the Senate bill until September. The general opinion in Washington was that this would probably derail the reform agenda until after the midterm elections as there would be too little time to reach a compromise. Tancredo noted: 'Odds were long that any so-called "compromise bill" would get to the president's desk this year... The nail was already in the coffin of the Senate's amnesty plan. These hearings probably lowered it into the grave.' (Weisman and Murray, 2006, p. A-1)

Comprehensive reform may have died, but House conservatives returning after the summer recess were determined to push the enforcement-only solution, spurred by their summer hearings, the president's declining popularity, dismaying projections about midterm seat losses, and several poorly attended immigrants-rights demonstrations in early September. The House's December 2005 bill was broken up into a series of mini bills, which were quickly passed and dispatched to the Senate. Despite the Senate's long-standing opposition to the enforcement-only approach, it approved several of the House-inspired measures to secure the border. Most notably, the Secure Fence Act [SFA] mandated an additional 700 miles of fence along the 2,000 mile U.S.-Mexico border, but did not authorize funding for construction.[11] A $35 billion DHS spending bill signed by the president on 4 October allocated $1.2 billion for the border fence, but this represented only 20 percent of the estimated $6 billion cost. The measure further undermined the SFA by giving the executive branch considerable flexibility in how to spend the monies – for example on 'virtual fencing' and 'tactical infrastructure' – and by giving local elites a say in the fence's location (Branigin, 2006). Other immigration-security measures approved by the upper chamber ended Americans' ability to travel outside the U.S. without a passport, increased again the number of border patrol agents and expanded the number of beds at detention centers for captured undocumented persons. While senators were prepared to move some way toward the House's more conservative position, they did not capitulate on the more radical enforcement-only provisions, such as requiring the DHS to stop all unlawful entry within 18 months, state and local law enforcement officials to enforce federal immigration law, and mandatory photo ID for voting. The outcome was a relatively moderate and modest legislative achievement but nonetheless surprising given the general sense in Washington in mid to late 2006 that Congress was deadlocked on the immigration issue. Many Democratic and some Republican senators were disappointed to not have approved either a temporary worker program or path to citizenship, but concluded that legislation promoting border security was a prerequisite for liberal reform. 'Many people have told me they will support comprehensive immigration reform if we secure the border first. I hope we can use passage of this bill as a starting point toward long-term, comprehensive immigration reform,' noted Republican Senator Sam Brownback (Kansas) (quoted in Gaouette, 2006c). Bush took the same line: 'Yes, I'll sign it into law. I would view this as an interim step. I don't view this as the final product' (Weisman, 2006d, p. A-3). Others thought any legislative achievement was better than none, and still others thought that it would help motivate core conservatives to turn out and vote.

After more than a month of vacillation following the SFA's passage, Bush staged a public signing of the law on 26 October in an attempt to motivate his base to turnout in the midterms, but did so at the risk of antagonizing Latinos. The short-term imperative of winning elections triumphed over the Bush–Rove strategy of building a long-term majority coalition. The administration's outreach to the social conservatives was reinforced in late October when Bush and Cheney appealed personally to key religious and conservative leaders for support and performed dozens of interviews on conservative talk shows. Also, 42 radio

---

[11]   The bill passed the House easily, 283–138, on 14 September 2006. Ultimately the fence bill passed the Senate with some ease, 80 to 19 on 29 September. It was approved by 54 Republicans and 26 Democrats. Only one Republican (Sen. Lincoln Chafee, RI) voted against and was joined by 17 Democrats and the one independent (Jim Jeffords, Vermont). See Gaouette, 2006c; and Hsu, Spencer S. (2006) 'In Border Fence's Path, Congressional Roadblocks,' *Washington Post* (6 October), p. A-1.

hosts – the vast majority conservative – broadcast live from the White House lawn, with many top officials including Rove, Rice and Rumsfeld available for interview.

The Shifting Politics of Immigration Reform

Immigration reform in the 109th Congress was a divisive and damaging experience for the GOP. The presidential-driven reform agenda looked to the party's future, but was resisted by rank-and-file House Republicans more concerned with their short-term reelection prospects. The latter complained privately that the White House had underestimated the electoral liability of supporting the Senate bill, while administration officials complained that members of congress had overestimated the immediate danger and underestimated the long-term damage of further alienating Latino voters (Nogourney et al., 2006). But the president also faced an ideological as well as electoral barrier. His increasingly conservative House colleagues simply did not share his liberal beliefs on immigration. With security an overriding concern after 9/11 and his professional and public reputation diminished by Iraq and Katrina, Bush's prospects of persuading congressional colleagues to do his bidding on immigration were remote and grew remoter still as the debate matured. Yet he continued to invest time and energy and, most importantly, political capital in the issue. Bush's televised national address in May 2006 raised the political stakes but the gamble backfired when conservative Republicans in the House rejected his comprehensive reform agenda. Many were bemused that the president was prepared to invest so much on an issue that so divided the party and appeared to run counter to the electoral instincts of House members, but Bush was ideologically and strategically committed to reform.

The failure of comprehensive reform and the partial success of the enforcement-only agenda clearly represent a victory for the conservative approach over the liberal one. However, it is important to note how far the debate has progressed in little over a decade. In the mid-1990s Republican politicians aspiring to national office tried hard to portray themselves as anti-immigrant – not just in favor of closing the door on illegal immigrants but reducing the number of legal immigrants and cutting their benefits, too. Even Democrats joined in. Yet today legalizing the status of over 10 million people illegally resident in the United States and setting up an extensive guest-worker program are firmly on the political agenda, put there by a Republican president. As the Latino population grows in size and becomes ever more politicized, so the electoral imperatives of liberal immigration reform will become more irresistible. What appears to many House Republicans as a distant political change will perhaps in the next decade be a short-term electoral consideration.

The politics of reform changed again when the Democrats recaptured Congress in the November 2006 midterms, opening up the possibility of a pro-liberalization alliance between the president and his partisan opponents. The new congressional leadership is unquestionably better aligned to the White House's thinking on the immigration issue. New Speaker Nancy Pelosi of California and Senate Majority Leader Harry Reid of Nevada expressed hope that they could work with the president on immigration reform. Moreover, at his first post-election press conference Bush said it was 'a vital issue... where I believe we can find some common ground with the Democrats.' However, a significant minority of House Democrats would not support a bill that included a guest-worker or legalization program, so Bush faced a hunt for votes among the limited number of moderate Republicans. The fact that the GOP caucus in the lower chamber – and indeed the Democratic one – was more conservative after the midterms appeared to work against him. It remained to be seen whether the failure of the enforcement-first electoral strategy would convince some Republicans to rethink the political policy merits of comprehensive reform.[12] Bush's choice of Mel Martinez, co-author of the Senate's liberal immigration bill, to be general chair of the Republican National Committee reaffirmed the national GOP leadership's determination to pursue Latino voters. In contrast, it was by no means clear how the Democrats would deal with the issue, which had not featured as a priority in their midterm campaign. Their support for reform would likely depend on whether they could claim credit for its passage rather than hand the president a personal victory and with it the keys to the Latino vote as his legacy to his party. While the stars appeared to be better aligned in favor of reform in the 110th Congress than in the 109th, success was far from assured. The reform agenda was intimately tied to electoral, partisan and institutional politics, with differing short- and long-term imperatives further complicating matters. It was clear, however,

---

[12]   A number of prominent enforcement-first Republicans lost their seats, including House immigration subcommittee chair John Hostettler in Indiana, J.D. Hayworth in Arizona and Rick Santorum in Pennsylvania. Minutemen co-founder Randy Graf failed to win an open seat in Arizona. The *National Election Pool* exit poll shows that Latino support for Republican candidates in the 2006 midterms was about 27 percent, a fall of 11 points from 2002 and considerably less than the 44 percent who supported Bush in the 2004 presidential election. Twenty-nine percent said illegal immigration was 'extremely important' in determining their vote choices (multiple responses permitted) but there was no significant bias among these voters in favour of Republican candidates. See Cummings, Jeanne (2006) 'Hispanic Voters Shift Allegiance to Democrats,' *Wall Street Journal* (8 November), p. A-6; Fletcher, Michael A. and Cohen, Jon (2006) 'Moderate Voters Lean Toward Democrats,' *Washington Post* (8 November), p. A-30.

that the tone and content of the immigration debate had evolved considerably in little over a decade. The harsh rhetoric of the 1990s was still heard in the early twenty-first century but was increasingly challenged by liberal voices.

Bibliography

'Border Illusions' (2006) Editorial, *New York Times* (16 May).

Branigin, William (2006) 'Bush Signs U.S.-Mexico Border Fence Bill,' *Washington Post* (26 October).

Brownstein, Ronald (2006) 'Immigrant Bill Snared by Web of Suspicion,' *Los Angeles Times* (8 April).

Congressional Quarterly Almanac (1995) vol. LI (Washington DC: Congressional Quarterly Inc.).

Congressional Quarterly Almanac (1996) vol. LII (Washington DC: Congressional Quarterly Inc.).

Congressional Quarterly Almanac Plus (2005) vol. LXI (Washington DC: Congressional Quarterly Inc.).

Congressional Research Service (2006) 'Immigration Legislation and Issues in the 109th Congress' (12 May).

Durand, Jorge, Massey, Douglas S. and Charvet, Fernando (2000) 'The Changing Geography of Mexican Immigration to the United States: 1910–1996,' *Social Science Quarterly* vol. 81.

Gaouette, Nicole (2006a) 'Senate Toughens Border Stand, Approves Miles of New Fence,' *Los Angeles Times* (18 May).

Gaouette, Nicole (2006b) 'House GOP Not Budging on Border,' *Los Angeles Times* (24 May).

Gaouette, Nicole (2006c) 'Border Barrier Approved,' *Los Angeles Times* (30 September).

Gaouette, Nicole and Simon, Richard (2006) 'House GOP Fails to Warm to Bush Border Proposal,' *Los Angeles Times* (17 May).

Gimpel, James G. and Edwards, James R. (1999) *The Congressional Politics of Immigration Reform* (Allyn and Bacon).

Gorman, Anna, Miller, Marjorie and Landsberg, Mitchell (2006) 'Immigrants Demonstrate Peaceful Power,' *Los Angeles Times* (2 May).

'Honor Our Immigrants' (2006) Editorial, *Washington Post* (19 April).

Los Angeles Times, October 19, 1994a. Ronald Brownstein and Patrick J. McDonnel, 'Kemp, Bennett and INS Chief Decry Prop. 187'.

Los Angeles Times, November 22, 1994b. James Bornemeier, 'Kemp, Bennett Warn of GOP Rift on Prop. 187'.

Los Angeles Times, March 23, 1996a. *Times* Staff Writers, 'Dole Uses State Visit to Attack Clinton on B-2'.

Los Angeles Times, June 11, 1996b. *Times* Staff Writer, 'Clinton, Dole Partisans Spar on Illegal Immigration'.

Los Angeles Times, April 8, 2000. Cathleen Decker, 'Bush Courts Latinos, Other Californians'.

Los Angeles Times Exit Poll (1996).

National Election Study Cumulative Data File, 1948–2000. Latest version of ANES data file can be found at www.electionstudies.org.

National Election Study Survey (1992).

New York Times, September 18, 1994. *Times* Staff Writer, 'Reno Initiative Aims to Control Immigration'.

New York Times, December 13, 1994. B. Drummond Ayers Jr., 'Stepped-Up Border Patrols Halve Unlawful Crossings'.

Nogourney, Adam, Hulse, Carl and Rutenberg, Jim (2006) 'Bush's Immigration Plan Stalled as House GOP Grew More Anxious,' *New York Times* (25 June).

Office of the Press Secretary (2004a) White House Press Release, 'Fact Sheet: Fair and Secure Immigration Reform' (January 7).

Office of the Press Secretary (2004b) White House Press Release, 'President Bush Proposes New Temporary Worker Program' (January 7).

Reno, Janet (1994) 'President Clinton's Attorney General, referring to a new federal program, Operation Gatekeeper,' *New York Times* (18 September).

State of the Union Address, 24 January 1995 (delivered version).

Swarns, Rachel (2006) 'Senate Deal on Immigration Falters,' *New York Times* (7 April).

U.S. Census Bureau (2004) 'US Interim Projections by Age, Sex, Race, and Hispanic Origin,' www.census.gov/ipc/www/usinterimproj/.

Watanabe, Teresa and Becerra, Hector (2006) '500,000 Pack Streets to Protest Immigration Bills,' *Los Angeles Times* (26 March).

Watanabe, Teresa and Gaouette, Nicole (2006) 'Next: Converting the Energy of Protest to Political Clout,' *Los Angeles Times* (2 May).

Weisman, Jonathan (2006a) 'Senate Republicans Agree on Immigration Bill,' *Washington Post* (6 April).

Weisman, Jonathan (2006b) 'Senate Pact Offers Permits to Most Illegal Immigrants,' *Washington Post* (7 April).

Weisman, Jonathan (2006c) 'Immigrant Bill Fallout May Hurt House,' *Washington Post* (12 April).

Weisman, Jonathan (2006d) 'Congress Resumes Immigration Efforts,' *Washington Post* (21 September).

Weisman, Jonathan and Murray, Shailagh (2006) 'GOP Plans Hearings on Issue of Immigration,' *Washington Post* (21 June).

Wroe, Andrew (2007, forthcoming) *The Republican Party and Immigration Politics* (New York: Palgrave).

14

The Cuban Adjustment Act and Immigration from Cuba

Jessica Gibbs

The Cuban population in the United States numbers some 1.5 million, of whom nearly 913,000 are foreign born. It is highly concentrated: more than two-thirds (68%) live in Florida, with smaller concentrations in New Jersey (81,000), New York (78,000), California (74,000) and Texas (34,000) (Pew Hispanic Center). Thus, while not particularly large, it has considerable electoral clout, especially in close-run presidential elections, and is able to exert a significant influence on U.S. policy towards Cuba. Not only has the Cuban American National Foundation, a conservative émigré lobby group founded in 1981, been effective in forming alliances with successive administrations and members of Congress, but more recently Cuban American politicians have themselves achieved prominence in Washington. Florida and New Jersey currently have one Cuban American senator each (Republican Mel Martinez and Democrat Bob Menendez), while there are three Cuban Americans in the House of Representatives (Ileana Ros-Lehtinen, Lincoln Diaz-Balart and Mario Diaz-Balart, all Republicans from Florida). This chapter will look at the circumstances leading to the formation of this community and use the case study of the Cuban Adjustment Act (CAA) of 1966 to cast light upon the difficulties of effective policymaking in the sphere of immigration and the danger of unintended consequences. As Steven Gillon argues in reference to the Immigration Act of 1965, 'Immigration policy is always unpredictable, dependent on many variables – population increase, natural disasters, international economics, changing expectations – that are beyond the control of policy makers' (Gillon, 2000, p. 178). In addition, as with the 1965 Act, the brief congressional debate on the CAA demonstrates a failure on the part of policymakers to anticipate accurately, or even to consider carefully, the impact the legislation would have over the following forty years.

The CAA was passed to address a specific problem: in the immediate aftermath of the revolutionary victory, large numbers of Cubans had left their country for the United States. Most of those who arrived between 1959 and 1966 did so with non-immigrant visas, visa waivers, or no documents at all, or, in the case of the 'Freedom Flight' participants, under executive parole, rather than with immigrant visas, so they did not have permanent resident status.[1] Rather than focus upon their reasons for leaving Cuba, or their experiences in the United States, this essay examines the legislative response to this situation, and the way in which Cold War foreign policy objectives obscured and overrode the normal criteria for migration to the United States. It highlights the unintended consequences flowing from an inadequately considered bill, the periodic challenges to the exceptional treatment of Cuban migrants, and the effect on the U.S. government of changes in the nature and perception of Cuban migration beginning in 1980. It also considers the increasingly important political influence of the émigrés, which, together with the lingering symbolism of the Cuban 'flight to freedom,' has served to keep the CAA in effect to this day.

Origins of the Cuban Exception

The CAA allows Cubans with temporary status in the United States, together with their spouses and minor children, to apply for adjustment to permanent residence at the discretion of the Attorney General and without the need to establish a political asylum case. The origins of the CAA lie in the position adopted by Washington towards immigration from Cuba between January 1, 1959 and the Cuban Missile Crisis of October 1962, when Castro cut off direct flights between the two countries. This stance pre-dates the legislation, but has come to be associated with it, leading several analysts to state, quite erroneously, that the CAA requires certain actions to be taken by the U.S. Coast Guard or the Immigration and Naturalization Service (INS).[2] During the first two years of the Cuban exodus, prominent defections were encouraged and even induced by Washington, but in general the State Department 'pursued a passive policy

---

[1]   Executive parole was first used on a large scale for thirty thousand of the Hungarians who had left for Austria after the failed uprising of 1956. It stems from a section of the Immigration and Nationality Act allowing the Attorney General to bring aliens temporarily into the United States 'for emergent reasons or for reasons deemed strictly in the public interest.'

[2]   See, for example, Olson, J.E. and Olson, J.S. (1995) *Cuban Americans: From Trauma to Triumph* (New York: Twayne Prentice Hall International), p. 69; Teitelbaum, M. and Weiner, M. (1995) 'Introduction,' in Teitelbaum and Weiner (eds.), *Threatened Peoples, Threatened Borders: World Migration and U.S. Policy* (New York: W.W. Norton), pp. 26–7; Zimmerman, W. (1995) 'Migrants and Refugees: A threat to security,' in Teitelbaum and Weiner (eds.), *Threatened Peoples, Threatened Borders*, pp. 112–3.

designed to let virtually any Cuban enter... without legal formalities' (Loescher and Scanlan, 1986, pp. 61–62). According to Wayne Smith, then a junior diplomat at the embassy in Havana, by the end of 1960 consular officers had noticed that few of the Cubans who were given non-immigrant visas in fact returned, so they requested guidance from Washington. When none was forthcoming, staff continued to relax standards for the issuance of visas (Engstrom, 1997, p. 33). The Coast Guard picked up many Cubans at sea and brought them to the United States, and the INS did not attempt to deport those who arrived or overstayed illegally.[3]

Quite apart from any humanitarian impulse, U.S. policymakers pursued both a short-term foreign policy goal – the creation of an exile leadership and fighting force capable of overthrowing the Cuban government – and the wider objectives of discrediting the Cuban example and impeding Cuban economic development by stimulating the emigration of professionals. American politicians and newspapers were quick to describe the Cubans as 'voting with their feet' against Castro's government (Jordan, 1959, p. I1). A July 1960 memorandum from Assistant Secretary of State Gerard Smith suggested that special treatment for Cubans would:

> ... demonstrate the rule that when given a chance people generally
> flee toward freedom and away from communism. Our case would
> be improved if Castro took military steps to block the flow of
> refugees. A few pictures of Castro's men shooting refugees attempt-
> ing to escape would do more to hurt Castro than a host of economic
> sanctions. (*Foreign Relations of the United States*)

The Eisenhower administration established a Cuban refugee center in Miami in December 1960, and, following the closure of the U.S. embassy in January 1961, many Cubans took advantage of dedicated visa waiver programs to migrate (for details see Torres, 1999, pp. 62–67). The failure of the Bay of Pigs invasion in April 1961 disrupted neither the stream of Cubans nor their welcome in the United States.

In the wake of the Missile Crisis, Washington briefly experimented with a new policy of migration restriction aimed at creating an internal uprising.

---

[3] Coast Guard figures from 1959–69 show that a total of 14,367 people were assisted, while statistics from May 1967–May 1970 indicate that 78 percent of arrivals had received assistance from the Coast Guard (See U.S. Congress (1970) House, Committee on Foreign Affairs, Subcommittee on Inter-American Affairs, *Cuba and the Caribbean*, 91st Cong., 2nd sess., July 8, 9, 10, 13, 20, 27, 31, (August 3), p. 1493).

Following Castro's September 28, 1965 announcement that Cubans with family in the United States could leave if their relatives petitioned for them, however, this policy was swiftly abandoned in favor of one that used the would-be migrants to send a message to the wider world. On October 3, at a Liberty Island ceremony to mark the signing of the 1965 Immigration Act, President Johnson declared that those who sought 'refuge' would find it:

> Once again, it stamps the mark of failure on a regime when many of its citizens voluntarily choose to leave the land of their birth for a more hopeful home in America. The future holds little hope for any Government where the present holds no hope for the people...
> (*Congressional Record*, 1965)

Since the new act made no provision for the admission of refugees from the Western Hemisphere, Johnson decreed that the Cubans would receive executive parole. One month later, when Cubans from the United States had already arrived at the port of Camarioca to take up Castro's invitation, the two governments signed a Memorandum of Understanding which neither limited the total number who could participate nor ruled out the emigration of people with no relatives in the United States, although it did establish priorities and the rate of arrival (three to four thousand a month). This astonishingly open-ended presidential commitment formed the basis of the 'Freedom Flights.'

Special Legislation

In 1966, the Johnson administration and influential members of Congress such as Senator Edward Kennedy (Democrat, Massachusetts) came to an agreement on the need for special legislation to allow Cubans to adjust to permanent residence. As introduced in the House in 1966, H.R. 15183 provided that:

> The status of any alien who is a native or citizen of Cuba who was inspected and admitted or paroled into the United States subsequent to January 1, 1959, may be adjusted by the Attorney General, in his discretion and under such regulations as he may prescribe, to that of an alien lawfully admitted for permanent residence if (1) the alien makes an application for such adjustment, and (2) the alien is eligible to receive an immigrant visa and is admissible to the United States for permanent residence.

The adjustment provisions applied to co-resident spouses and minor children, regardless of their citizenship and place of birth.

Debate in Congress focused on the difficulties experienced by Cubans as a result of their temporary status, particularly the many professionals unable to practice because of inflexible state licensing regulations. It was generally agreed to be a terrible burden for Cubans to travel to a U.S. consulate in Canada or Mexico to be issued with immigrant visas – for which they did not have to obtain Department of Labor certification that their skills were in demand in the United States – despite the fact that some 75,000 of those in temporary status had managed to do so. Undersecretary of State George Ball told the House subcommittee that humanitarian motives and foreign policy interests in the proposal could not be separated. Congress would be 'demonstrating to the world our sympathy for people who do not want to live under totalitarian regimes,' while, if the legislation was not passed, 'the condition of Cubans in the United States – who are having to work at tasks which are beneath their qualifications – is going to be a pretty unedifying spectacle to many nations of the world' (U.S. Congress, 1996, pp. 12–13). It appears that the Johnson administration wished to make it easier for Cubans to flourish in their new environment, so that their success would provide a more telling contrast to the austerity prevailing in a homeland under U.S. embargo.

Only one member of the subcommittee, Representative William Cahill (Republican, New Jersey), seemed aware of the possible implications:

> ... we are adopting a permanent policy. We are really saying in effect
> we will accept all Cubans who want to come into the United States
> regardless of the number for however long they want to come in
> and, after coming in, we will then see to it that they have the
> opportunity of becoming American citizens ... A great deal of
> thought, however, should be given to it because we are indeed, in
> my judgment, setting a precedent that will have far-reaching effects
> in the future. (U.S. Congress, 1996, pp. 18–19)

Yet little debate took place. The differences between adjustment for a continuing movement from Cuba, and the Hungarian adjustment legislation, which, though cited several times as a precedent, had dealt with a more defined group, were hardly explored (*Congressional Record*, 1966b and 1966c). Although mention was made of the Freedom Flights, some members of Congress continued to refer to 164,000 Cubans (those in temporary status as of July 1, 1966), as though the numbers were not constantly increasing (*Congressional Record*, 1966a). The discussion touched only briefly upon the Cuban boat-people, who arrived without prior U.S. screening but were not excluded from adjustment by the terms of the bill. While the INA required that an immigrant visa be immediately available to an applicant before he or she could adjust to permanent residence, there was no such requirement in the CAA, nor was there any discussion of what impact Cuban adjustment would have on the future Western Hemisphere immigration ceiling, due to come into effect on July 1, 1968. The neglect of such topics strongly suggests that adjustment legislation was seen as one of several special measures aimed at promoting the advancement of Cubans and not as part of an overall immigration policy (for further details see Garcia, 1996, pp. 26–30, 36–37, 40–45).

The House passed the bill by 300 to 25 votes in September, the conference report passed Congress unanimously a month later, and the CAA became law on November 2. The only additional requirement was that the applicant must have been 'physically present in the United States for at least two years' (amended to one year in 1980). In other respects, however, the conference report was more generous than the House version, for it established that the Attorney General should create a record of the applicant's admission for permanent residence as of thirty months previous to the adjustment to permanent residence, or the date of arrival in the United States, whichever was later.

Unintended consequences

The inadequate debate soon gave rise to problems. In 1968 the INS announced that Cuban adjustments would be counted toward the Western Hemisphere ceiling. Despite some congressional protest, no immediate action was taken on any of the bills introduced to counter this administrative interpretation, but legislation passed in 1976 provided that the adjustment of Cubans present in the United States on or before January 1, 1977 should not be charged to the ceiling. In November 1976, a class action *Silva v. Levi* on behalf of all Western Hemisphere natives with visa priority dates after July 1, 1968, challenged the previous visa allocation practice, arguing that extra visas should be issued to those on the waiting list to compensate for the 144,946 visa numbers already used for Cuban adjustment. Looking at the legislative history, the Carter administration concluded that as the CAA 'had been perceived by all concerned as a special act, designed to deal with a unique and pressing problem,' outside of quota limits, the previous administrative interpretation had been incorrect. Consequently, it suspended the deportation of tens of thousands of Western Hemisphere migrants and began to process the additional visas.[4] Although the 1976 legislation did not require that the no-offset policy be applied to the per country limits due to come

---

[4]   See the series of memoranda included in U.S. Congress (1977) House, Committee on the Judiciary, Subcommittee on Immigration, Citizenship, and International Law, *Indochina Refugees – Adjustment of Status*, 95th Cong., 1st sess., (May 25, June 2), pp. 113–28.

into effect in 1977, it became administrative practice not to charge Cuban adjustments to any quota. The fact that other applicants for immigrant visas do not compete with Cubans adjusting under the act helps to explain its longevity.

Hearings in 1977 on adjustment of status for Indo-Chinese refugees provide further evidence that the CAA had been carelessly drafted. State Department witness Barbara M. Watson recommended that the Indo-Chinese legislation should have a cut-off date, since the open-ended CAA 'encouraged the further influx of Cubans resulting in an astronomical number over which you have no control' (U.S. Congress, 1977, pp. 9–10, 20, 22–23). While Watson was being disingenuous about the extent to which executive action, rather than the terms of the CAA itself, had produced this result, there were certainly some surprising consequences of the legislation. In one early example of the CAA benefiting an individual for whom it had clearly not been designed, in 1968 the Bureau of Immigration Appeals found a Cuban who had moved to Haiti in 1936 (twenty-three years prior to the Cuban Revolution) and had entered the United States on a tourist visa eligible for adjustment (Eig, 1996, pp. 93–253).

During this period there were some signs of concern in Congress over preferential treatment for Cubans. African American representative William Clay (Democrat, Missouri), a founding member of the Congressional Black Caucus, in 1970 offered an amendment to remove funding from the Freedom Flights. While mainly concerned about the 'unjustifiable drain on the taxpayers' purse,' he also argued that the program was unfair to other would-be immigrants, citing 'the people of Haiti or Brazil who want to escape oppression in their countries' (*Congressional Record*, 1970). Yet, Congress backed President Johnson's commitment until Havana ended the flights in 1973, by which time more than 300,000 had benefited from the program. Furthermore, although U.S. policy continued to focus on Castro's overthrow, the Johnson and Nixon administrations disregarded growing evidence that he was manipulating the flights to rid Cuba of potential troublemakers. A former Cuban spy, for example, testified that contacts of foreign correspondents were given exit permits to get them out of the way (U.S. Congress, 1970, pp. 159–61; U.S. Congress, 1971, p. 1650).

The Mariel Crisis and Its Consequences

Cuban migration suddenly became far more salient in 1980, when Havana converted an embarrassing episode at the Peruvian embassy into a crisis for the United States by inviting émigrés to pick up relatives from the port of Mariel. The ensuing boatlift brought some 125,000 to the United States, including thousands of convicts and people with mental health problems encouraged (and in some cases forced) to join the exodus by the Cuban authorities. A new Refugee Act, on which the ink was hardly dry when these Cubans were brought to shore, and the coincident arrival of thousands of Haitian boat-people, complicated the Carter administration's handling of the crisis. Rather than admit just the Cubans as refugees, which would offend congressional supporters of the Haitians, the administration recommended that Congress pass legislation to create a new 'Cuban–Haitian Entrant' category for all Cubans and Haitians in INS custody. Under the administration's proposal – which was never actually enacted – the 'entrants' would have been able to adjust to permanent residence after two years in the United States.[5]

Beyond the immediate political fallout for the administration, which appeared powerless to halt and inept in dealing with the influx – and for Arkansas Governor Bill Clinton, whose 1980 re-election bid failed after he called in the National Guard to control rioting Cuban detainees – the boatlift impacted upon U.S. policy toward Cuba, perceptions of Cuban arrivals and treatment of Western Hemisphere migrants more generally. While Mariel contributed to making improved relations with Cuba highly unlikely during what remained of the Carter presidency, the inclusion of undesirables – a hostile act construed by Reagan officials as proof that Carter had employed the wrong approach – paradoxically increased U.S. motivation to negotiate with Havana. It also produced a new awareness that Cuban migration was a double-edged sword. Whatever the propaganda costs of a massive exodus, the benefits to Castro of exporting the disaffected and the costs to the United States had become all too obvious. A May 1980 Gallup poll found that 59 percent of respondents believed that the boatlift was bad for the United States, while only 19 percent welcomed the Cubans on the grounds that their migration revealed 'widespread dissatisfaction with the Government of Fidel Castro' (*Most in Poll Concerened*, 1980, p. A32). The 1983 film *Scarface*, in which Al Pacino plays the Mariel entrant as a cocaine king, revealed how the episode had taken the shine off the 'Golden Exiles' of the 1960s. Even Cuban Americans, enticed into participation in the boatlift by the prospect of family reunification, reacted against their manipulation by Havana. Many agreed with Miami Mayor Maurice Ferre that Castro had 'flushed these people on us' (Garcia, 1996, p. 70). Finally, in the words of one analyst, 'Mariel was translated into an unarticulated policy that the United States was not to become the Thailand of the Western Hemisphere' – a policy which reached its apogee in the September 1981 interdiction agreement between the Reagan administration and Haitian President Jean-Claude Duvalier (Keely, 1995, p. 227).

---

[5]   In 1984, the Reagan administration allowed the Cuban entrants to apply for adjustment under the CAA.

Yet the Reagan administration's attitude towards Cuban migrants after Mariel is more opaque. While the *Washington Post* reported in April 1981 that officials 'say they already have a clear-cut policy should Castro ever again open his country to unlimited emigration,' the correspondent was unconvinced, commenting that it 'remains unclear whether any administration would have the resources and political willpower to stop thousands of Cuban Americans from bringing their relatives to freedom in the United States' (Walsh, 1981, p. A1). Conservative Cuban Americans, part of Ronald Reagan's natural foreign policy constituency, had recently been encouraged by his officials to form a lobby group, but neither the Cuban American National Foundation (CANF) nor the wider Cuban American community were bound to defer to the executive on migration. In July 1981, Assistant Secretary of State for Inter-American Affairs Thomas Enders described the boatlift arrivals as 'a group of people that are essentially not refugees' and confirmed that if Havana attempted a repeat performance it would be U.S. policy to intercept boats on the high seas and turn them back to Cuba (U.S. Congress, 1981a, p. 5). Three months later the administration proposed legislation, which granted the executive sweeping powers in the event of an immigration emergency, addressed the status of the entrants and, importantly, repealed the CAA (U.S. Congress, 1981b, pp. 1075–77, 1082–86). In the meantime, however, the Coast Guard continued to bring Cuban boat people to the United States. Cuban American outrage after the deportation of one young stowaway in January 1982 discouraged the administration from repeating the exercise (Skoug, 1996, p. 90).

While the Reagan administration acknowledged that the CAA was anachronistic, the return of the so-called 'excludables' – the few hundred Mariel Cubans who had been detained continuously since their arrival and those who had committed serious offences in the United States – was a far higher priority (U.S. Congress, 1984, pp. 10, 36; U.S. Congress, 1986, p. 81). In April 1983, in an attempt to induce the Cuban government to accept the excludables' return, the Justice Department suspended the processing of preference visas at the U.S. Interests Section in Havana, opened during Carter administration efforts to improve relations (Skoug, 1996, pp. 11–12). When talks finally took place between July and November 1984, Havana initially pressed the United States to refuse entrance to those who left Cuba without exit permits and to grant 30,000 immigrant visas a year, but eventually agreed to accept 2,746 named excludables in exchange for normal immigration (up to 20,000 preference visas and the unlimited entry of spouses, parents and minor children of U.S. citizens) plus in-country refugee visa processing for up to 3,000 Cubans (former political prisoners and their relatives) a year (Skoug, 1996, pp. 65–79). Some analysts have overlooked the significance of the Reagan administration systematically returning Cubans – albeit only this stigmatized group – yet Jorge Dominguez points out that Reagan officials even testified that the Cuban government would respect the returnees' human rights (Dominguez, 1992, p. 50). Robert Bach further argues that the agreement 'essentially redefined the linkage that had existed since the early 1960s between opposition to the Cuban Revolution and the strategic use of anyone leaving the island as a symbol of the failure of that revolution' (Bach, 1990, p. 13). The agreement was suspended by Cuba in May 1985, when the U.S. government-funded surrogate broadcasting station Radio Marti went on air, and restarted in November 1987.

Despite the ostensible 'normalization,' the Reagan administration's failure to induce Congress to repeal the CAA meant that Cubans continued to receive exceptional treatment. This failure may be explained by the fact that, in the absence of a migration crisis, repeal was not a high enough priority for the administration or for Congress, and by opposition from Cuban Americans. Certainly, it was with regard to migration from Cuba that CANF first demonstrated real independence from the administration, using congressional allies in 1987 to sponsor legislation that conflicted with efforts to pressure Havana into resumption of the migration agreement.

New Challenges to the Cuban Exception

By the end of the 1980s, another simultaneous influx of Cuban rafters and Haitian boat-people revived protests over 'double standards.'[6] While many observers attributed the rafter phenomenon to a Cuban government policy of restricting migration, the situation was in fact more complicated. The fortunate few who obtained U.S. visas were rarely prevented from emigrating, as the State Department human rights report for 1993 acknowledged (U.S. Congress, 1994a, p. 177). Most of the rafters, on the other hand, did not qualify for visas (they might also have been unable to pay the high exit fees imposed by Havana), but once they arrived in the United States they were received with open arms. Regarded as a health risk – first for tuberculosis and then for AIDS – the Haitians conversely were unwelcome in Florida, where, according to one account, 'the local elite goaded the federal authorities into an unparalleled policy of rejection' (Stepick, 1992, p. 153). Thus, while Cubans were brought to shore, paroled after a sketchy INS inspection, not required to apply for asylum and eligible for adjustment to permanent residence after one year, Haitians were intercepted on

---

[6]   Although many of the 'rafters' prior to the crisis of August–September 1994 used boats rather than home-made rafts to make their exit, the term *balseros* or rafters has become generalized.

the high seas and returned to Haiti, detained in the United States if they managed to elude the Coast Guard and only granted asylum in exceptional cases.[7]

Although it was hoped that congressional and media exposure of such disparities would lead to improved treatment of Haitians, a few members of Congress challenged the continued relevance of the CAA. At congressional hearings, officials in George H.W. Bush's administration responded with a mixture of obfuscation and openness. In November 1991, for example, INS Commissioner Gene McNary maintained that it was necessary to parole rafters because Havana would not accept their return. However, the Cuban government's 1984 suggestion that the United States return Cubans who left without exit permits and its later cooperation in rafter repatriation suggest that the Bush administration was really expecting resistance from Cuban Americans rather than from Havana. Yet McNary acknowledged that the CAA was a substantial incentive for Cubans, and that most either arrived by sea, for which the penalty in Cuba if caught was normally a short period of detention, or on non-immigrant visas, a practice Washington was trying to reduce by screening out those most likely to overstay (U.S. Congress, 1991d, pp. 75–78).[8] Six months later, however, testifying against the repeal of the CAA proposed by Romano Mazzoli (Democrat, Kentucky), chair of the House Subcommittee on International Law, Immigration and Refugees and an opponent of ideologically based refugee policies, McNary argued that it was not the time to send a message that might be 'misconstrued.' Directly contradicting his earlier testimony, he stated that any Cuban who 'flees' was subject to a three-year prison sentence on return (U.S. Congress, 1992a, pp. 67, 80). Another witness at this hearing, Dan Stein of the Federation for American Immigration Reform, expressed rather different views. He observed that the CAA 'had stood as a monument to the degree to which the Nation will tolerate gross deviations in basic legislative and judicial fairness when overarching foreign policy interests are perceived to be at stake.' He further argued that the CAA had allowed Castro to stay in power by exporting his opposition. Notwithstanding the powerful constituencies opposed to change, Stein urged that 'reason, justice and equity demand rectification.' (U.S. Congress, 1992a, pp. 257–58)

---

[7] For details on the treatment of Haitians, see Koh, H. H. (1994) 'The "Haiti Paradigm" in United States Human Rights Policy,' *Yale Law Journal* vol. 103, pp. 303–314.

[8] Overstaying increased in the early 1990s in part because the Cuban government progressively loosened age restrictions on travel for personal reasons. Initially restricted to men over 65 and women over 60, by July 1991 any Cuban above the age of 20 was in principle allowed to travel if they had a personal invitation from a foreign friend or relative, a Cuban exit permit and a visa. Cuban analyst Ernesto Rodríguez Chavez calculates that 31.7 percent of the 47,500 Cubans who migrated to the United States between 1990 and 1993 arrived with non-immigrant visas. See Rodríguez Chavez, E. (1997) *Emigración Cubana Actual* (Havana: Editorial de Ciencias Sociales), pp. 93–94.

Clearly, the argument that the CAA in itself allows Castro to export opponents to the United States is overstated. Successive administrations had facilitated migration from Cuba – even picking up rafters at sea – prior to 1966. Furthermore, the CAA neither governs admission nor obliges the Attorney General to adjust the status of applicants. It is permissive, not directive. Yet as the Cuban economy staggered under the impact of the collapse of the Soviet bloc in Eastern Europe, more and more Cubans looked to the greener grass on the other side of the Florida Straits. A long tradition of 'exile' had created a sense of entitlement to the American dream among the Cuban population, and seeking an exit from Cuba was a far more attractive option than seeking an outlet for dissatisfaction at home.

Operating alongside the CANF Exodus program, another example of Cuban American lobbying success which brought in nearly 10,000 Cubans from third countries as privately sponsored refugees between 1988 and 1993, the in-country refugee program established in 1984 became a way out for broadly defined opponents of the Cuban government. In 1990, the Bush administration, disregarding reports that Havana used it to dispel discontent, announced that in the fiscal year 1991 it would be available to political dissidents, religious activists and former U.S. government employees who met the refugee definition (U.S. Congress, 1990, pp. 50, 314–17). Following voluntary agency testimony that Cubans were being forced on to rafts by processing limitations, the administration extended the program to 'members of persecuted religious minorities ... forced labor conscripts, persons deprived of their professional credentials or subjected to other disproportionately harsh or discriminatory treatment resulting from their perceived or actual political or religious beliefs or activities, and other refugees of compelling concern to the United States,' criteria maintained by the Clinton administration (U.S. Congress, 1991c, pp. 175, 219; U.S. Congress, 1992b, pp. 13–14; U.S. Congress, 1993b, p. 58).

Conspicuously lacking in the debate in the judiciary committees was a sense of how the provision of numerous refugee visas under a program whose parameters were repeatedly expanded, and the acceptance of large numbers of rafters and visitors who were able to adjust under the CAA, interacted with U.S. efforts to bring Castro's rule to an end. Only the restrictionist Stein touched on this aspect. Nor was there much discussion elsewhere in Congress about the role of emigration in reducing pressures for change in Cuba. One of the few exceptions was its invocation by House Western Hemisphere subcommittee chair Robert Torricelli (Democrat, New Jersey) in 1991. In response to his inquiry whether a recent Cuban decision to reduce penalties for illegal exit and the age requirement for visits abroad represented 'a plan to abuse the system,' State Department witness Michael Kozak remarked that emigration was 'always a safety valve' for Castro

(U.S. Congress, 1991b, pp. 42–43). A few days later, Kozak's superior Bernard Aronson acknowledged that Havana prevented opponents from organizing by imprisoning dissidents or forcing them to emigrate (U.S. Congress, 1991a, p. 115). Torricelli argued that Castro would hold power indefinitely if he could export all his economic problems and political dissidents, but if the administration 'spoke honestly' to the American public and Cuban Americans they would understand the need for change. The 'legal Mariel' represented by the flood of Cuban applications for non-immigrant visas demanded a policy response 'as it has very real ramifications for our national objectives of change of regime in Cuba' (U.S. Congress, 1991a, p. 130). In July, by when non-immigrant visa processing for Cubans had been temporarily suspended, both Jorge Mas Canosa of CANF and Cuban American academic Jaime Suchlicki endorsed the suspension on the grounds that it would increase internal pressure. Torricelli also called for a new policy 'which deals with the reality that this immigration policy has something to do with political change inside Cuba' (U.S. Congress, 1991a, pp. 173–74).

Yet there was little reference to the role of emigration in sustaining Castro's rule during hearings or floor debate on the legislation Torricelli himself sponsored in 1992 (the Cuban Democracy Act). The rafters were used as shorthand for all that was rotten in Cuba, rather than read as a warning that a policy which sought to create an uprising against Castro was unlikely to succeed. The fact that Torricelli dropped the issue suggests a calculation that increasing economic pressure while simultaneously expanding contact with the Cuban people (the approach of the Cuban Democracy Act) appealed more to Cuban Americans than attempts to shut down Castro's safety valve. The Bush administration also appears to have been convinced that adopting a different interpretation of the CAA – or providing fewer refugee visas – would spark protest at home. As Suchlicki had acknowledged in 1991, not all Cuban Americans agreed that limiting emigration was a necessary means to a desirable end (U.S. Congress, 1991a, p. 175). Those who had close family members in Cuba naturally wanted to keep all emigration avenues open. Nor did the discourse typically surrounding the subject make it easy to campaign for a change of policy. Although Cuban Americans – like other observers – were aware that the Cuban economic crisis explained much of the new migration, they were reluctant to admit this in public.[9] A continuing insistence that all who came from Cuba were political refugees, forced into exile like their predecessors, made it harder to argue that Washington should reverse course.

---

[9]   See for example the testimony of Maria Dominguez of the American Immigration Lawyers Pro Bono Project, U.S. Congress, *Cuban and Haitian Immigration*, p. 154–63.

The first nineteen months of Bill Clinton's administration saw no change in policy towards Cuban migrants, despite rising rafter numbers, higher levels of hijacking and a congressional campaign on behalf of Haitian boat-people. In 1992, candidate Clinton had censured the Bush administration for the direct return of Haitians, creating the impression that he would allow Haitians picked up in international waters to be brought to shore by the U.S. Coast Guard just like Cubans. However, days after the election and amid reports that tens of thousands of Haitians were preparing to set sail as soon as he took the helm, Clinton decided to continue the Bush policy for the time being (see Koh, 1995, pp. 139–173). Members of the Congressional Black Caucus, an important Democratic constituency, were angry at this reversal. But while they persevered in alleging racial discrimination and introducing bills to benefit Haitian boat-people, other legislators attacked the CAA in an effort to level the playing field (U.S. Congress, 1994b, pp. 34–35, 52, 54, 64, 66, 95, 101). In June 1994, amidst polarized and partisan congressional debate over a possible invasion of Haiti, Mazzoli opened a hearing on Haitian asylum seekers by calling for repeal of the CAA (U.S. Congress, 1994b, p. 28). Yet his attempt to focus attention on the inequity in the legislation was thwarted by administration testimony still more misleading than that provided by McNary in 1992. Clinton's Deputy Commissioner Chris Sale maintained not only that Havana did not accept the return of Cubans beyond the Mariel excludables, but also that the CAA 'prescribed' the parole of Cuban rafters (U.S. Congress, 1994b, pp. 138–39).

There was also increasing concern about the impact on the United States of possible Cuban developments. As early as October 1992, State Department adviser Richard Nuccio had warned the transition team that 'a Clinton administration will very likely confront a crisis in Cuba during its first two years,' which could involve 'threats of massive illegal migration to Florida and other Southern states' (Nuccio, 1999, pp. 10–11). A rare open hearing of the Senate Select Committee on Intelligence in 1993 touched upon the possibility that a violent transition might produce 'the catastrophe of mass migration' (U.S. Congress, 1993a, p. 5). At a March 1994 hearing on Representative Charles Rangel's proposal to lift the embargo on Cuba, Representative George Miller (D-California) told his colleagues that many believed this move 'would avert possible chaos in Cuba, resulting in a flood of tens of thousands of new Cuban immigrants to the United States' (U.S. Congress, 1994a, pp. 18–20).

A New Interpretation of the CAA

The rafter crisis of 1994, like Mariel, came in the context of limited opportunities for legal migration to the United States and an open-arms policy towards
Cuban hijackers, who were attracted towards more violent methods because of
the risks and low success rate of rafting.[10] On June 5, sixty-one Cubans hijacked
a 125-foot freighter to Florida. On July 13 another group hijacked the tugboat
13th of March. When the boat, laden with seventy-two passengers, was some miles
out at sea, it was intercepted by Cuban government vessels, which fired water
cannon and rammed the boat, causing it to sink. At least thirty-seven people
were killed (Human Rights Watch, 1994, p. 86). The survivors, who were later
picked up by the Cuban Coast Guard, were detained upon their return and the
men imprisoned. Despite this outcome, the hijacks continued. On August 5,
after a day of rioting, Castro appeared on television to warn that Cuban restrictions on sea departures would be lifted 'if the United States does not take quick
and sufficient measures to stop incentives for illegal exit' (Colomer, 2000,
p. 438). Following another hijack on August 8, in which a naval officer was
killed and the hijackers received assistance from the U.S. Coast Guard to reach
Florida, the Cuban government gave confidential instructions to the police not
to impede the rafters, who began to take to the seas in increasing numbers
(Perez, 1999, p. 202). Between August 12 and August 16, the U.S. Coast Guard
picked up 868 Cubans, and the one-day total on August 17 reached 537.

In public, and despite pressure from the Democratic governor of Florida,
Lawton Chiles, who faced elections in November, Clinton officials insisted that
everything was under control. At an August 18 afternoon press briefing, by
which time Chiles had already declared a state of emergency, a White House
press officer declared that the administration was legally bound to treat Cubans
differently from Haitians. If Cubans were 'picked up at sea by the Coast Guard,
or if they come to the United States, there is a law in place passed by Congress
that sets a certain standard for handling them' (Myers, 1994). Yet a principals'
meeting chaired by National Security Adviser Anthony Lake decided that –
rather than follow what had been Coast Guard practice since 1959 – Cubans
intercepted at sea should be taken to 'safe haven' outside the United States.
Attorney General Janet Reno announced the policy change that night.

At the following day's press conference, omitting any mention of the welcome previously extended to rafters and hijackers by Washington, Clinton

---

[10] Between 1985 and 1993, 25,723 people were intercepted by the Cuban authorities, while only
9,447 reached the United States. It is not known how many died at sea, and estimates vary wildly.
See Martínez, M. et al (1996) Los Balseros Cubanos (Havana: Editorial de Ciencias Sociales), pp. 34–35.

accused Castro of encouraging Cubans 'to take to the sea in unsafe vessels to escape their nation's internal problems... He is trying to export to the United States the political and economic crisis he has created in Cuba in defiance of the democratic tide flowing throughout this region.' He rejected one journalist's suggestion that he take 'a few small, albeit brave steps to negotiate a possible movement toward democracy with Cuba,' reiterating his support for the embargo. The 'illegal refugees' – a curious phrase – who reached land, Clinton promised, would be 'apprehended and... treated like others,' while those picked up at sea would be taken 'first to Guantanamo, where we will seek safe havens for them.' Above all, he stressed, no one wanted 'another Mariel boatlift.' (*Excerpts from President Clinton's News Conference*, 1994, pp. A10–11) For her part, Reno informed the press that the CAA 'is not relevant to entry into this country' (Reno, 1994). Yet neither press briefing satisfactorily explained how the 'safe haven' concept applied to the rafters. While Haitian detainees then at Guantanamo were awaiting an imminent resolution to the conflict back home, there was little sign that the Cuban situation would soon change.

The congressional reaction underwent a dramatic shift once it became evident that Havana was no longer obstructing departure. On August 10, Cuban American Representative Bob Menendez (Democrat, New Jersey) – precipitously forecasting the 'beginning of the end for the Castro dictatorship' – called on Cuban Americans to show 'restraint' and refrain from facilitating a new exodus which would release the pressure building up in Cuba (*Congressional Record*, 1994). Florida representatives called upon the Clinton administration to prevent a 'slow motion Mariel,' while Mazzoli and Michael Kopetski (Democrat, Oregon) asked for co-sponsors for their bill to repeal the CAA. The Guantanamo detention policy led to accusations of illegality from Newt Gingrich (Republican, Georgia), Menendez and the two other Cuban American representatives. In an attempt to mollify criticism, Clinton announced new measures to 'punish' Castro, presenting these as concessions to CANF chair Jorge Mas Canosa.[11]

As the huge search-and-rescue operation in the Florida Straits attracted growing numbers of rafters who continued to hope that somehow they would make it to Miami, Clinton officials announced that requirements for legal immigration would be relaxed. But while willing to discuss migration with Havana, the administration rejected all calls for a higher-level dialogue or a new approach. In

---

[11] These measures were along the lines of those suggested by Menendez in Congress – an end to remittances from Cubans in the United States to their relatives on the island, an end to family visits, save in exceptional circumstances, a removal of the general license for academic researchers and freelance journalists to visit Cuba, an expansion in U.S. efforts to broadcast to Cuba and a commitment to focus on Cuban human rights abuses in international fora.

response to an August 27 announcement of limited bilateral talks, the Cuban Coast Guard started patrolling beaches to stop children departing on unseaworthy rafts, and 20,000 Cuban Americans marched in protest in Miami.

Domestic Factors Complicate the U.S. Negotiating Stance

The Clinton administration did not have a strong hand going into the September talks. Keen to keep CANF onside, the administration ruled out the satisfaction of Cuban demands in any sphere other than migration. Clinton officials refused to discuss even the punitive measures introduced in response to the crisis. Nor was it possible, given the anti-immigrant mood in Florida and in Congress, to accept all would-be immigrants, as the Cubans suggested. Yet, though the administration was prepared to make few concessions in exchange for Cuban cooperation to impede the exit of rafters, Havana eventually – after more than ten thousand additional rafters had been intercepted – agreed to the original proposal of increased legal immigration. Whether this was because Castro now wanted to end a crisis that was hindering efforts to develop tourism, or because he hoped for future rewards from the administration, is unclear (Werlau, 1996, p. 480).

On September 9, the two governments issued a joint communiqué recognizing 'their common interest in preventing unsafe departures... which risk loss of human life' (U.S. Department of State Despatch 37, 1994). The United States was to accept a minimum of 20,000 Cubans a year, not including immediate relatives of U.S. citizens, and Cubans currently on the preference visa waiting list would be admitted as a one-off measure.[12] Both countries would take steps to stop hijacks and people-smuggling, Havana would prevent 'unsafe departures' by 'mainly persuasive methods,' and Cubans intercepted at sea would not be permitted to enter the United States but would be taken to safe haven. One further statement, that 'the United States has discontinued its practice of granting parole to all Cuban migrants who reach U.S. territory in irregular ways' could be interpreted as a commitment, but has not been read as such by Washington (Smith, 2002). Despite Reno's insistence in May 1995 that 'Cubans who reach the United States through irregular means will be placed in exclusion proceedings

---

[12] On October 12, 1994, the categories for expanded legal migration were announced. The 20,000 annual total was to be met by preference immigrants and broadly defined 'refugees,' at least 6,000 of whom would be admitted in the first year. In addition, public interest parole would be granted to unmarried adult children, as well as family members residing in the same household, of Cubans issued immigrant or refugee visas, and to Cubans who obtained visas in the special lottery.

and treated as are all illegal migrants from other countries, including giving them the opportunity to apply for asylum,' this has not been the case (Reno, 1995). Cubans who arrive by irregular means continue to be paroled into the country and are allowed to adjust under the CAA whether or not they qualify for asylum. In April 1999, INS Commissioner Doris Meissner issued a memorandum clarifying that this policy had not been superseded by the 1996 Immigration Act (U.S. Department of Justice, 1999). Almost as soon as the agreement had been reached, Cuban Americans began to campaign for the Guantanamo group to be allowed into the United States. Still hopeful of achieving their objective, very few Guantanamo rafters went home to apply for visas, despite the new lottery open to Cubans who neither qualified as refugees nor had U.S. relatives.

In the spring of 1995, by which time more than 10,000 detainees had been granted humanitarian parole by the United States, the Clinton administration considered how to deal with Guantanamo (where the remaining 20,000 were being held at a cost of $1 million a day) without encouraging more Cubans to take to sea. Rafter numbers had already started to increase in April, and Senator Bob Graham (Democrat, Florida) and Representative Porter Goss (Republican, Florida) returned from a visit to the base predicting riots in the camps and another exodus from Cuba during the summer. It was finally decided that the Guantanamo group – with very few exceptions – would be paroled into the United States, counting against three years' worth of Cuban visas.[13] In order to prevent another outflow, ultra-secret bilateral talks produced an agreement that future migrants intercepted at sea – 'wet-foots' – would henceforth be sent back to Cuba. Although the Cuban law penalizing illegal exit remained on the books, Havana promised that those returned by the U.S. Coast Guard would not be punished and would have access to U.S. Interests Section staff in the case of mistreatment. Only Cubans who appeared to have a genuine asylum claim would be taken to Guantanamo, where their cases would be assessed more fully. As stated above, however, those who reached land – 'dry-foots' – and those who arrived with non-immigrant visas, or even visa waivers, were still eligible for parole and adjustment under the CAA. This arbitrary distinction was clearly intended to appease Cuban Americans, who would have greeted any further alteration to established practice with a storm of criticism. Although Reno had acknowledged in August 1994 that the CAA did *not* require this treatment, the Clinton administration continued to behave as if it did. Nor was there any support from the

---

[13]   Only camp residents who failed to meet health or criminal record eligibility were excluded from this agreement and, due to the large number who already qualified under the administration's humanitarian parole program and were being progressively admitted, only 15,000 Cubans (5,000 per year) counted against the annual minimum of 20,000 visas.

administration for attempts by Senator Alan Simpson (Republican, Wyoming) to repeal the CAA. Evasion, not repeal, was the preferred approach.

When debate on Simpson's proposal came to a head in 1996, the CAA's chief champion was Senator Graham. He had acted pragmatically in supporting the Clinton administration's May 1995 migration agreement but marshaled some extremely misleading arguments in favor of the legislation as he responded to the interests of his Cuban American constituents (*Congressional Record*, 1996). Graham's amendment to preserve the CAA until Cuba had a 'democratically-elected government,' as defined by the exacting criteria of the Helms-Burton Act of 1996, was co-sponsored by the top recipients of Cuban American campaign contributions in the Senate and passed by 62 votes to 37. Yet during any kind of transition period, when there is no guarantee that Cuban authorities will have either the will or the capacity to restrict migration by sea, it is likely that tens if not hundreds of thousands of Cubans will set sail for Florida. Graham's successor, Senator Mel Martinez, acknowledged the danger of a new mass migration in August 2006, when hopes were high in Miami that Castro's temporary transfer of power to his brother Raul was finally the 'beginning of the end' for Castro (*Senator Martinez*, 2006).

Conclusion

Both the Clinton government's position on repeal, and the brief Senate debate on the issue demonstrated the difficulties in dealing with a migration issue when it is not high on the news agenda, and the only people likely to notice the change are those who will be adversely affected by it. The almost un-remarked inclusion of Cubans in the 1997 Nicaraguan Adjustment and Central American Relief Act (NACARA) is further testimony to the strength of the Cuban American lobby in Congress.[14] Senator Edward Kennedy's description of NACARA as 'unjust and shamefully discriminatory' is fully deserved (*Congressional Record*, 1997). In the full glare of media scrutiny, however, lobby power may be reduced. The Clinton administration's handling of the Elian Gonzalez affair suggests that a mass migration episode which could plausibly be attributed to executive mismanagement is to be avoided even at the cost of Cuban American displeasure. Although some hoped that the case of the small

---

[14]   The act provided some redress for Guatemalans and El Salvadorans badly affected by the 1996 Immigration Act, but allowed any Nicaraguan or Cuban continuously present in the United States since December 1, 1995 – including Cubans who had entered without INS inspection and therefore were ineligible under the CAA – to apply for adjustment to permanent residence.

boy rafter would expose the inequity of the CAA and lead to its repeal, it became a test not of the legislation but of adherence to the wet-foot/dry-foot compromise of May 1995. As a wet-foot, Elian should have been sent straight back to Cuba, but instead he became the center of both a U.S. media circus and a Cuban campaign for his return. The argument used by the Clinton administration to justify the seizure of the child from his Miami relatives, that it was a question of family rights, disguised fears that a disgruntled Castro might release another flood of rafters. Despite attempts by members of the Florida congressional delegation and others to grant Elian citizenship, defusing this threat took higher priority for the administration than satisfying the desires of Cuban Americans, who were almost unanimous in their belief that Elian should remain in the United States. However, while some commentators suggested that the case had damaged the standing of Cuban Americans in the United States – as their attacks on family, flag and police dismayed the general public – frontrunners for the Democratic nomination in 2004 took note of the Florida defeat in 2000 of Al Gore, who had tried unsuccessfully to distance himself from the administration's decisions on Elian. Both John Kerry and Howard Dean altered existing positions on the embargo in an attempt to woo back the Cuban American vote.

With regard to the CAA itself, the incentives for politicians to respond to Cuban American pressure have thus far proved more compelling than any interest they might have in consistent immigration legislation. Admittedly, the Cuban government's campaign against the 'murderous' Cuban Adjustment Act for inciting unsafe departures and people smuggling overstates the case, since these phenomena would hardly disappear in its absence. Nevertheless, it is clear that the act makes illegal migration from Cuba even more attractive than it would otherwise be. Only one member of a family need take any risks – the more vulnerable can wait behind for a visa under family reunification provisions of U.S. immigration law once the adventurer has adjusted to permanent residence. Furthermore, as currently interpreted, the CAA extends an open invitation for Cubans living elsewhere in the world to relocate to the United States without the formality of an immigrant visa – an aspect of the legislation which has received very little attention in the U.S. media. It may well be, however, that as national debate over immigration in general intensifies, the anomalies of the Cuban American situation will come under more critical scrutiny.

Beyond the difficulty of policymaking in the sphere of immigration, this case study demonstrates the increasing importance of intermestic issues such as migration in international relations. The generous initial reception of Cubans and the CAA itself were conceived in a climate of global Cold War. The CAA allowed Washington to demonstrate both humanitarian regard for Cubans fleeing communism and the superiority of the American system as the émigrés prospered.

The dominance of such overarching foreign policy concerns explains why so little consideration was given to the CAA as immigration legislation or indeed as part of an overall policy towards Cuba. While such concerns did not subside entirely in 1980, the Mariel boatlift shocked policymakers and the public into seeing Cuban migration less as a symbolic representation of Castro's iniquity and the humanity of the United States and more as a threat to U.S. borders. Furthermore, the fall-out from Mariel and the specter of a new 'immigration emergency,' which has loomed large in U.S. policy towards Cuba ever since, led Washington to provide Castro with special refugee processing in 1984 and special immigration processing in 1994. Both of these programs continue to reduce pressures for internal change and undercut the declared object of U.S. policy – a replacement of Castro's government. Although this line of argument has occasionally been voiced in academic and political circles (notably in the Western Hemisphere Subcommittee in 1991) it has not won much support among policymakers who have preferred more politically palatable explanations for Castro's survival, and who have silently sacrificed the prospect of a more effective policy towards Cuba for the sake of migration deterrence.

Bibliography

Bach, R. (1990) 'Immigration and U.S. Foreign Policy in Latin America and the Caribbean,' in R.W. Tucker, C. B. Keely and L. Wrigley (eds.), *Immigration and U.S. Foreign Policy* (Boulder: Westview).

Colomer, J.M. (2000) 'Exit, Voice, and Hostility in Cuba,' *International Migration Review* vol. 34, no. 2, pp. 423–43.

Congressional Record, October 6 1965, 26153.

Congressional Record, September 19, 1966a, 22913–17.

Congressional Record, September 19 1966b, 22917, 22920.

Congressional Record, October 21 1966c, 28608.

Congressional Record, June 4 1970, 18409–12

Congressional Record August 10 1994, 20894.

Congressional Record, April 29 1996, S4384.

Congressional Record, November 9 1997, S12264.

Dominguez, J. I. (1992) 'Cooperating with the Enemy? U.S. Immigration Policies Toward Cuba,' in Christopher Mitchell (ed.), *Western Hemisphere Immigration and United States Foreign Policy* (University Park, PA: Pennsylvania State University Press).

Eig, L. (1996) *Congressional Research Service Report for Congress: Cuban Adjustment Act of 1966* (Washington: Congressional Research Service, Library of Congress).

Engstrom, D.W. (1997) *Presidential Decision Making Adrift: The Carter Administration and the Mariel Boatlift* (Lanham: Rowman & Littlefield).

'Excerpts from President Clinton's News Conference' (1994) *Washington Post* (Federal News Service) (August 20).

Foreign Relations of the United States: 1958–1960. Washington, United States Government Printing Office, 1991, pp. 1010–1

Garcia, Maria Cristina (1996) *Havana USA: Cuban Exiles and Cuban Americans in South Florida, 1959–1994* (Berkeley: University of California Press).

Gillon, S. (2000) *"That's not what we meant to do" Reform and Its Unintended Consequences in 20th Century America* (New York: W.W. Norton).

Human Rights Watch (1994) *Human Rights Watch World Report 1995* (New York).

Jordan, W.J. (1959) 'Parley on Refugees Hears Plea to U.S. To Step Up Its Aid,' *New York Times* (May 23).

Keely, C.B. (1995) 'The Effects of International Migration on U.S. Foreign Policy,' in Teitelbaum and Weiner (eds.), *Threatened Peoples, Threatened Borders: World Migration and U.S. Policy* (New York: W.W. Norton).

Koh, H.H. (1995) 'America's Offshore Refugee Camps,' *University of Richmond Law Review*, vol. 29.

Loescher, G. and Scanlan, J.A. (1986) *Calculated Kindness: Refugees and America's Half-open Door* (New York: Free Press).

'Most in Poll Concerned Over Influx of Cubans' (1980) *New York Times* (May 18).

Myers, D. (1994) 'Press Briefing by Dee Dee Myers' (August 18), www.clintonfoundation.org/legacy/081894-press-briefing-by-dee-dee-myers.htm.

Nuccio, R.A. (1999) 'Cuba: A U.S. Perspective,' in R. N. Haass (ed.), *Transatlantic Tensions: The United States, Europe, and Problem Countries* (Washington: Brookings Institution Press).

Perez, L. (1999) 'The End of Exile: A New Era in U.S. Immigration Policy Toward Cuba,' in M.J. Castro (ed.), *Free Markets, Open Societies, Closed Borders?: Trends in International Migration and Immigration Policy in the Americas* (Miami: North/South Center Press)

Pew Hispanic Center, 'Cubans in the United States,' http://pewhispanic. org/files/factsheets/23.pdf

Reno, J. (1994) 'Press Briefing by Reno on Cuban Immigration Policy' (August 19), www.clintonfoundation.org/legacy/081994-press-briefing-by-reno-on-cuban-immigration-policy.htm.

Reno, J. et al. (1995) 'Press Briefing by Reno Et Al on Cuban Immigration and OK City' (May 2), www.clintonfoundation.org/legacy/050295-press-briefing-by-reno-et-al-on-cuban-immigration-and-ok-city.htm.

'Senator Martinez Holds a News Conference on Cuba' (2006) *Washington Post* (CQ Transcripts Wire) (August 1), www.washingtonpost.com.

Skoug, K. (1996) *The United States and Cuba under Reagan and Schultz: A Foreign Service Officer Reports* (Westport: Praeger).

Smith, W. S. (2002) 'U.S. Should Honor 1994 Agreement,' *South Florida Sun-Sentinel* (September 20).

Stepick, A. (1992) 'Unintended Consequences: Rejecting Haitian Boat People and Destabilizing Duvalier,' in Christopher Mitchell (ed.), *Western Hemisphere Immigration and United States Foreign Policy* (University Park, Pennsylvania: Pennsylvania State University Press).

Torres, M. (1999) *In the Land of Mirrors: Cuban Exile Politics in the United States* (Ann Arbor: University of Michigan Press).

U.S. Congress (1970) House, Committee on Foreign Affairs, Subcommittee on Inter-American Affairs, *Cuba and the Caribbean*, 91st Cong., 2nd sess., July 8, 9, 10, 13, 20, 27, 31 (August 3).

U.S. Congress (1971) Senate, Committee on the Judiciary, Subcommittee to Investigate the Administration of the Internal Security Act and Other Internal Security Laws, *Communist Threat to the United States through the Caribbean*, 92nd Cong., 1st sess., part 23 (February 25), p. 1650.

U.S. Congress (1977) House, Committee on the Judiciary, Subcommittee on Immigration, Citizenship, and International Law, *Indochina Refugees – Adjustment of Status*, 95th Cong., 1st sess. (May 25, June 2).

U.S. Congress (1981a) Senate, Committee on the Judiciary, Subcommittee on Immigration and Refugee Policy, *The United States as a Country of Mass First Asylum*, 97th Cong., 1st sess. (July 31).

U.S. Congress (1981b) House, Committee on the Judiciary, Subcommittee on Immigration, Refugees, and International Law, *Immigration Reform*, 97th Cong., 1st sess. (October 14, 15, 21, 26, 27, November 12, 17, 19).

U.S. Congress (1984) House, Committee on the Judiciary, Subcommittee on Immigration, Refugees and International Law, *Cuban-Haitian Adjustment*, 98th Cong., 2nd sess. (May 19).

U.S. Congress (1986) House, Committee on the Judiciary, Subcommittee on Immigration, Refugees and International Law, *Immigration and Naturalization Service*, 99th Cong., 2nd sess. (March 13).

U.S. Congress (1990) Senate, Committee on the Judiciary, *U.S. Refugee Programs for 1991*, 101st Cong., 2nd sess. (October 3).

U.S. Congress (1991a) House, Committee on Foreign Affairs, Subcommittees on Europe and the Middle East and on Western Hemisphere Affairs, *Cuba in a Changing World: The United States–Soviet–Cuban Triangle*, 102nd Cong., 1st sess. (April 30, June 11, July 31).

U.S. Congress (1991b) House, Committee on Foreign Affairs, Subcommittee on Western Hemisphere Affairs, *Recent Developments in United States-Cuban Relations: Immigration and Nuclear Power*, 102nd Cong., 1st sess. (June 5).

U.S. Congress (1991c) Senate, Committee on the Judiciary, *U.S. Refugee Programs for 1992: Annual Refugee Consultations*, 102nd Cong., 1st sess. (September 24).

U.S. Congress (1991d) House, Committee on the Judiciary, Subcommittee on International Law, Immigration, and Refugees, *Cuban and Haitian Immigration*, 102nd Cong., 1st sess. (November 20).

U.S. Congress (1992a) House, Committee on the Judiciary, Subcommittee on International Law, Immigration, and Refugees, *Immigration and Naturalization Housekeeping Amendments of 1992*, 102nd Cong., 2nd sess. (May 20).

U.S. Congress (1992b) Senate, Committee on the Judiciary, *U.S. Refugee Program for 1993: Annual Refugee Consultations*, 102nd Cong., 2nd sess. (July 23).

U.S. Congress (1993a) Senate, Select Committee on Intelligence, *Prospects for Democracy in Cuba*, 103rd Cong., 1st sess. (July 29).

U.S. Congress (1993b) Senate, Committee on the Judiciary, *U.S. Refugee Programs for 1994: Annual Refugee Consultations*, 103rd Cong., 1st sess. (September 23).

U.S. Congress (1994a) House, Committee on Ways and Means, Subcommittees on Select Revenue Measures and on Trade, *H.R. 22229, Free Trade with Cuba Act*, 103rd Cong., 2nd sess. (March 17).

U.S. Congress (1994b) House, Committee on the Judiciary, Subcommittee on International Law, Immigration, and Refugees, *Haitian Asylum-Seekers*, 103rd Cong., 2nd sess. (June 15).

U.S. Congress (1996) House, Committee on the Judiciary, Subcommittee No. 1, *Adjustment of Status for Cuban Refugees*, 89th Cong., 2nd sess. (August 10, 11, 17).

U.S. Department of Justice (1999) 'Clarification of Eligibility for Permanent Residence Under the Cuban Adjustment Act' (April 26), www.uscis.gov/propub/ProPubVAP.jsp?dockey=ba292568ad9164fee0202e446c1ae1fd.

U.S. Department of State Dispatch 37 (1994) 'U.S–Cuba Joint Communique on Migration', Sept 9, 1994, New York City: U.S. Department of State.

Walsh, E. (1981) 'Next Cuban Exodus May Not Get As Warm a Welcome as '80 Boatlift,' *Washington Post* (April 28).

Werlau, M. (1996) 'Foreign Investment in Cuba: The Limits of Commercial Engagement,' *Cuba in Transition*, vol. 6, pp. 456–95.

15

Urban Electoral Coalitions in an Age of Immigration: Time and Place in the 2001 and 2005 Los Angeles Mayoral Primaries

Raphael J. Sonenshein and Mark H. Drayse

Urban politics have been reshaped by large-scale immigration. What coalition patterns are likely to arise in an urban environment that has experienced dramatic demographic and political change?

This study examines the 2001 and 2005 Los Angeles mayoral primary elections. Such non-partisan primary elections provide effective vehicles to measure core coalitions of citywide candidates. Our dependent variable is voting for Antonio Villaraigosa, a liberal Latino candidate associated with the rise of immigrant communities, running against James Hahn, a white candidate with roots in the African American community. Three core coalitions appeared in the primaries. In both 2001 and 2005, Villaraigosa benefited from a stable coalition that combined Latino mobilization with some white liberal support. Hahn's core was among African Americans although that base had eroded for him by 2005. There was little evidence of a coalition of color in either primary election. A third alliance, a white-led moderate coalition drawing support from neither African Americans nor Hispanics, emerged unexpectedly as having great stability over both elections. If Los Angeles had partisan elections like New York City, candidates riding that coalition would have had a clear path into the general election by winning the Republican primary.

A significant spatial dimension emerged in the vote in both primary elections. Racial and ethnic bloc voting was reinforced by the residential concentrations of ethnic groups in Los Angeles. We conclude that space and time are related to each other in the construction and maintenance of political coalitions surrounding immigration.

Introduction to Coalitions

Coalitions are at the heart of all politics (Riker, 1962), but for racial and ethnic minorities in American cities, coalitions are especially poignant reminders of the need to multiply their limited political resources. Even as minority groups gain great numbers, they usually require the support of other groups to obtain the political resources needed to win a share of urban power.

Leading cities are no longer black and white, but are highly diverse due to immigration (Table 1). In an era of immigration, how will rising new groups forge the alliances necessary to win power and shape public policy? With the gap between immigration and citizenship, coalitions may be even more critical.

This article seeks to bring together political and geographical analysis in the understanding of urban coalitions in an era of immigration. O'Loughlin (2000) argues that many political scientists interested in contextual effects on political behavior equate geography with distance. A place-based perspective on politics combines analysis of macro-level processes that influence a city or region (e.g., migration and economic globalization) and micro-level processes (e.g., neighborhood formation and the emergence of place-based identities). Through a place-based analysis, O'Loughlin suggests, we can generate a more productive relationship between political science and geography.

We explore the development of urban coalitions by focusing on mayoral primary elections in 2001 and 2005 in the City of Los Angeles, a place that has been transformed by immigration. These particular elections offer an excellent case study of urban coalitions in an age of immigration. Like many cities in the American West, Los Angeles has non-partisan elections. In non-partisan primary election, all candidates for the same office run on a single ballot without party designations. If no candidate receives more than 50 percent of the primary vote, a runoff election is held between the top two finishers. In the primary, multiple possible coalitions can be explored. In non-partisan primary elections, voters have the opportunity to make sharply focused choices as compared to a two-person runoff that may require voters to select their second or third choice. Primary coalitions are likely to be somewhat more tightly constructed, therefore, than runoff coalitions.

Recent immigration has transformed the possibilities for electoral coalitions in Los Angeles. In 2000, 41 percent of Los Angeles residents were born in other countries. Nine in ten foreign-born Los Angeles residents were from three regions: Mexico and Central America, Pacific Asia and Southwest Asia. Mexicans are the largest national group, followed by Salvadorans, Guatemalans, Filipinos, and Koreans.

Figure 1 shows the spatial distribution of foreign-born residents in the City of Los Angeles in 2000. There are two major clusters of immigrants: (1) the central

Table 1: Ethnic and Foreign-Born Population of Major U.S. Gateway Cities, 2000
(Cities Ranked By Number of Foreign-Born Residents)

City	Total population	Foreign born		White (Not Hispanic)		Hispanic or Latino		African American		Asian	
		Number	Percent	Number	Percent	Number	Percent	Number	Percent	Number	Percent
New York	8,008,278	2,871,032	35.9	2,801,267	35.0	2,160,554	27.0	1,962,154	24.5	780,229	9.7
Los Angeles	3,694,820	1,512,720	40.9	1,099,188	29.7	1,719,073	46.5	401,986	10.9	364,850	9.9
Chicago	2,896,016	628,903	21.7	907,166	31.3	753,644	26.0	1,053,739	36.4	124,437	4.3
Houston	1,953,631	516,105	26.4	601,851	30.8	730,865	37.4	487,851	25.0	102,706	5.3
San Jose	894,943	329,757	36.8	322,534	36.0	269,989	30.2	29,495	3.3	238,378	26.6
San Diego	1,223,400	314,227	25.7	603,892	49.4	310,752	25.4	92,830	7.6	165,895	13.5
Dallas	1,188,580	290,436	24.4	410,777	34.6	422,587	35.6	304,824	25.6	31,626	2.7
San Francisco	776,733	285,541	36.8	338,909	43.6	109,504	14.1	58,791	7.6	238,173	30.7
Phoenix	1,321,045	257,325	19.5	736,844	55.8	449,972	34.1	63,756	4.8	23,453	1.9
Miami	362,470	215,739	59.5	42,897	11.8	238,351	65.8	72,190	19.9	2181	0.6
United States	281,421,906	32,107,889	11.1	194,552,774	69.1	35,305,818	12.5	33,947,837	12.1	10,123,169	3.6

Sources: U.S. Census Bureau, 2000 Census Summary File 1 (SF 1), Table P8 – Hispanic or Latino by race; Summary File 3 (SF 3), Table QT-P15 – country of birth, foreign-born population.

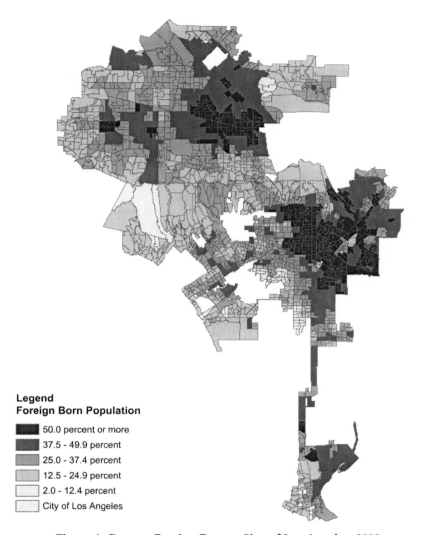

Figure 1: Percent Foreign Born – City of Los Angeles, 2000

core neighborhoods around Downtown Los Angeles; and (2) the eastern San Fernando Valley. Smaller concentrations of foreign-born citizens are located in the western San Fernando Valley and Westside Los Angeles. Figure 2 shows these major areas in Los Angeles. By 2000, the City of Los Angeles's population was 47 percent Latino, 11 percent African American, and 10 percent Asian American. Of the ten major gateway cities in the United States, only Miami had a higher proportion of Latinos and a lower proportion of whites (Table 1).

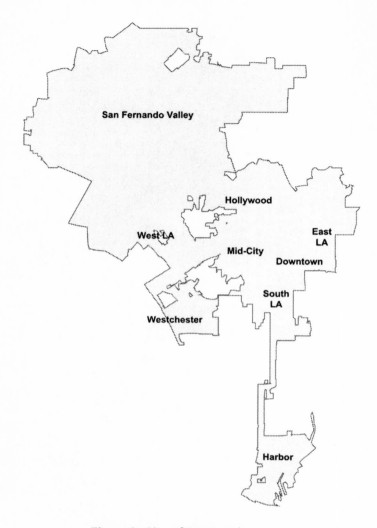

Figure 2: City of Los Angeles Areas

The City of Los Angeles is the core of the Los Angeles metropolitan area, one of the world's major immigrant gateways. The City rests within the County of Los Angeles. The City represents only 39 percent of the population of Los Angeles County, and 23 percent of the population of the five-county metropolitan area. Its ethnic composition is now very similar to that of the rest of Los Angeles County. Even the peripheral counties of Orange, Riverside, San Bernardino, and Ventura are experiencing a growing Latino population. The higher concentration of Latinos in the urban core gives them greater potential political power in the City of Los Angeles, compared with the periphery. While the City of Los Angeles was 47 percent Latino and 30 percent non-Hispanic white in 2000, the peripheral counties were 34 percent Latino and 44 percent white. On the other hand, possible confusion between residence in the City or County of Los Angeles may reduce ease of political participation.

Between 1973 and 1993, Los Angeles politics was dominated by a biracial coalition of African Americans and Jewish liberals. Built around Mayor Tom Bradley, this coalition featured strong interracial leadership ties and a high degree of coherence and coordination over a long period of time (Sonenshein, 1993). After a devastating riot in 1992 and a painful economic recession (a consequence of the post-Cold War restructuring of the aerospace industry in Los Angeles), Los Angeles voters turned in a more conservative direction, electing Republican businessman Richard Riordan as mayor in 1993 over a liberal Asian American who sought to construct a more diverse version of the Bradley coalition. While Riordan's victory marked the defeat of the liberal biracial coalition, the two sides in the election were quite similar to the long-standing pattern of blacks and white liberals on one side, and white conservatives on the other. Eight years later, with the rise of new immigrant-based voting blocs, the stable structure of Los Angeles coalitions underwent major changes.

In 2001, the campaign for an open mayoral seat generated new types of competing coalitions in this demographically, politically and geographically transformed city. In 1993, Latinos cast 8 percent of all votes in the mayoral primary election; by 2005, Latinos represented 25 percent of all votes cast in the runoff election (Sonenshein and Pinkus, 2005). The rise of Latinos in Los Angeles politics was dramatized by Antonio Villaraigosa's campaigns to become the first Latino mayor of Los Angeles in over 130 years. His main opponent in both elections was fellow Democrat James K. Hahn, son of Kenneth Hahn, who was a white politician with tremendous appeal to African Americans because of his long service representing South Los Angeles on the City Council and the County Board of Supervisors.

In the 2001 primary, Hahn parlayed his strong base in the African American community into a place in the runoff election against Villaraigosa, who drew votes from Latinos and white liberals. Villaraigosa finished first in the primary, and Hahn edged out a white Republican, Steven Soboroff, for the second spot. In the runoff, Hahn ran a very harsh campaign against the Latino candidate and won a decisive victory (Sonenshein and Pinkus, 2002). But after making some decisions that cost him politically with his base (such as firing African American police chief Bernard Parks, and fighting a secession measure backed by white conservatives), Hahn was in trouble by the 2005 election.

The 2005 mayoral election developed as one of those relatively rare urban rematches that helps illuminate emerging coalition patterns. The two mayoral races in Los Angeles between Sam Yorty and Tom Bradley in 1969 and 1973 generated an explosion of research (e.g., Hahn and Almy, 1971; Halley et al., 1976; Hahnet al., 1976; McPhail, 1971; Maullin, 1971; O'Loughlin and Berg, 1977) that helped define the emerging lines of biracial politics. The Rudolph Giuliani versus David Dinkins elections of 1989 and 1993 provided data for the analysis of coalition patterns over time in New York City (Mollenkopf, 1994).

Hahn, a vulnerable incumbent, faced strong challenges not only from Villaraigosa, but also from Bob Hertzberg, a prominent Jewish politician from the San Fernando Valley; former police chief Bernard C. Parks, now a city councilman; and Richard Alarcón, a Latino state senator from the east Valley area that is a major node of foreign-born residents.

The candidates faced each other in a non-partisan primary on March 8, 2005. Villaraigosa finished first with 33 percent of the votes, to Hahn's second place finish of 24 percent. A runoff election between the two top finishers was set for May 17, 2005. Villaraigosa won easily.

What types of coalitions developed in the 2001 and 2005 mayoral elections? How did place-based factors influence the development of electoral coalitions in these elections?

Urban Coalitions in Time and Place

Political scientists analyze coalitions in terms of the interests and beliefs of the members of the groups, the motivations and actions of group leaders and how these factors influence coalitions over time. Political geographers seek to understand how localized processes of social interaction, the historical and geographical development of cities (internally and as a part of larger scale systems), and the development of place-based identities influence urban politics and coalitions. We hope, in this chapter, to join the two approaches together. In our analysis, urban coalitions exist as political packages of interests, ideologies, and leaders that cannot be separated from the places within which groups live. As immigration continues to reshape the neighborhoods of American cities, we expect that this approach will help illuminate evolving coalition behavior.

The political analysis of urban coalitions grows out of the African American urban experience in the latter half of the twentieth century. The theory of minority political incorporation developed by Browning, Marshall, and Tabb (2001) established that, for African Americans, winning political power required a major mobilization of their group combined with the backing of white liberals (Browning et al., 2001; Sonenshein, 1993).

The rise of African Americans was marked by consistency in coalition patterns. In virtually every city with a black candidate for mayor, support came from highly mobilized black voters and supportive white liberals, usually younger and better educated than other whites, and to some degree from Latinos (Pettigrew, 1971). Opposition to these interracial coalitions emerged from conservative whites, as racial division and ideological disputes tinged with racial overtones increasingly framed urban and even national politics (Edsall and Edsall, 1991). In other words, urban coalitions were consistently patterned, both racially and ideologically.

While racial ideology among whites and mobilization of African Americans were consistent elements of minority incorporation, the interplay of interests and leadership played important roles as well. Where liberal whites and African Americans had conflicts of interest, and where interracial leadership did not develop to surmount those conflicts, biracial coalitions failed, as in New York City (Sonenshein, 1993). Conversely, strong biracial leadership prevented potential interest conflicts from jeopardizing the biracial coalition, as in Los Angeles (Sonenshein, 1993).

Political structure helped influence the outcome of these forces. One of the most critical structural differences between American cities is whether elections are held on a partisan or non-partisan basis. Non-partisan elections are prevalent in Western U.S. cities where the progressive reform movement had its greatest impact. Party designations do not appear on the ballot, and there are no party primaries. In more traditional cities in the East and Midwest, partisan election structures are more common and are often associated with strong party organizations. In a partisan city with huge public sector resources like New York City, there are greater opportunities for conflict over public goods than in a non-partisan city with fewer public resources like Los Angeles and this structural difference helped shape coalition politics (Sonenshein, 1993).

In exploring coalitions over time, we draw on the work of Barbara Hinckley. Rather than a set of isolated transactions between self-interested political actors, Hinckley (1981) saw coalitions as built over time between and among trusting partners. Hinckley complained that much of the study of coalitions involved single games played one time:

> [I]n sharp contrast, real political games occur in time. They occur as one of an experienced or expected series, where players know each other and expect to meet and play again. Bargaining is shaped by historical alliances. Deception is constrained by the risk of retaliation. The single-game situation, then deliberately excludes the temporal context within which political activity occurs. (1981, p.66)

Coalition partners operate within a framework of human choices:

> [W]ith both a past and a future, players may reason that a stable
> coalition will bring the greatest return and prefer to stay with a past
> partner, despite present resource distribution, to maximize returns
> over all games. Thus in any one game in a series, the past choice of
> partner may be the best predictor of present coalition formation. (68)

Real political games occur in time *and* place. The types of coalitions that develop are conditioned by the geographical context of urban politics. Agnew (2002) argues that three dimensions of place influence voting behavior: place as (1) a locale or setting for everyday life; (2) a location situated within regional, national, and global systems of places, and (3) a source of identity and sense of place.

Voting decisions occur in a spatial context that has an independent effect on voting. As Agnew (2002) notes, the 'identities, values, and preferences that inspire particular kinds of political action are embedded in the places... where people live their lives' (2001, p. 3). Two identical voters are less likely to make the same voting decisions if they live in different neighborhoods, because of spatial differences in context and information. These differences can be due to the diffusion of information horizontally, through formal and informal social interaction, and vertically, through dissemination by mass media or activities of political campaigns and other organizations. Whom individuals talk to, what media they read and listen to, and how they perceive their locale affect, how they think and how they vote (Books and Prysby, 1991; Burbank, 1995; Cox, 1969; Johnston et al., 2001).

Place-based political analysis, which meets the practical needs of electoral politics, may in turn contribute to a contextual effect on voting. For example, political campaigns and organizations may target certain neighborhoods for canvassing and leafleting during an election campaign because that is the most effective way to reach concentrations of favorable voters, in turn influencing the information available to voters (Huckfeldt and Sprague, 1995). And the fact that voters were contacted at all may be due to their residence in a neighborhood that generally favors the contacting party or candidate.

A neighborhood's situation with respect to processes operating at larger scales is also important. For example, gateway cities are being transformed by immigration, but in different ways. The proximity of gateway cities to other countries influences migration flows; for example, most immigrants to Los Angeles are Mexican, while most immigrants to Miami are Cuban. Processes of economic globalization are contributing to uneven spatial patterns of prosperity, stagnation, and decline within and between cities that can affect voters' attitudes and behavior.

Place-based identity can be an important spatial influence on voting behavior. Individuals may develop emotional attachments to their perceived neighborhoods or communities that transcend bonds of ethnicity or class. Neighborhood residents may vote for a candidate whom they think will address local concerns that they perceive through observation of their environment (Johnston et al., 2004). The strength of place-based identity and its influence on voting are likely to be stronger in stable neighborhoods with higher proportions of long-term residents, which is likely to increase both the extent and strength of social interaction and the depth of attachment to place on the part of local residents (Books and Prysby, 1991). In some cases, place-based identity may be the main explanation for political behavior. For example, O'Loughlin, Witmer, and Ledwith (2002) show that the most important factor explaining neighborhood votes in 1999 and 2001 for the Democratic Socialists (PDS) in Berlin was location east or west of the old Berlin Wall. The destruction of the Wall and the reunification of Berlin have not erased the distinct ideologies and concerns of residents in eastern Berlin, who have a regional party to promote their interests.

The foundation of a coalition is bloc voting – for example, common voting preferences by members of an ethnic group, who are usually concentrated in space due to processes of ethnic residential differentiation. Bloc voting is strengthened by local social interaction and place-based identities. To the extent that different groups have converging interests, we may see the development of voting coalitions that may or may not persist through time. Gimpel and Tam Cho (2004) analyzed township-based voting in three presidential elections in New England. They found that European ethnic groups (e.g., Italians, Irish and French Canadians) exhibited distinct patterns of spatial concentration that helped to explain common voting behavior. Although common voting was not as strong in these assimilated groups as it was for other ethnic groups, it was still significant.

The context of politics varies between cities, and place-based factors influence politics within cities. The relative size, political cohesiveness and electoral strength of particular ethnic groups will vary from city to city. Urban coalitions will be influenced by place-based factors including ethnic residential geography, the relationship between municipal boundaries and the geographic distribution of ethnic groups, and the development of place-based identities. A place-based analysis of voting behavior, which is the basis of this study, provides an ideal way to bring together political and geographical interpretations of urban coalition behavior in an age of immigration.

New Immigration, New Coalitions

Massive immigration to American cities now has the potential to shatter the orderly structure of urban racial and ethnic politics built around the racialized politics of the African American movement for incorporation. Cities in which politics could easily be framed as black and white may crack open, with the building blocks of coalitions re-forming with different partners. The presence of potential new coalition partners and competitors, mostly Latinos and Asian Americans, has changed the equation of local politics. The impact on non-immigrant communities of the presence of large numbers of immigrants may even create the conditions for both pro-immigrant and anti-immigrant coalitions in a manner parallel to the racialization of urban politics in an earlier time.

What was once a relatively simple (if often extremely difficult) politics of black and white has now become a much more complex, diffuse, multidimensional politics of diversity. As Mollenkopf (2001, p. 136) has written: 'forming a dominant political coalition will depend on who can construct broader and more complex coalitions than the relatively simple biracial ones.'

Despite the difficulty of generating a new understanding of multiracial coalitions, there is some urgency to the task. Even though the foreign born and their children represent growing shares of the population, and comprise very significant blocs in major cities and states, their political incorporation will be severely limited without coalition development and the mobilization efforts that may be spurred by participation in coalitions.

We present here several possible permutations of coalition partnerships. The list is not meant to be exhaustive, but to be suggestive. We will explore the applicability of these models to two successive primary mayoral elections in Los Angeles in 2001 and 2005.

Coalitions of Color

One possibility for a coalition involving immigrant communities is a coalition of color. Given the primacy of racial divisions in American politics, racial identity has considerable importance. It is common, for instance, to keep track of when a city or a state becomes 'minority majority,' with the assumption that this will represent a political turning point. Interest in such a statistic makes sense if we assume a commonality between communities of color. To the extent that non-white groups share political attitudes based on their racial identity, there might be strong reasons to coalesce.

Whether or not coalitions of color develop is likely to be influenced by such factors as how groups define themselves on racial and ethnic dimensions, and whether or not there are conflicts or commonalities of interests and beliefs. Kaufmann (2003), for instance, found that African Americans felt closer to Latinos than Latinos did to blacks. One of the most ambitious efforts, by McClain and others (1990, 1998), examined both interest and ideology in multi-city studies of African Americans and Latinos. The study found numerous cities in which political interests of the two groups were opposed, some where they were not, and variety in group attitudes as well.

The construction of pan-ethnic identities and alliances is a complex process mediated by the interaction of diverse groups of people in specific historical-geographical settings (Saito, 1998). The development of distinct ethnic neighborhoods limits inter-group interaction and may reinforce the potential for conflict. Ethnic neighborhood transition is another source of conflict. For example, economic and political competition between African Americans and Latinos in South Los Angeles obstructs efforts to build coalitions (Johnson and Oliver, 1989). Similar struggles between African Americans and Korean Americans present challenges to liberal coalitions (Park and Park, 2001). Some African Americans, feeling threatened by new immigrant populations, might be drawn into anti-immigrant coalitions.

Alliance with Liberal Whites

On racial matters, there are profound differences between liberal and conservative whites (Browning et al., 2001). The rise of new immigrant communities may engender similar divisions. It would be possible that ideological lines among whites that involve race may also involve ethnicity and immigration. Some research suggests that those whites who are liberal on race are also liberal on immigration, and that the same consistency exists for white conservatives (Sears et al., 1995). If this is correct, then liberal whites should, all other things being equal, be more likely to join a coalition with immigrant communities.

Independent Power Politics

The go-it-alone strategy depends upon numbers and mobilization which are so great that alliance with other groups is not required. The circumstances for such a strategy for immigrant communities may be rare, especially given the lag between immigration and citizenship. However, for one immigrant group, Cuban Americans in Miami, the independent power politics strategy seems to have been feasible. With surging numbers, high citizenship and significant economic resources, Cuban Americans were able to rapidly win political power to the exclusion of native whites and African Americans (Grenier and Castro, 2001; Warren and Moreno, 2001).

The increasingly diverse populations of large American cities mitigate the feasibility of a go-it-alone strategy in most cases. This is more likely to occur in smaller cities in an urban region dominated by one ethnic group, such as Monterey Park and other Chinese 'ethnoburbs' in Los Angeles County's San Gabriel Valley (Li, 1998), and South Gate and other overwhelmingly Latino cities in Southeast Los Angeles County.

Alliance of Immigrant Communities

Another way to sort groups in an age of immigration is to place immigrant communities on one side, and native communities on the other. For example, Latinos and Asian Americans, both communities with very large percentages of immigrants, might find common ground against native whites and African Americans. They might be particularly likely to join forces when public issues involving immigrant rights take center stage.

Conservative Coalitions with Native Whites

Immigrant communities might find themselves in a conservative coalition with conservative native whites. Especially where there is conflict or competition with African Americans, who are politically distant from white conservatives, there might be a basis for alliance. The presumed conservative values of immigrant communities make them a desirable target for conservative political forces.

In both New York City and Los Angeles, white Republican mayoral candidates have been successful in winning the support of Latinos and Asian Americans, while facing strong opposition from African Americans (Sleeper, 1993; Sonenshein et al., 1996). Rudolph Giuliani was elected in 1993 and re-elected in 1997 with white backing combined with significant support from Latinos. In 2001, another Republican, Michael Bloomberg, won a considerable share of Latino votes even against a Latino candidate, Frederick Ferrer. Los Angeles Mayor Richard Riordan, another Republican, won more than 60 percent of Latino voters in his 1997 re-election campaign against a liberal Asian American candidate.

In 2001, Orlando Sanchez, a conservative Republican Cuban American seeking the Houston mayoralty, won 72 percent of the Hispanic vote in a mostly Mexican American Democratic community and a large share of white

Republican votes to nearly unseat African American Democratic mayor Lee Brown. However, when Sanchez ran again four years later against a white Democrat, Bill White, he received a smaller share of the Hispanic vote than he had in 2001 and lost by a large majority.

Data and Methods

Our study builds on a precinct-level database for the City of Los Angeles that we developed and previously applied to several Los Angeles elections. The precinct-level voting data include votes in the 2001 and 2005 primaries, and data from the Statewide Database (the State of California's redistricting database maintained by the Institute for Governmental Studies at the University of California, Berkeley), including number of registered Democrats and Republicans, and ethnic breakdowns of registered voters and the voting age population. Contextual data from the 2000 census by census tract were linked with the precinct-level data. Census variables include race, ethnicity, income, educational attainment, foreign-born and citizenship status.

We first tabulated votes for four groups of precincts that represented different ethnic blocs. The City of Los Angeles has more than 1,700 precincts, with an average population of 2,087. The precinct groups were identified based on the combined census and voting data. The precinct groups represented combinations of ethnicity and partisanship. These included Latino, white Democratic, white Republican and African American blocs (Figure 3).

Latino precincts are those in which at least 50 percent of the registered voters are Latinos. The actual Latino population is higher, especially in areas with high concentrations of Latinos without U.S. citizenship. White Democratic precincts are at least 70 percent white, with at least 52 percent of registered voters being Democratic. This equals the share of all registered voters in the City of Los Angeles stating a Democratic Party preference. White Republican precincts are at least 70 percent white and 40 percent Republican. This is 1.5 times the concentration of Republicans in the city. African American precincts have a population at least 50 percent African American. African American areas accounted for 125 precincts, while by contrast there were only eight precincts in which Asian Americans represented at least 50 percent of the population despite the fact that each group represents one-tenth of the city's population. This clearly shows the much higher degree of residential concentration of African Americans in Los Angeles compared with Asian Americans (Sonenshein, 2005).

White Republicans are located in the city's periphery – the foothills of the San Fernando Valley, Malibu and Pacific Palisades, Westchester, and San Pedro –

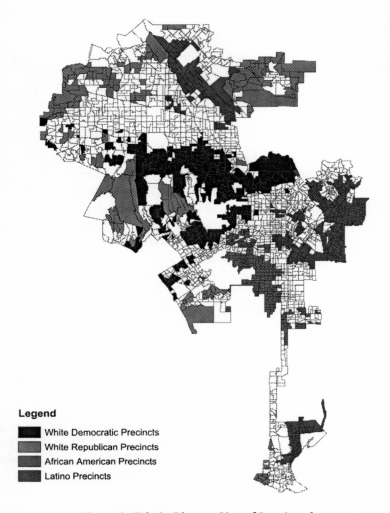

Legend

White Democratic Precincts
White Republican Precincts
African American Precincts
Latino Precincts

Figure 3: Ethnic Blocs – City of Los Angeles

while white Democrats are more centrally located in the southeast San Fernando Valley, the Hollywood Hills and Westside Los Angeles.

Next, we mapped the voting results for the 2001 and 2005 primaries. These maps allow us to visualize bloc voting and voting coalitions for different candidates. We mapped the votes for Villaraigosa and Hahn in the two elections. We also mapped the vote for Soboroff in 2001 and Hertzberg in 2005, two white candidates who sought to appeal largely to white voters.

In order to test for stability and coherence of coalitions over time, we utilized spatial correlation and spatial regression. Spatial autocorrelation is based on the relationship between the vote for a candidate in a precinct, and the average of the vote for that candidate in neighboring precincts. This analysis computes Moran's I statistic, which indicates spatial autocorrelation (a clustering of values). High Moran's I values (near 1.0) denote a high degree of spatial autocorrelation, confirming evidence of bloc voting obtained by mapping the voting results. We also generated results for serial correlation, which tests the relationship between the votes for a candidate in the same precinct in two elections.

These two tests can be combined into a space–time correlation, which relates the vote for a candidate in a precinct in an election with the average vote for the candidate in neighboring precincts in a later election. Thus, while spatial auto-correlation tests the degree to which a candidate's votes are spatially concentrated in any one election, the other two measures help to show the persistence in support for a candidate in place and over time (Anselin, 2005).

Finally, we analyzed voting results using spatial regression models. Using the GeoDa program developed by Luc Anselin, we began with ordinary least squares regression to identify the expected spatial autocorrelation in the values of the dependent variables. We developed models for the Villaraigosa vote in 2001 and 2005, the Hahn vote in 2001 and 2005, the Soboroff vote in 2001 and the Hertzberg vote in 2005.

Regression diagnostics suggested that both the spatial lag and spatial error models were appropriate alternatives to OLS regression. We show the results for the spatial lag models, which incorporate a row-standardized weights matrix based on queen contiguity of precincts. A significant spatial lag coefficient indicates that a candidate's vote in a precinct is partly explained by his or her vote in surrounding precincts, suggesting that place-based factors are influencing voting behavior.

Given aggregate voting data reported at the precinct level, what inferences can we make regarding voting behavior? The standard solution is ecological inference, in which independent variables (e.g., percent foreign born, percent Latino) are regressed against a dependent variable (e.g., vote for Candidate A). However, this method is vulnerable to the inherent ecological fallacy of inferring individual behavior from spatially aggregated data. Spatial autocorrelation is another unavoidable limitation in ecological analysis, since most variables of interest are not randomly distributed across space.

Nonetheless, in recent years there has been a renewed interest in ecological analysis in the social sciences (King, 1997; Palmquist, 2001; Sui et al., 2000; Tam Cho, 2001). When available, individual voter surveys can be used to strengthen ecological analysis (Johnston and Pattie, 2003). The problem of spatial autocor-relation can be reduced by using geographically weighted regressions, as we do here with the spatial lag models. This method assigns higher weights to data in neighboring areas, and lower weights to areas further away (Fotheringham, 2000).

Despite its recognized limitations, ecological analysis has advantages over surveys. Voter surveys have significant limitations in a city with a large, diverse electorate such as Los Angeles. Surveys are subject to statistical problems in inferring group behavior from individual-level sample data, including sampling errors and the reliability of self-reported data. They are very problematic in trying to understand social phenomena occurring across numerous spatial districts, such as the roughly 1700 voting precincts in the City of Los Angeles. Mollenkopf, Olson, and Ross (2001) indicated that ecological analysis 'can provide insights that elude sample surveys because it analyzes the entire universe of activity, allows consideration of the role of place and context, and does not rely on self-reported behavior' (2001, p. 50).

Results and Analysis

The 2001 and 2005 City of Los Angeles mayoral primaries provide a striking comparison. Antonio Villaraigosa won a plurality in each primary, followed by James Hahn (Table 2). Moderate Jewish candidates from the San Fernando Valley, one a Republican and one a Democrat, came in third in each primary. Hertzberg narrowly missed the opportunity to face Villaraigosa in the May 2005 runoff election. In terms of ethnicity, the main difference in the primaries was the presence of former Los Angeles police chief Bernard Parks, an African American, in the 2005 primary.

Table 2: Official results: City of Los Angeles' mayoral primaries, 2001 and 2005

2001 primary			2005 primary		
Candidate	Votes	Percent	Candidate	Votes	Percent
Antonio Villaraigosa	152,031	30.4	Antonio Villaraigosa	136,242	33.1
James Hahn	125,139	25.0	James Hahn	97,049	23.6
Steve Soboroff	106,189	21.3	Bob Hertzberg	90,495	22.0
Joel Wachs	55,016	11.0	Bernard Parks	55,808	13.6
Xavier Becerra	29,851	6.0	Richard Alarcón	14,815	3.6
Other candidates	31,415	6.3	Other candidates	17,195	4.2
Total votes for mayor	499,641	100.0	Total votes for mayor	411,604	100.0

Source: City of Los Angeles, Office of the City Clerk, Election Division.

Table 3: Voter preference by ethnic bloc: 2001 mayoral primary

Ethnic bloc	Villaraigosa		Hahn		Soboroff		Wachs	
	Number	Percent	Number	Percent	Number	Percent	Number	Percent
Latino precincts	28,707	55.6	4,750	9.2	3,085	6.0	1,559	3.0
White Democratic precincts	17,026	28.9	8,871	15.1	17,302	29.4	10,752	18.3
White Republican precincts	4,023	16.4	4,153	16.9	10,176	41.5	3,852	15.7
Black precincts	5,922	16.2	26,222	71.9	839	2.3	441	1.2
City total	152,031	30.4	125,139	25.0	106,189	21.3	55,016	11.0

Table 4: Voter preference by ethnic bloc: 2005 mayoral primary

Ethnic bloc	Villaraigosa		Hahn		Hertzberg		Parks	
	Number	Percent	Number	Percent	Number	Percent	Number	Percent
Latino precincts	23,622	63.2	5,298	14.2	1,763	4.7	1,934	5.2
White Democratic precincts	14,157	29.5	10,078	21.0	17,262	35.9	2,476	5.2
White Republican precincts	4,458	18.1	6,302	25.6	9,189	37.3	1,812	7.4
Black precincts	5,807	22.0	4,056	15.4	667	2.5	14,353	54.5
City total	124,561	33.1	89,189	23.6	83,420	22.0	50,341	13.6

In the 2001 primary, Villaraigosa received strong support in Latino precincts, far outpacing Hahn (Table 3). Hahn's core strength was in the African American neighborhoods. Soboroff and Joel Wachs (another moderate independent) ran strongly in white precincts, with the Democratic bloc showing a stronger preference for Wachs, and the Republican precincts displaying stronger support for Soboroff. Overall, voters in white neighborhoods were split among several candidates.

Villaraigosa's support in Latino precincts was even greater in 2005 (Table 4). Hertzberg ran strongly in white precincts, receiving a similar share of the vote in both Democratic and Republican blocs. Parks siphoned off much of Hahn's African American vote. Hahn's strongest support came from white Republican precincts, but even here his showing was relatively unimpressive. In geographic terms, Hahn appeared to be a man without a base except in his own harbor neighborhoods in the south, strong enough everywhere to inch into the runoff, but not potent enough anywhere to have a springboard for further growth.

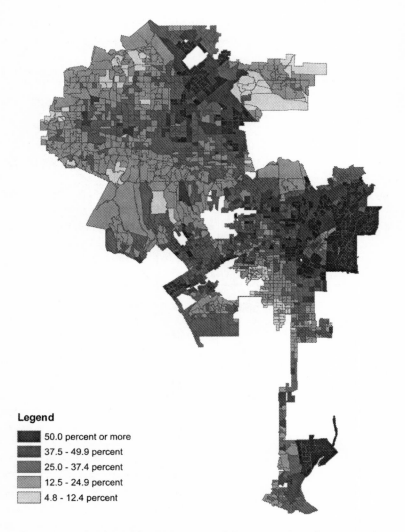

Legend

■	50.0 percent or more
■	37.5 - 49.9 percent
■	25.0 - 37.4 percent
■	12.5 - 24.9 percent
□	4.8 - 12.4 percent

Figure 4: Vote for Villaraigosa, 2001 Primary – City of Los Angeles

Clearly, Villaraigosa managed to unify Latino voters to a significant degree in both primary elections. The ability of Latino candidates to unify and mobilize the Latino vote is undoubtedly a necessary factor in coalition development, and its success cannot be assumed in advance simply because of ethnicity.

The spatial pattern of the vote, related to ethnic bloc voting, is shown in Figures 4 through 9. Villaraigosa's core neighborhoods are in the heavily Latino central core, eastern San Fernando Valley, and Wilmington. Despite the

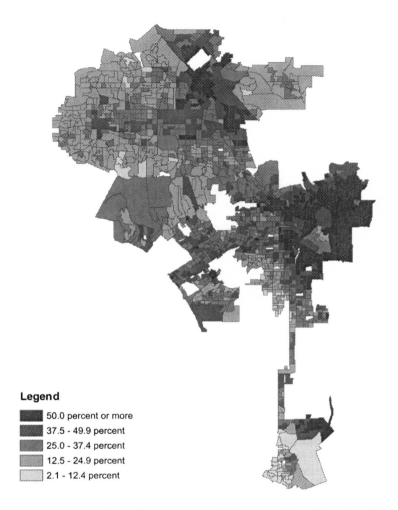

Legend

- 50.0 percent or more
- 37.5 - 49.9 percent
- 25.0 - 37.4 percent
- 12.5 - 24.9 percent
- 2.1 - 12.4 percent

Figure 5: Vote for Villaraigosa, 2005 Primary – City of Los Angeles

geographic and sociological distance between Latino communities on the urban eastside and the more suburban East Valley, Villaraigosa was equally strong in both areas. Significant support was also seen in the Westside of Los Angeles, along the Venice Boulevard corridor, which has a growing Latino population, and in some white Democratic neighborhoods.

Soboroff and Hertzberg received strong support across white precincts, but especially in white Republican precincts. The western and southern San Fernando Valley, Hollywood–Santa Monica uplands, and Westchester showed

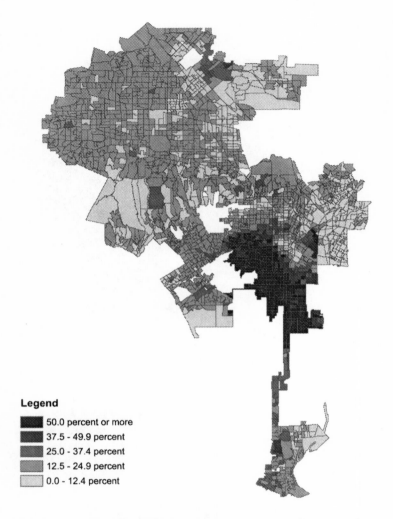

Legend

■ 50.0 percent or more
■ 37.5 - 49.9 percent
■ 25.0 - 37.4 percent
■ 12.5 - 24.9 percent
□ 0.0 - 12.4 percent

Figure 6: Vote for Hahn, 2001 Primary – City of Los Angeles

strong support for these candidates. The map of Hahn's 2001 vote reveals the strong support he received in African American neighborhoods in South Los Angeles and Mid-City – support that evaporated in 2005, when Hahn's home area of San Pedro was the core of his support.

The stability of electoral coalitions was evaluated by comparing regression coefficients for three pairs of models: (1) Villaraigosa 2001 and 2005; (2) Hahn 2001 and 2005; and (3) Soboroff 2001 and Hertzberg 2005. In the spatial regression models, the dependent variables were the percent of votes for Villaraigosa in

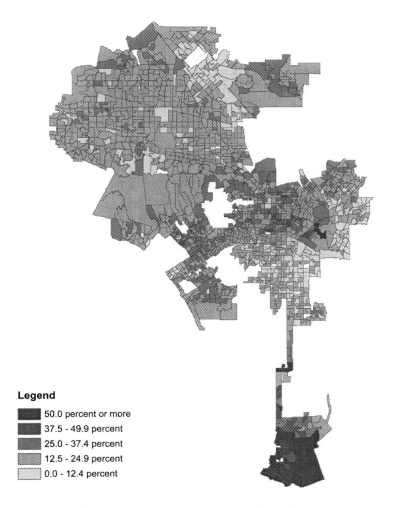

Legend

- 50.0 percent or more
- 37.5 - 49.9 percent
- 25.0 - 37.4 percent
- 12.5 - 24.9 percent
- 0.0 - 12.4 percent

Figure 7: Vote for Hahn, 2005 Primary – City of Los Angeles

2001 and 2005, Hahn in 2001 and 2005, Soboroff in 2001 and Hertzberg in 2005. Explanatory variables in the models included indicators of *ethnic and immigrant population concentration* (percent foreign born, percent recent immigrants, percent Latino, percent Asian American, percent non-Hispanic white, percent Jewish, percent African American), *education and income* (percent with college degree, median household income), and *partisanship* (percent Democratic and percent Republican). We also included a dummy variable for location in the San Fernando Valley to test whether or not Valley residence had an independent

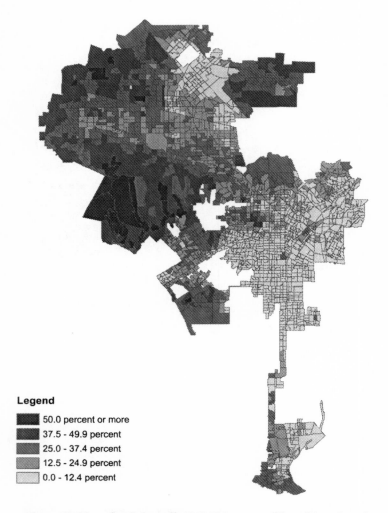

Figure 8: Vote for Soboroff, 2001 Primary – City of Los Angeles

effect on voting in the mayoral primaries, especially in light of the recent Valley secession movement. To complement the spatial regression analysis, we also derived measures of serial and space–time correlation of the 2001 and 2005 votes.

Following Anselin (2005), we first ran classic ordinary least squares regression models. Diagnostic tests showed clear evidence of spatial autocorrelation (Table 5). In each of the six models, the Moran's I, Lagrange Multiplier (lag), and Lagrange Multiplier (error) were highly significant – the dependent variable and the error term for each precinct were correlated with values in neighboring

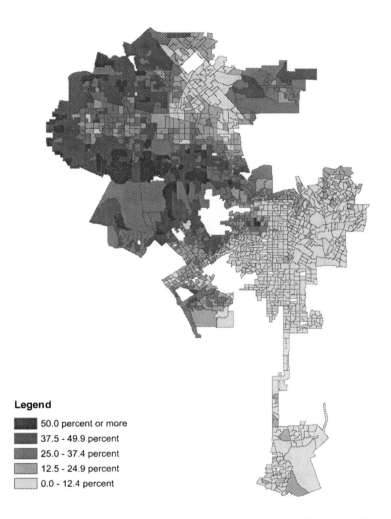

Legend

■ 50.0 percent or more
■ 37.5 - 49.9 percent
▨ 25.0 - 37.4 percent
▨ 12.5 - 24.9 percent
□ 0.0 - 12.4 percent

Figure 9: Vote for Hertzberg, 2005 Primary – City of Los Angeles

precincts. We elected to run the spatial lag model, in which the spatially autoregressive coefficient is the weighted dependent variable.

In both elections, Villaraigosa's support is strongly associated with concentrations of Latino voters (Table 6). Other ethnic variables are negatively associated with support for Villaraigosa, especially in 2005 when percent white, percent Jewish, percent black, and percent Asian are all statistically significant and negatively associated with the vote for Villaraigosa. In both primary elections, there was a strong Jewish candidate and either a strong black candidate (Parks in 2005)

Table 5: Row-standardized Moran's I City of Los Angeles mayoral primaries, 2001 and 2005

	Moran's I	Z-value
Villaraigosa 2005	0.347	16.121
Villaraigosa 2001	0.184	8.650
Hahn 2005	0.721	33.255
Hahn 2001	0.304	14.167
Hertzberg 2005	0.439	20.317
Soboroff 2001	0.181	8.508

or a candidate strongly preferred by blacks (Hahn in 2001). While this suggests that Villaraigosa was riding a go-it-alone Latino coalition, his support was also positively related to educational attainment. This indicates the possibility of a Latino-white liberal coalition. The persistence of Villaraigosa's Latino-based coalition between 2001 and 2005 was also shown by the spatial correlation analysis. The serial correlation of the precinct-to-precinct vote for Villaraigosa was 0.961, and the space-time correlation between neighboring precincts in 2001 and each precinct in 2005 was 0.684.

By contrast, there is relatively little consistency between Hahn's support over the two elections. While Hahn's primary coalition in 2001 could be described as a black-led mobilization, in 2005 he received most of his primary support from white conservatives. An additional element of support for Hahn in 2005 were Asian voters – as percent Asian increases, support for Hahn increases. This was the strongest coefficient in the model of Hahn's 2005 vote.

In particular, we can see the evaporation of Hahn's support in the black community based in South Los Angeles. The correlation between the Hahn votes in 2001 and 2005 was very weak: the Moran's I for the Hahn vote was -0.11 for space-time correlation, and the slope of the serial correlation between the two votes was -0.14. There was nonetheless some spatial structure evident in Hahn's vote, as is shown by the spatial autocorrelation tests in the regression models and the high Moran's I in the 2005 vote.

Hahn made certain key decisions that alienated both elements of his coalition. Both came in 2002, when he fired African American police chief Bernard Parks, and when he led the campaign against Valley secession. This is an unusual political phenomenon, in which a skilled, experienced politician essentially loses his entire electoral coalition within one year after taking office.

We suggest that there is something in the nature of inter-group coalitions that helps explain this rather bizarre phenomenon. Interests and ideology mediated

Table 6: Spatial lag models City of Los Angeles mayoral primaries, 2001 and 2005

	Villaraigosa 2005	Villaraigosa 2001	Hahn 2005	Hahn 2001	Hertzberg 2005	Soboroff 2001
Constant	47.904***	81.642***	-8.964	-17.405***	5.489	1.745
Spatial lag (weighted dependent variable)	0.116***	0.083***	0.531***	0.120***	0.322***	0.104***
Percent Democratic	-0.121*	-0.502***	0.221***	0.734***	-0.110*	-0.142***
Percent Republican	-0.654***	-1.097***	0.170**	0.524***	0.337***	0.602***
Percent Latino	0.311***	0.330***	-0.055*	-0.446***	-0.021	0.001
Percent White	-0.101***	-0.025	0.133***	-0.171***	0.064**	0.072***
Percent Black	-0.312***	-0.343***	-0.029	0.353***	0.031	0.070***
Percent Asian (Pacific Asia)	-0.115*	-0.053	0.379***	0.073*	-0.041	-0.007
Percent Jewish	-0.302***	-0.312***	-0.375***	-0.307***	0.848***	0.471***
Percent with college degree	0.217***	0.189***	-0.016	-0.044***	-0.010***	-0.012
Median household income (in thousands)	0.013	-0.004	-0.018	0.002	0.021	0.057***
Citizens-percent foreign born	-0.015	-0.129***	-0.020	0.017	0.033	-0.031
Percent recent immigrants	0.112**	0.003	0.046	-0.078**	-0.037	0.149***
Valley	-0.212	0.048	0.134	0.428	0.877**	0.268
Log likelihood	-4622.160	-4249.770	-4763.940	-4121.550	-4371.870	-3985.360
N	1,399	1,399	1,399	1,399	1,399	1,399

*$p < 0.05$, **$p < 0.01$, ***$p < 0.001$.

by leadership tie coalitions together (Sonenshein, 1993). In 2001, African Americans and white Republicans seemed to share a concern about the changing city and its demographics, and helped elect Hahn. But on a host of issues, they had little in common and much in conflict. On each of the controversial decisions Hahn had to make, his coalition allies were in opposite camps. Privatization of city services and secession were most heatedly opposed by African Americans and supported by white Republicans. African Americans suspected that the police union, long a darling of white conservatives, was behind the Parks firing. No group supported secession as actively as white conservatives, and no block opposed secession as vociferously as blacks. Thus the high stakes of the choices Hahn had to make exemplified the strangeness of his coalition. Time did not knit it together; rather, it tore it apart. When Sam Yorty had a similar coalition in 1961, he simply chose white conservatives, abandoned African Americans, and rode that right-wing alliance to victory (Sonenshein, 1993). Hahn had less choice in a city with a far smaller proportion of whites or African Americans in the electorate.

We also examined consistency in the third coalition, the white alliance that third-place candidates built in 2001 and 2005, in each case nearly winning a spot in the runoff. We compared the vote for Soboroff in 2001 with the vote for Hertzberg in 2005. The vote for both candidates is positively related to percent white, percent Republican, percent Jewish, and income. This suggests a voting bloc united by ethnicity and class – upper income whites. The Hertzberg vote was the only one in which the Valley variable was significant. This suggests that place-based identity may have been a factor in this race, as many Valley voters coalesced behind a moderate Democrat from their side of the Santa Monica Mountains.

The spatial correlations of the Soboroff and Hertzberg votes were especially strong. The Moran's I was 0.771 for space–time correlation, and 0.845 for spatial autocorrelation, even higher than the respective values for the Villaraigosa votes. Such consistency is particularly striking because they were both losing candidates who failed to make the runoff and because they were different politicians, and even of different political parties.

The coalition patterns that emerged in these two elections present a tri-polar framework for a city election system that only has room for two seats at the runoff table.

In terms of the coalition models presented above, each primary coalition can be seen as a potential base from which to build a citywide majority alliance in a runoff election. With three strong contending primary candidates, the two runoff candidates would seek to monopolize the vote of the third candidate and others who do not make the runoff. At the same time, any primary candidate who has broad and deep support in one community can pre-empt other candidates from poaching in those neighborhoods. Villaraigosa's strength in Latino neighborhoods marked those areas as off-limits to other candidates, as did Hahn's 2001 support in African American neighborhoods. Had either failed to make the runoff, though, another candidate would have tried to pick up those core neighborhoods.

Hahn's option in 2001 was to start with African American voters and get to a majority where votes were available to him, which meant white Republicans and conservatives especially in the San Fernando Valley. Villaraigosa's chance was to expand his base among white liberals, especially on the westside of the city. While Hahn's alliance of blacks and white conservatives prevailed in 2001, it proved highly unstable, and collapsed in 2005. The surprisingly stable white base behind the third-place candidates in the two mayoral primaries could become the basis for a majority coalition but only if such candidates could greatly increase their appeal to either African American or Latino voters as happened in New York City's recent mayoral elections.

Coalitions of color would face some significant obstacles, but because of the fluctuating stance of African Americans, could be formed on a pragmatic basis. The potential for white candidates to win minority support or for minority candidates to win white support would depend heavily on the ideological identification of the candidates.

Conclusion and Implications

In the new world of urban politics in an age of immigration, new coalition patterns are likely to rise and fall, and perhaps rise again. Immigrant communities are not a unitary political phenomena, as African Americans had been to a significant degree. Politics may become a framework for 'mix and match' coalitions.

As this process of coalition formation, collapse, and re-formation occurs in numerous cities, it will be valuable to study it in time and place. A single election measured by surveys will not yield enough information either about durability or about the geographic shape of community attachments.

In 2001, a coalition of Latinos and white liberals emerged in the Villaraigosa campaign, and was ultimately defeated by Hahn's unlikely voting alliance of African Americans and white conservatives (Austin et al., 2004; Sonenshein and Pinkus, 2002). As surprising as the winning alliance was in light of the long-standing political hostility between African Americans and white conservatives, it raised the possibility that the vote against Villaraigosa reflected the new role of African Americans as threatened political 'ins' in the face of the rising immigrant political participation. The coincidence of voting between these two groups had been foreshadowed in 1994 when Proposition 187, a statewide ballot measure to deny public benefits to undocumented residents, won overwhelming support from white conservatives and was backed by half of African Americans (Meyerson, 2001).

This preliminary examination of two successive Los Angeles mayoral primary elections with similar electoral dynamics reveals that our tendency to treat winning or competitive coalitions as the most significant may have limitations. In this case, only one of the two candidates who advanced to the runoff election had a durable, deeply rooted coalition. Villaraigosa's coalition was consistent in place and time. Hahn's was utterly transformed and unstable. By contrast, the 'losing' candidates, Soboroff in 2001 and Hertzberg in 2005, rode a consistent and potentially durable alliance to third-place finishes. The analysis of coalitions in place and time leads to the prediction that the white-led coalition in some form will play an ongoing role in the coalition process of Los Angeles politics; in other political circumstances, it may have a chance to win.

Here political structure plays a role. If Los Angeles had partisan elections, as does New York City, the Hertzberg–Soboroff base (similar to that of previous Mayor Richard Riordan) would be enhanced by the availability of a Republican primary. All the Democrats would be forced to compete against each other in the Democratic primary. Once in the general election, one on one, the Republican nominee would have visibility and a real chance to win. The overlap between and among Republicans Riordan and Soboroff, and Democrat Hertzberg, suggests that there is a center-right leaning base, which anyone with the appropriate credentials can tap. In this light, it is less surprising that a New York City Democrat, Michael Bloomberg, saw the value of the Republican primary in 2001, and switched his party registration to Republican in the election year. And today, he is New York City's mayor, easily re-elected in 2005.

The fragility of the Hahn coalition suggests that the factors of ideology and interest can still be profitably examined in the era of immigration. African Americans are certainly conflicted about immigration, a stance that emerges in polls and in voting on such measures as Proposition 187. Yet, the most durable opposition to immigrant advancement is most likely to come not from African Americans whose interests are threatened by immigrants, but rather from white conservatives whose opposition to immigrant advancement may be more ideological. Furthermore, the interest and ideological conflicts between African Americans and conservative whites are about as wide as any political gap in the nation, and are unlikely to be bridged simply by common reservations about immigration.

Our research also suggests the fragility of the African American political position in an age of immigration. After years of uphill struggle to win political incorporation at city hall, African Americans have found themselves playing catch-up in a new era of diverse city politics. Forging alliances with available groups on a self-interested, pragmatic basis will inevitably be a key part of the new black politics, but building stable, long-term coalitions will be a challenging task indeed. Evidence of a community in flux could be found in the New York City mayoral election of 2005, in which African Americans were divided among themselves when faced with a choice between Republican incumbent Michael Bloomberg and Latino Democratic challenger Frederick Ferrer (Fernandez, 2005).

Though weakening, the situation of African Americans is still considerably stronger than that of Asian Americans who also make up about 10 percent of the city's population. Asian Americans have yet to become a significant force in Los Angeles politics in part due to the lag between immigration and citizenship. Asian Americans are also divided by ethnicity and neighborhood, limiting the development of a cohesive pan-Asian bloc. In Los Angeles, Filipinos are the largest Asian ethnic group, comprising 27 percent of the city's Asian population. Distinct communities of Korean, Chinese, and Japanese descent, and numerous smaller groups, also reside in the city. This is very different from the situation of Latinos. Latinos represent almost half of the city's population, and are dominated by one national group, Mexicans, who represent 64 percent of the city's Latinos. Despite considerable success in winning offices in the State Legislature from constituencies outside Los Angeles, Asian Americans in the city have been virtually shut out of public office (Sonenshein, 2005).

An implication of this research is that time and place provide useful ways to augment the knowledge we have already accumulated about urban coalitions in an age of immigration through surveys, interviews and voting analysis. This approach will hopefully help add a ground-level dimension tested over time to the tools of coalition analysis. The further linkage between urban politics and geography will undoubtedly benefit both fields.

Acknowledgments

This article is based on a paper presented at the 2005 annual meeting of the Western Political Science Association. The research for this paper is being funded by a grant to the authors from the Russell Sage Foundation. We thank Janelle Wong, Ali Modarres, and Jason McDaniel for comments on an earlier version of this article. We also acknowledge the editor of *Political Geography* and anonymous referees for their constructive comments.

Reprinted from Sonenshein, Raphael J. and Drayse, Mark H. (2006) 'Urban electoral coalitions in an age of immigration: Time and place in the 2001 and 2005 Los Angeles mayoral primaries,' *Political Geography* vol. 25, pp. 570–595, Copyright (2006), with permission from Elsevier.

Bibliography

Agnew, J. (2002) *Place and Politics in Modern Italy* (Chicago: University of Chicago Press).

Anselin, L. (2005) *Exploring Spatial Data with GeoDa: A Workbook* (Urbana-Champaign: University of Illinois, Department of Geography and Center for Spatially Integrated Social Science).

Austin, S., Wright, D. and Middleton IV, R.T. (2004) 'The Limitations of the Deracialization Concept in the 2001 Los Angeles Mayoral Election,' *Political Research Quarterly*, vol. 57, no. 2, pp. 283–93.

Books, J. W. and Prysby, C. L. (1991) *Political Behavior and the Local Context* (New York: Praeger).

Browning, R., Marshall, D. R. and Tabb, D. (eds.) (2001) *Racial Politics in American Cities* (3rd ed.) (New York: Longman).

Burbank, M. (1995) 'The Psychological Basis of Contextual Effects,' *Political Geography*, vol. 14, pp. 621–35.

Cox, K.R. (1969) 'The Voting Decision in Spatial Context,' *Progress in Geography*, vol. 1, no. 2, pp. 81–117.

Edsall, T.B. and Edsall, M.D. (1991) *Chain Reaction: The Impact of Race, Rights, and Taxes on American Politics* (New York: W.W. Norton).

Fernandez, M. (2005) 'Black Voters, No Longer a Bloc, Are Up For Grabs In Mayor's Race,' *New York Times* (September 26).

Fotheringham, A. S. (2000) 'A Bluffer's Guide to a Solution to the Ecological Inference Problem,' *Annals of the Association of American Geographers*, vol. 90, pp. 582–86.

Gimpel, J. G. and Tam Cho, W.K. (2004) 'The Persistence of White Ethnicity in New England,' *Political Geography*, vol. 23, pp. 987–1008.

Grenier, G. J. and Castro, M. (2001). Blacks and Cubans in Miami: the Negative consequences of the Cuban Enclave on Ethnic Relations, in M. Jones-Correa (ed.), *Governing American Cities*, pp. 137–57. (New York: Russell Sage Foundation).

Hahn, H. and Almy, T. (1971) 'Ethnic Politics and Racial Issues: Voting in Los Angeles,' *Western Political Quarterly*, vol. 24, pp. 719–730.

Hahn, H., Klingman, D. and Pachon, H. C. (1976) 'Cleavages, Coalitions, and the Black Candidate: the Los Angeles Mayoralty Elections of 1969 and 1973,' *Western Political Quarterly*, vol. 29, pp. 521–30.

Halley, R. M., Acock, A. C. and Greene, T. (1976) 'Ethnicity and Social Class: Voting in the Los Angeles Municipal Elections,' *Western Political Quarterly*, vol. 29, pp. 507–20.

Hinckley, B. (1981) *Coalitions and Politics* (New York: Harcourt Brace Jovanovich).

Huckfeldt, R. and Sprague, J. (1995) *Citizens, Politics, and Social Communication* (Cambridge and New York: Cambridge University Press).

Johnson J. Jr., and Oliver, M. (1989) 'Interethnic Minority Conflict in Urban America: the Effects of Economic and Social Dislocations,' *Urban Geography*, vol. 10, pp. 449–63.

Johnston, R.J. and Pattie, C.J. (2003) 'Evaluating an Entropy-Maximizing Solution to the Ecological Inference Problem: Split-Ticket Voting in New Zealand, 1999,' *Geographical Analysis,* vol. 3, pp. 1–23.

Johnston, R.J., Pattie, C.J., Dorling, D.F.L., MacAllister, I., Tunstall, H. and Rossiter, D.J. (2001) 'Social Locations, Spatial Locations and Voting at the 1997 British General Election: Evaluating the Sources of Conservative Support,' *Political Geography*, vol. 20, pp. 85–111.

Johnston, R.J., Jones, K., Sarker, R., Propper, C., Burgess, S. and Bolster, A. (2004) 'Party Support and the Neighbourhood Effect: Spatial Polarisation of the British Electorate, 1991–2001,' *Political Geography*, vol. 23, pp. 367–402.

Kaufmann, K.M. (2003) 'Minority Empowerment in Denver, Colorado: How Black and Latino Voters Respond to Each Other's Political Leadership,' *Political Science Quarterly*, vol. 118, pp. 107–25.

King, G. (1997) *On a Solution to the Ecological Inference Problem: Reconstructing Individual Behavior From Aggregate Data* (Princeton: Princeton University Press).

Li, W. (1998) 'Los Angeles's Chinese Ethnoburb: From Ethnic Service Center to Global Economy Outpost,' *Urban Geography*, vol. 19, pp. 502–17.

Maullin, R. (1971) 'Los Angeles Liberalism,' *Trans-Action*, vol. 8, pp. 40–50.

McClain, P. and Karnig, A.K. (1990) 'Black and Hispanic Socioeconomic and Political Competition,' *American Political Science Review*, vol. 84, pp. 535–45.

McClain, P. and Tauber, S.C. (1998) 'Black and Latino Socioeconomic and Political Competition: Has a Decade Made a Difference?' *American Politics Quarterly*, vol. 26, pp. 237–52.

McPhail, I. R. (1971) 'The Vote for Mayor in Los Angeles in 1969,' *Annals of the Association of American Geographers*, vol. 6, pp. 744–58.

Meyerson, H. (2001) 'A House Divided,' *LA Weekly* (June), pp. 15–21.

Mollenkopf, J. (1994) *A Phoenix in the Ashes: The Rise and Fall of the Koch Coalition in New York City* (Princeton: Princeton University Press).

Mollenkopf, J. (2001) 'New York: Still the Great Anomaly,' in R. Browning, D. Tabb and D. Marshall (eds.), *Racial Politics in American Cities* (3rd ed.) (New York: Longman), pp. 115–41.

Mollenkopf, J., Olson, D. and Ross, T. (2001) 'Immigrant Political Participation in New York and Los Angeles,' in M. Jones-Correa (ed.), *Governing American Cities* (New York: Russell Sage Foundation), pp. 17–70.

O'Loughlin, J. (2000) 'Geography as Space and Geography as Place: the Divide Between Political Science and Political Geography,' *Geopolitics*, vol. 5, pp. 126–37.

O'Loughlin, J. and Berg, D.E. (1977) 'The Election of Black Mayors, 1969 and 1973,' *Annals of the Association of American Geographers*, vol. 67, pp. 223–38.

O'Loughlin, J., Witmer, F. and Ledwith, V. (2002) 'Location and Political Choice in Post-Unification Berlin: Explaining the PDS (Party of Democratic Socialism) Vote, 1999 and 2001,' *Eurasian Geography and Economics,* vol. 43, pp. 349–82.

Palmquist, B. (2001) 'Unlocking the Aggregate Data Past: Which Key Fits?,' *Historical Methods*, vol. 34, pp. 159–69.

Park, E. J. W. and Park, J. S. W. (2001) 'Korean Americans and the Crisis of the Liberal Coalition: Immigrants and Politics in Los Angeles,' in M. Jones-Correa (ed.), *Governing American cities: Inter-Ethnic Coalitions, Competition, and Conflict* (New York: Russell Sage Foundation), pp. 91–108.

Pettigrew, T. F. (1971) 'When a Black Candidate Runs For Mayor: Race and Voting Behavior,' in H. Hahn (ed.), *People and Politics in Urban Society* (Beverly Hills: Sage), pp. 99–105.

Riker, W. (1962) *The Theory of Political Coalitions* (New Haven: Yale University Press).

Sears, D.O., Citrin, J. and van Laar, C. (1995) 'Black Exceptionalism in a Multicultural Society,' Paper presented at the annual meeting of the American Political Science Association, Chicago (August 31–September 3).

Saito, L. T. (1998) *Race and Politics: Asian Americans, Latinos, and Whites in a Los Angeles Suburb* (Urbana and Chicago: University of Illinois Press).

Sleeper, J. (1993) 'The End of the Rainbow? America's Changing Urban Politics,' *The New Republic* (November), pp. 20–25.

Sonenshein, R. J. (1993) *Politics in Black and White: Race and Power in Los Angeles* (Princeton: Princeton University Press).

Sonenshein, R. J. (2005) 'Do Asian Americans Count in LA?,' *Los Angeles Times* (February 28).

Sonenshein, R. J. and Pinkus, S. (2002) 'The Dynamics of Latino Incorporation: the 2001 Los Angeles Mayoral Election as Seen in *Los Angeles Times* Polls,' *PS: Political Science and Politics*, vol. 35, no. 1 (March), pp. 67–74.

Sonenshein, R. J. and Pinkus, S. (2005) 'Latino Incorporation Reaches the Urban Summit: How Antonio Villaraigosa Won the 2005 Los Angeles Mayor's Race,' *PS: Political Science and Politics*, vol. 38, no. 4 (October), pp. 713–21.

Sonenshein, R.J., Schockman, H.E. and DeLeon, R. (1996) 'Urban Conservatism in an Age of Diversity: a Comparative Analysis of the Mayoralties of San Francisco's Frank Jordan and Los Angeles's Richard Riordan,' Paper presented at the 1996 annual meeting of the Western Political Science Association, San Francisco, CA.

Sui, D., Fotheringham, A.S., Anselin, L., O'Loughlin, J. and King, G. (2000) 'Book Review Forum: On a Solution to the Ecological Inference Problem: Reconstructing Individual Behavior From Aggregate Data, by Gary King,' *Annals of the Association of American Geographers*, vol. 90, pp. 579–606.

Tam Cho, W.K. (2001) 'Latent Groups and Cross-Level References,' *Electoral Studies*, vol. 20, pp. 243–63.

Warren, C.L. and Moreno, D.V. (2001) 'Power Without a Program: Hispanic Incorporation in Miami,' in R. Browning, D.R. Marshall and D. Tabb (eds.), *Racial Politics in American Cities* (3rd ed.) (New York: Longman), pp. 281–308.

16

California and the Third Great Demographic Transition: Immigrant Incorporation, Ethnic Change, and Population Aging, 1970–2030*

Dowell Myers

California today stands at a crossroads. In many ways the state is in transition, because it is passing from one era to another. The crossroads entails both demographic change and political decisions about the change. How we work this out will have some importance beyond the state, because California is leading the nation, even the world, in a great transition that will become commonplace as we traverse the twenty-first century.

In the old version of California, circa 1970, the population was largely native-born and of native-born parentage. The state was also largely composed of white residents who were non-Hispanic in origin. And the state was full of baby boomers and their parents, and later the baby boomers as parents themselves. Today, in the new version of California, all is becoming reversed: already half of the state's population is comprised of immigrants and their children. And the non-Hispanic white population has fallen to less than half of the state total, marking the first time a large state has ceased to hold a white majority. Just ahead, the Baby Boom generation will be retiring, and the weight of a senior population will suddenly grow heavy. A rising new generation, predominantly Latino, will be replacing them in the work force. California's voters reside in the present, making so many judgments based on self-interest, but more often reacting to preferences from the past rather than desires about a likely future.

This paper surveys the demographic transition in California and highlights its ethnic divisions. Part of a much larger project, the emphasis here is on the political demography that characterizes a great imbalance between voting power and population size. The problem that will need to be resolved in California is not solely that a minority of the population is dominating the electorate. Rather, the

---

* This essay draws on material that appears in Myers, Dowell, *Immigrants and Boomers: Forging a New Social Contract for the Future of America* (New York: Russell Sage Foundation, 2007).

problem is that the voting majority may not share the political preferences of the incoming population majority. Differences in preference include the value placed on immigrants, fears about population growth, and desires to increase taxes and spending.

In essence, we find that California's outgoing majority, although already a minority of the population, still holds a two-thirds electoral majority. And it uses that majority to vote policies that shape the future to be borne by the incoming majority. These policies appear more devoted to the past, or designed to avoid burdens in the present, than they are aimed at the best interests of the state and its residents in the future ahead. At the crossroads of California's transition, the state's residents, as well as elected officials, need to effect a shift in their thinking so that they can make decisions that are more rewarding in the long term. This chapter aims to advance that understanding.

A Third Great Transition

The changes underway in California and other developed regions of the globe are so momentous that they can be characterized as a great transition. Twice before in the world we have faced transitions of such sweeping magnitude. The notion of a demographic transition describes an intimate transformation of population change, involving family formation, race, and life and death. Originally, a classic theory of demographic transition was developed to explain the population explosion first commencing in Western and Northern Europe around 1800, and thereafter spreading to other countries around the world. Improvements in nutrition and public health broke the longstanding balance of high fertility and high mortality. When mortality was reduced, other social customs continued as before and fertility remained high. There followed nearly a century of rapid population growth, with population overflow emigrating to other countries, until norms for childbearing finally adjusted. As these norms took hold, a prolonged decline in fertility rates ensued. Thus the nations of Western and Northern Europe transitioned from a regime of high mortality and high fertility to one with low mortality balanced by low fertility (and low outmigration). The U.S. and other nations around the globe have followed a similar transition path, although the least developed nations are only just beginning to reduce fertility to the new level that balances their reduced mortality. The example of Mexico illustrates change so rapid that few Americans have yet realized it. As recently as 1970, the Mexican total fertility rate was 6.8 births per woman, but by 2000 that had declined to 2.4, just above the replacement level of 2.1 lifetime births per woman.

More recently, in the 1960s, a second demographic transition was identified as emerging in Europe and the United States. First proposed by Dutch demographers Ron Lesthaeghe and Dirk J. van de Kaa, this transition theory describes a bundle of changes in family formation behavior, sexuality, and economic roles for women.[1] Accompanying the economic transformation to a post-industrial economy, as well as the low fertility phase of the first demographic revolution, the new emphasis was on individual self-fulfillment. This transition was grounded in new attitudes about intimate behaviors and gender equality, as indicated in sharp changes in public opinion data after about 1965. [2] If the first demographic transition emphasized rebalancing of fertility and mortality, under the second transition reproduction has become underemphasized and fertility has fallen so low as to create a growing 'birth dearth.' As of 2005, not a single European nation had a replacement level of fertility. The highest were Albania and Ireland at 2.0, but most nations were near the level of Italy and Germany, which have a total fertility rate of 1.3 (Population Reference Bureau, 2005). Countries of east Asia have joined in the fertility plunge, registering only 1.2 or 1.3 births per women in Japan, Taiwan and South Korea. The mega-countries of China and India have fertility rates of 1.6 and 3.0, respectively, but throughout Africa fertility rates are roughly five or six births per woman. The imbalance in fertility between the developed and developing nations poses a grave problem, with some countries brimming with young people while others are aging and suffer a lack of workers (Kent and Haub, 2005). If the stresses of the first demographic transition pushed migrants out of Europe, those of the second demographic transitions are pulling migrants in.

---

[1]   The second transition was first identified by Ron Lesthaeghe and Dirk J. van de Kaa in a publication in the Dutch language in 1986. Publications in English soon followed: van de Kaa, Dirk J. (1987) 'Europe's Second Demographic Transition,' *Population Bulletin* vol. 42 (March), pp. 3–57, and Lesthaeghe, Ron (1995) 'The Second Demographic Transition in Western Countries: An Interpretation,' in Karen Oppenheim Mason and An-Magritt Jensen (eds.), *Gender and Family Change in Industrialized Countries* (Oxford: Clarendon Press), pp. 17–62. A more recent summary can be found in Coleman, David (2005) 'Facing the 21st century: New Developments, Continuing Problems,' in Miroslav Macura, Alphonse L. MacDonald and Werner Haug (eds.), *The New Demographic Regime: Population Challenges and Policy Responses* (New York and Geneva: United Nations), pp. 11–43.
[2]   Van de Kaa (1987) Table 1, cites numerous evidence from Dutch surveys, among them that the percent of residents agreeing that voluntary childlessness of a couple is acceptable increased from 27 percent in 1966 to 60 percent in 1970 and 79 percent in 1980. Also, the percent of residents agreeing labor force participation of a married women with school-age children is acceptable rose from 17 percent in 1965 to 56 percent in 1970. Similar evidence in the case of the U.S. is reported by Reynolds Farley in a chapter titled, 'The 1960s: A Turning Point in How We View Race, Gender, and Sexuality' in *The New American Reality* (New York: Russell Sage), pp. 22–63.

Within the U.S., there is considerable variation in the extent of the second demographic transition, and in fact the states are widely split. A recent study by Ron Lesthaeghe and Lisa Neidert found that California is among the leading states in the U.S. with respect to such indicators as delayed fertility, never married status, and cohabitation. [3] The authors also found a striking political association between states with low prevalence of second demographic transition indicators and a high voting percentage for George W. Bush in the last presidential election. This is indicated by a very strong negative correlation of -0.88, '...to our knowledge one of the highest spatial correlations between demographic and voting behavior on record' (Lesthaeghe and Neidert, 2006).

Today, a third demographic transition, with a very different character, is now underway in the developed world. Building for some time, we can begin to see how several forces have converged. For the first time in history we are learning to accommodate an aging society, a transition common to much of the industrialized world (Kinsella and Phillips, 2005). In many ways this aging is a direct consequence of the lowered mortality and sharply reduced fertility of the first two demographic transitions. As shown in Exhibit A, there is a connection from the first demographic transition to the second, and from the first two to the third. An aging society creates many challenges, but one consequence of aging is a slowdown in labor force growth. The easiest remedy to the emerging shortage of workers is an increase in immigration, particularly from countries that may have higher fertility than employment growth (Holzman, 2005). In addition, as a result of international migration, which has been accelerating in Europe, Canada and Australia, as in the U.S., we are witnessing a reshaping of the population across age and racial groups, and between native and foreign born populations. Prior waves of immigration to the U.S. did not have this character of racial transformation.[4] More importantly, the prior waves of immigration did not coincide with an era when the U.S. population age structure was made top heavy by such a large number of seniors.

The new, third demographic transition that now characterizes the twenty-first century takes its unique importance from the political, social, and economic interactions at its core. In essence, the older generation is comprised of the established

[3] These indicators were reported for non-Hispanic white women. Lesthaeghe, Ron and Neidert, Lisa (2006) 'The Second Demographic Transition in the U.S.: Spatial Patterns and Correlates,' unpublished paper (Ann Arbor: University of Michigan, Population Studies Center).

[4] The notion of racial identity has changed over time, with some ethnic groups who we now consider white, such as the Irish, once treated as if they were a separate race. On this and the racial effects of recent immigration, see Bean, Frank D., Lee, Jennifer, Batalova, Jeanne and Leach, Mark (2005) 'Immigration and Fading Color Lines in America' in Reynolds Farley and John Haaga (eds.), *The American People: Census 2000* (New York: Russell Sage), pp. 302–31.

First Demographic Transition

'Rebalancing Fertility and Mortality'

Decline of mortality,   *1800 to 1900*
  followed by fertility   *Western/Northern Europe*
    6.0 children
    |
   3.0
    |

   1.5   Second Demographic   *1965 to 1980*
         Transition   *Western/Northern Europe/US*

       ## 'New Sex Roles and Values'

       Women's equality
       Fulfillment, not reproduction
       Support for new family relationships
       Very low fertility
             but
       Labor shortages and aging society

       A Third Demographic Transition

       ## 'Intergenerational Ethnic Diversity and Political Incorporation'

       International migration of workers
       Racial and ethnic diversification
       Growing burdens of an aging society
             but
       Political inability to incorporate

Figure 1: The Sequence of Demographic Transitions

majority group that existed before, while the younger generation is infused by immigration and has a different racial mix. This distinction between generations – racial, immigrant, and relative size – is straining the political relations that foster cooperation in a democratic society. The new demographic transition embodies this overt political dimension. Despite racial and cultural differences, the older generation needs to negotiate a new relationship with the incoming generation that will carry such a large portion of society's burden in the near future. Thus, the new demographic transition, unlike the prior transitions, entails the forging of a new social contract that spans racial and generational divisions.

European nations continue to lead the world in fertility decline and aging. However, the immigration and ethnic dimensions of the transition have been recognized and accepted more slowly in countries of Europe. A recent United Nations report concludes that, in comparison to the U.S. and Canada which accept immigration as a permanent feature of their populations and encourage settlement:

> 'Most European countries do not consider themselves immigration countries and so follow ad hoc and control-oriented policies... Pursuing a deliberate and systematic immigration policy, which balances human rights, human capital requirements and integration concerns, is the best option to ensure that future migration is beneficial for both individual migrants and their children as well as for their receiving and sending countries... [Also] immigration brings diversity and the necessity to manage increasing cultural pluralism and multi-ethnicity' (quotation from the *Final Document of the Forum*, 2005, p. 290–91).

Despite the greater experience with immigrant incorporation in the U.S., and some would say the great success, the current phase in California is illustrating the enormous challenges yet to be surmounted in Western democracies. In following sections we review the evidence on specific dimensions of the demographic transition, including a close examination of the current political strains.

The Long-Term Decline and Rebound in the Foreign Born Share

Immigration works its effects across generations, and therefore it is useful to see it in a longer run perspective. The rise and fall of foreign-born presence in the population is startling in its magnitude. Viewing this trend over 150 years, from 1880 to 2030, what is most remarkable is the steep decline followed by a sharp rebound in the percent of residents who are foreign born in both California and the U.S. (Figure 2).[5] In the nation as a whole, a steady-state percentage foreign born of just under 15 percent was achieved in the latter half of the nineteenth century through 1910. The percent foreign born increased after each wave of renewed immigration but the figure was moderated by the bulk of the native

---

[5]   These data are derived from several sources. Gibson, Campbell and Lennon, Emily (1999) 'Historical Census Statistics on the Foreign-Born Population of the United States, 1850–1990,' Population Division Working Paper no. 29, U.S. Bureau of the Census. Census 2000 Public Use Microdata Sample. U.S. Census Bureau (2000) Population Division. Final projections consistent with the 1990 census. (NP-T5) Projections of the Resident Population by Race, Hispanic Origin, and Nativity: Middle Series, 1999 to 2100. California Demographic Futures projections by John Pitkin, version 5.0.

born population, including the children of the new immigrants who were born in the U.S. Moreover, immigration had been running so long that deaths to immigrants who had arrived decades earlier also offset the numbers of new arrivals. After 1910 the percent foreign born began its long decline to a low point of 4.7 percent recorded in the nation in 1970. At that time, many of the foreign born were concentrated in older age groups because they had aged since their arrival many decades earlier.[6]

Immigration has always been more prominent in California than the nation as a whole, both because its geographic position on the Pacific and bordering Mexico makes it a natural port of entry, and also because the storied attractions of California drew many to settle in the state. The foreign-born percentage reached a high of 38.6 percent in 1860, following the Gold Rush that brought new settlers from around the world. Thereafter, the percentage foreign born steadily declined for 100 years, reaching its low point of 8.5 percent in 1960. From 1970 to 1990, with the resurgence of immigration, the percentage foreign born rocketed upward to 21.7 percent. So sudden was this rise in the foreign born population that understandably this was profoundly startling and even unsettling to the established population. No matter that this percentage was well below its levels of a century before, recent memory extended only to 1950 when the foreign born percentage was 10 percent or less. The relative change within a generation was truly striking.

After 1990, the percentage foreign born continued to rise in California, but more slowly, reaching 26.2 percent in 2000, and this is expected to level off at about 30 percent in 2030, according to projections developed by John Pitkin for the California Demographic Futures project at the University of Southern California (Myers et al., 2005). Similar information is available for the nation as a whole from the Census Bureau, but those projections were last updated before the 2000 census and by 2000 they already underestimated the nation's percentage of foreign born, calling into question their projections for future decades as well.[7] Nonetheless, it appears that the U.S. percentage foreign born is headed back to the 15 percent level that was the long term average in the nineteenth century. This level is about half that likely to be reached in California. Other large states that the 2000 census showed to have unusually high foreign born percentages (and which could be expected to rise higher in the future) include New

---

[6] In 1970, 34.3 percent of the foreign born were age 60 or older, compared to only 12.9 percent of the native born. Special tabulation of the public use microdata sample from the 1970 census.

[7] Note that the Census Bureau projections only extend to nativity not to second generation or decade of arrival for the foreign born. U.S. Census Bureau (1999) 'Projections of the Resident Population by Race, Hispanic Origin, and Nativity: Middle Series, 1999 to 2100,' (NP-T5), Population Division.

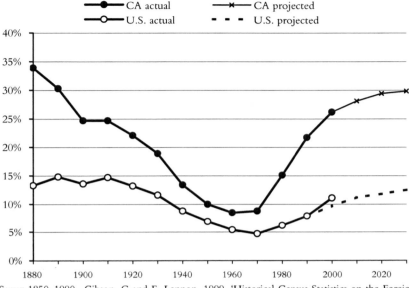

Figure 2: Long-Term Trend in Percentage Foreign Born Among Residents of California and the U.S., 1880–2030

Source: 1850–1990   Gibson, C and E. Lennon. 1999. 'Historical Census Statistics on the Foreign-Born Population of the United States, 1850–1990'. Population Division Working Paper No. 29, US Bureau of the Census. U.S. Census Bureau 2000 Census PUMS 5 percent data

2010–2030   California Demographic Futures projections by John Pitkin, version 5.0.

2010–2030   U.S. Census Bureau, Population Division. 2000. Final projections consistent with the 1990 census. (NP–T5) Projections of the Residential Population by Race, Hispanic Origin, and Nativity: Middle Series, 1999 to 2100

York (20.4 percent), New Jersey (17.5 percent), Florida (16.7 percent), Texas (13.9 percent), and Illinois (12.3 percent) (Malone et al., 2003).

A Shrinking White Share of the Population

California is not only well advanced beyond the nation as a whole in terms of its growing foreign born share but also in terms of the racial and ethnic aspects of the great transition. In 1970, California already had a population with a substantial Hispanic or Latino presence, 12.1 percent, and in total 22.7 percent of the state's population was identified in some group other than white non-Hispanic.[8]

[8]   Historical data for California are taken from 'Race/Ethnic Population with Age and Sex Detail, 1970–1989 [and 1990–1999],' issued by the Demographic Research Unit of the California Department of Finance in December 1998 [and May 2004].

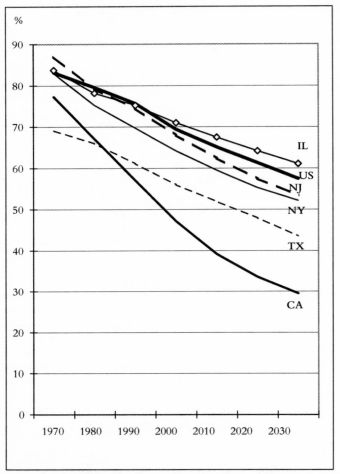

Source: Decennial census of 1970, 1980, 1990, and 2000; Population Projections for States by Age, Sex, Race, and Hispanic Origin: 1995 to 2025 (PPL 47) U.S. Census Bureau; Extrapolations by author from 2025 to 2030

Figure 3: The Declining White, Non-Hispanic Population Share in California, Texas, New York, New Jersey, Illinois, and the U.S., 1970–2030

In comparison, in the U.S., Latinos were a much smaller share of the population at that time, 4.7 percent, and instead African Americans were the largest minority group, comprising 11.1 percent of the total.[9]

[9] Historical data for the U.S. are taken from Gibson, Campbell and Kay, June (2005) 'Historical Census Statistics on Population totals by Race, 1970 to 1990, and by Hispanic Origin, 1970 to 1990, for Large Cities and Other Urban Places in the United States,' Working Paper no. 76, U.S. Census Bureau, Population Division. The 2000 data are drawn from the decennial data of Census 2000.

Over the decades, the racial makeup of both California and the U.S. has shifted rapidly. The pace of change was especially abrupt in California. The Latino share of the population surged to 26.0 percent by 1990 and is projected to be 38.7 percent in 2010 and 46.8 percent in 2030.[10] The Asian and Pacific Islander portion of the California population also has grown rapidly, from 3.3 percent in 1970 to 9.2 percent in 1990, but this group is expected to grow more slowly, reaching 12.4 percent in 2010 and leveling at 13.2 percent in 2030.

A focal point of concern among voters and others is the trend in the white non-Hispanic portion of California's population. The white share is expected to continue its decline, falling from 77.3 percent in 1970 to 57.1 percent in 1990, 39.2 percent in 2010, and reaching 29.5 percent in 2030. How steep is that decline can be seen in a comparison with other major immigrant receiving states (Figure 3). The white share is decreasing much more rapidly in California than in Texas, New York, New Jersey, Florida, or Illinois.[11]

White decline is not simply a major feature of California's demography; it also figures prominently in the state's politics. As discussed below, the white population retains a voting majority and often exercises that majority to block initiatives supported by the population majority. Already achieving minority status by 2000, when the white non-Hispanic share fell below 50 percent of the total state population (48.8 percent), the white group will fall behind Latinos and become the second largest minority group shortly after 2010. Indeed, California is expected to remain a state of minorities until 2040 when Latinos grow to 50 percent of the population. In a later section, we examine a projection of race/ethnicity among the voters, as opposed to residents as a whole. With no ethnic group clearly dominant in future years, political success will require multiethnic coalitions built around shared visions of what is good for the state.

Aging of the Population and the Racial Divide

Racial change is sweeping the California population from the bottom up – that is from younger to older. In 1990, over half the state's population under 20 years of age was already comprised of Latinos and others who were not white

---

[10] Latinos are expected to reach 50 percent of the total in 2040. Projection data for California cited in the text and for the accompanying figure are taken from 'Race/Ethnic Population with Age and Sex Detail, 2000–2050,' issued by the Demographic Research Unit of the California Department of Finance in May 2004.

[11] Data are not shown for Florida because the trend line of that state is virtually indistinguishable from that for the U.S. as a whole.

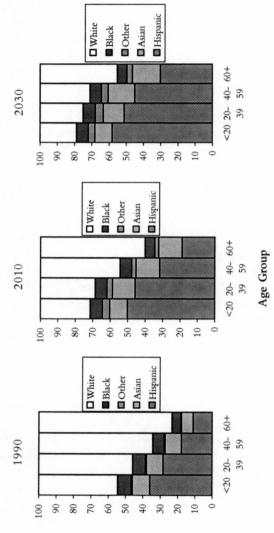

Figure 4: Race and Ethnic Composition of Age Groups in California

Source: U.S. Census Bureau 1990 census; California Department of Finance. Demographic Research Unit projections issued in 2004

non-Hispanic (see Figure 4). Whites were a majority, however, of all other age groups, and the white majority was successively greater in older age groups, reaching 76.7 percent white among those aged 60 and older. By 2010 we anticipate the white shares will have decreased in all age groups, falling under 30 percent among those under age 20 and declining to 60 percent among those aged 60 and older. Looking ahead to 2030, we see that the white population will have lost its majority in the older age group as well, and its share among the other age groups will range only from 29.0 percent at ages 40 to 59, down to 21.3 percent among those under age 20.

Whereas whites were once the majority, or at least the largest group at every age, by 2010 they will be outweighed by the number of Latinos in the younger two age groups, and by 2030 they will be outweighed by Latinos in all age groups save the oldest. Indeed, in the prime age range of 20 to 59, white residents will amount to little more than one-quarter of the state's population, while Latinos will amount to one-half. Not only will the group age 60 and older, largely retired from the labor force, be predominantly white, but the prime working ages in California will be filling with Latinos and, to a smaller degree, Asians.

The challenge is made more acute by the very large size of the baby boom generation that will be retiring. That is a lot to support. As shown in Figure 5, the ratio of elderly aged 65 and older to working age population, ages 25 to 64, jumps markedly after 2010. In longer perspective we can appreciate how remarkable is the aging dimension of the great transition. During the first half of the twentieth century, this dependency ratio hovered around 100 seniors for every 1,000 working-age adults. For most of the latter half of the twentieth century, the ratio held steady at 200 (climbing to 250 in the U.S.). However, after 2010 the senior dependency ratio will surge, in 2030 reaching 350 per 1,000 working-age adults (410 in the U.S.). Thus, the seniors in California and the nation, who are predominantly white, are about to place unprecedented weight on the shoulders of a working age population made up largely of Latinos and others.

Some of the most crucial questions in California concern whether this future generation of workers will be able to replace the highly skilled baby boomers who are retiring and whether they will be able to carry the tax burdens required to support services for this large population of retirees. David Hayes-Batista and co-authors have termed this challenge Latinos' 'burden of support' (Hayes-Bautista et al., 1988). A similar question regarding the demographic challenge of labor force preparation has been raised in other states, most notably in Texas, through the work of state demographer Steven Murdock, which has gained considerable attention in its state legislature, and also through the efforts of Marta Tienda and Teresa Sullivan in the domain of higher education (Murdock et al.,

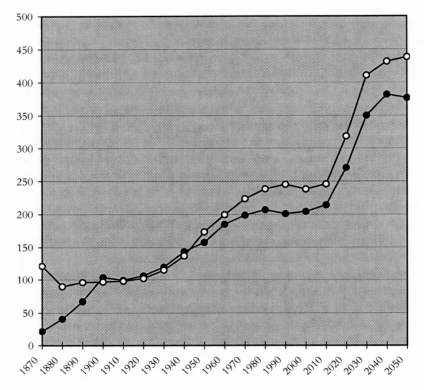

Source: U.S. Census Bureau decennial censuses and predictions; California Department of Finance. Demographic Research unit projections issued in 2004

Figure 5: Ratio of Elderly per 1000 Working Age (25–64) Residents

2003; Tienda and Sullivan). In California, the demographic challenge of preparing for 2025 was recently addressed by Hans Johnson, Mark Baldassare and others at the Public Policy Institute of California, as well as by Henry Brady, Michael Hout, and Jon Stiles at the University of California, Berkeley (Johnson, 2005, pp. 23–49; Brady et al., 2005).

Continued Political Dominance by the Former Majority

In the context of this demographic change, the present chapter adds the further question of relative political power. Will the older group command sufficient political power to sustain priority public support for seniors, and at what point might the younger group acquire sufficient voting strength to shrug off the demands of these seniors? Answers found in California may well foreshadow outcomes in other parts of the nation.

Changes in political representation have been postulated to often lag a good 20 years behind population growth (Logan and Mollenkopf, 2004). Here we examine the dynamics behind that lag and the resulting imbalances among population size, voting, and political representation. To preview this portion of the argument, whites hold this advantage for many reasons, the strongest being that they are older and more established. That seniority position means they are more likely to register to vote than are the newer groups who are often under age 18 or not yet citizens. And longer term residents are also much more likely to be politically active.

Statewide elections have grown ever more important in an era of direct democracy that makes policy by voter initiatives and referenda (Matsusaka, 2004). This context enhances the political power of whatever groups hold the largest share of the statewide electorate. Despite a shrinking proportion of the California population (about 45 percent in 2005), white non-Hispanics' percentage of voters is far larger. The actual share varies somewhat between elections, with higher percentages in less publicized elections and lower percentages in presidential elections that draw a stronger turnout from other groups. For example, the spring 2004 primary election, which included a major state-wide bond issue for education, drew a turnout of whom 74 percent were white, whereas the fall 2004 presidential election in California drew a record high turnout of whom 67 percent were estimated to be white.[12] Thus, the presidential elections record a lower share of voters who are white but a relatively larger share who are Latino or other.

Voting Strength Lags Decades Behind Population Growth

The imbalance between population size and voting strength is clear cut among Latinos and Asians. How long will this under representation persist before greater equity is achieved? John Logan and John Mollenkopf have posited a

[12] Exit poll determinations of race of voter are inexact, depending on whether this is a visual observation by the interviewer (problematic for cases of persons of mixed ancestry) and also on the differential refusal rates when recruiting interviewees who are exiting the voting centers. The data reported are drawn from exit polls conducted by the Los Angeles Times, published March 5, 2004, A20, and by the *Los Angeles Times* and Edison Media Research/Mitofsky International, reported in the *California Opinion Index* (Table 3), January 2005, Field Research Corporation, San Francisco.

'twenty-year representation lag' based on a study comparing New York City and
Los Angeles:

> Whites hold political office in both cities at far higher rates than
> their population share and blacks hold offices at about parity with
> their population or a little more, but Latinos and Asians hold much
> less representation than their population share. Indeed, their current
> level of representation matches their much smaller population share
> twenty years ago. (Logan and Mollenkopf, 2004, p. 5)

No matter the dramatic increase in Latino population, the Latino share of the
electorate is far below their share of the California population. Conversely, the
white population may have fallen to less than half the state total, but the white
share of all voters remains at two-thirds or more. This voting strength is most
important for statewide ballots, such as the gubernatorial election or the increasingly popular ballot initiatives.

We need to better understand how it is that larger populations garner fewer
voters. Likely the most reliable assessment of relative voting strength is provided
by the federal government's November 1998, 2000 and 2002 Current Population
Surveys (CPS), among the most scientific of general social and economic surveys.
The CPS has the advantage of including not only questions about race and voting participation (while avoiding questions about voting choices or political party),
but also questions about age and citizenship. Thus we can draw a relatively more
precise profile of who the voters are, permitting also a comparison of California
and the nation. Pooling the three survey years together, and averaging results to
represent the year 2000, we also obtain a much larger sample for analysis.

The size of the voter representation gap is clearly shown in Table 1. In
California, of the total population in 2000, 46.6 percent were white non-
Hispanic, and 32.3 percent were Hispanic, with other groups much less numerous. California is the first large state in the nation to become majority minority,
meaning that whites are less than 50 percent of the total and, instead, the population is now a composite of minority groups. Nonetheless, despite its minority
status, the white population in California accounts for 71.3 percent of the regular voters in these data.[13]

In contrast, Latinos comprised only 13.8 percent of the regular voters even
though they held a 32.3 percent share of the California population. Given that

---

[13] Regular voters are defined in this case as those who said they voted in the Fall elections, pooling results from one presidential year and two off years, and thus creating a composite profile of
'regular voters.'

Table 1: Contrast Among Shares of Total Population, Eligible Citizens and Voters

California

	Total	% Age 18+	% 18+ Citizens	% Registered	% Voted
All	100.0	100.0	100.0	100.0	100.0
White	46.6	51.0	64.1	69.1	71.3
Black	6.4	6.2	7.8	7.5	7.1
Asian	11.1	11.6	9.3	7.5	7.0
Hispanic	32.3	28.0	17.7	14.8	13.8

United States

	Total	% Age 18+	% 18+ Citizens	% Registered	% Voted
All	100.0	100.0	100.0	100.0	100.0
White	68.2	71.0	77.6	80.3	81.3
Black	11.8	11.0	11.9	11.4	11.2
Asian	3.7	3.7	2.5	1.9	1.8
Hispanic	13.7	12.1	7.1	5.8	5.1

Note: All percentages are ethnic shares of the specific category
Source: Current Population Survey, November, 1998, 2000, and 2002 adjusted to 2000 census population base.

many Latinos are children or non-citizens, fewer are eligible to vote. Table 1 shows how their share shrinks to 28.0 percent among adults and then more drastically among adults who are citizens (17.7 percent). Conversely, whites' share steadily rises as a percentage of each of these categories.

In the U.S., a similar imbalance is observed, although whites have a far larger share of the population (68.2 percent) and the Latino share is far smaller than California (13.7 percent). As in California, whites constitute a disproportionate share of the voters, rising to 81.3 percent, while Latinos fall to a much smaller share (5.1 percent). African Americans retain a voting strength that is much closer to their population numbers, but Asians suffer the same fall off as Latinos.

What underlies each group's share of a jurisdiction's voters is not only the relative size of the group but also its per capita rate of voting participation. Some groups may have a large share of their population under age 18 or non-citizens, and hence be ineligible to vote. Other groups may have a low percentage of their eligibles registered to vote, or a low percentage of those registered may actually turn out on election day. The hurdles to voting for those not born in the U.S. are substantial and have been described as 'a three-step process – naturalization, registration and turning out – that involves, at each turn, a set of costs,' and, as a consequence, this leads to substantial delays in achieving full voting participation (Lien et al., 2001).

Table 2: Translation of Population into Voting Numbers

California

Successive Probabilities

	Total Group	Proportion Age 18+ of Total Group	Proportion Citizens of Age 18+	Proportion Registered of 18+ Citizens	Proportion Voted of Registrants	% Voted of Total Pop in Group
All	100	72.8	80.7	64.1	78.5	29.5
White, non-Hispanic	100	79.6	95.5	69.1	80.9	42.5
Black	100	70.3	96.6	61.5	74.2	31.0
Asian	100	76.4	63.2	52.0	72.6	18.2
Hispanic	100	63.2	53.8	53.8	73.1	13.4

United States

Successive Probabilities

	Total Group	Proportion Age 18+ of Total Group	Proportion Citizens of Age 18+	Proportion Registered of 18+ Citizens	Proportion Voted of Registrants	% Voted of Total Pop in Group
All	100	74.3	92.2	67.7	74.3	34.5
White, non-Hispanic	100	77.4	97.9	70.0	75.2	39.9
Black	100	68.9	95.1	64.6	72.9	30.8
Asian	100	76.0	60.0	50.1	70.8	16.2
Hispanic	100	65.8	61.5	55.2	65.7	14.7

Source: Current Population Survey, November, 1998, 2000, and 2002 adjusted to 2000 census population base.

Thus a closer understanding of the under representation of Latino and Asian voters can be gained if we trace the conversion of each group's total population into numbers of eligible age citizens, registrants and actual voters (Table 2). In California, 79.6 percent of white non-Hispanics are aged 18 or older and, of those, 95.5 percent are citizens. These eligible citizens are not all registered to vote – only 69.1 percent – and of those who are registered, only 80.9 percent say they are actual voters. The net result of all these successive probabilities is that 42.5 percent of the total white population are voters. By comparison, among Latinos, a somewhat smaller share are aged 18 or older – 63.2 percent – but only 53.8 percent of those are citizens who are eligible to vote. In turn, of the eligibles, a lower ratio than among whites have registered to vote, 53.8 percent, and 73.1 percent of those registrants report they voted. Compared to whites, these successive probabilities are all lower, with the greatest discrepancy among citizenship of adults and registration of citizens. The net result is that only 13.4 percent of the total Latino population are voters. A very similar pattern of conversion of population into voters occurs for Asians, and their voting numbers amount to only 18.2 percent of their population, slightly more than Latinos but far below whites. In the U.S. as a whole, each ethnic group follows a translation process into voting numbers that closely resembles the pattern prevailing in California (see Table 2).

How much difference does each factor make in the translation of population numbers into voting strength? Put another way, how much of the gap between white, non-Hispanics and other groups is contributed by relative age, citizenship, registration, or voter turnout? In the case of California Latinos, their 13.4 percent of population who are voters is 29.2 percentage points lower than is the case for whites. Over one-half of that gap would be closed, 15.8 points, if Latinos who were age 18 and older were citizens as often as are whites.[14] Another 5.8 points of the gap would be closed if Latinos who were citizen adults registered to vote as often as whites. And only 2.2 points more of the gap would be closed if those Latinos who were registered turned out to vote at the same rate as whites. The remainder of the gap is due to the higher proportion of Latinos who are under age 18 and thus not eligible to vote. Lack of citizenship is also the

---

[14]   The factor contributions described in the text are derived from a modified components of change analysis applied to the conversion factors displayed in the previous table. Those factors form a sequential chain of probabilities – of being age 18 or older, of being a citizen, of being registered to vote, and of turning out to vote. The analysis systematically replaces one factor at a time with the respective value for the white, non-Hispanic population and calculates the overall reduction that equalization makes in each group's overall voting gap with whites. The summation of single-factor contributions accounts for most of the voting gap, and the residual amount due to interactions among multiple factors is allocated proportionally to each of the single factors.

largest factor in the case of California's Asian residents, while under-registration is an even greater impediment in their case. Indeed, other California researchers have noted that the under registration of Asians is particularly striking, especially in view of the otherwise supportive factors of higher education and income (Citrin and Highton, 2002, pp. 27–32).

Under-Representation Among Local Activists

There is an additional element of population seniority, beyond simple citizenship and voting registration, that is the cause of under representation in local politics. It takes time for a group to build up a sufficient number of political organizers to be competitive in local politics. In the context of demographic transition, the longer established group holds a key advantage over the more numerous newcomers. One study in Los Angeles county found that the majority of both Democratic and Republican party activists comprised longtime residents (Guerra and Marvick, 1986). Despite rapid population growth and migration flux in the area, among activists of both parties and among all ethnic groups the average length of residence in California exceeded 30 years and the average years at the same address exceeded 12 years. A major study of immigrant voting and political participation in America also found that length of time at the same address – over and above age or length of time in America – led to higher rates of active voting. The explanation offered was that longer resident citizens are more vested in their community and have more stable networks of friends and neighbors (Ramakrishnan, 2005, pp. 56–58).[15] Thus, it takes time to grow a committed cadre of local political players, giving an added advantage to the declining former majority group because of its seniority.

Outlook for Continued Dominance in the Electorate

How many years might it take for white residents in California to fall below 50 percent of all voters, and how many years might it take for Latino voters to exceed 50 percent of the total? That is a question often speculated on, but one lacking much careful analysis. Here we offer a reasonably well-grounded

---

[15] In addition, those residing longer at the same address may be self-selected for willingness to participate politically, because they are more likely homeowners with large investment stakes, and they also have implicitly elected to express 'voice' to shape their local environment, rather than 'exit.' Hirschman, Albert O. (1970) *Exit, Voice, and Loyalty: Responses to Decline in Firms, Organizations, and States* (Cambridge, MA: Harvard University Press).

projection. To establish its credibility we must examine the data and calculations that can lead to an informed judgment. It also is helpful to compare a projection prepared independently by political scientists Jack Citrin and Benjamin Highton. In fact, the original analysis offered here yields results that are comparable, in key respects, to the conclusion reached by those scholars. The preferred approach for projecting future voting shares combines long-term population projections with recently observed rates of voting participation among each detailed population subgroup. However, we should first consider results from an alternative approach that extrapolates recent shifts in ethnic shares of voting turnout.

The simplest approach, and the one most often used by local commentators, is the extrapolation of recent shifts observed at the polls, but that method also may be the least reliable. To demonstrate, we can extrapolate the recent change in ethnic participation achieved in two comparable elections. A good candidate would be the presidential elections of 2000 and 2004, as reported in the exit polls conducted at the voting place, or in the Current Population Survey's (CPS) November Voting Sample.[16] In just four years, the white share reported in the CPS survey declined by 5.0 percentage points (four points in the exit polls), while the Latino share increased by 2.5 percentage points (or by a greater amount, four points, in the exit polls). We immediately note a discrepancy in the two sources, and this will have major consequences for any projections. Indeed, the extrapolations of these short-term trends into the future can yield erratic or exaggerated rates of change because they embed and then magnify any errors and erratic features of the recent elections or of the survey methodology. As shown in Table 3, the extrapolation of voting shares in the CPS suggests black voters will grow to 11.6 percent of the electorate in 2030, while extrapolation of exit poll shares suggests blacks will decline to 0.3 percent of the electorate in the same year. Neither is at all plausible given the steady share of black residents expected in the population over coming decades. Similarly, Asian voters are anticipated to increase to 22.5 percent of the electorate in 2030, based on extrapolation of recent shifts in the CPS, whereas they are expected to grow to only 14.9 percent based on extrapolations from exit polls. The projection from the CPS data is clearly implausibly high. Not surprisingly, projections for whites and Latinos also bounce up and down between the two alternative extrapolations. While informative, the risk of exaggeration and misleading conclusions is substantial from this method of extrapolating voting shares.

[16] An alternative set of data derives from exit polls conducted on the day of the election. A comparison of available poll data shows broadly similar results to those employed here. *California Opinion Index* (2005) Table 3. For a variety of reasons these data provide a less accurate representation of race and Hispanic origin than does the Current Population Survey, including their smaller sample size, the visual method by which race is assigned, and other features.

Table 3: Alternative Projections of Future Ethnic Shares
of the California Electorate

	2000	2010	2020	2030	Year reaching 50%
A. Composition–Based Projection					
White	70.4	63.5	56.9	50.8	2031
Latino	14.5	19.1	24.2	29.0	2073
Asian	7.4	9.7	11.4	13.1	—
Black	7.8	7.7	7.4	7.0	—
Total	100.0	100.0	100.0	100.0	—
B. Extrapolation of Voting Shares (exit polls)					
White	70.4	60.4	50.4	40.4	2020
Latino	14.5	24.5	34.5	44.5	2036
Asian	7.4	9.9	12.4	14.9	—
Black	7.8	5.3	2.8	0.3	—
Total	100.0	100.0	100.0	100.0	—
C. Extrapolation of Voting Shares (CPS)					
White	70.4	57.8	45.2	32.6	2016
Latino	14.5	20.8	27.0	33.3	2057
Asian	7.4	12.4	17.5	22.5	—
Black	7.8	9.1	10.3	11.6	—
Total	100.0	100.0	100.0	100.0	—

Source: Calculations by the author, with assistance from Seong Hee Min.

Two alternative projections were carried out, as described here.

The composition-based projection applies per capita voting rates to projected population from the California Demographic Futures, detailing that population by ethnicity, age, nativity, and duration in the U.S. Per capita voting rates are derived from the Current Population Survey November Voting Supplements of 2000 and 2004.

Alternatively, the extrapolation of voting shares affords a crude projection by assuming the rate of change in shares recorded between the presidential elections of 2000 and 2004 is continued indefinitely. Two variations on these extrapolations are provided, one based on exit polls, the other based on CPS estimates.

A more stable means of estimating future voting shares is to construct a projection of voting shares based on the changing composition of the population. The extrapolation method only treats the voters in an aggregate manner, not refining the expected level of voting due to aging of the population group or other factors. Significant differences need to be accounted for. For example, among Californians who are white, non-Hispanic, the likelihood of voting increases from 46.0 percent, at ages 25 to 34, to 73.7 percent at ages 65 to 74. Similarly, Latino voting increases from 15.0 percent of those aged 25 to 34 to 45.6 percent at ages 65 to 74. Of course, voting also depends on nativity: Latinos who are native-born are all citizens and consequently have much higher voting rates – for example, 39.8 percent at ages 25 to 34 – albeit still below those of whites.

The alternative method of projecting voting, the compositional method, directly accounts for these differences among different segments of each race or ethnic group. Detailed voting rates per capita are defined for the base year and then applied to the future population composition as we have projected it to evolve over the decades. Despite the merits of this detailed approach, it suffers the clear drawback that voting rates for each age and nativity group are assumed to hold constant for decades. Within each population segment, there is no allowance for increases in registration or turnout in future elections. Nonetheless, the compositional method captures the enormous effects on likelihood of voting as the population of each ethnic group shifts into segments that are generally more likely to vote. This includes not only aging of the population, but also growing shares of Latinos and Asians in the future who will be native born, and the lengthening residence of the foreign born.

According to the composition-based projection, white voters can be expected to decline from 70.4 percent of the electorate in 2000 to 50.8 percent in 2030, falling to the 50 percent majority line in 2031 (Table 3). Latinos, in contrast, are expected to increase their share of the electorate from 14.5 percent in 2000 to 29.0 percent in 2030, not reaching the 50 percent majority status until 2073. Meanwhile, the share of voters comprising African Americans will hold steady between 7 to 8 percent, reflecting their stable population share (varying only from 6.5 percent to 6.6 percent) much more closely than the erratic projections based on the extrapolation method. At the same time, the Asian share is projected to nearly double from 7.4 percent to 13.1 percent, nearly matching their share of the total population in 2030. These projections for Asians and blacks appear far more credible than in the crude extrapolations, and they lend some confidence in the greater accuracy of the projections for whites and Latinos as well. Nonetheless, it is possible that the Latino share could grow a little faster than projected in future decades if registration and voting turnout rates within each segment were to be escalated beyond what was observed in 2004.

Other researchers have arrived at projections of ethnic voting representation that are similar to those presented here. Jack Citrin and Benjamin Highton followed a similar compositional strategy of applying 2000 voting rates to future population changes, but added some variations (Citrin and Highton, 2002, pp. 67–77). In their status quo projection, they found that whites will hold a 53 percent majority of voters even as late as the year 2040, which suggests the 50 percent line will not be reached until 2046. In 2040, Latinos would constitute 26 percent of the electorate, and at this rate they would not reach 50 percent until the next century, 2120. These projections afford a highly exaggerated outlook on future majority status, largely because of inadequacies in the population projections on which they relied. (Their analysis of voting rates in 2000 is exceptionally well executed and is not a likely weakness in their voting projection.) The population projections they obtained from the California Department of Finance do not detail nativity (immigrant generation) and length of residence in the U.S.. Accordingly, Citrin and Highton's voting projections fail to pick up the added participation of Latinos and Asians that we expect to take place as these populations grow longer settled. To compensate for that deficiency, they offer hypothetical simulations of voting participation if citizenship and turnout were to increase (Citrin and Highton, 2002, pp. 71–74).

What seems most plausible in light of the present analysis is their assumption that citizenship might increase among Latinos and Asians by 50 percent. Something like that can be expected because of the population shift to native-born and longer settled status that we already incorporate in our own projections. Based on that assumption, Citrin and Highton compute a projected white share of voters that falls to 50 percent by 2030, virtually the same as our projection. They also find a Latino share of 29 percent that year, suggesting that this share would not reach the 50 percent line until 2083, a decade longer than the projection we have presented. When they add an additional, more extreme assumption, if turnout in each population segment also were to equal that of whites, they reduce the date of Latino voting majority to 2068 and shorten the tenure of the white majority to 2016.

No matter what projection of future voting is to be believed, clearly the imbalance of population and voting is not going to be eliminated any time soon. California will need to manage this problem for decades to come. And the rest of the nation will be encountering the imbalance with greater urgency in coming years, because the numbers of Latinos and Asians in many states will continue to outpace the growth of whites and blacks. Whether this is more than a philosophical and ethical problem of equal representation, whether it has practical policy consequences, remains to be seen. We turn to that question now.

Conflicting Political Views of the Old and New Populations

The great transition we have described has three demographic dimensions, including the growing foreign born population, the shrinking white non-Hispanic population, and the surging numbers of elderly. The older population that belongs to the outgoing majority has retained its political hold on the state's electorate, even if it does not represent either the current population or the population of the future. With time, the political transition will follow the demographics, but it lags at least 20 years. In the meantime, the current electorate, satisfying the present interests of the majority, is making crucial policy decisions that will shape the state's future.

The final section of the paper explores the degree to which the outgoing majority of the population holds political preferences that are opposed to those of the incoming majority. Racial and ethnic difference aside, members of the outgoing group have a fundamentally different orientation than members of the rapidly growing groups. Among the differences to be explored, the incoming groups are more future-oriented, and more optimistic about the future, while members of the outgoing majority are more nostalgic and pessimistic about the future. As we will show, the native-born residents are more resentful of immigrants, whites especially so, and they are also more likely to view population growth as a bad thing for their quality of life. Finally, we will examine the preferences of these groups for greater taxes and spending, something especially needed for investing in the well-being of young families with children who will comprise the future.

Orientation to the Past, Not the Future

Members of the outgoing majority have a wholly different temporal orientation. Long settled in California, they remember a time past when life was easier in California: traffic congestion was much less, housing prices were far lower, and the environment cleaner. In contrast, incoming residents are much younger. They remember the past less and instead look forward to the future. Indeed, Latino and Asian residents are much less pessimistic about the future, 41 percent and 30 percent, respectively, than are whites (52 percent) and blacks (45 percent).

Rapid population growth is widely seen as a problem that is a bad thing, including nearly two-thirds of voters. It is this factor that people blame most for traffic congestion and poor quality of services. The recent opinion of residents statewide was tapped by a survey in May/June 2004 by the Public Policy Institute of California that asked: 'Between now and 2025, California's population is estimated to increase by 10 million people from 35 to 45 million. On

Table 4: Undesirable Population Growth: Factors Explaining the Probability that California Voters Believe Population Growth is a Bad Thing

Category	Variable	Value	Factor	Condition	Value
Race	Asian	-1.2	Public education system	Get worse	2.8
	Black	-9.7 **		Other (ref)	....
	Hispanic	-8.0 **	Air quality	Get worse	3.2
	White NH (ref)	....		Other (ref)	....
	Other	-1.9			
Age	18–24	-10.7 **	Job opportunities & economic conditions	Get worse	7.7 ***
	25–34	-9.3 **		Other (ref)	....
	35–44	-1.8			
	45–54 (ref)	....	Traffic conditions	Get worse	5.9
	55–64	1.1		Other (ref)	....
	65+	-1.4			
Gender	Male (ref)	....	Affordable housing	Get worse	6.6 **
	Female	5.5 **		Other (ref)	....
			Place to live	Get worse	20.0 ***
				Other (ref)	....
Nativity	Native-Born (ref)	....	Confidence in state planning	Low confidence	2.6
	Foreign-Born (citizen)	-7.2 *		Other (ref)	....
Education	Less than HS	2.6	Confidence in local planning	Low confidence	4.0
	HS (ref)	....		Other (ref)	....
	Some College	-4.5			
	BA+	-7.1 *			

Income	Less than 20,000 (ref)	....
	20,000–39,999	4.7
	40,000–59,999	8.8 ★
	60,000–79,999	9.2 ★
	80,000+	2.6
Political leaning	Conservative	2.6
	Liberal	4.3
	Moderate (ref)	....
Homeownership	Owner	-2.3
	Renter (ref)	....
Expected population growth	Rapid	2.6
	Other (ref)	....
Intercept		34.7 ★★★
Obs.		1,456
R-Square		0.139

Notes: Linear probability model of belief that population growth is a bad thing rather than a good thing or of no consequence; statistical significance indicated by ★★★p<0.01   ★★p<0.05   ★p<0.1

Source: PPIC Statewide Survey, August 2004, Public Policy Institute of California; subsample of regular voters defined by those who indicated they always or usually voted.

balance, do you think this population growth is a good thing or a bad thing or does it make no difference to you and your family?' (Baldassare, 2004b) Fully 59.2 percent of all residents judge this population growth to be 'a bad thing,' including an even larger share (67.4 percent) of the white voters.

Most Californians are well aware that the growth is being driven by immigration (see following discussion) and they see from their daily life how much of the growth stems from the rapid increase in numbers of Latinos and Asians. Accordingly, we might expect that white residents view this population growth with less favor than do Latinos and others. It remains to be seen whether this supposition is true, once we control for factors such as age, education and political leaning, or for voters' fears about specific features of declining quality of life. If we control for the latter, physical and economic conditions feared by voters, that could remove much of the fears they have about population growth. Any remaining dislike might then be interpreted as representing attitudes toward the unmeasured social content of population growth.

For this background, respondents were asked to consider whether or not a series of things would happen 'in your part of California.' They were asked whether the population would grow rapidly or not, and if a series of living conditions would improve or grow worse: the public education system, air quality, job opportunities and economic conditions, traffic conditions, and the availability of affordable housing. A follow-up question then asked: 'Overall, do you think that in 2025 your part of California will be a better place to live than it is now or a worse place to live than it is now, or will there be no change?' Two additional questions to include in our analysis concern voters' confidence that state and local planners have the ability to mitigate the effects of growth.

We can bring all the above information to bear in determining whether voters think population growth is a bad thing, estimating this as a linear probability model.[17] The results displayed in Table 4 show that, controlled for all other factors, Latino voters are 8.0 percent less likely to think population growth is a bad thing than are white non-Hispanic voters. Black voters are even less likely to think it is a bad thing. Controlled for these racial differences, young adults are 9.3 percent to 10.7 percent less likely than middle-aged adults to judge

[17] Multiple regressions were estimated as linear probability models, where belief that population growth is a bad thing, rather than good or of no consequence, was coded as 1 and non-bad as 0. Given the binary nature of the dependent variable, a more statistically efficient design would utilize logistic regression. Although logistic and linear probability regressions yield similar statistical conclusions, logistic regression is preferred in cases where the mean of the outcome variable has a mean that lies near the extremes, either 0 or 1. Given that our outcome measure lies in the mid-range, this concern is less warranted. Moreover, the coefficients of the linear probability model are directly interpretable as percentage increases in voting support. Accordingly, we utilize the linear probability specification to facilitate ease of interpretation.

population growth unfavorably, perhaps because they have less experience witnessing its impacts over time. In contrast, women are more likely to judge growth unfavorably than men, for reasons that are not clear.[18]

Voters' expectations about the future pace of growth have no significant impact on how they judge its results. Moreover, quite a few other factors prove insignificant as well. It is surprising that no effect on growth opinion is drawn from either political leaning or the amount of confidence in the ability of state and local planners to mitigate the effects of growth. We also introduced in the model a series of indicator variables to measure whether respondents fear specific negative trends impacting their daily life. Only three of those trend evaluations are statistically significant. Voters with an expectation that job opportunities will get worse are 7.7 percent more likely to think growth is bad. Similarly, voters who think the availability of affordable housing will get worse are 6.6 percent more likely to think growth is bad. The largest effect, however, is found for the overall evaluation of living conditions: those who think life will grow worse are 20 percent more likely to feel growth is a bad thing. What is most striking is that this factor is evaluated after specifically controlling for trends in education, jobs, traffic, housing, and air quality. There must be something else fairly major that voters do not like about the anticipated future living conditions in their part of California. Unfortunately, the available survey data do not include a question on perceptions of the changing ethnic mix of the population.

Net of all these factors, white voters and older voters are much more likely to view population growth with disfavor. As we will see later, their dislike may transfer to an unwillingness to support it financially. First we turn to the matter of immigration, which voters widely assume is a very important factor in population growth.

Immigrants as a Burden or Benefit

The most prominent part of population growth in many people's eyes is immigration. In fact, just over half the residents in California in 2005 believe that immigration from other countries is the biggest factor causing the state's population to grow.[19] Given the widespread dislike of population growth, it surely is no

---

[18] One possible explanation is that women are more sensitive to deterioration in their local living conditions and/or less sensitive to the economic opportunities that may accompany growth.

[19] Surveys in May 2001 and November 2005 found that 55 percent and 53 percent, respectively, of residents believed that immigration was the biggest growth factor. Baldassare, Mark (2005) 'Special Survey on Population,' PPIC Statewide Survey (December) (San Francisco: Public Policy Institute of California), p.11.

surprise that immigration could be disliked as well. But immigrants have been sin-
gled out in political discourse for special attention with regard to the burdens they
impose. Indeed, next to the matter of illegal immigration, debate over the incidence of burdens has become the central feature of debates about immigration.[20]

The feelings of California voters were revealed in their November 1994 vote to
deny services to illegal immigrants in Proposition 187. The changes in voter opinion since then are of considerable interest. Comparison of the available survey data
could reveal how much the discontent with regard to immigration may have moderated in recent years. Although it would be ideal to capture the public mood in
1988 and 1994, as well as 2004, surveys of California voters with comparable questions are not available to facilitate analysis for those years. Here we examine opinion polls conducted in 1998 and 2004 that asked voters an identical question,
namely, which of the following statements was closest to their views: 'Immigrants
today are a benefit to California because of their hard work and job skills;' or
'immigrants today are a burden to California because they use public services'
(Baldassare, 2004a and 1998). These opinions, expressed in April 1998, were collected just three and a half years following the vote for Proposition 187, and it is
instructive to compare them to opinions collected in February 2004. Among all
adult residents, the proportion judging immigrants to be a burden fell in six years
from 41.5 percent to 34.8 percent, a reduction of 6.7 percentage points. However,
among *voters* the proportion fell only 2.5 points, and among white voters by only
1.5 percentage points. Here we find a clear instance where the attitudes of voters
are lagging behind changing opinions in the population as a whole. Nonetheless,
we report evidence below that opinion of some segments of white voters is moving much closer to that of the population majority.

How large is the difference in opinion between white and other voters? How
much of the difference can be accounted for by other factors, such as education,
income, or general political leaning? Again a multivariate statistical analysis is
employed to help sort out the effect of these various factors.[21] In these models,
the various effects are measured relative to the opinions of middle-aged white
men, who are native-born, with low income, and who are politically moderate.
Controlling for these factors, we test how much effect each difference in voters'
characteristics can make. In 2004, voters who were Latino or Asian were at least

[20]   Estimates of contributions and burdens have been a prominent part of scientific inquiries to
inform policy about immigration, such as the major investigation organized by the National Academy
of Science, published in Smith James P. and Edmonston, Barry (eds.) (1997) *The New Americans:
Economic, Demographic, and Fiscal Effects of Immigration* (Washington, D.C.: National Academy Press).
[21]   Multiple regressions were estimated as linear probability models, where belief that immigrants
pose a burden, rather than a benefit, or equally a burden and a benefit, was coded as 1 and non-
burden as 0. On the relative virtues of this method, see note 17.

Table 5: Undesirable Immigrants:
Factors Explaining the Probability that California Voters Believe Immigrants
Pose More of a Burden than a Benefit

		1998	2004
Intercept		45.2 ★★★	37.0 ★★★
Race	Asian	−3.4	−21.5 ★★★
	Black	1.3	6.4
	Hispanic	−17.2 ★★★	−22.2 ★★★
	White NH (ref)	....	....
	Other	−8.4	−9.0
Age	18–24	−6.3	9.8
	25–34	0.1	−4.2
	35–44	0.9	−2.1
	45–54 (ref)	....	....
	55–64	1.1	6.0
	65+	2.6	−6.8
Gender	Male (ref)	....	....
	Female	6.5 ★★	3.1
Nativity	Native-born (ref)	....	....
	Foreign-born citizen	−16.9 ★★★	−6.8
Income	Less than 20,000 (ref)	....	....
	20,000–39,999	−1.1	5.2
	40,000–59,999	−3.8	7.3
	60,000–79,999	−4.9	10.0 ★
	80,000+	−6.1	4.6
Political	Liberal	−4.6	−12.3 ★★★
Leaning	Moderate (ref)	....	....
	Conservative	9.1 ★★★	18.4 ★★★
Obs.		1,246	1,157
R-Square		0.059	0.131

Notes: Linear probability model of belief that immigrants pose a burden rather than a benefit or no difference; Statistical significance indicated by ★★★$p<0.01$ ★★$p<0.05$ ★$p<0.1$
Source: PPIC Statewide Survey, April 1998 and February 2004, Public Policy Institute of California; subsample of regular voters defined by those who indicated they always or usually voted.

20 percent less likely than whites to believe immigrants posed a burden (Table 5). No significant differences were found due to any other demographic factors in 2004. Aside from ethnicity, the other strong factor appears to be political leaning. Compared with moderates, liberals are 12 percent less likely, and conservatives 18 percent more likely, to view immigrants as a burden. Thus the gap between liberals and conservatives is a full 30 percentage points on this issue.

The changes between 1998 and 2004 are of considerable interest. Rather than moderating in recent years, differences between white and other voters appear larger in 2004, especially in comparison with Asians. The persistence and strengthening of these racial differences may be surprising, because they are net of all other important factors, as described here. Back in 1998, women voters were 6 percent more likely than men to view immigrants as a burden, but that difference subsided and was insignificant in 2004. An even greater change is seen when foreign-born voters are compared with the native-born. Whereas the foreign born were 17 percent less likely to see immigrants as a burden in 1998, the difference is insignificant in 2004.

Perhaps the most important change from 1998 to 2004 is the effect of political leaning on attitudes toward immigrants. Back in 1998, the differences between liberals and conservatives were half as great, only 13.7 percent, compared with 30.7 percent in 2004. From this statistical model, we cannot tell what has narrowed this gap: whether it is liberals who grew more tolerant of immigrants or conservatives who grew less tolerant.[22] Turning to the raw data on immigrant views of white voters by political leaning, we find that liberals' view of immigrants as a burden decreased from 40.1 percent to 28.5 percent. Meanwhile, there was no change among moderates, but we find among conservatives that the burden assessment *increased* from 53.9 percent to 61.9 percent. Thus, while liberals grew 12 percent more likely to be tolerant of immigrants, conservatives grew 8 percent less tolerant over the six years, and the resulting gap widened by nearly 20 percentage points between the two political groups of white voters. Adjusted for other factors, and assessed among all voters, we find that the gap doubled in size from 13.7 percent to 30.7 percent (Table 5).

By way of summary, a rough generalization can be offered with regard to the changing profile of opposition to immigrants. Between 1998 and 2004 there has been a widespread increase in acceptance of immigrants. Back in 1998 the native-born voters were fairly unified in their opposition, Latinos excepted. By 2004, however, native-born opinion had converged on that of the foreign-born

---

[22] The lower intercept for the linear probability regression in 2004 indicates that the reference group in the model, the middle-aged, native-born white men who are political moderates, decreased their view that immigrants are a burden.

citizens, and women had ceased their greater opposition. During this time, all ethnic groups had increased their acceptance of immigrants to roughly the same degree, so that the sharp ethnic differences observed in 1998 were sustained in 2004. Nonetheless, the evidence is that the opinion of white voters was fracturing along lines of general political leaning, indicating a growing polarization in the electorate with regard to immigration. While liberal voters became much more accommodating, we find that it is the conservative wing among white voters that has grown less tolerant. It is this conservative wing whose preferences are most divergent from those of the incoming population majority.

Preferred Level of Spending and Taxing

California voters are deeply ambivalent about taxing and spending, expressing a strong desire to 'have their cake and eat it too.' Survey data show they want to pay less in taxes, but even conservatives also want to avoid any spending cuts in services. This tendency is commonplace among voters, being long recognized (see, for example, Hansen, 1998). Of particular interest are the findings of voter experiments showing that people will support budget cuts in the abstract, but not on a program-by-program basis, perhaps because the benefits are more easily imagined (Baron and McCaffery, 2006).

The only realistic way to understand the choices voters are willing to make is to pose a trade off of how much they prefer services against how much they prefer cutting taxes. A survey in June 2003 by the Public Policy Institute of California presented the following choice: 'In general, which of the following statements do you agree with more – I'd rather pay higher taxes to support a larger government that provides more services, or I'd rather pay lower taxes and have a smaller government that provides fewer services?' Unlike the responses to unconstrained questions about desired spending, this question uncovers greater acceptance of spending cuts by some, but not all, important segments of the electorate. In particular, Latino voters (68.0 percent) were far more likely than white voters (38.6 percent) to prefer higher taxes and more services rather than lower taxes and fewer services.

Several sets of factors may explain willingness to support higher taxes and spending. Demographic characteristics such as race, age, gender and nativity could prove important. Economic factors are also important, measured here by income, education level, and homeownership. In addition, political leaning and trust in government could prove to be crucial factors. To better understand the net effect of all these factors, a simple statistical analysis is constructed of voters' opinions, as summarized in Table 6. The first model incorporates just the

Table 6: Support for Higher Taxes and Spending: Factors Explaining the Probability that California Voters Want to Expand Support for Services

(Percentage point increase or decrease in support due to each factor)

		Model 1 Based on Demographics and Economics	Model 2 Factoring in Trust in Government	Model 3 Factoring in Political Leaning
Political Leaning	Liberal			21.4 ★★★
	Moderate (reference)		—	
	Conservative			−17.9 ★★★
Trust in Government	Trust		12.4 ★★★	7.9 ★★★
	Not trust (reference)		—	—
Race	Asian	11.6 ★	11.1	9.7
	Black	21.4 ★★★	24.1 ★★★	18.2 ★★★
	Hispanic	18.7 ★★★	18.8 ★★★	14.6★★★
	White (reference)	—	—	—
	Other	4.3	4.5	1.7
Age	18–24	26.2 ★★★	24.5 ★★★	19.8 ★★★
	25–34	10.7 ★★	10.4 ★★	10.2 ★★
	35–44	−3.8	−3.4	−0.9
	45–54 (reference)	—	—	—
	55–64	−7.6	−7.0	−5.3
	65+	−15.2 ★★★	−14.5 ★★★	−8.8 ★
Gender	Female	11.8 ★★★	11.5 ★★★	7.0 ★★
	Male (reference)	—	—	—
Nativity	Foreign-born citizen	9.8 ★	8.2	10.6 ★★
	Native-born (reference)	—	—	—
Education	Less than HS	4.5	3.9	3.3
	HS (reference)	—	—	—
	Some College	−6.9	−6.3	−6.5
	BA+	2.7	3.4	−3.0
Income	Less than 20,000 (ref)	—	—	—
	20,000–39,999	3.6	4.4	5.9
	40,000–59,999	−2.8	−2.2	0.4
	60,000–79,999	−5.2	−4.9	−3.8
	80,000+	−9.1	−9.6 ★	−4.6
Home-ownership	Owner	−10.3 ★★★	−10.1 ★★★	−7.7 ★★
	Renter (reference)	—	—	—
Constant		46.1 ★★★	41.3 ★★★	42.7 ★★★
Number of observations		1,064	1,064	1,064
R-Square		0.159	0.172	0.272

Notes: Linear probability model of preference for higher taxes and spending versus lower or don't know: Statistical significance indicated by ★★★p<0.01 ★★p<0.05 ★p<0.1

Source: PPIC Statewide Survey, June 2003, Public Policy Institute of California.

Subsample of regular voters is defined by those who indicated they always or usually voted.

demographic and economic factors, to which we add trust and political leaning in models 2 and 3.

Primary attention is directed to the differences between voters belonging to different race-ethnic groups, observing how much those differences persist once we control demographics, economic factors, and political opinions. We see that black voters are 21.4 percent more likely than whites to support higher taxes and spending, and Latino voters are 18.7 percent more likely (Model 1 of Table 6). Although Asians are 11.6 percent more likely to be supporters, this has marginal statistical significance. These estimates are controlled for major demographic and economic differences among the groups. When we introduce the factors of trust in government and political leaning, the racial and ethnic differences are only slightly altered. Thus, there appears to be a fairly firm base of difference between white voters and others (although Asians are not appreciably different from whites).

Some of the control factors are very interesting in their own right. Trust in government has the effect one would assume, raising willingness to increase taxes by 12.4 percent among all voters. But the largest single explanatory factor, not surprisingly, is that liberals are 39.3 percent more willing than conservatives to tax and spend. Controlled for these powerful political influences, it is impressive how much distinctive influence is commanded by voters' demographic and economic positions. In model 3, we find that young voters are much more supportive of raising taxes than are the elderly. Compared with the middle-aged reference group, voters ages 25 to 34 are 10.2 percent more supportive and those age 65 and older are 8.8 percent less supportive. Women are 7.0 percent more supportive of increasing taxes and spending than are men, and foreign-born citizens are 10.6 percent more supportive than are the native-born. Surprisingly, education and income have no effect of any significance, but homeowners are systematically 7.7 percent less supportive of increasing taxes and spending. Homeowners may fear that any tax increases will fall disproportionately on them. Conversely, the young may judge that any increase in spending is more to their advantage, whereas the elderly might assume the opposite.

All of the above factors have an even stronger influence on willingness to tax and spend in model 1, before we take account of the political factors of trust and leaning in models 2 and 3. This underscores the sharp divisions in preference between voters who are white, older and native-born and those who are part of the growing new generation – younger, foreign born and Latino. The members of the incoming generation want a California that invests in its developing young population by providing more public services. Members of the outgoing majority, especially those of a conservative leaning, would prefer to shrink government and invest less in others. The consequence of those preferences is to resist development of the incoming generation.

Conclusion: the Outlook for the Future

California has reached an awkward point in its demographic transition. The white non-Hispanic population has now fallen to a minority of the state's residents, but it still retains a two-thirds majority at the polls. This majority position in the electorate may well persist another 25 years. In the meantime, California voters are making many decisions that will dictate the quality of life in the future. One hopes that they are forward looking.

We have seen how dramatic is the demographic transition now underway in California. This change is sweeping from the bottom up in the age distribution, thus allowing the established population in a seniority position to prolong its electoral dominance. The imbalance between voting and population in California would take on tragic proportions if the outgoing group of the voting majority supported the interests of the past, not the interests of the incoming group which is destined to be the future. Acting in their short-term interests, how great is the risk that the voting majority will undermine investments needed to support a more successful future, such as greater funding for education of the young or new infrastructure? Why should we assume that the outgoing majority would vote for future-oriented investments requiring higher taxes today but not benefiting them personally?

It is this temporal disconnect implied in the mismatch of interests and voting power that is the most dysfunctional potential outcome of the political imbalance. How California negotiates the political dimension of its great transition should be closely monitored. Other states and nations may well benefit from learning about the pitfalls of democratic dominance that plague the process of demographic transition.

Bibliography

Baldassare, Mark (1998) 'Untitled,' PPIC Statewide Survey (April) (San Francisco: Public Policy Institute of California).

Baldassare, Mark (2004a) 'Californians and Their Government,' PPIC Statewide Survey (February) (San Francisco: Public Policy Institute of California).

Baldassare, Mark (2004b) 'Special Survey on Californians and the Future,' PPIC Statewide Survey (August) (San Francisco: Public Policy Institute of California).

Baron Jonathan and McCaffery, Ed (2006) 'Starving the Beast: The Psychology of Budget Deficits,' paper prepared for a conference on Fiscal Challenges: An Interdisciplinary Approach To Budget Policy, held at the USC Gould School of Law (February).

Brady, Henry, Hout, Michael and Stiles, Jon (2005) 'Return on Investment: Educational Choices and Demographic Change in California's Future,' report from the Survey Research Center, University of California, Berkeley.

Citrin, Jack and Highton, Benjamin (2002) *How Race, Ethnicity, and Immigration Shape the California Electorate* (San Francisco: Public Policy Institute of California).

'Final Document of the Forum,' in Miroslav Macura, Alphonse L. MacDonald and Werner Haug (eds.), *The New Demographic Regime: Population Challenges and Policy Responses* (New York and Geneva: United Nations), pp. 279–93.

Guerra, Fernando J. and Marvick, Dwaine (1986) 'Ethnic Officeholders and Party Activists in Los Angeles County,' Working Paper, Institute for Social Science Research, UCLA.

Hansen, John Mark (1998) 'Individuals, Institutions, and Public Preferences Over Public Finance,' *American Political Science Review*, vol. 92, no. 3 (September), pp. 513–31.

Hayes-Bautista, David E., Schink, Werner O. and Chapa, Jorge (1988) *The Burden of Support: Young Latinos in an Aging Society* (Stanford, CA: Stanford University Press).

Holzmann, Robert (2005) 'Demographic Alternatives for Aging Industrial Countries: Increased Total Fertility Rate, Labor Force Participation, or Immigration,' Discussion paper no. 1885 (December) (Bonn, Germany: Institute for the Study of Labor).

Johnson, Hans P. (2005) 'The California Population in 2025,' in Ellen Hanak and Mark Baldassare (eds.), *California 2025: Taking on the Future* (San Francisco: Public Policy Institute of California), pp. 23–49.

Kent, Mary M. and Haub, Carl (2005) *Global Demographic Divide*, Population Bulletin, (Washington D.C.: Population Reference Bureau).

Kinsella, Kevin and Phillips, David R. (2005) *Global Aging: the Challenge of Success*, Population Bulletin (Washington D.C.: Population Reference Bureau).

Lesthaeghe, Ron and Neidert, Lisa (2006) 'The Second Demographic Transition in the U.S.: Spatial Patterns and Correlates,' unpublished paper (Ann Arbor: University of Michigan, Population Studies Center).

Lien, Pei-te, Collet, Christian, Wong, Janelle and Ramakrishnan, S. Karthick (2001) 'Asian Pacific-America Public Opinion and Political Participation,' *PS: Political Science and Politics* vol. 34, no. 3 (September), pp. 625–30.

Logan, John and Mollenkopf, John (2004) *People and Politics in America's Big Cities*, (New York City: Drum Major Institute for Public Policy).

Malone, Nolan, Baluja, Kaari F., Costanzo, Joseph M. and Davis, Cynthia J. (2003) 'The Foreign-Born Population: 2000,' Census 2000 Brief, C2KBR-34 (Washington, D.C.: U.S. Census Bureau), Table 1.

Matsusaka, John G. (2004) *For the Many or the Few: The Initiative, Public Policy, and American Democracy* (Chicago: University of Chicago Press).

Murdock, Steve H. et al. (2003) *The New Texas Challenge: Population Change and the Future of Texas* (College Station: Texas A&M University Press).

Myers, Dowell, Piktin, John and Park, Julie (2005) 'California Demographic Futures Projections to 2030, by Immigrant Generations, Nativity, and Time of Arrival in U.S.,' Population Dynamics Research Group, University of Southern California, www.usc.edu/schools/sppd/research/popdynamics.

Population Reference Bureau (2005) World Population Data Sheet.

Ramakrishnan, S. Karthick (2005) *Democracy in Immigrant America: Changing Demographics and Political Participation* (Stanford, CA: Stanford University Press).

Tienda, Marta and Sullivan, Teresa 'The Texas Higher Education Opportunity Project,' www.texastop10.princeton.edu.

Recent and forthcoming titles in the ISA series:

Making Institutions Work in Peru: Democracy, Development and Inequality since 1980
edited by John Crabtree

Right On? Political Change and Continuity in George W. Bush's America
edited by Iwan Morgan and Philip Davies

Francisco de Miranda: Exile and Enlightenment
edited by John Maher

Caciquismo in Twentieth-Century Mexico
edited by Alan Knight and Wil Pansters

Democracy after Pinochet: Politics, parties and elections in Chile
by Alan Angell

The Struggle for an Enlightened Republic: Buenos Aires and Rivadavia
by Klaus Gallo

Mexican Soundings: Essays in Honour of David A. Brading
edited by Susan Deans-Smith and Eric Van Young

America's Americans: The Populations of the United States
edited by Philip Davies and Iwan Morgan

Football in the Americas: Fútbol, Futebol, Soccer
edited by Rory Miller

Caribbean Literature After Independence. The Case of Earl Lovelace
edited by Bill Schwarz

Contesting Clio's Craft: New Directions and Debates in Canadian History
edited by Christopher Dummitt & Michael Dawson

Printed in the United States
200332BV00004B/73-213/A